That Other World

That Other World

Nabokov and the Puzzle of Exile

آن دنیای دیگر: تاملی در آثار ولادیمیر نباکف

Azar Nafisi

آذر نفیسی

Translated from the Persian by Lotfali Khonji
Edited by Azar Nafisi and Valerie Miles

Yale

UNIVERSITY PRESS

New Haven & London

Yale University Press books may be purchased in quantity for educational, business,
or promotional use. For information, please e-mail sales.press@yale.edu
(U.S. office) or sales@yaleup.co.uk (U.K. office).

Set in Bulmer type by Tseng Information Systems.
Printed in the United States of America.

Library of Congress Control Number: 2018957963
ISBN 978-0-300-15883-0 (hardcover : alk. paper)

A catalogue record for this book is available from the British Library.

This paper meets the requirements of ANSI/NISO z39.48-1992 (Permanence of Paper).

10 9 8 7 6 5 4 3 2 1

To my students in Iran,
and my family, Bijan, Negar, and Dara Naderi

One day while disrupting the strata of sense
and descending deep down to my wellspring
I saw mirrored, besides my own self and the world,
something else, something else, something else.

— "Fame"

Contents

Introduction to the English-Language Edition
Volodya

It all started with this book. I mean the way I have written my other books has been shaped by the process of writing this one. Like a life story, a book has its own murky history, shaped by complex circumstances, unexpected events, and strange coincidences. In this case, the story of those diverse factors, coming together at a specific time and place can provide a reasonable answer to the question, why Nabokov? Why write a book about Nabokov in a country now called the Islamic Republic of Iran, that was once called Iran and before that Persia? What makes Nabokov relevant to life in the Islamic Republic?

I could, of course, count all my connections—real or imagined—to Nabokov, beginning with the long and tumultuous history of the relations between Iran and its northern neighbor Russia, and Russia's influence on shaping Iran's modern history and culture. There is an undiminished sense of humiliation and grievance among Iranians about their country's devastating defeats in the nineteenth century at the hands of Russians, which led to Iran ceding the Caucasus and half of the Caspian Sea to Russia, and then there is Russia's and later the Soviet Union's immense influence in shaping Iran's modern political ideologies as well as its literary taste and tendencies—influences in the best and the worst sense of the word: great literature and Communist ideology. Iran seems to have followed Russia—thankfully, on a smaller scale—in its rebellion against political dictatorship, creation of a short-lived liberal interim government, and finally a violent ideological totalitarian revolution.

I can also cite the influence of Russian literature on Iranian intellectuals, and on my own education. By the time I was fifteen I had read many of the books Nabokov had read: not just Hugo, Stendhal, Austen, and Dickens, but also Tolstoy, Gogol, Dostoevsky, Turgenev, and Chekhov. To stretch the similarities, I might reference my own liberal education in a family that was part of the upper class, yet disdainful of it. My father became the youngest mayor of Tehran, very popular, and my mother was one of the six women first elected to the Iranian parliament in 1963; both were rebels against the very institutions they served. My mother did not last more than a term, and my father was rewarded for "insubordination" toward the prime minister and the minister of interior with four years without a trial in a "temporary jail," until his actual trial and full exoneration. Not just my parents but most of the Nafisi clan were unimpressed by or uninterested in wealth and class, though they were informed by education and culture, about which they could become tediously snobbish. And then of course, like Nabokov, I became an exile in America. All these facts could have had some effect on how I connect to Nabokov. But I don't think any of them was a real factor in shaping my views of Nabokov or my fascination with his work. Nor do I believe in using a work of fiction as an extension or allegory for my own or any other life story.

In writing this book I wanted to get away from the kind of learned literary essays that were popular in Iran and that I had been writing. I was bored with that kind of essay, I felt I was still writing college term papers — but even in college I had strayed from the conventional way of writing those often uninspiring texts. My book was to be about Nabokov, but not just a literary analysis of his fiction. My focus would be the interdependence of fiction and reality and the intersections where the two meet, each turning into a metaphor for the other. I wanted to narrate rather than explicate how different times and circumstances have shaped my views and interpretations of Nabokov's fiction, and how reading his books has reflected those realities while changing and subverting my perceptions of them. The book was to be a narrative of my experiences and Nabokov's fictional works.

I spent many exciting and anxious hours trying to find the right balance between my real and fictional experiences. For one thing, I discovered that reality is not as concrete and indisputable as it appears, or as we want it to be, and fiction is not as unreal as we believe it to be. But that was not a problem; the main drawback was related to the very reality I was trying to articulate: that reality itself would become the key obstacle standing in the way of writing my book. *And* perhaps one of the biggest incentives for writing it.

I remember vividly the moment I discovered how I wanted to write the first sentence of my book. I had just visited the Iranian poet Bijan Elahi, one of the two people I knew in Iran of that time who really knew Nabokov—not simply familiar with his work, he was genuinely passionate about it. (The other expert was a brilliant and reclusive literary critic whom I called "the magician.") The day had been one of those sunlit fall days. Elahi's house was situated in the older part of northern Tehran, close to the mountains, still preserving its dusty quality, the aroma of earth, and the leaves rising with the dust as I walked the narrow alley to his house. The living room was cool and dark, large French windows opening into a shaded, tree-filled garden, the evergreens keeping the sun out. It seemed as if that particular garden had deliberately resisted the colors of fall. I had enthusiastically explained to Elahi why I wanted to write about Nabokov, why I felt this was so relevant to the times we lived in—and yes, yes, I knew that did not really matter, that great literature is timeless, but then, there we were: even if we were not living in exceptional times, our times in one way or another affect how we read and write.

I left his leafy green world with its own choice of seasons and stepped out into the early afternoon light, dazzled by the impossible colors of leaves, not just yellow, red, and brown, but the color I identified as fall copper. From the dusty alley, I turned toward the more naked light and bare asphalt of the main street. I felt elated and fidgety with excitement, chasing multitudes of scattered ideas that, like mischievous children, were running wild and evading my attempts to catch them. The street was on a steep slope, and as I walked down, I came to a sudden stop, having gotten hold of one of those evasive ideas and not wanting to let my captive go. I took out my notebook from my bag and wrote these words: "The first book I read by Nabokov was *Ada*. My boyfriend Ted gave it to me, writing on the flyleaf, 'for Azar, my Ada, Ted.'" My first encounter with Nabokov was thus joyous and deeply personal, its mood coloring all my later readings of his work. It felt like "the tingle in the spine" that he had demanded of reading and readers.

I read *Ada* as a fairy tale, never once opening a dictionary to look up words or search the allusions, fervently discussing it with Ted. We were very young and we were in love and passionate about literature. This seemed like a good opening for my first book.

But right after writing those words, I knew that I would not be able to publish them. Not just political dissent or criticism but the public articulation of unruly passions of youthful love, or love in general, were also banned. It was a sign of the kind of regime the Islamic Republic had become that alongside of political offenses and crimes, public expression of love in any form or shape, including poetry, was not just banned and censored but also punished. In the poem "In This Blind Alley," the poet Ahmad Shamlu had written about the murder of love, joy, and poetry in the Islamic Republic, starting with these words:

> They smell your breath
> lest you have said: I love you,
> They smell your heart:
>> These are strange times, my dear.
>
> They flog love
> at the roadblock.
> Let's hide love in the larder.
>
> In this crooked blind alley, as the chill descends,
> they feed fires
> with logs of song and poetry.
> Hazard not a thought:
>> These are strange times, my dear. . . .

I knew that the very first sentence I had thought of for my book had already become the first victim of the reality I wanted to narrate. If to write of falling in love with a man (and a foreign man at that) was forbidden by law, then its mutilation and censure was sure to follow in print. Its appearance in print would, after all, be proof that such things did exist and could be celebrated despite censorship—that fact in itself was considered too dangerous. The center of every narrative is the individual, her concrete experiences, feelings, and emotions, as well as her relation to the wider world. All this is the microcosm of the world at large. The Islamic regime, like all totalitarian systems, instinctively reacted against anything that created space for the unique and the individual, anything it could not control and redefine. Its targets were not merely political but those that ensured the diversity and individuality of voices, lifestyles, beliefs, and viewpoints, namely women, culture, and minorities.

For a while I spent a rather pleasant if melancholy time brooding over my fate in the Islamic Republic. My notes of that time show a marked fondness for the word "confiscation." I had written several pages on how—to deprive Iranians of our reality—the regime had to justify its actions by confiscating our history, for if the past was not what we knew it to be but what the Islamic Republic had rewritten, then the present, as confiscated and reshaped by the Islamic Republic, was justified. According to the regime, we were not Iranians with three thousand years of history, composed of different ethnicities and religions, but were instead all Muslims—and not Muslims with different interpretations and belonging to different denominations of religion; we were limited to only one interpretation and denomination, the most extreme and backward. Religion itself had become a victim of the regime used as an ideology to maintain power over the Iranian society. Within this context we were all to uniformly obey the laws of the Islamic Republic that had come to us, not just in the name of religion but as *representative* of the word of God. How we dressed, acted, expressed ourselves, how we felt and imagined and thought, all was subject to confiscation. This was how it should be in their view. In confiscating history, culture, and tradition, the regime also confiscated our identities as individual citizens, with the right to freedom of expression and choice. "They" know what "they" are doing, "they" know the threats to "their" rule, or so I wrote in my notebook, on and on . . .

■

These thoughts brought me closer to Nabokov, his celebration of individuality and individual dignity, his commitment to a life of imagination, his uncompromising stance against any form of totalitarianism not only at state level but also in terms of personal relationships. I seemed, too, to be getting signs and guidance from the master himself: suddenly everywhere I went a book of his was beckoning — in one of the few English bookstores left in Iran I discovered *Speak, Memory;* on one of the top shelves in my father's library I noticed *Lolita* side by side with *King, Queen, Knave* and *Laughter in the Dark* (on whose flyleaf Father had written, "Washington, 1953"); and my magician friend offered me the use of his collection of Nabokov editions. I started rereading *Ada,* this time finding more demons behind those fairy-tale trees and in the corners of opulent mansions . . . one by one, I went through the books I had already read and those that I hadn't. There was something so deeply resonant in the texture of Nabokov's work, something that I had not caught before, too struck at first by the deceptive and seductive beauty of his words.

One theme that caught my eye, recurring in book after book, was the idea of exile. Exiled was how I was feeling, living in the Islamic Republic of Iran. I had returned home in 1979 to discover that home was not home anymore, that the people who ruled my country were more alien to me than others who lived thousands of miles away. The confiscation of Iran's history, the loss of my identity as a person of certain principles and beliefs (as a woman, a teacher, a writer, and a reader) made me feel orphaned, homeless, in the beloved country of my birth. This went beyond politics; it became an existential matter.

At first I felt detached and marginalized, alone and disoriented, in a perpetual state of exile from the country I knew; then I started to connect with those who shared the same sentiments. Escaping social and political reality, we, like many others, created our own self-sufficient island. Gradually I realized that I was not alone, that it was not just people like me, but that many among the Iranians were now in exile, having lost their past and feeling bewildered in the present, with little or no connection to their current state of being. No wonder Nabokov's sense of tragic absurdity seemed so familiar to me. For him exile was not just a physical migration. His protagonists were often aliens, either in physical exile or exiled in their own homes, experiencing a feeling of unreality, orphanhood, isolation. His characters like Cincinnatus or Krug were aliens and exiles in their native countries, living under similar circumstances to many of us in the Islamic Republic. As my book began to take shape, each chapter revolved around a particular dimension of exile, each one independent of but overflowing into the other.

■

My preoccupation with Nabokov made me eager to share his work with my students. He was unknown to most of them and it was a bit risky teaching a writer so "difficult," at least linguistically, yet that element of risk was itself intriguing and challenging. I began with one of his most abstract but relevant books, *Invitation to a Beheading,* and after the students' unexpected and joyous response I added *Pnin.* Later, in my private class, we read *Lolita.* Before teaching each book, I would ask myself the same questions: Would they "get it"? Would they connect? Will they run after the White Rabbit and risk jumping down the hole? Well, I must say they most certainly did "get it," and connected, and most of them eagerly followed the White Rabbit and showed little hesitation in jumping down the famous hole. How to get them out again was another matter. I remember Mr. Sami reproaching me for not introducing them to Nabokov earlier, and another student, a petite girl with delicate features and a shy demeanor, choking and breathless with excitement, telling me that, the night before, she had been pacing up and down her dorm room, waving her copy of *Invitation to a Beheading* at her startled if bemused roommate and her two friends, hurling at them the words that Cincinnatus addressed to his jailers: "I obey you, specters, werewolves, parodies."

What was it that so attracted us to Nabokov? The same students who had complained about having difficulties with Henry James's *The Ambassadors* were treating the difficult and highly formalized *Invitation to a Beheading* as if it had been written specifically for them. It was not just a passionate readerly appreciation of a book (my students had felt that about the majority of texts we studied): many among them felt a kinship with Nabokov's protagonists, instinctively connected to his books as, in more ways than one, they resonated with their reality. This was true both of his "political" novels like *Invitation to a Beheading* or *Bend Sinister* and his "nonpolitical" fiction, *Pnin* and *Lolita*. They connected, then, not because of the books' content, but because of how that content was shaped, by how the reading experience led to the Joycean kind of epiphany and the Nabokovian tingle in the spine!

I am not trying to use Nabokov's books as allegories for our reality, however; there was not a one-to-one relationship between that reality and his fiction. Nor do I advocate treating books as remedies or therapeutic sessions for the soul. But there needs to be a form of connection, an empathy between reader and text that goes beyond a simple equation to reflect the universal nature of books, their celebration of difference, and their simultaneous appreciation of our common experiences, values, and needs. Just as difference is vital to a great work of fiction, so too is empathy, the shock of recognition about our common humanity, when we realize not how different we are but, despite our differences, how alike we are, sharing the best and the worst. Nabokov, an immigrant who connected to so many different cultures, instinctively grasped the interdependence and interactions of particularity and universality.

We empathized with the tone and texture of Nabokov's novels, which gave rise in us to a sense of anguish and trauma, a feeling of irretrievable loss. The intensity of our response—the weight of its reality, the everlasting presence of our oppressive state in the shape of the specters and werewolves that Cincinnatus raged against—intruded on every aspect of our lives, in public and in our most private moments. When the sensations were not there, fear of their intrusion was ever present. I did not want the Islamic Republic to dominate my fictional experiences as well as my everyday life. It was imperative that I not simply teach or write about that reality without focusing on fiction, on the world of imagination that Nabokov saw as the alternative to the phantasmagorical world created by his and our rulers. My students' reactions to Nabokov's fiction strengthened my faith in the power of ideas and the imagination to resist and challenge the totalitarian powers that appeared otherwise to be beyond our control.

One way of survival was to acknowledge our shared sense of absurdity in what had come to pass, to share it, to turn it into art. But in that, too, reality was ahead of us. No work of fiction could compete with the absurdity imposed on our everyday reality by the solipsism of the Islamic regime: who could invent the blind censor reigning over Iran's theater and later a television channel? Who could create an anecdote about airbrushing out the figures of ballerinas from Degas's *Ballerinas at the Barre* in an art book, or concealing women's bodies in copies of *Newsweek* and *Time?* Who could think of deleting Olive Oyl from most of the Popeye episodes on television because Olive is a loose woman, not married to Popeye? And who would put headscarves on the drawings of female chickens in a children's book? How could an absurd play or a story compete with that? Nabokov had succeeded in reflecting perfectly the atmosphere and the texture of that absurd life we lived, and, just as important, he demonstrated how the antidote to such absurdity was real imagination, cleansing and refreshing our vision, such that we could see and articulate the truths hidden and silenced by that absurd reality.

We felt threatened not just by a political dictatorship (it wasn't only about politics, not something that a social revolutionary novel could decipher) but by the fact that the totalitarian mindset had extended into the most private corners of our lives to such an extent that our most personal gestures, like holding hands in public, wearing ties, or showing a bit of hair, had become political statements. There were few or no boundaries between public and private, political and personal. More frightening was the danger that we who were victims of this mindset could ourselves unintentionally adopt its approach, using the same tactics and rhetoric, becoming just as blind toward others, just as inflexible. To challenge the state meant fighting for a way of living, of being, that was now in danger of extinction. Nabokov had experienced that kind of danger. The tone in his fiction gave voice to a deep traumatic and anguished existence, a sense of irretrievable loss. That pained silence articulated through fiction prompts great empathy. More than the works of any other modern novelist, his are variations on the evils of solipsism. Yet in both the "nonpolitical" and the "political" novels, and in the most tragic, like *Lolita,* you will find an undertone of the absurd, a defiant mockery, almost a parody of some form of cruelty. Pathos in his work is accompanied by bathos. The "innocent"—Lolita, Pnin, Krug, Cincinnatus, or Lucette—suffer tragic fates, but those who impose tragedy upon them, the solipsists, the "monsters," were parodied, providing the absurd component of the stories. It was with that sense of absurdity that I empathized too. I am reminded now of all our jokes about the Islamic Republic. They were extremely funny at times, but the tragedy was that this absurdity, the joke and the parody, was *our* reality, an integral part of *our* everyday life; it was our condition and there was not much fun in that. We had to turn it into an existential joke to resist it, to make reality tolerable.

The relation to Nabokov's fiction was not one way. I felt then as I feel now that, like any passionate reader, my students and I not only took from the books but also gave something back, brought our own fresh experiences to the novels, and with that a fresh perception of the whole work. Novels are written to be read, and each reading adds a new dimension to the book, resurrects the work in a sense; without active reading, works of fiction simply wither and die. We too illuminated certain hidden aspects of Nabokov's work, we too brought forth what might have been unseen until then. Something in *Lolita,* for example, in the very texture of the book, reminded me profoundly of our own reality in the Islamic Republic. The intensity of that reality, like an open wound, created a sensitivity in us, illuminating the hidden depths and dimensions of Nabokov's multidimensional stories.

■

Like most great books, Nabokov's novels were far more subversive and effective in questioning not just their worlds but their readers too, jolting them out of a complacency fueled by the predictable plots of lesser works with their stock characters, with preachy language trying to force a "message," a political or moral agenda, down the poor reader's throat—an insult to readers' intelligence and their desire for truth. We did not need to be told that the regime was bad and we were good, we did not need to be made to feel self-righteous and beyond reproach; we needed to go beyond that, to spurn the reality imposed upon us, and to do so we needed a new way of looking at that reality in search of revelation, not condemnation, of understanding, not judgment. We needed the kind of illumination that comes through imagination and ideas, and a connection to the world that had been taken from us. This was why my students ignored most socially committed novels but loved Nabokov—not because they were not politically committed, but because Nabokov's fiction did not merely question politics of the day but went far beyond that to put on trial all forms of tyrannical mindset.

In the process of writing my book I kept recalling Nabokov's saying, "Fancy is fertile only when it is futile." This writer, like the majority of writers I taught, was not overtly political in his public life; he in fact shunned politics, and when he did pay attention to it, he supported many conservative causes. Compared to a revolutionary author like Sholokhov or Gorky, Nabokov was both the greater writer and the more enduring, the more essential. Remember Sholokhov, a Soviet functionary who won the Nobel Prize for literature? How many people in the world and in his own country remember him? Nabokov won the bigger prize: continuing to live in the hearts and minds of millions of readers the world over. He does not criticize a specific government at a specific time; what his books target is the totalitarian mentality, be it in the dystopian works like *Invitation to a Beheading* and *Bend Sinister* or on a more personal level in Humbert's blindness toward Lolita as a separate and distinct being with her own aspirations and feelings. Humbert's greatest crime turns out to be not Quilty's murder but his confiscation of a child's life and her transformation into a figment of his disturbed imagination, into an object of his desire. Such wicked transformations spoke volumes to me and to my students. We also empathized with the victims, and with the defenses by Cincinnatus, Krug, and Lolita of their rights as individuals, their refusal to give up their individual identities and their sense of dignity. These matters did not merely concern the totalitarian societies but were/are quite relevant to life in a democratic society. Remember that *Lolita* happens in the United States of America and the victim in the novel is a little American girl. Nabokov in that book has drawn a portrait of both the victim and the perpetrator in such a poignant and heartbreaking manner that it becomes almost unbearable. Rape is not just a physical act, it is a violation of our identity as individuals, pointing to the victim's helplessness, fear, self-loathing, and loss of identity and confidence. Whether in Iran or America, it is the same: the act is ultimately a violation and a confiscation of the victim's self-esteem and identity.

■

After spending a great deal of time brooding, doubting that I could ever write a book under such circumstances, I decided to shelve my original idea but not abandon it entirely. I created two columns in my diary, under the heading "Things I have been silent about." In one column, I wrote all the strange and absurd things we were confronted with in Iran, and particularly in the capital: going to parties in Tehran, going to concerts in Tehran, reading *Lolita* in Tehran, reading *Huck Finn* in Tehran, translating Langston Hughes in Tehran, lecturing on *Madame Bovary* in Tehran, teaching *Jacques le Fataliste* in Tehran, watching the Marx Brothers in Tehran, listening to the Doors in Tehran. . . . In the second column I wrote the name of books relevant to these realities. When I came to the United States, every book I wrote in English was a continuation and a response to the difficult and painful birth of this first book in Farsi—addressing not what I had put into this book but what I had been obliged to leave out.

Instead, in this volume, I tried to find a different way to write about the relationship between our reality and Nabokov's fiction. I called its structure metaphoric. I wanted to see whether I could write a book without once mentioning the Islamic Republic, a straight book of literary analysis that also illuminated our reality then in Iran while going beyond Iran and revealing the general totalitarian mindset and its targets. It took me five years to write, and never again will I have the kind of experience I had over those five years. Everyone close to me, from family and friends to students, became involved in one way or another. My brother and friends who lived abroad sent me books on Nabokov. In our place near the mountains outside Tehran I organized groups of my own and our friends' children to chase butterflies, the swarm of blue butterflies gracing that part of the country, and made up stories for them about where the butterflies might lead them. We even had a drawing contest where the children drew portraits of Nabo-

kov and his butterflies. I wrote my book for my students and those who
flocked to my classes from across the city because of their love of literature,
especially those who did not have access to Nabokov's works, and were deprived of a public space to freely discuss them, but who had the passion and
the tenacity to create the space.

In 1990 I was permitted to leave the Islamic Republic for the first
time and started traveling abroad for conferences and on fellowships, and I
spent a great deal of time researching the latest books on Nabokov; not just
Tehran but Oxford, Philadelphia, Los Angeles, Washington, London, also
became parts of my Nabokov memory. I remember how excited I was when,
after a talk at the University of Pennsylvania, I received my first paycheck for
a speech. It was a generous sum, if you came from postrevolutionary Iran.
The first thing I did was buy my very own copy of Brian Boyd's biography
of Nabokov's Russian years.

My book played a small role in the conflicts between what are called
Iran's hardliners and reformists. My publisher was a reformist and a former
official at the Ministry of Islamic Culture and Guidance. He had taken some
risk by publishing a book by a "formalist" writer—formalism in the Islamic
Republic of Iran, as in the Soviet Union and Nazi Germany, was frowned
upon and criticized and banned as decadent. My publisher was repri-
manded in print. After publication in 1994 the book was well received but
went out of print rather quickly. A second printing was denied; for a while
copies were sold on the black market at exorbitant prices and then the black
market ran out of stock as well. When I first found my opening sentence to
the book I never wrote, I would never have imagined that the book I finally
wrote would not be found in its country of birth but become available in
English in a country that would also become my home, the book itself being
reborn in exile.

■

Why Nabokov in America? How relevant is he to this society in times
of such deep crisis? The answer is quite simple: whenever we are obliged
to justify the necessity of imagination and ideas, we have proved why we

need more than ever ideas and imagination—which is why we also need Nabokov.

Nabokov's response would probably be to repeat that "fancy is fertile only when it is futile." Before literature becomes useful to us on political and social levels, it is essential to our existence as human beings—like breathing, you don't question its necessity, you simply breathe. What Nabokov called the "tingle in the spine" is the main purpose of literature, at least great literature, and like true love, the tingle keeps coming back each time one reencounters the beloved. It is only through the tingle that fancy becomes useful to us in other ways, illuminating the past, subverting and clarifying the present, predicting the future. As for literature's relevance today, maybe if we had paid more attention to imagination and ideas, maybe if we had not dismissed genuine knowledge in favor of short-term gain and ideological agendas, we would have discovered that this crisis (which, by the way, is not going away) is not merely political or economic, it is one of vision, the result of moral timidity, cynicism, intellectual and imaginative sclerosis, and ignorance. Perhaps the relevant question for lovers of literature in these times should be: is there something wrong with a society where the importance of ideas and imagination must be proved?

When I returned to the United States in 1997, I missed the tingle in the spine: I found little passion for meaning and purpose in life or the will to confront and resist obstacles, but rather a sort of complacency and a desire for intellectual comfort. Until then I had not realized the depth of both Nabokov's joy and his frustrations in America, what he called the "gloom and glory of exile." When I migrated to America I brought with me my "portable world," a term I have stolen from *Pnin* and use to explain the world of memories and imagination. I never imagined the degree to which Nabokov's fiction would be relevant to my life in this country. Ever since my return I have witnessed with increasing bitterness and sorrow the denigration of most activities involving the imagination and the world of ideas. I came back at a time when not just Nabokov's books but books classified as literature were increasingly being labeled irrelevant to our reality—as if books were responsible for the mess the country was getting itself into. Publishers were becoming more commercial in focus, paying more attention to the celebrity status of authors than the quality of their work. Book-stores were in deep financial trouble, libraries were being closed, the arts and humanities were belittled especially by the ideologues (on the right and on the left) who dominated the think tanks and academia. Perhaps most in-sidious was and still is the relentless assault by a corporate mentality on all aspects of life in America, including that of the universities and the whole system of education.

Worse still, the individuality that Nabokov and so many great Ameri-can writers had cherished here has been vanishing alongside the pub-lic spaces that created bridges between our private and public selves — connecting us to others, helping in the creation of communities that offer a sense of belonging and loyalty without compromising individual integrity. That individualism has been gradually replaced by the solipsism that Nabo-kov so beautifully evoked in his best work, as the archvillain of his stories. Surely "absurd," with all its tragic connotations, is an apt term to apply to an age identified with Donald Trump. An era when all who are different from the male white establishment represented by him, especially women, immigrants, minorities, and in general his critics, are shunned, treated as outsiders. In great works of fiction, the individual is always central, but that individual's growth, the process of individuation, occurs through relation-ships with others, both friends and enemies. I refer not to the dog-eat-dog world, not to that kind of individualism. Observe how Cincinnatus and Krug, just like Huck Finn, grow through the choices they make and the les-sons they learn through their interactions. How could so many Americans miss the symptoms that led to this disease? Any creative mind, no matter what field, would feel in this country today something of the way Cincin-natus felt in that staged and fabricated world he was forced to endure. Who would have thought that the dictator/clown Paduk of *Bend Sinister,* a man without imagination and therefore without empathy, ruled by his inferi-ority complex, trying to prove his superiority by eliminating those superior to him in intelligence and integrity, would predict the reign of a reality TV star, ready to destroy the world if need be to prove his superior self to non-believers? Nabokov, after all, saw in his time his fair share of mad dictators, far worse than anything we are experiencing today.

■

There are some similarities between the years that Nabokov spent in America, the two decades beginning in 1940, and our times. He migrated to America at another time of crisis and confusion while a vicious world war unfolded on an unprecedented scale. Those experiences are reflected in his work. *Pnin* is a litany of mishaps based on Nabokov's own experiences. Pnin's primary problem, like that of his creator, is lack of appreciation by most of his peers, their blindness to his immense scholarly talents and unique personality. Pnin does not complain, but Nabokov does. He had written Edmund Wilson, "Funny—to know Russian better than any living person—in America at least,—and more English than any Russian in America,—and to experience such difficulty in getting a university job." Pnin must also deal with the ignorance of people who insist on imposing on him their own misguided views and images of him and his country. They are not necessarily bad people, evil people, they are just ordinary people, careless when it comes to others, without empathy. From Pnin's wife Liza and her lover (and later husband) to the "nice" lady hosting him for a lecture (introducing him as "Professor Pun-neen," mistakenly claiming that Pnin's father was "Dostoevski's family doctor, and he has travelled quite a bit on both sides of the Iron Curtain"), to the student who enrolls in his class because she has been told that by the time one has mastered the Russian alphabet one could practically read "Anna Karamazov" in the original language, to the head of the French literature department who hates French *and* literature, to the president of his college (who pays compliments to what the narrator calls "another torture house" as follows: "Russia—the country of Tolstoy, Stanislavski, Raskolnikov, and other great and good men"), and finally to his nemesis, Jack Cockerell, trolling Pnin around the campus, telling derisory anecdotes behind his back, none of them true. There is also a special breed of immigrant, people like the painter Komarov and his wife: "Only another Russian could understand the reactionary and Sovietophile blend presented by the pseudo-colorful Komarovs, for whom an ideal Russia consisted of the Red Army, an anointed monarch, collective farms, anthroposophy, the Russian Church and Hydro-Electric Dam."

Perhaps Nabokov's worst experience both in Europe and America was the generalization of immigrants and vocal opponents to the Soviets as White Russians, courtiers and their apologists, mourning the loss of money and power. No matter how hard Nabokov avoided the political and ideological battles over his home country, he could not be entirely immune from them. Time and again he had to explain that his quarrel with the Soviet regime had nothing to do with his lost wealth but with his lost culture, his lost childhood. He had an aversion to Western intellectuals who at the height of Stalinist terror sought to justify Stalin's crimes and blame the victims and their supporters. The result was an extreme anticommunism leading at times to extreme political positions on the right. His writing transcended political bias, however, targeting totalitarian mindsets left or right.

It hurt to feel as if he was losing Russia all over again in the attitudes and images created here of that beloved homeland. Nabokov paid the price for being intractable enough not to tone down his criticism of Soviet crimes in an era when the Soviet Union was becoming an ally in the war against Hitler. His chapter in *The Gift* on the socialist revolutionary Cherneshevsky, already banned in Europe, remained censored until 1952. The *New Yorker*, serializing *Pnin*, refused to publish chapter 2 because of its anti-Soviet stance, with its references to "medieval tortures in a Soviet jail," and a "Bolshevik dictatorship." The *New Yorker*, according to Robert Roper in his brilliant book, *Nabokov in America*, also cut "bright dog dirt" from a short story, and changed the last line of his poem "On Translating Eugene Onegin" from, "Dove-droppings on your monument" to "The shadow of your monument." Mildred McAfee, president of Wellesley College, had wanted Nabokov to tone down his biting critique of the communist regime, to which he responded, "Governments come and go but the imprint of genius remains." That did not prevent her from refusing to renew his contract after Stalin changed sides to join the Allies. In the end, though, it was Nabokov who was in the right.

I find myself empathizing with him, wondering how, while things change, they also remain the same. I returned to the United States to discover that the dominant view and image of the beloved country I had left had been reduced to its regime. In the Trump era this viewpoint was extended to all citizens of Muslim majority countries, who were turned into caricatures of themselves, all defined as potentially dangerous fundamentalists and terrorists. Twice my country of birth was taken from me, once by the regime and again by the ignorance and intellectual biases of ideologues, politicians, and pundits. What I am left with are my memories, and the knowledge that the past is irretrievable in reality; I know my only weapon is writing, writing to resurrect another Iran, the Iran I lived in and the imaginary Iran I carry with me. I would use any occasion to bring in that other Iran. I wonder how Americans would feel if people in Iran accepted and repeated Trump's narrative of America? If they believed that America is a place where white supremacists are guardians of its history and culture, a place where women and minorities are denigrated, where people believe that General Pershing killed Muslims with bullets soaked in pigs' blood? If that is fair, then the images created of Iran, the Soviets, and Eastern Europe behind the Iron Curtain are also fair.

   Yet for Nabokov, as for Pnin, it was not all gloom—life in America was not, is not all about ignorance and complacency: in the end America, for Nabokov, was more about glory. Before the gloom came the glory, and glory came after it too. In America, he wrote to his sister Elena, "my most sacred dreams have been realized." His biggest loss, which he mourned time and time again, was the loss of the Russian language. To follow Nabokov's life (as well as the fiction it produced) during the so-called American years is to discover a great deal about America's gloom and glory. America provided Nabokov with a kind of freedom he had been deprived of in progressively repressive and poverty-ridden Europe. The price exacted from him for glory was to give up the last precious gift he had brought with him from Russia: the language. He had made a home away from home in that language, for if he could write in Russian, he was *in* Russia, the pristine land of his childhood. Through the long years of exile in Berlin and France, suffering near poverty and the growing threat of fascism and repression, he had what he called his "malleable" and beloved Russian in which to take refuge. Being an exile was nothing new to him; he had been one since the age of nineteen, when he left Russia forever. What had kept him going was writing, writing in Russian, a language he was adamant not to lose, one that had become his "portable home."

But there was something else—with the loss of language, the last "possession" he had from the country of his birth, Nabokov had nothing more to lose. Having lost everything brought with it great pain and anguish and an inconsolable sense of loss, but also a great sense of liberation and possibilities. He had to start from scratch, to invent another world, a job seemingly impossible while tauntingly exhilarating. America was perhaps the best place for him to achieve that goal.

On my return to the United States in the late nineties, while rereading Nabokov, I was struck by the fresh beauty and maturity of most of Nabokov's American novels. I am not suggesting that they are better or worse than his Russian novels, but they are different and they do pay homage to the place of their birth, to America. I feel he illuminates America—in its vulgarity and also the simple and majestic beauty at its core. While he never became rich until the publication of *Lolita*, almost two decades after his migration to the United States, there was a world of difference between living in Europe in a one-room apartment and having to write with frozen fingers on the bidet (his makeshift desk) in order to not disturb his young son, and writing in the homes of college professors away on sabbatical.

In America he found new ways of pursuing his passions. The country was so new, so clear and transparent, in contrast with Europe with its centuries of history and layers of tradition and culture. Nabokov had belonged to that old world, and he imported it to America, but he bloomed in the novelty, the fresh audacity, the allure of America. That feeling of discomfort in the new language remained a challenge to him, a feeling of restlessness, and perhaps the curiosity to see how far he could bend the English language to his will. The resonances of his Russian that he brought to his English all added a new dimension not just to his language but also to American fiction. Rereading him, at times I feel that he is playing with the English alphabet and words with the same buoyant joy as he did with his mother's jewelry when he was a child.

Nabokov is not Humbert, although they both hail from "old Europe," and *Lolita* is not an allegory for America, although she is a typical American girl. Nabokov reveals to us about America what Humbert discovered about Lolita: that beyond that callow and vulgar if seductive appearance there is in America, as in Lolita, "a garden and a twilight, and a palace gate—dim and adorable regions . . ." That insight is what adds such luminosity, such poignancy to an ordinary unrefined American girl. On a different level, in *Pnin,* we discover the joyousness of America, its generosity, its humble beauty. Nabokov was not blind to American superficiality, consumerism, or vulgarity, all of which he describes in both his fiction and his lectures, but like another fellow European (of British descent), Rebecca West, he discovers the beauty in constant bloom at the heart of all that appears brash, the beauty summarized in the seemingly infinite and ever-varying landscape, offering seemingly endless possibilities—a landscape he traveled constantly in search of butterflies. Rebecca West, writing about Sinclair Lewis's novel *Babbitt,* claimed that its eponymous protagonist must have been struck by "the majestic creativeness of his own country, its miraculous power to bear and nourish without end countless multitudes of men and women." She added: "There is in these people a vitality so intense that it must eventually bolt with them and land them willy-nilly into the sphere of intelligence; and this immense commercial machine will become the instrument of their aspiration." Nabokov said: "I love this country. . . . Alongside lapses into wild vulgarity there are heights here where one can have marvelous picnics with friends who 'understand.'"

As both writer and scientist he thrived in America's newness, its glorification of the concrete and the actual, its vastness and variety, its innocence and ignorance, its callowness and its poignancy, its vulgarity and its hidden depths. This limitless space somehow translated into the vast landscapes of his American novels, and a new openness to the world while he continued to examine, even more forensically now, the most monstrous aspects of being human.

In America his fictional characters become more complex. While in his Russian fiction he had mainly praised the poet, the artist, and the lover, in his American novels, things turn darker as he goes deeper into their stories—to be a poet or a lover does not necessarily mean you are a good person, one with a heart. You can be or become too self-involved, too self-indulgent to see or feel others. A monstrous and almost evil character emerges in Humbert and later, in a different way, in Kinbote; even the lovers, Ada and Van, who have great imagination and a poetic language, are also blind toward others, they have little heart. These characters all have an affinity with the great heroes of American novels, inasmuch as they are outsiders, orphans, in a sense homeless, but—unlike the American fictional protagonists—they do not make their heart their home: Humbert and Kinbote take refuge in their obsession, and Van and Ada are too enmeshed in each other to develop empathy with others. It took courage to bring out the monster in characters who in one sense were very close to him: the creative individuals and the lovers. These villains are different from the more straightforward totalitarian villains of novels like *Invitation to a Beheading* or *Bend Sinister*. They are deceptive, seductive, they are in one sense far more dangerous because they come in so many attractive guises, but not in the usual garb of a villain. In reality they appear as statesmen, men of God, poets, actors, philanthropists, they appear as billionaire businessmen out to rescue the poor and the needy. To detect them you need to have what Nabokov calls the "third eye of imagination." He not only created new forms of protagonist in his American novels but added a new dimension to and insights into the nature of love, writing, and art as explored in English-language fiction. If only for that, Nabokov is relevant to reality today in both totalitarian and democratic societies.

In book after book, *Pnin, Lolita, Invitation to a Beheading, Bend Sinister, Pale Fire,* and *Ada,* the villains are the solipsists, those who for one reason or another are too self-involved to hear, see, or feel empathy for others, those who impose not just their will but their prefabricated images and ideas upon real living human beings. These new and compelling monsters are among Nabokov's great contributions to modern fiction.

Two decades and half have passed since the initial publication of this book in Iran. Many books on Nabokov, as well as new editions of books by Nabokov, have appeared since then, and much has happened, but I have chosen to only replace the initial introduction with a new one and make minor changes to the translation, with some updates, including mention of Nabokov's unfinished and since published novel, *The Original of Laura*

(2009). I have not talked about issues that have come to light since I published this book, such as Nabokov's love affair, his dalliances with young women, or the main reason for his troubled and guilt-ridden relationship with his gentle, cultured, and kind gay brother Sergey. In the second chapter I mention Nabokov's guilt and strained relations with his younger brother, but I did not know then that his discovery of Sergey's homosexuality was perhaps the main factor to strain their relationship. I find no justification for his attitude toward Sergey. My intention in making no substantive changes has been to keep the book as it is: it belongs to a specific time and place, and I am curious to know how it will do in exile, and how much it will belong to these times and this place. Another reason, as I mentioned before, is that this book has shaped every other book I have written. Together with *Reading Lolita in Tehran* and *The Republic of Imagination* (setting aside my memoir, *Things I Have Been Silent About*), it creates a sort of trilogy. The last chapter in this book anticipates the first chapter of *Reading Lolita in Tehran,* and the last chapter of that book leads into the first chapter of *The Republic of Imagination.*

I have not talked about the thrill and freedom of reading Dmitri Nabokov's note complimenting *Reading Lolita in Tehran;* of discussing Nabokov and his family with the gracious Ivan Nabokov (the author's cousin, and a distinguished publisher in France); of participating in a panel with Stacy Schiff and Alfred Appel, or hearing from Nabokov scholars whom I once read in Iran; of hearing my students tell me of their amazement over hearing a reader at the Johns Hopkins SAIS library laughing out loud while reading *Pnin;* or of my American students going to libraries and bookstores in search of new books by and on Nabokov.

First and last: I cannot imagine having written this particular book without my students in Iran, without their resilience in the face of cruel and oppressive times, their passion for literature, and their love for Nabokov. As I write these lines I hear Mr. Sami demanding that I teach more of Nabokov's works, I see the tall young woman who audited a few of my classes handing me a piece of paper on which she had formed with a few blue colored flowers the word "UPSILAMBA," and I recall, too, the glow in Nima's eyes and the joy in Manna's voice as we discussed with affection our esteemed "Volodya."

That Other World

Life

Speak, Memory

1

"A colored spiral in a small ball of glass; this is how I see my own life."[1] Vladimir Nabokov wrote this line toward the end of his autobiography, *Speak, Memory,* which was first published in 1966. If we move a few sentences back toward the opening paragraph of chapter 14, we find his explanation of the spiral as a spiritualized circle, one that is uncoiled, unwound, and set free, and for that reason no longer a vicious circle. He came up with the idea as a schoolboy, he admits, but he also discovered it later in Hegel's triptych ("so popular in old Russia"), which expresses merely the essential "spirality" of all things in their relation to time: thesis, antithesis, and synthesis. As applied to Nabokov's own life, the first twenty years growing up in his native Russia (1899–1919) draws his "thetic" arc. The following twenty-one years of voluntary exile in England, Germany, and France (1919–1940) make up the antithesis, and the next twenty, the years he spent in America, his adopted country (1940–1960), constitute the synthesis — and the new "thesis." Of course, he first wrote these lines from *Speak, Memory* a few years before returning to Europe and settling in Switzerland. And his autobiography ends with the second twenty-one-year period of antithesis. He began a second volume to *Speak, Memory,* intending to cover the years in America, and even speculated on calling it *Speak on, Memory,* but unfortunately he never completed it.[2]

I open this book with Nabokov's life story not simply to obey the age-old idea that the most obvious entry point for analyzing a writer's work is his biography, but because in Nabokov's particular case, his life was an essential and indissoluble part of his work. His real life and the life of his imagination are shadows of each other. And his autobiography stands as a powerful work of art in its own right. The world he lost as a youth lingers like an aura and permeates the imaginary worlds he created. If *Speak, Memory* can be categorized as both "memoir" and "fiction," then his novels, written during his long years in exile, were undeniably composed within the radiant recollected space of his childhood. When he refers to Russian émigrés as "free citizens of [their] dreams" at the tenth anniversary of the 1917 Revolution, what he's really putting forward is an image that largely describes *him*.[3]

This spiral relationship with time is not only present in Nabokov's autobiography but runs through most of his work. It is no accident that both the beginning of *Speak, Memory* and the final chapter of *Ada* (his novel that most closely resembles *Speak, Memory* in tone and atmosphere) deal with time. In fact, they are not only about time; they attempt to defy time, struggle against it in order to negate it. The essential role that time plays in the contemporary novel is taken more or less for granted, yet few writers have invested themselves so deeply in exploring its possibilities as Nabokov did. In Marcel Proust's *In Search of Lost Time,* the concept of time functions as a "now" that is saturated with sorrow and nostalgia for a "past" that has been lost. In Nabokov's work, however, time doesn't follow this Proustian notion of continuity.[4] Nabokov's childhood and adolescence were truncated, split off from the rest of his life in the aftermath of the Russian Revolution in 1917, and as a result remained forever an incomplete experience. The physical ties to his memories and the remnants of that cherished time were severed completely. As a result, his novels are not an attempt to recreate the remembrances of a past, as they are not solely constructed from a place of sorrow or nostalgia. Instead, his writing endeavors to build a bridge across this inexorable gap in his own life. Perhaps this is why *Speak, Memory* opens with the image of an infinite, timeless abyss: "The cradle rocks above an abyss, and common sense tells us that our existence is but a brief crack of light between two eternities of darkness."[5] This first sentence pauses to contemplate existence, shackled as it is in the everlasting darkness of time's prison. And this image is not unique. One of Nabokov's major themes is the aching struggle to preserve intact every moment of a person's life, both as a writer and as one partaking of universal experience. But this struggle ultimately comes face to face with the passage of time, which makes a travesty of even our most resolute ambitions.

Nabokov's first memory offers an extraordinary image of the moment he becomes aware of time. There he is, toddling along, tumbling every now and then, with his left hand in his mother's (she wears "soft white and pink"), right hand in his father's (he is in the "hard white and gold" of a military uniform). The boy asks his parents how old they are (thirty-three years for his father, twenty-seven for his mother), and in the process discovers his own age (four). The association of differences is what brings him to the perception of his own identity. His first gleam of consciousness acts as a second baptism. Nabokov intuits that his father must have completed military training long before he himself was born. And that it must have been his mother's birthday, as his father had dressed up in his old uniform to celebrate. So Nabokov owes his first spark of full consciousness to a joke, and concludes that according to the theory of recapitulation, "the first creatures on earth to become aware of time were also the first creatures to smile."[6]

Nabokov's ideas eventually take shape in light of this "time as prison" metatheme. It is what lays the foundations for his body of work, what sculpts its bends and curves. In this book I set out to explore the evolution of these thematic designs in depth. Exile, reality versus dream, cruelty and pain, art and love (or love and art): these are the building blocks with which Nabokov constructs his narrative world. It is important to keep in mind that these words are cultivated from within Nabokov's novels; it is there that they acquire flesh, bones, and skin. Outside the context of his imagination, words such as "exile" and "pain" lose their corporality, revert to being concepts devoid of form or identity. This book is less the outcome of a conscious decision than the result of a fascination with Nabokov's themes and the awakening they provoked in me as a reader. I see Nabokov's spiral glowing in my mind. I see its incandescence from the depths of an absolute darkness, its coil radiating colors.

2

Vladimir Vladimirovich Nabokov was born in St. Petersburg on April 23, 1899. He was the firstborn son and darling of the family. His siblings were Sergey (born in 1900), Olga (1903), Elena (1906), and Kirill (1911).[7] We learn in *Speak, Memory* that Vladimir was born on the same day as Shakespeare and in the year of Pushkin's centennial. Two of Nabokov's principal biographers, Andrew Field and Brian Boyd, call attention to these coincidental anniversaries. Shakespeare and Pushkin were Nabokov's absolute models of literary accomplishment and his most beloved writers. This becomes even more significant when taking into account how much Nabokov used plot to give shape and meaning to his work. This is evident in *Speak, Memory*, where he describes his own life and then comments on it as if he were appraising a novel, thereby discerning meaningful events and storied associations. This, for him, is how the past predicts the future and the future explains the past.

Nabokov's childhood mirrors the same terrestrial paradise we find in *Ada*. He remarked several times throughout his life that it wasn't his family's wealth and privilege that distinguished this period. What made him feel so fortunate, what he loved and adored so much about his parents, was the value they placed on cultural refinement. His father had engaged in political activities before and after the Russian Revolution as a response to the cultural dearth in Russia at the time, and later in the Soviet Union, and in this sense Nabokov followed suit with his own publications in exile. For years, his family welcomed and entertained the most exceptional artists. Their private library housed thousands of volumes. Nabokov's father, Vladimir Dmitrievich, was a great patron of the theater, and following the Revolution he was tasked with supervising the reconstruction of state theaters. Later still, in exile in Berlin, he was asked to welcome the Stanislavsky theater group.[8] V. D. Nabokov wrote devotedly on many of his favorite writers, including Tolstoy, Flaubert, and Dickens. After his father's death, Nabokov proudly remembered that a friend had sent his recently widowed mother a special copy of *Madame Bovary*, on whose flyleaf Nabokov's father had written, "The unsurpassed pearl of French literature."[9]

The struggle for freedom in Russia began, in fact, during Nabokov's paternal grandfather's lifetime: with Dmitri Nikolaevich himself, who was Tsar Alexander II's reformist minister of justice. But it was Nabokov's father who truly raised these implicit notions of freedom and culture to the level of explicit actions, rejecting the generalizing force of sociology in favor of a fervent defense of individual rights.[10] V. D. Nabokov was a progressive activist and by nature a rebel. He was a professor of criminal law, a journalist, and a deputy in the First Duma, who championed the notion of individual freedom in the face of state pressure. In 1900, he wrote against capital punishment, which was to become a recurring theme throughout his son's work. Following the Kishinyov pogrom in 1903, he wrote a celebrated article in the *Pravo* review titled "The Bloodbath of Kishinyov," berating the police for not having made any attempt to stop it from happening.[11] It cost him his university post and title in the royal court. Later, when the tsar dissolved the First Duma, V. D. Nabokov and a group of deputies gathered in Vyborg, Finland, and signed a resolution called the Vyborg Manifesto. This earned him a three-month prison term, which he spent in solitary confinement. Even stripped of his political rights, though, V. D. Nabokov could not be deterred from his activism. It is alleged that he placed an advertisement in the press to sell off his formal court garb, and he made good use of his incarceration by reading Dostoevsky, Anatole France, Victor Hugo, Oscar Wilde, Nietzsche, and the New Testament. He studied Italian and wrote several articles that were published upon his release.[12]

Nabokov's adolescence coincided with this politically tumultuous period, when his father was deeply involved in fighting for radical reforms, yet the sociopolitical upheavals are not what bestow color and scent to his autobiography. Reality, for Nabokov, was something that could only be found hiding somewhere else. This "elsewhere," this "other place" (Antiterra) cloaks his work in a sort of haze. It is the same "other place" that meets the eye in the empty spaces on every page of *Speak, Memory*. It is in the design of the extraordinary worlds envisaged in characters like Cincinnatus and Krug. Nabokov believed, like the make-believe French philosopher Pierre Delalande in *The Gift*, his last novel written in Russian, that contrary to what people think, life is not only a journey along one road leading to another destination.[13] There is another world, another place right here, surrounding us at all times. "In our earthly house, windows are replaced by mirrors; the door, until a given time, is closed; but air comes in through the cracks." It is this theme that inspired one of his finest pieces of Russian verse in March 1942, the long poem titled "Fame": "and descending deep down to my wellspring / I saw mirrored, besides my own self and the world, / something else, something else, something else."[14]

Vladimir is a child. There's a framed aquarelle hanging on the wall above his bed. It depicts a shadowy path disappearing into the depths of a forest of European beech trees. His mother has read him an English fairy tale about a boy who leaves his bed for the painting. As a result, young Vladimir hurries through his prayers every night, imagining how he will climb into the painting above his bed before he falls asleep. The painting appears again in Martin's room in the novel *Glory*.[15] At the end of the novel, Martin, the story's protagonist, somehow achieves what young Vladimir so desired: he disappears into a painting. But the painting becomes Russia: the Russia transformed by the Revolution into a land of dreams for Nabokov and the characters in his novel. We catch recurring glimpses of this world throughout Nabokov's oeuvre, hovering just beyond the everyday world: in *Pale Fire*, in *Ada*, and even in apparently realistic novels such as *Lolita*. It also materializes in other guises in novels such as *Invitation to a Beheading* or *Bend Sinister*. It seems as though from his earliest childhood, Nabokov fantasized about creating his own secret world, free of censorship: a nomadic empire where "we are free citizens of our dreams." His lost Russian childhood became transfigured as a tangible instance of this world.

3

Few writers have enjoyed such a magical childhood. It was a safe place, serene and pleasurable, overflowing with the beauty of nature, literature, art, and love. This is the world Nabokov carried with him like a treasure during the years of exile. Yet even the colors of this magical childhood were no match for the vibrancy of Nabokov's formidable imagination. For as long as he could remember, Nabokov was visited by what he called "praedormitary visions," or mild hallucinations. More important, he was synesthetic, seeing words and letters as having colors.[16] He shared this trait with his mother, who praised and encouraged the exceptional peculiarities of her favorite child. A half-century later, in *Speak, Memory,* Nabokov recalled that his mother would take out her jewels for young Vladimir to commit their sparkling colors to memory.[17] What persisted in his young mind (and what was precious to him, even as an adult) wasn't the material value of the jewelry but their charmed, twinkling kaleidoscope of colors.

His mother taught him the importance of remembering details. When strolling together through Vyra, the family's country estate, she enjoyed drawing her son's attention to the "intangible property," the ephemeral beauty of nature, whispering *Vot zapomni* (now remember).[18] It provided good training for the losses that were shortly to befall them. Vyra is also where Nabokov's father first inspired a passion for butterflies in his son, teaching him how to catch and collect them. This became Nabokov's lifetime obsession: literature and butterflies are what endured as the two main features of his indissoluble link with Russia. The paradise that was Vyra, that supremely significant place and model for all the enchanted lands of Nabokov's fiction (especially in *Ada*), was eventually occupied by the German Army in 1942, serving as its Russian headquarters until a fire gutted it in 1944. For some time afterward, the villagers would carry the bricks away to use as material for their chimneys.[19]

Nabokov narrates the episode of his first beguilement with the opposite sex in a short story titled "First Love."[20] The story was incorporated later and in a slightly different form in *Speak, Memory.* This first romantic awakening happened when he caught sight of a little French girl in Biarritz during the family's summer vacation.[21] They are both ten years old. Little Vladimir cannot bear the idea of her being hurt. There is a slight bruise on her forearm where her mother has pinched her, and the sight of it causes him pain. He later gets into a fistfight with a red-haired boy who is rude to her. And oh, how deeply he aches over the bites the mosquitoes leave on her neck at night. He resolves that they must elope; he will take her somewhere far away from her bourgeois parents. Their last encounter takes place after their summer vacation has ended, when they meet in a park in Paris. The little girl gives Vladimir's younger brother a box of candied almonds as a farewell gift, but Vladimir knows the gift is intended for him alone. The last image he remembers is of the little girl rolling a glinting metallic hoop with the aid of a stick. She continues rolling it in the light and in the shade, tap-tapping it around a fountain choked with shriveled, fallen leaves. In Nabokov's memory, the sound of dead leaves mingles with the leather of the little girl's shoes and gloves. A feature of her clothes, maybe the ribbon on her Scottish cap or the pattern of her stockings, reminds Vladimir of the rainbowlike spiral inside a glass marble.

Nabokov's first love affair took place when he was sixteen, over the course of an enchanted summer in Vyra, in 1915. His object of desire was fifteen-year-old Valentina (Lyussya) Shulgin.[22] In *Speak, Memory,* Nabokov gives her a pseudonym, the "concolorous" name of Tamara.[23] She is exceptionally beautiful, probably with a drop of Tartar or Circassian blood. She is witty, she loves poetry (Nabokov says the "minor" poetry of jingles), and she enjoys writing her name. Even before they meet, Valentina's arrival has been announced to Vladimir because he sees her name written in the sand, carved into the wood of a bench, penciled on a whitewashed wicket. Vyra was the setting for all Nabokov's first (significant) experiences in life: his first butterfly, his first romance, his first poem. In *Speak, Memory,* he details the composition process of his first verse: a sudden thunderstorm passes overhead, and he runs to take shelter in a pavilion. When the rain subsides, he looks around and sees a leaf bow beneath the weight of a raindrop; "what looked like a globule of quicksilver performed a sudden glissando down the center vein, and then, having shed its bright load, the relieved leaf unbent"; the poem ensues.[24] It is as if through his first poem and his first love, which flourish at the same moment, poetry and love become for Nabokov bound together.

Before long the woods and copses of Vyra and its adjoining estate, which belonged to Nabokov's uncle, form the lovers' secret meeting spots, even though the dalliance was not much of a secret from the adults. We find traces of this affair and the reaction of the people around them in the story of the young lovers in *Ada:* in the furtive meetings between Ada and Van, in the peeping servants, and in the stories and songs in the villages nearby. The gardener who tended his uncle's estate reported to Vladimir's mother that he had caught the tutor spying on the young lovers. She had already learned about the affair by reading her son's poems and could not abide the idea of someone snooping on them. She ordered the butler to leave a plate of fruit out on the veranda every night.

Vladimir and Valentina's relationship lasted two years. Back in St. Petersburg, however, they were no longer free to stroll around informally as they had in Vyra, and the harsh winter weather proved problematic. The magical days of that first summer in Vyra could never be recovered, and eventually the 1917 Revolution came between them forever. Their last encounter was accidental; they met on a suburban train the summer before the Revolution. Valentina stood in the coach's vestibule, nibbling small pieces of chocolate that she broke off a bar that she held in her hand. She told Vladimir about the office where she was working. She glanced back at him once more before descending and disappearing into a huge amber sunset and the "jasmin-scented, cricket-mad dusk of a small station." Shortly thereafter, Vladimir and his brother would board a train in St. Petersburg bound for Crimea. The young lovers continued exchanging letters for a time, and despite his many betrayals, there was nobody else who could fill the void left by Valentina.[25] Nabokov's family was eventually forced to leave Crimea and Russia altogether, and all that remained were memories. Before departing, Vladimir had been tempted to join Anton Denikin's White Russian Army—not because he felt called to fight heroically against the Reds, but because he thought he might find a way back to the Ukrainian hamlet where Valentina was.[26]

4

Nabokov nurtured the memories of his childhood years, keeping them alive in his mind as a form of sustenance: wandering amid the natural beauty of Vyra, its colors, its butterflies, rummaging in the vast family library, and giving free rein to his imagination. English was his first language because his early education had been entrusted to English governesses. It seems as though fate, something he strongly believed in, had been trying to prepare him early to survive the years of exile to come. Along with his native Russian, he was also educated in French and read books in all three languages.

He had devoured Jules Verne in French by the time he was ten; Doyle, Kipling, Conrad, Chesterton, and Wilde in English; and in Russian, Pushkin's *Eugene Onegin,* and Tolstoy's *Anna Karenina.*[27] At twelve he became obsessed with Dostoevsky, but by nineteen the passion had faded, never to be revived. He composed a cheeky poem after rereading some of Dostoevsky's work when he was in Crimea: "Listening to his nightly howl, / God wondered: can it really be / that everything I gave / was so frightful and complicated?"[28]

By fifteen, he had read the complete works of Shakespeare in English, Flaubert in French, and Tolstoy in Russian.[29] He was favorably biased toward all three of these artists throughout his life, as he was for Pushkin, Gogol, and Chekhov. He also appreciated the work of philosopher William James, who was first read to him by his father, but he was never able to rouse interest in Henry James, William James's brother.[30] V. D. Nabokov had known Tolstoy personally, and Nabokov could remember their stopping to exchange a few words with a small, bearded man one day, when they were out for a stroll. "That was Tolstoy," his father said afterward.[31] Nabokov was in his teens at the time of the Russian Symbolist movement and the Acmeist and Futurist responses to it. The Symbolists fascinated him, especially the work of Alexander Blok and Ivan Bunin.[32] Years later, in exile, Bunin was awarded the Nobel Prize. He was one of the first to pronounce Nabokov's work extraordinary, voicing admiration and even astonishment. Bunin also appreciated the lesser-known Vladislav Khodasevich, another of Nabokov's favorites. In his introduction to the English translation of *The Gift,* Nabokov called Khodasevich "the greatest Russian poet that the twentieth century has yet produced."[33]

Nabokov was also home-schooled in drawing and painting, though he never excelled in the visual arts. Half a century after the fact, he learned from a friend that one of his teachers thought him the most hopeless pupil he'd ever had. Yet he did have the gift of being able to see letters of the alphabet in colors, so his imagination was always bursting with different hues. His sentences that teem with light and shadow have produced some of the most beautiful images in the history of the novel. He studied with M. V. Dobuzhinsky, one of the most celebrated Russian painters of the time and one of young Vladimir's favorite teachers. Dobuzhinsky taught him to be attentive to detail, how to visualize properly and depict from memory objects he had seen a thousand times: a lamppost, a mailbox, "the tulip design on the stained glass of our own front door."[34]

In 1911, twelve-year-old Vladimir was sent to Tenishev School, which was liberal, progressive, and democratically egalitarian. He was admitted four years after Osip Mandelstam.[35] He received excellent grades, but was standoffish and tended to shy away from participating in extracurricular activities or clubs. As a result, he was accused of displaying aristocratic behavior. He also refused to touch the filthy towels in the washroom. His being driven to school in an automobile with a liveried chauffeur was considered offensive in the school's democratic atmosphere. But the worst offense of all was his lack of interest in the political climate, which unnerved the more revolutionary or reformist teachers. But he never buckled or let himself be bullied, and was never afraid to stand up for himself. He took boxing lessons as a boy, and to defend a friend, stood up to school bullies who were stronger than he, earning the respect of his classmates.[36]

It is important to reiterate how influential his parents' refined cultural sensibilities were in shaping Nabokov's personality. His father had focused passionate attention on the ideals of individual freedom and expression. Literature became his son's bedrock, the enduring presence in his life that would allow him to withstand adversity. This heritage allowed fifteen-year-old Vladimir to compose his earliest poems while World War I raged in the background. At sixteen he had already begun contributing verse to his school's newspaper, along with his translations of Alfred de Musset. One of his poems was printed in a highly prestigious publication of the time, the liberal magazine *Vestnik Evropy*. Later in life he returned to the experience, declaring that when his father's private librarian finished typing the poem and mailed it to *Vestnik Evropy,* he had felt "utter surrender" to literature. Though it was juvenilia, the magazine accepted it straightaway. For Vladimir, however, the printed item caused "much less of a thrill than the preliminary process, the sight of my live lines being sown by the typist in regular rows on the sheets, with a purple duplicate that I kept for years as one does a lock of hair or the belltail of a rattler."[37]

When his uncle died in 1916, Nabokov, who was his heir, inherited a two thousand-acre estate worth several million dollars at the time.[38] Together with his own family's wealth, this made him one of the wealthiest seventeen-year-olds in all of Russia. Naturally, his first book of poetry, comprising sixty-eight poems, was published at his own expense. The verses were written to Valentina, about Valentina, and for Valentina, and the dedication reads "To Valentina Nabokov." In *Speak, Memory,* he recounts that his Russian literature teacher (a lesser-known poet whom young Vladimir thought was first-rate) brought the book to class one day to ridicule him in front of his classmates, applying his fiery sarcasm to some of the dreamier lines. This and other (deserved) criticism quickly cured him of any interest in literary fame forever.[39] Vladimir also received (undeserved) praise in an article written by a talentless journalist trying to ingratiate himself with the young man's father. Not to be easily thwarted, however, he had his second collection ready by early 1918, along with his first play in verse. In the interim, two governments had been overthrown, and a revolution had taken place. Young Vladimir went on composing his poems, catching butterflies, falling in love, and losing his sweetheart to the Revolution. But when word came announcing that the Red Army had occupied Vyra, it triggered a composition of a different kind. "In Radiant Autumn" is the first poem in which Nabokov looks back at Vyra and first love through the prism of exile.[40]

On the afternoon of October 25, 1917, V. D. Nabokov and other members of the Council of the Russian Republic were summoned to a meeting in the Winter Palace.[41] V.D. was the only member of the Council to actually show up. After two hours of arguing, he finally concluded that the ministers in the Provisional Government were only wasting time, and he left. Twenty minutes later, the Bolsheviks stormed the Winter Palace. Nabokov had continued writing poetry throughout that tumultuous year, and on the night when these seismic events took place, he put the final touch on one of his poems and then jotted down the circumstances around him; the sound of rifle fire and the crackle of machine guns in the streets.

Vladimir inherited the qualities of sangfroid and self-confidence from his father. V.D.'s even temper and self-control could unnerve anyone, from the tsar to Trotsky. Even his enemies acknowledged his boundless courage and remarkable honesty. The records show V. D. Nabokov as a legendary figure, even greater than the heroes in his son's oeuvre. Two stories illustrate these qualities. When the attendees of a secret meeting received word that the Cheka, the Soviet state security organization, had been tipped off about the gathering, V. D. Nabokov was the only person willing to stay long enough to warn the approaching Mensheviks, who had recently broken from the Bolsheviks, thereby risking his own life. He did so even though he disagreed with their ideas.[42] A second example has V.D. out walking with his friend Hessen when skirmishes broke out in the street, followed by gunshots. Hessen suggested that they take refuge in the public library, but V. D. Nabokov responded that "the bullet destined for him had yet to be cast," and continued on his way.[43]

In March 1917, Tsar Nicholas II abdicated in favor of his brother Mikhail, though Mikhail also refused the throne. V. D. Nabokov wrote and signed the abdication document himself, effectively heralding the end of the Romanov Dynasty. In November 1917, the young Vladimir wrote the last of the poems to be composed during his St. Petersburg period. He dedicated it to his mother, the loving companion with whom he would never again be able to stroll through the trees of their beloved Vyra.[44]

To avoid conscription into the Red Army, Vladimir and Sergey were sent to Crimea, which was still a free zone. Soon afterward their mother, sisters, and younger brother joined them. They stayed at an inconspicuous villa in Gaspra on the estate of Countess Sofia Panin, who had been a colleague of V. D. Nabokov's in the Provisional Government. In 1901, Tolstoy had been Countess Panin's guest on the same estate, and in 1902, Chekhov and Gorky had visited Tolstoy there.[45] For Nabokov, however, Crimea was the first link in a chain of exiles that extended farther and farther away from his cherished land.

In November 1917, V. D. Nabokov and twelve others were arrested on Lenin's orders in Smolny, and were released only five days later. Freed, V. D. Nabokov went immediately to a performance at the Mariinsky Theater. The show was a fund-raiser for the Literary Fund, of which he was still acting president. The following day, the family heard the news that several friends and colleagues had been detained, including Countess Panin. The time had come for V.D. to flee St. Petersburg and join his family in Crimea. They stayed there until the Red Army broke through in the north and occupied the peninsula in March 1919. The Nabokovs were witness to many events during this relatively brief stay, including the temporary victory of the White Army. V. D. Nabokov vehemently opposed its violent behavior, as he did the viciousness of the Reds. The family also experienced the short-lived occupation of the German Army. The people, remembering the merciless comportment of the other armies, had welcomed them. Young Vladimir patrolled the house at night, together with his father and brother, but was otherwise busy with his usual pastimes: poems and letters, butterflies, and chess. It was in Crimea that he composed his first chess problem.[46]

They left Russia and sailed for Greece in April 1919, on a small and decrepit old ship named *Nadezhda* ("hope" in Russian) in the company of six other ministers of the Provisional Government. Nabokov wrote about these last moments in *Speak, Memory,* recalling their departure: "Over a glassy sea in the bay of Sebastopol, under wild machine-gun fire from the shore (the Bolshevik troops had just taken the port)." As they zigzagged out of the bay, young Vladimir tried to concentrate on the game of chess he was playing with his father: "One of the knights had lost its head, and a poker chip replaced a missing rook." His awareness of leaving Russia was eclipsed by the notion that Valentina's letters would continue to arrive, only to find nobody to open them, and "weakly flap about like bewildered butterflies set loose in an alien zone, at the wrong altitude, among an unfamiliar flora."[47]

5

Following a three-week stay in Greece, they continued on to Paris and London. V.D.'s brother Konstantin was still deputy ambassador at the soon to be obsolete Russian embassy in London. Their lives from this point forward would be punctuated by poverty, homesickness, separation, and death, though they had no inkling yet of the future disasters that were in store. The jewelry that had encouraged young Vladimir's aesthetic sensibilities now became the means of their survival, though the Nabokovs had been able to squirrel out only a few pieces, hidden in talcum powder.[48] In October 1919,

Vladimir was admitted to Trinity College, Cambridge. His education was funded by his mother's string of pearls.

One of Nabokov's obsessions took shape while he was studying in Cambridge. How could he preserve his native Russian, his only surviving memento and link to his life before tragedy struck? His deepest horror was the thought that he might forget it. Though his first language was English, and he was no stranger to English literature, and even though he was active in university events, especially sports, he strongly identified himself as Russian. He focused heavily on the differences between him and the other students, more than on any similarities. Yet he meticulously took stock of new social conventions: never shake hands, never nod your head, never ask how anyone is doing; just smile; never venture out in Cambridge wearing an overcoat or a hat, even in the coldest weather.[49]

In *Speak, Memory* he says that the narrative of his college years in England is the story of how he became a Russian writer.[50] Cambridge acted as a frame for his deep, rich nostalgia for Russia. At first, he was unable to express what he was feeling because the words fell flat and seemed inadequate. In his autobiography, he writes: "My old (since 1917) quarrel with the Soviet dictatorship is wholly unrelated to any question of property. My contempt for the émigré who 'hates the Reds' because they 'stole' his money and land is complete. The nostalgia I have been cherishing all these years is a hypertrophied sense of lost childhood, not sorrow for lost banknotes."[51]

In Cambridge he encountered another problem, one that remained with him throughout the years in exile: the prejudices held by even the most liberal Western intellectuals against the "White" Russians. One such intellectual was a fellow Cambridge classmate he assigns the pseudonym Nesbit in *Speak, Memory*. Later we find that Nesbit was in fact Richard Austen Butler, whose ministerial career in Conservative governments carried him as far as the post of deputy prime minister in the 1960s. A young socialist as a student, "Nesbit" cut a perfect prototype of the well-meaning *intellectual*. Intellectuals, who were otherwise opposed to any form of cruelty, were somehow able to find ideological justification for the executions, tortures, and concentration camps in the Soviet Union. They "lumped together as 'Czarist elements' Russian émigrés of all hues," Nabokov writes in *Speak,*

Memory, "from peasant Socialist to White general—much as today Soviet writers wield the term 'Fascist.'"[52]

In his autobiography, Nabokov remarks on some of the truths he would have liked to share with Nesbit, if the latter had not been so firmly entrenched in his ignorance, regarding them as mere fancies. Given the chance to explain, one such truth he might have affirmed was that Russian history could be seen from two vantage points: one was the emergence of the police, and the second was the development of a splendid culture. "Under the Tsars," he wrote later, "despite the fundamentally inept and ferocious character of their rule, a freedom-loving Russian had had incomparably more means of expressing himself, and used to run incomparably less risk in doing so, than under Lenin."[53] But that wasn't even the principal problem. What distressed Nabokov even more deeply was another group that liked to rally around him from an ultraconservative, even reactionary stance. Their support of an immigrant like Nabokov was fueled not by respect for freedom and love of culture but out of sheer hatred for left-wing intellectuals.

Six weeks after arriving in Cambridge, Nabokov took part in a debate about the Soviet Union, arguing against Russia's postrevolutionary Bolshevik government (and losing). He repeated verbatim one of his father's articles, which he had committed fully to memory. He spoke for eighteen minutes and fifty seconds, reciting every single sentence by heart. Then he dried up and fell silent. It was the first and last time he ever took part in political debate.[54]

Over these years, Nabokov's poems appeared in Cambridge University's *Trinity Magazine,* as well as in Russian-language émigré periodicals. More important, he began collaborating in a new émigré project titled *Rul'* (The rudder), founded in part by V. D. Nabokov, living with the rest of the family in Berlin. Three of his poems appeared in the inaugural issue in early 1921, along with a short story signed by "Vlad. Sirin," the first use of this nom de plume. He took the name less to hide his identity than to differentiate his byline from his father's, now that they were both writing for the same publication. Yet he remained "Sirin" for years to come, and everything he wrote during his time in Europe (and in Russian) was signed with this pseudonym. Sirin is the name of a fabulous, imaginary bird that supposedly lived in Russian forests centuries ago. Nabokov wrote about it in an English piece that he signed with another pseudonym, V. Cantaboff, saying, "This wonder-bird made such an impression on the people's imagination that its golden flutter became the very soul of Russian art."[55]

Calamity struck the following year. A political meeting had been organized on March 28, 1922, for Pavel Milyukov, a leader in the émigré community, to deliver a lecture. V. D. Nabokov strongly disagreed with Milyukov's ideas. They had been political colleagues in the past, but a bitter schism had divided them. As a result, V. D. Nabokov was reluctant to attend the lecture, but out of politeness and a sense of duty, he welcomed Milyukov in an editorial column he wrote for *Rul'*. Milyukov addressed a crowd of more than fifteen hundred people that evening in the Berlin Philharmonic. He spoke for an hour before calling for a brief break. Suddenly, a short, dark man jumped from his seat and shouted, "for the tsar's family and Russia," firing several shots at Milyukov. In an extraordinary act of bravery, V.D. raced toward the assailant, disarmed him, and pinned him to the ground. But then the attacker's accomplice, taking advantage of the chaos, jumped onstage, shouting and firing several more shots. V. D. Nabokov was pronounced dead a few minutes later. Milyukov narrowly escaped death that evening, and the assassin would later rise to high office within the Russian Nazi movement.[56]

In *Speak, Memory,* Nabokov recounts a particularly disturbing day when he was twelve years old. At school, he learned the news that his father had challenged another man to a duel. When he came home, he could hear the sound of laughter coming from the landing at the top of the staircase. He immediately assumed the adversary must have apologized for the offense and called off the duel. Young Vladimir rushed up the stairs anyway, desperate to feel the soft weight of his father's hand stroking his hair. At the end of this long passage, Nabokov condenses the incidents of his father's death, ten years later, into the space of a few lines. Though he did his best to behave stoically in public, he recorded in detail the events of that night in a private notebook. The memory of his father's death became one of those absences that overshadow the events in several of his works.[57] Later that year, during final exams in Cambridge in May, he wrote a letter to his mother telling her that his father was appearing often in his dreams. In another he wrote: "At times it's all so oppressive I could go out of my mind — but I have to hide. There are things and feelings no one will ever find out." In his autobiography, his father's death takes up only a few lines. But the vivid shadow of his larger-than-life remembrance, and his devastating murder, recur over and over again. The memory of his father's death weaves threads of pain and loss into the web of his novels.

By the time Nabokov had graduated from Cambridge University and joined his family in Berlin, he had already produced a small body of work. His third and fourth poetry books were in preparation, his Russian poems had appeared in a variety of different publications, he had completed two English poems, and he had translated English and French works into Russian. He had also written a verse drama, a short story, and an article on butterflies.[58]

6

Due to increasing financial difficulties, Nabokov's family moved from Berlin to Prague en masse in 1923, though Nabokov himself stayed on in Berlin for another fifteen years. That year, he became engaged to a young girl named Svetlana, though her parents put an end to the engagement almost immediately, asserting that Vladimir had no money and hence no future.[59] Eventually, both Vladimir and his brother Sergey found positions in a German bank. But Vladimir lasted all of three hours, and for Sergey it was a matter of three weeks. Vladimir earned a living mainly as a private tutor. He taught English, French, tennis, and even boxing. He earned five dollars for his translation of *Alice's Adventures in Wonderland* into Russian, which, as he explains in *Speak, Memory,* was a considerable sum of money in those inflation-ridden times in Germany. According to Brian Boyd, the twenty-three-year-old Vladimir's translation of *Alice* is regarded as the best translation of the book into any language.[60]

On May 8, 1923, Nabokov met a young girl at a charity ball given by a Russian émigré organization. She was hiding behind a black demimask

with a wolf's profile. The girl never took it off throughout the entire evening, as if she did not want to allow her beauty to be her only charm. This
was how Vera met Nabokov for the first time, though she was already acquainted with some of his work. Years later, when the biographer Andrew
Field asked Vera what her life would have been like had the Revolution
never occurred, Nabokov interrupted her answer to say: "There would have
been no difference. You would have met me in St. Petersburg and we would
have married and been living more or less as we are now."[61] Nabokov always
looked for patterns to his life, and after meeting Vera he realized that they
might have met several times in the past. When they were children, Vera had
often walked past the Nabokov home on 47 Morskaya. During adolescence,
they could have met several times at balls. And in Berlin, Nabokov had once
accompanied a friend to Vera's father's publishing house. Vera had even
been there at the time, working in an adjacent room. Nabokov wrote a poem
three weeks after they met titled "Encounter." The last line reads: "But if
you are to be my fate . . ."[62]

Vera Yevseyevna Slonim was born in St. Petersburg in 1902 to a family
of Jewish intellectuals. Her father had graduated with a law degree, but following a decree by the Ministry of Justice restricting the practice of law by
Jews, he went into the lumber export business. He was very successful, and
in exile was able to build again some of the wealth they had lost during the
Revolution, though the economic mayhem of Germany at the time eventually forced him into bankruptcy. Vera had been a precocious child. Her first
memory reached back to when she was six or seven months old; she could
read bits of the newspaper by the time she was three. Like Nabokov, she had
learned Russian, English, and French as a child. Her memory was extraor-
dinarily keen for retaining anything in verse, not only as a young girl, but
also into old age. She had already written poems by the time she turned ten
or eleven, and hoped to study physics. But her father was convinced that
study would take too much of a toll on her weak lungs, exacerbating her recurring bouts of bronchitis.[63]

Vladimir and Vera were married on April 15, 1925. From that moment
forward, Nabokov dedicated every one of his books to her. Vera devoted
her entire life to Nabokov and his art, even though she was astonishingly

gifted herself. Brian Boyd points to how expansive a role she played in their partnership, which went beyond simply being Nabokov's wife: she was the inspiration behind everything, and more important, his ideal reader. She performed the duties of secretary, typist, editor, proofreader, bibliographer, and translator. She was his literary, financial, and legal adviser, and acted as chauffeur, research assistant, teaching assistant, and professional understudy. Though Vera stressed in her conversations with Boyd that Nabokov had never modeled a single character on her, many critics see in her the prototype for several of Nabokov's "positive" female protagonists.[64] Of course, these women lack the allure of characters like Lolita and Ada. Some of the same critics contend that Vera's sustained presence in Nabokov's life impeded the objectivity supposedly so necessary to create high art. Obviously the deep ties between some of the male and female characters in Nabokov's work draw upon the strong and loving marriage between Vladimir and Vera, which lasted more than half a century, and remained joyful to the end.[65]

Vladimir and Vera's first and only child was born at dawn on May 10, 1934, when, in Nabokov's words, the shadows were on the wrong side of the street. They named him Dmitri Vladimirovich. Nabokov was a kind and caring father, and the young couple looked upon their child with a jealous eye; he was their only justified extravagance. Dmitri's life should not be allowed to drift too far away from the "incunabula" of his parents' opulent past.[66]

Although Nabokov gradually gained acclaim in Russian émigré circles, his writing alone was not enough to provide for the family. This would continue to be true until Nabokov was in his late fifties, when *Lolita* finally brought worldwide fame and financial respite. Until then, the Nabokovs were constantly "hard up," especially given that Nabokov was also supporting his mother and other relatives who were scraping by in Prague.[67] In Berlin he continued tutoring, traveling from house to house by bus and on foot. He also earned small fees reciting his work. One of the most successful events took place the first time he read in Paris, in 1932. He recited some poetry and the first two chapters of his novel in progress, *Despair*. The reading had been organized by Ilya Fondaminsky, whom Nabokov considered not only highly cultivated but one of the noblest human beings in the Russian émigré community. Fondaminsky eventually urged Vera and Vladimir to leave Berlin for Paris, and helped them relocate. They finally settled in Paris in 1937.[68]

Nabokov described one of these readings in an interview he gave in 1966, which constitutes the sixth chapter of *Strong Opinions.* He had been asked to step in at the last minute for a Hungarian writer who had fallen ill. She was "very famous that winter, author of a best-selling novel, I remember its title, *La Rue du Chat qui Pêche.*" The sudden change from the Hungarian woman to Nabokov's lecture on Pushkin made his friends worry that they would be faced with an empty house. A few Hungarians who showed up, unaware of the change, hung around anyway to listen, and Nabokov's friends did their best to round up as many of his readers as they could. According to Nabokov, the "unforgettable consolation" came when he caught a glimpse of James Joyce "sitting, arms folded and glasses glinting, in the midst of the Hungarian football team."[69]

The two great writers finally met one evening at the home of their mutual friends Lucy and Paul Leon. A long and sociable conversation ensued, though later Nabokov couldn't recall much about it, while Vera remembered clearly how keen Joyce was to know the exact ingredients of "myod," the Russian mead, and that no two people gave the same reply. Joyce presented Nabokov with a copy of *Haveth Childers Everywhere,* an advanced excerpt version of *Finnegans Wake.* Nabokov had not published in English yet, so was unable to respond in kind.[70] Nabokov considered *Ulysses* a towering novel and one of the greatest works of the twentieth century, but *Finnegans Wake* he found unconvincing. In a letter to Vera he wrote, "The abstract puns, the verbal masquerade, the shadows of words, the diseases of words . . . in the end wit sinks behind reason, and, while it is setting, the sky is ravishing, but then there is night."[71] Notably, there are many critics who have the same opinion of Nabokov's own latter works.[72]

7

Life in France was no easier for the Nabokovs. They were forced to rent a cramped, one-room apartment. Dmitri spent all his time either sleeping or playing, and as a result, Nabokov was forced to write in the bathroom. He explained in letters that he would place a suitcase on top of the bidet, and this served as a makeshift desk. By the time the sun went down, his fingers would be numb from the cold and the long hours of writing.[73] He received word of his mother's failing health, but the Nazis were tightening their grip on Czechoslovakia, and a trip to Prague was unthinkable at the time. These compounding circumstances are what led him to make the most important decision of his life: to write in English. It was not ambition that led him to it, but practicality: Hitler and Stalin were quickly getting rid of the émigré community. It is apparent in his letters and interviews (and sometimes in his books) that it was a heartbreaking choice for him to make, as painful as it was to leave his homeland. The Russian language had kept him tethered to his childhood and to his past, the only thing he had left. And this despair plagued him even after his English-language work brought unprecedented success. It was in Paris that he wrote his first novel in English, in 1939: *The Real Life of Sebastian Knight.*

Nabokov had a keen sense of humor. He loved joking around, especially in private, teasing others and being teased. According to Field, Nabokov walked into a room on May 2, 1939, where a few friends had been concocting a prank on him. He preempted the joke, though, telling them point-blank that his mother had passed away that morning and then stood silently for a few minutes, rubbing his forehead with his fingertips.[74] After his father's death, this was the bitterest blow in Nabokov's life. He had been unable to provide financial support to his mother when she needed it. He had been unable to visit regularly. Now he would miss her funeral. The bond with his mother had been a close one and irreplaceable. She had been the first person to hear and read his poems since he was a child, painstakingly documenting them in chronological order and organizing them into albums. She had been a tender, gentle soul, with a serene character, and a deep appreciation of nature and beauty. She had first taught him the value of transparent things, and more important, the value of remembering.

Nabokov dreamt of his brother Sergey one night in the autumn of 1945. He saw him in agony, prostrate on a bunk in a German concentration camp. As far as Vladimir knew, Sergey was still living in an Austrian castle with his lover, Hermann. The following day, a letter arrived from his younger brother, Kirill, with the news that Sergey had died of malnutrition in a camp near Hamburg. Nabokov had always felt guilty over the peculiar relationship he had with his reclusive brother and was racked with the feeling of never having shown enough fraternal regard. Vladimir had been the spoiled and coddled child, while Sergey had always received less attention. This is the theme that runs through *The Real Life of Sebastian Knight*.[75] It also emerges in different forms throughout *Ada,* in the way Ada and Van treat Lucette: how little we know about the ones who are supposedly the closest to us. Nabokov parses the concealed feelings of hostility, the taunting and dismissal, the lack of real concern in interactions with siblings and other relatives, and the inevitable regret over not appreciating family until it is too late.

In 1964 word came of Kirill's fatal heart attack in Munich. Kirill had been arranging a Radio Liberty program, which broadcast from West Germany into the Soviet Union. The program was to be a profile on his brother Vladimir. Kirill's notes were found scattered all around his room. Nabokov had neglected to keep in touch with Kirill, too, although occasionally he would listen to his brother read and critique his poems. Vladimir's relationship with his sister Olga had always been distant. He had been working to find a way to bring Olga's son Rostislav Petkevich from Czechoslovakia to the United States, but the communist coup of 1948 ruined this prospect. His younger sister, Elena, had always been his favorite sibling. Eventually she had chosen Switzerland as her home, and the Nabokovs were able to renew their convivial relationship when he and Vera moved there later on.[76]

Nabokov was private about his personal affairs and never expressed in public his affliction, like his grief over losing his father. At times some victims emphasize this aspect of their experience, until they are defined by it. His success and prominence were a long time coming, largely because he insisted on excellence in everything, and kept his focus on the work itself, paying little heed to extraliterary life. He avoided political propaganda of any sort and didn't care to engage the sympathy of the reader. It would seem that everything he lost over the course of his life was due to external factors, while everything he gained (apart from his genius) was the result of his astonishing self-confidence, and his love for work, work, and more work.

Following his transition into English as a writing language came the inevitable idea of actually migrating to America. The Fascists had won further victories in Europe, and the Communists appeared to be consolidating their power for the long term. Yet emigrating was a complicated process, and he could not even find a publisher willing to take on *The Real Life of Sebastian Knight.* As luck would have it, though, Stanford University had been in touch with a friend of his, Mark Aldanov, to offer a summer residency. Aldanov was not planning on a move to America at the time, so in his stead he recommended Nabokov. Even with their American visas in order, though, the crucial question was how the Nabokovs could leave France. And more important, how would they fund their journey? It took perseverance, fund-raising, and no small amount of assistance on the part of friends and acquaintances, but the impossible eventually became possible.[77]

Nabokov boarded yet another train toward exile. This time he departed with the family unit he had formed himself. Dmitri got sick as the train was pulling out of the station; he was suffering from a high fever. Luckily, he had recovered by the time they reached the port, and they were able to continue their journey. *Speak, Memory* ends with the image of Vladimir and Vera holding their six-year-old son Dmitri by the hand, subtly suggesting the image in the first chapter of the book: the four-year-old Vladimir tottering along, holding his mother and father's hands.[78]

Nabokov left some of his books and papers in a trunk in the basement of Fondaminsky's apartment building, together with his collection of European butterflies. The Nazis marched into Paris a few weeks later, and German bombs reduced the apartment where the Nabokovs had been living to rubble. Fondaminsky was arrested and his belongings ransacked, including Nabokov's butterfly collection. His books and notes were pitched and scattered about the street. Fondaminsky's niece carefully retrieved as much as she could at the time, and after years stowed away in a coal cellar, they finally caught up with Nabokov in 1950. Fondaminsky himself perished in a concentration camp.[79]

Sirin doesn't appear as a pseudonym in *Speak, Memory,* but instead is transformed into a real-life figure, another manifestation of the writer himself, examples of which can be found throughout Nabokov's oeuvre.[80]

Migration to America was not just another hop and a skip to somewhere else, but the end of Sirin's life, an incarnation that was contingent upon the Russian language. Nevertheless, Sirin left behind a noteworthy collection of novels: *Mary* (1926), *King, Queen, Knave* (1928), *The Luzhin Defense* (1930), *The Eye* (1930), *Glory* (1932), *Camera Obscura* (1933), *Despair* (1934), *Invitation to a Beheading* (1936), and, finally, *The Gift* (1937–1938), not to mention his poems, short stories, and two plays. By the time Nabokov left France, Sirin had become one of the finest Russian authors of the twentieth century, arguably the greatest. His last novel was recognized not only as one of Nabokov's best but also as one of the best examples of the form in contemporary Russian literature. Ivan Bunin, the doyen of émigré writers and a Nobel laureate (awarded in 1933), endorsed *The Luzhin Defense* in terms that clearly revealed Sirin's pivotal role during these years: "This kid has snatched a gun and done away with the whole older generation, myself included."[81]

Nabokov has this to say about Sirin in a chapter on émigré writers and poets in *Speak, Memory:* "But the author that interested me most was naturally Sirin. He belonged to my generation. Among the young writers produced in exile he was the loneliest and most arrogant one. Beginning with the appearance of his first novel in 1925 and throughout the next fifteen years, until he vanished as strangely as he had come, his work kept provoking an acute and rather morbid interest on the part of critics."[82] Nabokov goes on to comment that just as Marxists had condemned Sirin for his lack of interest in economic structures, so émigré "mystagogues" criticized his lack of religious insight and moral concerns. He upsets conventions and, especially, a Russian sense of decorum. Conversely, his admirers praised (perhaps too much, Nabokov writes) his "unusual style, brilliant precision, functional imagery." Russian readers accustomed to Russian realism "were impressed by the mirror-like angles of his clear but weirdly misleading sentences." And they also appreciated that "the real life of the books flowed in his figures of speech." Like a meteor, Sirin had shot through the dark sky of exile and disappeared, leaving nothing behind except a "vague sense of uneasiness."

8

Nabokov's life coincides with many of the key events that took place throughout the tumultuous twentieth century. Yet it is hard to identify clear-cut
signs of the changes that were taking place in Nabokov's own life. It seems
almost as though when facing external destructive forces, he walked deter-
minedly in the opposite direction. Not in the gallantry of empty heroics, but
instead out of a sense of perseverance and resolve in safeguarding his independence, and his integrity. He was truly swimming against the current,
keeping at arm's length the so-called revolutionary writers whose posturing
and bravado were a smokescreen for their ignorance and incompetence. In
Lectures on Russian Literature, he has this to say about Gorky: "As a creative artist, Gorki is of little importance. But as a colorful phenomenon in
the social structure of Russia he is not devoid of interest."[83] Exactly the
opposite can be said about Nabokov; his life can be summarized in one sentence: wherever he was, he just wrote . . . and wrote.

Nabokov's two consuming passions outside of literature were studying butterflies and composing chess problems. One of the Russian novels
he wrote in Berlin as Sirin was titled *The Luzhin Defense,* and it centers on
a chess grandmaster whose life and death are linked to the moves in chess
problems. His poetry collection titled *Poems and Problems* (1970) comprises
thirty-nine Russian poems (with their English translations), fourteen English poems, and eighteen chess problems and their solutions. In his introduction he wrote:

> Finally, there is the chess. I refuse to apologize for its inclusion.
> Chess problems demand from the composer the same virtues
> that characterize all worthwhile art: originality, invention, con-
> ciseness, harmony, complexity, and splendid insincerity. The
> composing of these ivory-and-ebony riddles is a comparatively
> rare gift and an extravagantly sterile occupation; but then all
> art is inutile, and divinely so, if compared to a number of more
> popular human endeavors. Problems are the poetry of chess,
> and its poetry, as all poetry, is subject to changing trends with
> various conflicts between old and new schools. Modern con-

ventionalism repels me in chess problems as much as it does in "social realism" or in "abstract" sculpture.[84]

Nabokov, in a 1963 interview, responded to the question of why he chose to study butterflies by saying: "They chose me, not I them." Butterflies became his emblem, his totem animal. Boyd explains that on the first page of his first book of poetry, beside the pseudonymous author's name and the title, "VI. Sirin. Poems. 1923," there is a hand-drawn sketch of a butterfly.[85] Many a letter to friend or relative had a butterfly drawn below his signature, and he inscribed books with multicolored hybrids. Boyd believed that Nabokov's development as a writer followed a process of imparting to his fiction the joys of entomology: "The pleasure of the particular, the shock of discovery, the intuition of mystery and playfully deceptive design."[86] The closer he got to nature as a young boy, the more deeply he observed and appreciated it, and the more mysterious the natural world became. He discerned that nature had a sense of humor. This idea can be found throughout his work: attention to crisp detail in every phenomenon, identification with the succession of deeper and deeper levels of specificity. All this mimics the relationship between phenomenon and knowledge on one hand, and nature on the other. What is the relationship between writing novels and being a lepidopterist, he was asked in an interview, and he explained that in a work of art, there is a "merging between the two things, between the precision of poetry and the excitement of pure science."[87] He was not attracted to butterflies because of their beauty, though; his interest was exclusively scientific. "All butterflies are beautiful and ugly at the same time—like human beings," he said in another interview.[88] What mattered to Nabokov most was that butterflies were singular, very special creatures.

Butterflies propelled Nabokov back to that sweet, adored place of his childhood. For example, the summer of 1906, when he was seven years old and caught his first butterfly, a rare and stunning swallowtail variety. He caught it and placed it in the wardrobe for safekeeping, but the next morning it escaped. It took him forty years of journeying to find it again, poised atop an "immigrant dandelion," under an endemic aspen near Boulder, Colorado.[89] His father had also been keen on butterflies, and Vladimir used to consult V.D.'s dusty old childhood collection, which he kept in Vyra's "magic room."[90] They were precious beyond words for young Vladimir. Years later, he would evoke the day his father burst into his room, grabbed his butterfly net, and shot out to hunt a rare female Russian Poplar Admirable he had just glimpsed.[91] Fyodor's father in *The Gift* constitutes what could be a loving portrait of Nabokov's own father. Here his fictional character is fashioned in the guise of a distinguished lepidopterist who disappears on an expedition to Tibet. Fyodor continues to feel his presence both when he's awake and while dreaming.

After that first summer, Nabokov's obsession with butterflies grew a little more every day. Not only did he catch and collect them as sport, but he began studying them in earnest. One can imagine how this early beguilement with lepidoptera and the idea of the butterfly's life cycle could occupy his imagination and eventually find its way into his books. The notion of metamorphosis is intrinsic: from life to death in the cocoon and death back to life. Consciousness might appear to be cut off with death, but instead it is simply transformed. In so many of his novels, the presence of a butterfly heralds a momentous event, and Nabokov's work glimmers throughout with the luminous shades of butterfly wings. According to Boyd, since butterflies serve as the reigning extended metaphor of Nabokov's life, they preserved and sustained the connection to his lost world, and his childhood's most hallowed place, Vyra: "Once butterflies were associated with the estate, Vyra's power over Nabokov's imagination became even more irresistible. Just as Humbert's pursuit of nymphets was an attempt to relive his idyll with dead Annabel Leigh, so Nabokov's lepping trips in adulthood would be in part the only possible continuation of a broken past." "We are the caterpillars of angels," Nabokov wrote in a poem when he was young, echoing Dante.[92]

Butterflies were not merely a pastime—Nabokov also wrote serious scientific articles about them. What he considered one of his true shining achievements, of which he was most proud, was having discovered and named a hitherto unknown species of butterfly. In the early 1940s, one of his Russian-language students, Dorothy Leuthold, offered to drive the Nabokovs from New York to Stanford in her new car. They were freshly arrived in America, and Nabokov had been invited to lecture at Stanford University, but the university would not cover his travel expenses. On the way, they stopped to see the Grand Canyon, and while they were walking along a trail in the morning chill, Dorothy's foot happened to kick up a midsized brown butterfly. Nabokov noticed that the butterfly belonged to an unclassified subspecies of *Neonympha* and promptly netted it. This was Nabokov's first American "discovery." He named the subspecies *Neonympha dorothea*, in honor of the woman who turned his first drive across America into an unexpected adventure.[93]

Not long afterward, after he began lecturing at Wellesley, he paid a visit to Harvard's Museum of Comparative Zoology. He found that most of the butterflies in the Old World section of the Weeks Collection were haphazardly arranged and housed in glassless trays, exposing them to dust and mites. Worse, they were not even classified properly. So he offered to rearrange the collection for free, and the head of entomology, Nathaniel Banks, accepted his proposition. Nabokov began working there once a week, after a tedious sixteen-mile journey to and from Harvard that included bus and train transfers. He soon became a fixture in room 402, and Harvard Museum eventually accommodated a part-time position for him. Late in 1942, during a visit to the American Museum of Natural History in New York, he saw the butterfly he had discovered announced with a red label, which designates a "type specimen." A red label is used instead of the traditional white when a find is considered a discovery. On his way to Washington, Nabokov wrote a poem in which he calls himself the godfather of an insect and its first describer, which is the only fame he cared for. "Dark pictures, thrones, the stones that pilgrims kiss, / poems that take a thousand years to die / but ape the immortality of this / red label on a little butterfly."[94]

9

Though Nabokov had come to the United States on an invitation from Stanford University, his time lecturing there lasted no more than six months. His academic teaching took place almost entirely at Wellesley College in the 1940s and Cornell University in the 1950s. He also lectured in different cultural centers whenever he had the opportunity. Even so, the Nabokovs were relentlessly beleaguered by financial concerns.[95] Other issues entered the mix, like the constant shifts in how Americans measured their relationship with the Soviet Union. For Boyd, the Hitler-Stalin pact had brought Nabokov, who was famously outspoken against the Soviets, closer to the interests of Mildred McAfee, president of Wellesley College. However, when the tide changed and the Soviet Union effectively became a U.S. ally in World War II, and especially after the Battle of Stalingrad, his contract was not renewed. This would seem a peculiar decision, given that the alliance between the nations had helped make Russian fashionable. Students were flocking to Russian language courses. In an exasperated letter to Edmund Wilson, Nabokov complained how funny it was to be faced with so many obstacles to academic employment when he knew Russian better than anyone else in America, and English better than any Russian in America.[96] He was forced to teach a wide array of subjects despite his eagerness to concentrate on Russian literature. And he had no choice but to teach the Russian language. His brilliance as a teacher of literature could not go unrecognized for long, however, and his lectures on Pushkin, Gogol, Turgenev, Tolstoy, and Chekhov were lauded. His lectures and fine analysis of the great European tradition, including Flaubert, Proust, and Kafka, together with Austen, Dickens, Stevenson, and Joyce, also distinguished him over time.

What made Nabokov's lectures stand apart in a traditionally dry academic setting was his uncanny capacity to beguile his students and stir in them the same passion for literature that he felt himself. His teaching methods were naturally unorthodox. Rather than getting lost in the "moonshine of generalizations," he preferred to "fondle details," and obliged his students to focus acutely on what they were reading.[97] During a lecture in Minnesota, when he had forgotten his notes and was forced to ad-lib, he gave his students a quiz on the approaches that distinguish a good reader. There are ten definitions, and the students had to choose a combination of four:

1. The reader should belong to a book club.
2. The reader should identify himself or herself with the hero or heroine.
3. The reader should concentrate on the social-economic angle.

4. The reader should prefer a story with action and dialogue to one with none.
5. The reader should have seen the book in a movie.
6. The reader should be a budding author.
7. The reader should have imagination.
8. The reader should have memory.
9. The reader should have a dictionary.
10. The reader should have some artistic sense.

In Nabokov's view, the readers should have imagination, memory, a dictionary, and an artistic sense.[98]

Nabokov's imagination and creativity extended even to his language training. He once explained in a letter to Edmund Wilson his method for teaching a class of one hundred girls how to pronounce Russian vowels: "Please take out your mirrors, girls, and see what happens inside your mouths . . . your tongue keeps back—independent and aloof—whereas in Я, е, и, ё, ю—the squashed vowels—it rushes and crushes itself against your lower teeth—a prisoner dashing himself at the bars of his cell."[99] His classes were at their fullest when he was teaching literature. Students would gossip outside of the classroom and comment on things he said or the dramatic skits he'd perform, for example, when walking into the classroom chattering to himself something like "the passion of the scientist and the precision of the artist." He'd pause, midstep, looking baffled: "Have I made a mistake?" he'd say. "Don't I mean 'the passion of the artist and the precision of the scientist?'" Another pause, an impish glance over his glasses at the students. He'd exclaim: "No! The passion of the scientist and the precision of the artist!"[100] Several of his now trademark phrases show how proximate Nabokov the teacher was to Nabokov the writer: "Caress the details, the divine details." Or his list of three factors that make up a great writer: "storyteller, teacher, enchanter." The storyteller entertains, and the teacher offers moral education or direct knowledge. But most important, "a great writer is always a great enchanter." So a "wise" reader's approach to a work of genius should not be with the heart and or even the brain, "but with his spine. It is there that occurs the telltale tingle."[101]

Nabokov was interested in reviving the art, the fervor, of reading "correctly." Consequently, even his exam questions deviated from the conventional and were designed to survey the student's attention to detail. For example: in *Madame Bovary*, was Rudolf Emma Bovary's first or second lover? (First.) What color was the bottle containing the arsenic with which Emma poisoned herself? (Brown.)[102] As another example, he told students to bring each novel to class, as the first lecture was largely so they could go over the wretched translations and make emendations. The course was about Emma's eyes, Emma's hairdo, her hands, sunshade, dress, shoes. And when he criticized the translator's laziness, it was as if Nabokov was telling the students how they should read his own novels.[103]

Nabokov would begin his semester-long European literary courses with a great show of mock-authoritarian flourish: "You will buy Austen today and start reading at once. Read *every word*. Suppress the radio and tell your room-mate to shut up." When he was teaching Austen's *Mansfield Park*, he would require the students to read the books the main characters read. For Kafka's *Metamorphosis*, he would sketch the insect into which Gregor Samsa was transformed ("It was a domed beetle, not the flat cockroach of sloppy translators") and require them to describe the arrangement of rooms and the positions of doors and furniture in the Samsa flat. In the case of Tolstoy's *Anna Karenina*, he drew the clothes that Kitty would have worn for ice-skating. And for Joyce's *Ulysses*, he consulted a street map in Dublin and drew out the crisscrossing routes used by Stephen and Bloom, expecting the students to learn it by heart.[104]

At times, Nabokov's zealous views triggered heated confrontations. Boyd points out that one student walked out of his classroom in protest twice, first when the lecturer targeted Dostoevsky and the other when he fiercely criticized Freud. Nabokov's sensitivity to bad literature, autocratic regimes, and racial, ethnic, or religious prejudice was evident not only in his lectures but also in his behavior. He withdrew from a project with the distinguished Russian linguist Roman Jacobson because Jacobson had traveled to Moscow to participate in a conference. (In Nabokov's words he made "little trips to totalitarian countries.") Another cantankerous response took the form of a letter to David Daiches, head of Cornell's Literature Division, praising his attack on T. S. Eliot's anti-Semitism. At a party for his students, he railed against Laurence Olivier's film adaptation of *Hamlet*. One student asked whether he had actually seen the film, and he replied: "Of course I haven't seen the film. Do you think I would waste my time seeing a film as bad as I have described?"[105]

In a review for the *New York Times Book Review* on Jean Paul Sartre's first novel, *La Nausée,* in March 1949, we see how strongly Nabokov derided the type of literature he disliked. He called it a "tense-looking but really very loose type of writing, which has been popularized by many second-raters — Barbusse, Céline, and so forth. Somewhere behind looms Dostoevski at his worst, and still farther back there is old Eugène Sue, to whom the melodramatic Russian owed so much."[106] He went on to excoriate: "When an author inflicts his idle and arbitrary philosophic fancy on a helpless person whom he has invented for that purpose, a lot of talent is needed to have the trick work. One has no special quarrel with Roquentin when he decides that the world exists. But the task to make the world exist as a work of art was beyond Sartre's powers." Afterward, the *New York Times* asked him to review Sartre's *What Is Literature?* But Nabokov declined, calling it "trash." "Frankly, I do not think it is worth reviewing."[107]

He was as ardent in his advocacy of the writers he loved (Shakespeare, Dickens, Pushkin, Gogol, Flaubert, Tolstoy, Chekhov, Wells, Proust, Kafka, and Joyce) as he was in his censure of those he considered bad or mediocre (Stendhal, Balzac, Dostoevsky, Mann, Pound, Eliot, Conrad, Faulkner, and Hemingway). In a television interview with Robert Hughes in 1965, he offered his list of the greatest masterpieces of twentieth-century prose, in order of importance: Joyce's *Ulysses,* Kafka's *Metamorphosis,* Bely's *Petersburg,* and "the first half of Proust's fairy tale *In Search of Lost Time.*"[108] In a later conversation with Alfred Appel, in 1970, he mentioned the contemporary European writers he most admired: Queneau, Robbe-Grillet, and the Belgian writer Franz Hellens.[109] Among the American writers, he praised Salinger and Updike. In 1972 he listed them again as among his favorite American short story writers, along with John Cheever, Herbert Gold, John Barth, and Delmore Schwartz. Following the publication of *Lolita,* which was feverishly circulated among young writers on the Cornell cam-

pus, he developed a cult following. One of them was his student Thomas
Pynchon, though Nabokov failed to remember him.[110]

10

Nabokov's first English novel, *The Real Life of Sebastian Knight,* was finally
published in December 1941. That year he also composed his first poem
in English (apart from the ones he wrote as a boy). In the poem, he begs a
fatal "farewell" to several things listed there, one of which is his native Russian language, the "softest of tongues."[111] This sorrow recurs repeatedly in
his books, in different forms. The poem's enumeration points to a crucial
element for Nabokov, another layer of his loss of Russian: the loss of his
Russia, his happy childhood, and his youthful sweethearts. At the close of
his epilogue to *Lolita,* written in 1956, we find a description of this private
tragedy: "I had to abandon my natural idiom, my untrammeled, rich, and
infinitely docile Russian tongue for a second-rate brand of English." Something that is not, he maintains, anybody else's concern.[112]

Regardless, he never lost the essence of his Russianness, and the remembrance of his past lingers on the pages he wrote in English. His linguistic flamboyance and literary technique were never mere side effects of his
abiding enchantment with language, or ways of showing off. He saw language as the essential form of consciousness: memory, love, and life itself.
As a result, his surrender to the English language was not an easy one. He
had to tame the language, digest it, and turn it into something that belonged to him. His extravagant use of English often fascinated English-
speaking critics (and in some cases horrified them, too), and underneath
these sentences one can intuit the cadences of his native Russian.[113] Nabokov rebelled against all tyrannies that would divest him of his homeland, his
father, his contemporaries, and his language. He rebelled against them, and
more than anything, defied the absolute concept of death. Nabokov's main
weapon in this rebellion (perhaps his only weapon) was language.

In one of his most famous English poems, "An Evening of Russian
Poetry" (1945), Nabokov depicts the surrender of his Russian language
as his "private tragedy": "Like a small caterpillar on its thread, / my heart

keeps dangling from a leaf long dead." The poet is addressing an audience only mildly interested in what they are hearing, that knows little about the Russian language and its literary tradition. He talks about the scepter that he lost "beyond the seas." He can still hear "the neighing of . . . dappled nouns" and the "soft participles coming down the steps."[114] There is despair over losing his language, a poet's prized possession, which intermingles with another sorrow: though he lays himself bare for listeners, they are ignorant of the problem and, naturally, cannot sympathize. This is the theme that emerges in a different form in the likable character of Pnin.

Nabokov began writing *Pnin* in 1953, and it was serialized in the *New Yorker,* chapter by chapter, except for the fifth, "Pnin under Pines," because he refused to remove references to Lenin and Stalin's regime, and phrases like "medieval tortures in a Soviet jail," or "Bolshevik dictatorship." *Speak, Memory* had also been successfully serialized in the magazine, and *Pnin* proved even more popular. The strange blend of tragedy and comedy in *Pnin,* the human pathos and misfortune, focus on the idea of pain. According to Brian Boyd, the fact that the title almost spells the word "pain" is clearly indicative.[115]

He wrote *Bend Sinister* in 1947, and together with *Invitation to a Beheading* (written in Russian), they are considered his most political novels. He had completed his autobiography, which was published in 1951 as *Conclusive Evidence.* He rewrote it, and the result of that effort was finally published in 1966 as *Speak, Memory.* Nabokov described it as "the meeting point of an impersonal art form and a very personal life story."[116] It is celebrated as a great work of literature, not only because it records a unique life but also because it is a complete work in and of itself. The writer re-creates the details of his own life on every page, as if he were trying to compete with the creator of this life—a life poised on the verge of its tipping point, which came with *Lolita.*

Nabokov completed *Lolita* on December 6, 1953 (after working on it for exactly five years), despite manifold interruptions and asides. He had been tempted to burn the manuscript once or twice, but was persuaded not to by "the thought that the ghost of the destroyed book would haunt my files for the rest of my life"—and, of course, there was Vera.[117] At first he intended to sign the manuscript using a pseudonym, and as a result had been wary of showing it to anyone outside of his circle. He was also concerned about how a conservative university like Cornell might react. *Lolita* was set to follow the same course of setbacks as Joyce's *Ulysses*. Art alters reality, yet there is the usual question, "What is *Lolita* about?" which leads to the inevitable answer, "It would have probably been better not to publish it."[118] *Lolita* is about a middle-aged man's obsession with a twelve-year-old girl. The novel doesn't attempt to defend the man's perversion. Nor does it overlook the fact that the girl is unprotected. This was not Nabokov's first literary exploration of the victim archetype and the abuse of power. Yet the unresolved problem of "What is the novel about?" remained. This question compresses the novel into a single, superficial dimension and lucidly illustrates the truth behind what Diderot said in 1773: "To me the freedom of [the author's] style is almost the guarantee of the purity of his morals."[119]

As was partly feared, American publishers rejected the book. Nabokov then decided to send the manuscript to Sylvia Beach in Paris, who had published *Ulysses*. Unfortunately, Beach's publishing days had come to an end by then, but the somewhat dubious publisher Olympia Press agreed to publish the book.[120] Despite his family advising him to wait, Nabokov felt he had no choice but to accept; he needed to be done with it. *Lolita* was finally published two years after it was completed, in Paris, in 1955. The story of how one of the greatest novels of the twentieth century came to be published in an uncertain, back-of-the-bookshop press is one of the most famous in contemporary literature. In France it was called "l'affaire *Lolita*." The novel became an underground sensation, and contrary to the writer's wishes, a *succès de scandale*. Before long, it brought along a whole new set of problems, too.

Early in 1956, Graham Greene kicked up a fuss when he named *Lolita* one of the best three books he had read the previous year. In a sharp reaction, John Gordon, the editor of the London-based newspaper *Sunday Times,* wrote that though he abhorred censorship, he found *Lolita* to be the filthiest book he had ever read and that anyone who published or sold it would certainly be sent to prison. Greene retorted ironically by proposing the constitution of a "John Gordon Society" to "examine and if necessary to condemn all offensive books, plays, paintings, sculptures and ceramics." A group of writers took up the idea to have some fun, and even held a preliminary "John Gordon Society" meeting in which writers Christopher Isherwood, Angus Wilson, and A. J. Ayer suggested that publishers use a bellyband with the words "banned by the John Gordon Society."[121]

Before long, the controversy seeped into the American press. At first, the author's name was withheld, but once the literary merits of the book were established and recognized, Nabokov's name was unveiled. A number of well-established American publishers began searching him out, but snatching the rights back from Olympia's talons proved a tricky matter.[122] The Olympia copies were selling very well on the American black market, and the United Kingdom became anxious about how to curtail books from being smuggled into its territory. As a result, the British Home Office formally asked the French government to ban the book. The French Ministry of the Interior capitulated, even though its most venerable publishing house—Gallimard, known for its conservatism—was in the process of legally translating the novel for publication. Spurred by the excellent reviews that were beginning to acclaim *Lolita*'s genius, Maurice Girodias, the owner of Olympia, sued the French government. The French press stepped into the fracas in defense of *Lolita*.[123]

Lolita transformed its creator's life at Cornell. The fifty-nine-year-old Vladimir Nabokov became a star. He inaugurated Cornell's Festival of the Contemporary Arts with a lecture titled "Readers, Writers, and Censors in Russia," one of his standard lectures given for public occasions since 1941, now presented in a new light, thanks to *Lolita*. The lecture hall was so crowded the Nabokovs' own arrival was delayed.[124] In one of the few passages actually composed for the unfinished second part of *Speak, Memory*, Nabokov relates that he and Vera could find only a parking spot so far away that they had to nearly run to make it to the hall on time. A lone Japanese man overtook them as they made their way toward the bustle of people waiting. "But the lecturer was still outside, almost paralysed by the weird feeling that a ghost must feel when debarred from the events of his relivable past." The scene later resurfaced in *Ada*, complete with the sprinting Japanese man.[125]

Lolita was finally published in the United States on Monday, August 18, 1958. Largely rave reviews had appeared in a dozen Sunday newspapers the day before. When Putnam later advertised *Lolita* in the *New York Times,* it claimed that 62,500 copies were in print and had sold out in the first four days. Three weeks later, the figure was 100,000 copies, making this the first time since *Gone with the Wind* that a book had reached that milestone so quickly. It stayed at the top of the American best-seller lists for seven weeks, and before long Stanley Kubrick showed interest in a Hollywood film adaptation. (Nabokov supplied a screenplay, though Kubrick used only part of it.) *Lolita* went on to sell more than fourteen million copies worldwide in the next thirty years. Despite all the naysayers and the misgivings, the novel is taught in high school literature classes as a twentieth-century classic.[126]

Meanwhile, Nabokov's intellectual life continued much in the same way as before. He had his pen and he had his butterflies. Nabokov wrote his most momentous work after the age of fifty. But now the tribulations of fame were proving disruptive. In *Lolita*'s wake, there was a double sort of publishing traffic that began to take place: his front-list English-language books were coming out as he was writing them, and his Russian backlist was gradually being translated and published in English. Publishers were fighting over anything signed by Nabokov. And of course his English books were finding their way now into Russian translation. By the end of his life, nearly all his Russian books had been translated into English. He translated some himself, or Dmitri translated them under his supervision. He supervised all translations, even into languages he did not fully command, such as Italian. Vera took it upon herself to crack Italian grammar for the sole purpose of being able to better supervise the translation process.[127]

In September 1959, the Nabokovs traveled to Europe. They had initially intended to spend a few months there, but then decided to extend their stay. *Lolita*'s success had freed Nabokov from academic burdens. Moreover, Dmitri had completed his studies at Harvard and was training in opera in Milan. Nabokov's favorite sister, Elena, now widowed, worked as a librarian in Geneva. He would clarify in several interviews that they were in Europe temporarily, that he was not renouncing his American citizenship (he had a U.S. passport and he paid his taxes to the United States government).[128] Yet they spent the rest of their lives in the deluxe Hotel Palace in Montreux, Switzerland. In an interview in the *New York Times Book Review*, he explained that it had always been his dream to live in a "large, comfortable hotel."[129] But all this had come about very late. In a letter to his sister in 1958, he adds, after referring to the incredible success of *Lolita*, "but all this ought to have happened thirty years ago."[130]

11

Nabokov continued to write prolifically following *Lolita*'s wild success, and was able to continue publishing work of an astonishing caliber. In fact, in the aftermath, Nabokov experienced a renewed and burgeoning creative period with his next two novels, *Pale Fire* (1962) and *Ada* (1969), each of which sent new ripples of excitement and commotion through the international literary community. *Pale Fire* proposed extraordinary new formal innovations (the novel is presented as the commentary on a long poem), and *Ada* brought him to the pinnacle of renown. *Pale Fire* squeaked onto the best-seller list, whereas *Ada* climbed to number four and stayed on the list for twenty weeks despite being his longest novel. It is also his most difficult novel to understand because the witticisms and linguistic puzzles are delivered in three languages (English, Russian, and French). True, some vexed critics found the novel self-indulgent and overcrowded. But Alfred Kazin wrote in the *Sunday Review* that it closed a trilogy—together with *Lolita* and *Pale Fire*—that had no contemporary peer.

In a 1967 *Paris Review* interview, Nabokov was asked for which books he would like to be remembered. He responded, "The one I am writing or rather dreaming of writing. Actually, I shall be remembered by *Lolita* and my work on *Eugene Onegin*."[131] Brian Boyd estimated that in sheer size and the amount of effort expended, Nabokov's work translating Pushkin's masterpiece dwarfs everything else and can be compared to *Lolita, Pale Fire,* and *Ada* combined.[132] He had written a book on Gogol in the early 1940s, and translated nineteenth- and twentieth-century Russian verse by Pushkin, Lermontov, Tyutchev, Fet, and Khodasevich. But *Eugene Onegin* was his definitive work, and what distinguished him as a matchless trans-

lator, scholar, and critic. The whole twelve hundred pages were first published in a four-volume edition in 1964, which included a word-by-word literal translation, his commentary, two appendixes, an index and a facsimile
reproduction. The rest is filled with Nabokov's descriptions and comments.

The years of obsessive research and translation that Nabokov dedicated to Pushkin are indicative of the prodigious regard he held for the
great writer. "Russians know," Nabokov once said, that "'homeland' and
'Pushkin' are inseparable, and that to be Russian means to love Pushkin."[133]
He first realized there was no adequate literal translation of *Eugene Onegin*
when he was teaching at Wellesley in the 1940s and often had to revise lines
of the existing translations. By the time he was at Cornell, he had become
tired of having to correct what he thought were shockingly and even dis-
gustingly rhymed paraphrases of Pushkin's boundless work. Obviously, he
knew that translating a masterpiece like *Eugene Onegin* would be no small
task, but once he set the process into motion, the challenge became his obsession. Through it, he was also evolving his own theory of literal translation: lexical exactitude with no accommodation for felicity or approxima-
tion to meter or style. Nabokov commented on his ideas in his introduction
to *Invitation to a Beheading:* "Fidelity to one's author comes first, no matter
how bizarre the result. *Vive le pédant,* and down with the simpletons who
think that all is well if the 'spirit' is rendered."[134]

Nabokov had in fact been more severe in the theory than in the practice of translating *Eugene Onegin* (according to his footnotes). And it was
never the ordinary reader he had in mind. Yet its publication raised one of
the mightiest brawls in contemporary literary history, which was first kicked
up by Edmund Wilson's caustic review in the very young *New York Review
of Books.* Many of the prominent intellectual figures of the time, including Robert Lowell and Anthony Burgess, joined the debate and egged the
two literary titans on. But what started as a skirmish quickly devolved into
an outright feud. Critics took issue with the flat literalism and minutiae of
Nabokov's commentaries, while he, incensed, defended its detail and precision. Generally, Nabokov's intention for the translation had been wildly
misunderstood; it was meant to help in reading the original, not to act as
a substitute for it. It had been done in the modesty of an explanation, a

species of concordance, not as an attempt to reproduce the genius of a work and its effect in another language. Burgess commented that even a translation as successful as Edward FitzGerald's rendering of Omar Khayyam's *Rubaiyat* completely betrayed the original text. And "if we want to read Omar, then, we must learn a little Persian and ask for a good, very literal, crib. And if we want to read Pushkin we must learn some Russian and thank God for Nabokov."[135]

The unhappy result of the literary commotion was that it ended a significant and long-standing friendship between Nabokov and Wilson, whose eminence as a critic and scholar had been key for Nabokov and his family during his first years in America.[136] Wilson had truly "discovered" Nabokov's work for the American audience, and had not only shown him compassion, a trait that Nabokov valued particularly, but extended himself in so many other, very tangible ways. In fact, behind every important literary outlet, Wilson had worked some machination or other. During those early years of hardship, Nabokov was also indebted to Katharine White, the fiction editor at the *New Yorker,* for breaking his work out for an American readership.[137] She was instrumental in bringing some financial succor to the Nabokovs when they were in need. Both Nabokov and Wilson were obstinate by nature and often intransigent, and their friendship, though deeply felt, had not been without its occasional squabbles over the years. They were competitive creatures, similar in a number of ways, divergent in others. Wilson's poetic sensibility was not as developed as Nabokov's, and Wilson's periodic phases of jealousy put a strain on their relationship. The tension led to a fissure when Wilson finally reacted to *Lolita,* telling Nabokov, "I like it less than anything else of yours I have read."[138] Nabokov did not believe that he had read it properly, and tried to get his friend to read the novel carefully. But the fissure finally ended in a complete rupture over *Eugene Onegin,* and their friendship never recovered. Wilson acrimoniously charged Nabokov with misunderstanding Pushkin. And in his merciless riposte, Nabokov belittled Wilson's superficial knowledge of Russian.

The controversy surrounding Nabokov's *Eugene Onegin* was not only directed at the translation, but extended also to the lengthy, scrupulous commentaries. Critics couldn't help but praise Nabokov's exhaustive research. John Bayley, a novelist and Pushkinist, wrote, "A better commentary on a poem has never been written, and probably not a better translation of one. . . . So sensitive is Nabokov's version that it becomes poetry in its own right."[139] Nabokov's method was unorthodox, based on a staunch form of individual scholarship that eschewed any reliance on secondhand sources. He had no patience for scholarship based on accumulated information or other people's findings instead of consultation with the original source material. Neither could he abide scholarship that pandered to ideology or the dictates of state. His only duty was to his own conscience, not to the established views or academic traditions, trends, or fashions. He trusted the details, and it was through this staunch fidelity to particulars that he reconstructed Pushkin's artistry. He scrutinized everything: the structure of poems, figures of speech, metaphors, details of the social structures in which the characters lived, and other minutiae such as the species of a tree lurking in the background. All generalities were relinquished in favor of the specifics, as the differentials to show readers what was unique about *Eugene Onegin*. Nabokov's dogged celebration of the individuality of phenomena is without a doubt the most significant characteristic in his approach to writing and scholarship. For Nabokov, reality was always extraordinary.

12

Once in Switzerland, Nabokov continued with a quiet routine during his final years, despite his having become a literary superstar. The only difference was the constant stream of admirers and reporters who made the pilgrimage to Montreux's Hotel Palace. A great deal of his time was occupied with overseeing the continuous flow of translations of his own work into several languages. But his days were mostly spent with butterflies and his writing. He shied away from public gatherings, though he actively continued to support Soviet dissidents and human rights. He did not care for Solzhenitsyn's writing but defended him nonetheless. When Solzhenitsyn was expelled from the USSR, Nabokov wrote to welcome him. They arranged to have lunch together in Montreux, but a misunderstanding occurred that seemed like something from one of his novels: the Solzhenitsyns drove past the Hotel Palace without daring to enter because the Nabokovs had not yet confirmed, while the Nabokovs sat at a private table in the Palace waiting for them.[140] From another quarter of the art world, Alfred Hitchcock approached Nabokov with some ideas to see whether he would be interested in developing a screenplay. They were mutual admirers, as can be gathered by the tone of their exchange. Though the screenplay never materialized, Hitchcock's sketches and Nabokov's proposals remain.

Nabokov's last novels were received more tepidly than the others, and *Transparent Things,* which came out in 1972, baffled many critics, among them John Updike. In Nabokov's opinion, "Amongst the reviewers several careful readers have published some beautiful stuff about it. Yet neither they nor, of course, the common 'criticule' discerned the structural knot of the story."[141] *Look at the Harlequins!* was published two years later and was similarly greeted with reviews that were split between his keen readers and "hacks" who found it less taxing than *Ada* or *Transparent Things.* Nabokov was compiling a book of interviews, and had already begun sketching the outline of a new novel; *The Original of Laura* was published posthumously after thirty years of debate, in 2009. Beleaguered with a chronic fever, he slipped into a coma during an extended hospital stay in 1976. Yet the illness was never diagnosed. He was writing and structuring the new novel in his head, as he always did before committing it to paper: "I must have gone through it some fifty times and in my diurnal delirium kept reading it aloud to a small dream audience in a walled garden. My audience consisted of peacocks, pigeons, my long dead parents, two cypresses, several young nurses crouching around, and a family doctor so old as to be almost invisible."[142]

Nabokov died on July 2, 1977.[143] Dmitri kissed his father's forehead when he left him the penultimate time before he passed, and saw that Nabokov's eyes were filled with tears. When Dmitri asked what was wrong, Nabokov replied that a butterfly was already on the wing. He would never see it. According to Boyd, in an unfinished and unpublished continuation of *The Gift,* Nabokov had written, "The bitterness of an interrupted life is nothing compared to the bitterness of an interrupted work."[144] In an interview he gave in 1971, he remarked, "My life thus far has surpassed splen-

didly the ambitions of boyhood and youth. . . . At fifteen, I visualized myself as a world-famous author of seventy with a mane of wavy white hair.
Today, I am practically bald."[145]

Leningrad recovered its original name, St. Petersburg, in 1986, and
Vladimir Nabokov was not only rehabilitated but gradually commemorated
as a national treasure. Evenings were devoted to his work and other memo-
rials took place at the Tenishev School, his alma mater, and in Vyra and
other childhood haunts. In 1988, *Invitation to a Beheading* and *The Gift*
were first published for Soviet readers, albeit in slightly censored versions.
In 1989, Melodia released a Soviet gramophone recording of his prose.
The note on the record's jacket places him in line with the greatest practi-
tioners of the Russian prose tradition: Pushkin, Lermontov, Chekhov, and
Bunin. It adds that "Nabokov creates his own mode of writing, unique in
its system of images and in the fluidity and musicality of its phrasing."[146]
The spiral of Nabokov's life and art followed the "synthesis" of his lifetime,
and now, once again, it has found the threshold where he crosses over to a
new "thesis."

Reality

The Gift, Look at the Harlequins!,
The Real Life of Sebastian Knight

1

In *Speak, Memory,* Nabokov shares a childhood anecdote. His father called him to his study one afternoon to greet General Kuropatkin, a family friend. The general spread out a handful of matches and arranged them end-to-end to craft a scene: "This is the sea in calm weather," he said. Then he tipped the matches into zigzags: "a stormy sea." But the general's visit was cut short by an urgent summons. Later they discovered that he had received orders to assume supreme command of the Russian forces in the Far East, in the Russo-Japanese War of 1904–1905.[1] Fifteen years later, Vladimir Dmitrievich is fleeing Bolshevik-held St. Petersburg en route to southern Russia when an old peasant in a sheepskin coat stops him and asks him for a light. V.D. is shocked to recognize him: it's General Kuropatkin. Perhaps what's more interesting than the story itself is Nabokov's reaction to their chance encounter and what he calls "the evolution of the match theme."[2] The general had been called away so abruptly that the matches were scattered and forgotten. At that time he had not been able to appreciate the significance of the magical matches. Nabokov explains that the purpose of autobiography is to track these patterns, these thematic designs that appear throughout one's lifetime. His unique perspective on the subject offers a way to explore not only the structure of *Speak, Memory* but of his entire oeuvre.

Nabokov had already introduced this concept in his first novel written in English, *The Real Life of Sebastian Knight,* a few years before writing his

autobiography. Toward the end of the book, the narrator explains the writer
Sebastian Knight's style, his penchant for "juggling with themes, making
them clash or blending them cunningly, making them express that hidden
meaning." He assures the reader that Knight perfected this method in his
last novel, where "it is not the parts that matter, it is their combinations."[3]

In *Speak, Memory,* Nabokov does not arrange the events of his life
chronologically; he instead juxtaposes a series of apparently unrelated
themes. The result is an autobiography that is at once a work of art. And
while examining Nabokov's interaction with art, we find indications of his
outlook on life, and his belief in a kind of pattern or logic that is always
looming behind apparently unrelated events. This is fate's way of expressing
itself creatively—in the continual recurrence of certain themes. A butterfly
escapes Nabokov's grasp when he is seven years old, only to be recaptured
forty years later in Colorado. His adolescence is forfeited in one country
but retrieved in another, through his fiction. If nature creates such sym-
metrical and meaningful coincidences, then nature, like art, is full of tricks
and able to conjure them cunningly into artifice. Art reveals its complexity
through hidden layers of light and shadow. Nabokov believed that skillful
magicians are at work in both nature and in art. And it is only through the
powers of perception and invention that the secrets of these skills are revealed, through the creative faculty. It follows then that though art is elusive, reality, too, is an unreliable variable.

The relationship between art and reality is one of the central themes in
most of Nabokov's novels. For Nabokov, in his own words, "reality" is "one
of the few words which mean nothing without quotes."[4] Reality is significant only in a relative or conditional sense, and the relationship is shaped
through patterns or models that may be either visible or veiled. Nabokov
tackles the theme of underlying associations or the interdependence of all
things in three of his novels: his last Russian novel, *The Gift;* his first English novel, *The Real Life of Sebastian Knight;* and his last completed novel,
Look at the Harlequins! All three deal in large measure with the dichotomy
between "life" and "biography." At once there is the life of a main character,
and at the same time, details of how his biography has been written. Can
we consider these three narratives as being more "realistic" because they

merge the narrator's life with his narration? Nabokov's work often explores how even the most impartial narrator imposes upon the plane of the novel's reality, recounting his own narrative alongside the story itself. In fact, it is impossible to get at the reality of an individual life unless, as in a fairy tale, one experiences that person's life by walking in his or her shoes.

The reader becomes acquainted with a main character in each novel: with Fyodor in *The Gift*, with Sebastian in *The Real Life of Sebastian Knight*, and with Vadim in *Look at the Harlequins!* Each is a writer by profession (either a novelist or a poet), and each novel corresponds with some point or period of Nabokov's own life. Of course, none of the characters is Nabokov himself, or his clear substitute, which is obvious and of negligible interest. What really matters, and what brings these three characters into Nabokov's most intimate space, is that each novel deals in some form with a creative mind struggling against the difficulties of exile. There are, however, some appreciable differences: Fyodor and Vadim are Russian-speaking writers outside of Russia, while Sebastian is of mixed heritage, having a Russian father and a British mother. The novel explores the theme of tension be-tween Sebastian's Russian and British identities: he has been deprived of everything that gives a human being a sense of fixed identity. And the Revo-lution has stripped him even of his childhood.

Life as a whole is an experience of death; every moment as we live it dies and is gone forever. A main concern of twentieth-century literature has been the question of how to regain one's past life. Exile has been referred to as a "double death" because it eliminates all vestiges of a person's past at once. The reality of this moment in time, the present, pales and desolidifies before a past that no longer exists. How can a person tend to basic needs in a new land, rebuild what he or she has lost, without being secure in the reality of that past—without documentary evidence of a previous existence in a place outside the current country of residence? Language is what keeps memories alive. Art is what bestows reality on absent or lost pasts, on what has significance only within the depths of a person's consciousness.

Nabokov lost his mother tongue and his fatherland. Yet he never suc-cumbed to the role of victim, even while suffering the void of exile. He was unwilling to surrender himself to the coercion of exile. And on a deeper level, neither would he yield to the coercion or fatalism of time, as we will come to see. His fiction gave him a space to fashion new circumstances so that he could create new realities. A governing characteristic of Nabokov's protagonists is their attitude toward exile and, more important, toward the passing of time. As a result, the so-called "real" themes of his novels are limited, and form a pattern in his narratives. A main concern, especially in his English novels, is the tension between the "reality" that exile imposes on the main character and the conduct of the character in the face of that tragedy.

Exile from one's homeland and exile from one's language both have roots in an even deeper form of exile. In 1841, the great nineteenth-century Russian literary critic Vissarion Grigoryevich Belinsky wrote in a letter to a friend: "We are men without a country—no, worse than without a country, we are men whose country is a phantom—is it any wonder then that we ourselves are phantoms, that our friendship, our love, our aspirations, our activities are phantoms?" In *Vladimir Nabokov: A Critical Study of the Novels* (1984), an unconvinced David Rampton quotes Belinsky at the end of his chapter on *The Gift*.[5] Perhaps it has always been this way. Isn't an exile's greatest affliction the loss of identity? Hasn't Russian intellectual culture always suffered this affliction, even before so many were forced to leave their homeland? Couldn't we extend this to all intellectuals from the first world to the third world, who live as exiles in their own countries? Nabokov explored this metamorphosis in meticulous detail, this process by which a person is abruptly rendered a "phantasm," and expanded on the notion's background, history, and literary tradition. The émigré Russians became like wandering ghosts because they had to forfeit all power to intervene or participate in local political matters, existing as mere spectators to the changes taking place in foreign lands. The painting above the bed is moved to the cellar and the striped trousers handed down to the poorer cousin, together with a tie that was used only once, in some long-forgotten wedding party. Rooms change gradually, curtains are altered, walls given a new coat of paint, the house is eventually sold, and the day comes when the removal van takes the largely unfamiliar furniture to another house, to an unknown place.

Nabokov reflects upon *The Gift*, the greatest of his Russian novels, and upon the "gloom and glory of exile," in *Speak, Memory*. With few exceptions, all the "liberal-minded creative forces" abandoned Russia under Lenin and Stalin. They all lived elsewhere, untethered, with impunity, suffering neither tsarist censorship nor the much more aggressive Bolshevik censorship. In fact, this apparently lucky group of expatriates enjoyed such unlimited autonomy that it raised the question of whether this "absolute mental freedom" was not due to being caught in an "absolute void."[6] True, the émigré community in Europe was large enough to sustain a writing community, but authors were now writing for a readership devoid of their identity. Indeed, they were writing for a country that had lost even its name: Russia. According to Nabokov, "Since none of those writings could circulate within the Soviet Union, the whole thing acquired a certain air of fragile unreality."[7] Later he admits that the detached observer could easily ridicule these "hardly palpable people who imitated in foreign cities a dead civilization, the remote, almost legendary, almost Sumerian mirages of St. Petersburg and Moscow."[8] They were like many of the great Russian writers, Nabokov asserts, who since the dawn of Russian literary tradition have always been rebels and insurgents. Writers on either side of the border were absorbed by the same threat of erasure. The ones who stayed in the Soviet Union forfeited their individuality. In exile, their identity was suspect. Writing opened a void. Like the first spark of our creation: the instant that is forever lost.

If Russian writers were like exiles even in their own country, it is also the case that the history of writing from exile was a long one. In *Lectures on Russian Literature*, Nabokov comments on the remarkable creativity of Russians when "working in a void," and cites Gogol as an example.[9] But the better example is Nabokov himself. What makes Nabokov and Gogol so much alike is not a question of subject matter or writing styles but their shared belief in imagination as a consequence of the surrounding void, the abyss. Nabokov views the "artist" as being an involuntary exile, a state which he therefore finds unbearable. The only way to survive the condition, then, is to transform the insufferable "reality" through art. The real world is transformed into a world of shadows so that memory and imagination can achieve the true state of "reality." Nabokov's novels teach us how to live in a void.

2

Nabokov explains the background of his novel *The Gift* (1962) in his preface to the English translation. He describes the exodus from Soviet Russia during the first years of the Revolution as "the wanderings of some mythical tribe whose bird-signs and moon-signs I now retrieve from the desert dust."[10] These figures remained largely unknown to American intellectuals, he points out, since the West was in the early stages of a turbulent honeymoon with the Soviet government at the time. Communist propaganda concealed the pale ghosts of émigré Russians within the folds of its red flag, in favor of the clenched fists of its workers and determined portraits of Stalin. "That world is now gone," he writes. "Gone are Bunin, Aldanov, Remizov. Gone is Vladislav Khodasevich, the greatest Russian poet that the twentieth century has yet produced."[11] Nabokov stresses that the world of *The Gift* was as much a phantasm as his other fictional worlds. He also announces that *The Gift* will be his last book written in Russian. The hero of *The Gift* is not Zina, whom Fyodor pursues amorously, but Russian literature itself.[12]

The Gift begins as a simple story. As we have seen, Nabokov reveals the structure of the book himself in the introduction. The first chapter centers on Fyodor's childhood and his poetry. The second follows Fyodor's infatuation with Pushkin and his attempt to write a biography of his father, a prominent lepidopterist who disappeared during a scientific exploration. In the third chapter, Fyodor shifts from Pushkin to Gogol, but his poem for Zina is its heart. The fourth chapter, which Nabokov describes as a "spiral within a sonnet,"[13] is Fyodor's book on Chernyshevski, the renowned Russian writer and social critic. And finally, the fifth chapter weaves all the themes of the previous chapters together and alludes to the book Fyodor dreams of writing one day: *The Gift*.

The Gift centers on the series of coincidences that lead to the encounter between Fyodor, the Russian poet and writer, and Zina. The Russian intellectual milieu in Berlin serves as a backdrop for the love story between these two young émigrés. We observe the development of Fyodor's literary life, with his persistent efforts to write and publish. The story unfolds in a logical sequence of events as in a realist novel. However, the reader occasionally comes across elements that raise certain doubts. Is the novel merely a love affair set in pre–World War II Berlin? From the first page, for example, the narration oscillates between the third and first persons, as if aiming to show both Fyodor's private and public personas. As we continue reading, we become aware that the story is replete with little tricks. Apparently meaningless digressions seemingly introduce unrelated or irrelevant events and characters. But of course these occasional asides are neither meaningless nor irrelevant. We gradually discover that the links among disparate elements constitute a key part of the novel's structure.

The novel opens with an ideal example. A friend (coincidentally named Chernyshevski, no relation to the famous writer) telephones Fyodor to congratulate him on the highly favorable review of his first poetry collection, and insists on having him over that evening to show him the newspaper where the review is published. Fyodor entertains himself on the way by trying to visualize this unknown critic, this literary twin who understands Fyodor better than Fyodor understands himself. But when he arrives, he discovers that it was all a practical joke; there was no kindly critic or glowing review. His host shows him the newspaper and tells him to pay attention to the date: it is April 1, and he has been fooled.[14] Despite feeling crestfallen, Fyodor realizes, or he thinks he realizes, that Chernyshevski believes he is able to see his own son's ghost. The youth, who has recently committed suicide, had resembled Fyodor, and even composed poems. So we ask, is Chernyshevski's belief that he can see his son's ghost less real than the existence of the imaginary critic? Perhaps it is more so. We ought not to forget that all this takes place at the novel's opening. Eventually, Fyodor himself hopes to see his dead father again,[15] and the theme of unreal reality recurs still later in the novel, when Chernyshevski is on his deathbed, considering the afterlife. "What nonsense," he exclaims, "of course there is nothing afterwards." He stops to listen to the trickling and drumming of the rain that can be seen just outside his window, and continues: "There is nothing. It is as clear as the fact that it is raining."[16] But Nabokov engages his delicious sense of humor here, for there is no rain; "outside the spring sun was playing on the roof tiles, the sky was dreamy and cloudless, the tenant upstairs was watering the flowers on the edge of her balcony, and the water trickled down with a drumming sound." It merely seems like rain to the dying Chernyshevski.[17]

Now let's return to the theme of love. The novel's first lines beautifully describe a couple moving their things into a new flat. Fyodor will eventually move in. We quickly lose sight of the couple but eventually discover that they were responsible for Fyodor and Zina's becoming acquainted, though their paths should have crossed several times before. Fate, it appears, has been trying to occasion encounters between Fyodor and Zina, but somehow the plans were foiled at every turn. This last attempt, however, is fateful. While seeking suitable lodgings, Fyodor was introduced to Zina's mother and stepfather. The stepfather didn't make a good impression on him, and later we find his intuition proved correct: the stepfather had long been an unwelcome and irritating presence for Zina. At first Fyodor decides against renting the unattractive room.[18] But at the end of the story, when Fyodor and Zina recall this episode together, Fyodor says it was that trickster fate that had the last laugh. It was when he had glimpsed a beautiful, pale blue, very short gauze dress of the kind worn to dances in an adjacent room that he decided to move in with the Shchyogolevs. He assumed that it belonged to their daughter. But Zina later explains that the dress was not hers; it belonged to a cousin who had left it with her to be altered.[19] The motif of lovers whom fate repeatedly tries to connect is also the theme of one of Sebastian Knight's own novels, and comes straight from the real lives of Nabokov and Vera. Many years later, Nabokov famously transformed this same circumstance of whether or not to rent a room into the magical scene of Humbert's first encounter with Charlotte and Lolita.[20]

Fyodor's reply to Zina when she solves the riddle of the blue dress is a sentence that Nabokov repeats in a number of different ways throughout his work: "The most enchanting things in nature and art are based on deception."[21] And Fyodor continues: "It began with a reckless impetuosity and ended with the finest of finishing touches. Now isn't that the plot for a remarkable novel? What a theme! But it must be built up, curtained, surrounded by dense life — my life, my professional passions and cares." Zina objects: "But that will result in an autobiography." Fyodor, however, is not worried: "Well, let's suppose that I so shuffle, twist, mix, rechew and re-belch everything, add such spices of my own and impregnate things so much with myself that nothing remains of the autobiography but dust — the kind of dust, of course, which makes the most orange of skies."[22]

Here, Nabokov offers one of the most succinct definitions of the art of writing novels. Experience cannot result in a work of art unless the writer is able to distance himself from his theme, "shuffle," "rechew," and recon-stitute. Those elements of a writer's life (and a writer's experience) that infiltrate the work are like a pale light glimmering through the shadows. But without this pale glow from within the work, it would remain a soul-less body. So what appears on the surface to be a deception, in fact holds hidden treasures at its core. And the key to these hidden treasures is how we confront "reality." It is Russian literature, as well as memory, that illu-mines Zina's significance for Fyodor. Zina is Fyodor's first and most serious reader. Through Zina, Fyodor is able to retrieve his lost world, the spirit of inspiration, and, above all, the twin critic he has created in his mind. What at first seems jocular and unreal ends up transformed into the most pleasant of realities. If Fyodor's approach is passive and responsive only in the beginning, he eventually becomes the active usurper of his own des-tiny (and Nabokov's spiral appears in the movements of this fate). When Fyodor, like Nabokov, becomes a creator in his own right through love and art, the reality of his inner world is no longer influenced by or sacrificed to external truth.

By comparing the biography that Fyodor does not write with the one he does (before his intellectual coming of age), we can measure the distance a writer must impose between himself and his subject. He forfeits writing his father's biography because he is worried that his own imagination might contaminate or dilute the narrative of his father's life and research. He is too close to his father to be able to maintain the crucial distance.[23] But he does write the biography of someone who has been moving in exactly the oppo-site direction of his father. The critic Chernyshevski holds views on the im-portance of social commitment and utilitarianism in literature that are the polar opposite of Fyodor's (and Nabokov's). Nonetheless, Fyodor writes Chernyshevski's biography, which is fully substantiated as the fourth chapter of *The Gift*. Chernyshevski's biography naturally causes trouble and controversy: both for Fyodor within the framework of the novel's reality, and for Nabokov in real life.[24] As a result, *The Gift* was published without this chapter, and the text remained incomplete for years. Not until 1952 was the novel first published in full. Nabokov considered the paradox "a pretty example of life finding itself obliged to imitate the very art it condemns."[25]

According to Nabokov, *The Gift* concerns Russian literature. As the novel progresses in its celebration of some of the great Russian writers, a particular stylistic trait begins to emerge, which Nabokov continued to refine and perfect throughout his subsequent novels: the presence of poetry intermingled with prose, and the weave of several different strands of narrative formatting from biography to reviews, lyric poetry to letters, and beautifully wrought descriptive passages. We realize just how deeply Fyodor's life is suffused with poetry through references to these Russian masters and quotations from Fyodor's own compositions. As life advances all around Fyodor, a poem begins to take shape in his mind. The poem heralds Zina and love. It is the beating heart from deep within the mist that suddenly speaks with a human voice: "Love only what is fanciful and rare; what from the distance of a dream steals through; what knaves condemn to death and fools can't bear. To fiction be as to your country true."[26] We are made privy to Fyodor's composition technique, to a kind of poetry that remains hidden behind the prose of everyday life. One of the best examples is when Fyodor's father climbs a hill after a storm in Ordos, and inadvertently steps into the "colored air" at the base of a rainbow. Nabokov doesn't hesitate: Fyodor's father takes one more step and exits to paradise.[27]

3

Fyodor emerges as a writer at the end of *The Gift*, attaining love and discovering his creative talent. In Nabokov's last novel published during his lifetime, *Look at the Harlequins!*, Vadim is an elderly writer who has probably already written his best works. Yet like Fyodor, Vadim encounters love

at the end of the novel, and the "reality" of his own life. The relationship
between these two novels comes into sharper focus when seen through the
reflection in the mirror of the third novel. *The Gift* and *Look at the Harlequins!* can be considered, respectively, as the introduction and the afterword to *The Real Life of Sebastian Knight*. Fyodor, Vadim, and Sebastian
are in many respects the closest of all of Nabokov's characters to himself.
They are similar not in personality or appearance but in the situation of
their existence. Each one of them is a distinctive personality, and as Vadim
explains, each one derives his identity not from nationality but from the
novels he writes and the worlds he creates in his imagination. All three dedi-
cate their lives to writing. And for each of them, his writing centers on a
single woman who becomes an ideal reader: the goddess of his inspiration.
And in this way, Vadim's life and body of work clearly imitate those of his
creator. But it does not end in mere imitation; the voice becomes a sort of
fast-talking parody.

    Look at the Harlequins! (1974) is the mock memoir of a Russian émigré
writer, Vadim Vadimovich. One of Nabokov's familiar artifices is to make
occasional camouflaged cameos in his novels under a pseudonym, creating
an intense authorial dimension, but here he keeps authorial intrusions to
a minimum. Mostly, Vadim Vadimovich recounts the story of his life as a
catalogue raisonné in the first person singular, and there's no evident trace
of the narrator's creator.[28] But in another sense, we find more of Nabokov's
presence in *Look at the Harlequins!* than in any other of his novels. This
authorial presence, which I will return to at greater length, invites an ob-
servation of relationships on different fictional planes: between the story's
main character and its narrator, between the narrator and the writer himself,
and as an allegory of face-to-face encounters.

    The themes of love and writing are braided throughout *The Gift*, but
also in *Look at the Harlequins!*, whose plotline traces the story of Vadim's
myriad loves and four marriages, together with descriptions of his novels.
First, as a young man in France, he marries the sunbathing Iris. After a
jilted lover murders Iris in the street, Vadim marries his frigid secretary,
Annette, who is a poor typist and an even shoddier reader. They have a
daughter, Bel, who stays with Annette when her parents separate, but is

sent to live with her father following her mother's death by drowning. The father and his pubescent daughter grow very close, a motive of concern for Vadim, especially when her penchant for walking around the house naked causes ripples of gossip. It is mainly for this reason that he throws himself into another marriage, with the ambitious seductress Louise, who thinks Vadim might secure an important literary prize. But the marriage sours the relationship between father and daughter, and Bel decides to elope with an American whose staunch left-wing views lead them to run off to the Soviet Union together. Vadim travels there under an assumed name, hoping to find Bel, but returns disappointed. The final love of his life is a woman who is never given a name in the narrative. She was one of Bel's classmates, so the same age as Vadim's daughter. She shares traits with other heroines in Nabokov's work, like Zina in *The Gift* and Clare in *The Real Life of Sebastian Knight*. She is Vadim's true companion and his ideal reader. Nonetheless, Vadim never gives her a name or refers to her in the third person singular. He calls her "You," and it is for this singular You that he writes. By this we understand that their private life transpires at a distance from others (and, of course, it recalls the "You" that refers to Vera in *Speak, Memory*).

   Look at the Harlequins! is about spouses and books. Though Vadim also summons another hero in his story: dementia.[29] Since childhood, Vadim has suffered a strange disorder that allows him to visualize what lies ahead, but he is unable to trace his steps backward to see the opposite direction. He has been careful to explain this condition to each of his three wives before getting married, but none of them has been able to gauge the true extent of Vadim's affliction. Furthermore, they remained indifferent to the center of gravity in Vadim's life: his art. Only "You" truly grasps the extent of his problem, and is in a place to provide Vadim with the solution. What is this saving grace? Vadim has a seizure shortly after proposing marriage to You, and slips into a coma, where he teeters between life and death, delirious, verging on madness. When he finally emerges from his deathlike trance, he cannot remember his own name. But he notices that one of the windows is open, and emits a "bellow of joy" when the door swings wide: "Reality entered," Vadim says, in the form of "You."[30]

   You is vaguer than any other character in the novel, and to the reader she remains the least real and most aloof of them all. But You is not only real for Vadim, she is the very embodiment of reality. She is at once the writer's source of encouragement and his only interlocutor, which leads to the inevitable question: what is "reality" for Vadim (or any writer, for that matter)? Vadim lives in exile, stripped of his identity; his documents mean nothing without context: a family background, an individual past, and a homeland (both Fyodor and Vadim belong to aristocratic families). Who is Vadim without the documents and context that identify him? The answer is obvious: his writing is what makes him recognizable. "Only the writing of fiction," Vadim confesses, "the endless re-creation of my fluid self could keep me more or less sane."[31] Thus readers who misunderstand his art also fail to identify him. By contrast, only the ideal reader of his novels understands and therefore recognizes him. Accordingly, You, his ideal reader, is able to bequeath the state of reality to Vadim. Just as Fyodor needed the ideal critic as a construct and incentive for living and for writing.

Part of what connects the real to the unreal depends upon the shifting concept of what being real actually means. A person's external reality cannot compare to his or her internal reality. For Vadim the writer, the reality of his novels matters only to the extent to which a reader is able to understand them. If a reader fails to grasp the meaning of his novels, then Vadim loses his raison d'être. As a result, love and writing become codependent. In his memoir, Vadim writes, "My wives and my books are interlaced monogrammatically like some sort of watermark or *ex libris* design; and in writing this oblique autobiography — oblique, because dealing mainly not with pedestrian history but with the mirages of romantic and literary matters — I consistently try to dwell as lightly as inhumanly possible on the evolution of my mental illness."[32] Vadim's attitude is clearly a sort of defense mechanism against the cruelty of intrusive external reality. We find some of these conflicts explained in the first few pages. His childhood was particularly disenchanted. His parents divorced, they remarried, and they "redivorced" so swiftly that Vadim was brought up by a great aunt, Baroness Bredow, incidentally née Tolstoy, who fretted over the boy's indolence. The young Vadim was an enthusiastic daydreamer. The baroness entreats him to stop moping around, and instead of sulking all the time, "Look at the harlequins!" He asks: "What harlequins? Where?" The baroness replies that they are everywhere. "Trees are harlequins, words are harlequins." She exhorts him, "Play! Invent the world! Invent reality!" The boy takes her advice and "invented my grand-aunt in honor of my first daydreams."[33]

The title of *Look at the Harlequins!* creates the acronym LATH, a word that describes a thin, narrow strip of wood used to provide a supporting framework for tiles or plaster. In Vadim's hands, this lath acts as a sort of magic wand that bestows life on any object, and the construction of the novel follows the movements of this magic wand. Although the plot may appear to follow a chronological order and the realistic descriptions of the characters propel the novel forward, in fact the trick is hiding in plain sight, and the skeleton key that reveals the secret is on display even before the novel opens. As is customary in many books, there is a page at the beginning that lists the author's previous works. The twist is that in *Look at the Harlequins!* the list is made up of Vadim's books, not Nabokov's, the narrator's, not the author's.[34] The list is divided into two sections: books in Russian and books in English, with six titles in each. The list is a conceptual innovation by Nabokov, who is continuously reminding the reader that story is artifice and not real life. Can it be that here the aim is *ostensibly* to pass the story off as being real? Is Nabokov trying to be more realistic than the realists? On closer examination of Vadim's bibliography, we find it a parodic mirror of the Nabokov canon: each work is a doppelgänger of an existing Nabokov publication. Each false rendition of a real title is nuanced and carries a coded message: Nabokov's *The Gift* becomes Vadim's *The Dare,* playing on the Russian word *dar,* meaning "gift."

Throughout the novel, we discover that the resemblance between novelist Nabokov and narrator Vadim runs much deeper than a few book titles. It extends to biographical similarities that are often distorted in mute, peculiar ways, as if to render Vadim's life a caricature of his creator's—as if Nabokov were exposing his most intense qualms not only to mock reality in general but deliberately to parody his own, specific reality. Aside from the mysterious similarities between each of Vadim's novels and Nabokov's, we gradually encounter characters in Nabokov's novels being referred to in ways that make them seem as if they were real people. Of course, there

is nothing new in this type of character-based cross-referencing in Nabokov. But here, the cross-referencing moves from the margins to the center
to form part of the actual plot. In other novels, it is the background that is
real—the references to other works by Nabokov or even other writers im-
bue the fiction with reality. But here the references are of a different sort;
they allude to Nabokov's imaginary worlds. The temptation when reading
Nabokov is to reject manipulated realities and redevise the novel's details.
By the same token, there has always been a latent tension between his two
worlds, the lost paradise of Russia and the reconstructed paradise in the
novel; between his two writing languages, Russian and English; and between his two identities, Sirin and Nabokov. Generally, this tension between real and imaginary forces creates the emergence of a synthesis, which
creates the world anew. In *Look at the Harlequins!*, however, the balance
between reality and fiction, one of Nabokov's main themes in his oeuvre, is
upset, and the novel descends completely into the world of fantasy.

Nabokov has been known to artfully deepen the authorial dimension,
differentiating the empirical author and his fictional instrument (mostly
through his own direct or indirect intrusion into the work) to remind the
reader that the story is a work of fiction, of the imagination. But Nabokov's
presence generally acts as a reference to the central movement of the novel.
In *The Gift*, we feel Nabokov's presence behind Fyodor. Similarly, in *The
Real Life of Sebastian Knight*, as we will see, the search for the narrator
would probably be impossible without Sebastian's (and Nabokov's?) inti-
mations or hints, and their (more or less imperceptible) assistance. But, in
Look at the Harlequins!, doubt is cast over the entire story as a result of the
constant intrusion of the implied author's presence. The question of the
singular You is an example. Vadim remains disinclined to reveal the identity
of this character—this You—even at the end of the novel. Astonishingly,
his reasoning, and the severity of his words, reminds one of how firmly
Nabokov protected his private life with Vera. Vadim's excuse for not wanting to narrate "what you know, what I know, what nobody else knows, what
shall never, never be ferreted out by a matter-of-fact, father-of-muck, muck-
ing biograffitist"[35] is that it would alter reality. This logic may be applicable
in the case of real people's lives, but when it comes to the characters in a

novel, it becomes much more problematic. The reader's interest in the book is a direct result of his or her desire—and right—to delve deeper into the story, its every detail. How can a writer want to obstruct this stream of interest? It would appear that Nabokov fell into the very trap he set for Vadim.

Vadim is undeniably caught in a trap. He suffers a recurring psychological malaise in which he's overcome by a sense of dual identity, as if he were an inferior, flawed copy of some other, more talented person who lives in another world. Stranger still, other people seem unable to distinguish Vadim from his doppelgänger: Oksman, a Russian book dealer, confuses him, the author of *Camera Lucida,* with the other author of *Camera Obscura* (later *Laughter in the Dark*).[36] The dealer continues to blunder, mentioning two occasions when he saw the narrator's father and brother. But Vadim's father died six months before he was born, so he could only be referring to relatives of the other, unnamed Russian novelist, Vadim's creator. Naturally, Vadim is furious over the confusion, and experiences a lurking dread over what this signifies. He runs into Oksman a few more times over the years, and the bookseller welcomes him "with a knowing twinkle as if we shared some very private and rather naughty secret." But the suspicion intensifies Vadim's notion that he might actually be impersonating somebody real, and it is an unbearable thought. Vadim has no idea what to do. "Should I ignore the coincidence and its implications?" he asks himself. He considers another course: "Should I abandon my art, choose another line of achievement, take up chess seriously, or become, say, a lepidopterist, or spend a dozen years as an obscure scholar making a Russian translation of *Paradise Lost* that would cause hacks to shy and asses to kick?"[37] Whatever course of action he chooses, whether chess, lepidoptery, research, or translation, all the choices inevitably belong to his creator. In the end, all he does is drop his pen name V. Irisin, just as his author did, abandoning V. Sirin.

Vadim alludes to other characters in Nabokov's novels as if they were real people. In fact, Vadim's father shares a name with the progenitor of the two main characters in *Ada.* So Vadim may be related to Ada. Some characters refer to Sebastian and Nina. And one of Vadim's lovers, Dolly von Borg, parodies Lolita. Just before Vadim finally rediscovers his identity, he gropes for his name and his father's name. He is sure it begins with an N, and conjures up a number of different possibilities, all of which in one way or another recall the name of his nemesis, the author, even comically (Naborcroft? Nabarro?).[38] But in his newly recovered state of awareness, he remains nameless and unreal. He's the figment of another writer's imagination. This state of unreality lasts until "reality" finally walks in the door in the form of You, who catalyzes Vadim's return to consciousness. Vadim unwittingly begins to see into that other world: a world that belongs to the protagonists of Nabokov's novels, a world free from the determinism of time and the abstraction of fate (things that are eventually accepted, for example, by Cincinnatus in *Invitation to a Beheading* or Krug in *Bend Sinister*), a world that coexists with the everyday world, but that belongs entirely to the writer and is of vital importance for Nabokov.

The three-part relationship between the writer and his characters, the writer and his book, and the writer and his reader, is highly significant in *The Gift* and likewise in *The Real Life of Sebastian Knight*. By contrast, in *Look at the Harlequins!*, what shapes the novel is the writer's conspicuous absence. Tension is developed not only between the opposing forces of reality and imagination but also between the real writer and the imaginary one. Nabokov does not permit access to Vadim's private space.[39] Nor does he allow the tension that operates in his other novels to permeate this one. As a result, the novel acts as a mirage to deceive the reader, who in the end comes away empty-handed. It seems ironic that Nabokov, who had so brilliantly and in such an original manner exposed the dangers and pitfalls of solipsism both in life and in fiction, would himself become its victim.

Nabokov reconfigures the world he lost into a world of dreams. In one of his early Russian novels, *Glory,* Nabokov endows his main character, Martin Edelweiss, with the memory of the painting above his bed, and the childhood longing of being able to travel from the material world into the abstract world of the painting. This is how Martin is able to visit the dreamworld (Russia) at the end of the novel. Though Nabokov does not endow Martin with creative faculties, his life is nevertheless transformed into a work of art: by remaining faithful to his dream, he disappears into the painting. He walks into what appears to be a Russian forest. But it's an imaginary world that also suggests death. While Fyodor and Sebastian refine the reality that was imposed upon them by their imaginative faculties and the worlds they create, Martin, who is not a writer, enters the forest of no return. This excursion, though, serves as a poetic flight in its own right. If lost Russia is now only a dream, then looking for it or trying to describe it in language within the Soviet Union is futile without the medium of poetry. All that matters now is keeping memory and imagination alive. In other words, keeping "Mnemosyne" and "Harlequin" alive. These two words are also names of two subspecies of butterflies. The poetics that inhabit Nabokov's prose, either openly or surreptitiously, unfurl from here.

Vadim is the only character in Nabokov's novels to return in person to the place that had once been Russia. Regrettably, he is unable to unpick the tangled knot of his feelings or understand what is taking place. Everything the reader gets by way of description is suspiciously tendentious, angry, and sneering, as if all Vadim cares to do is express his contempt for what he sees and hears. His journey, unlike Martin's, does not involve the plane of dreams (and death). Vadim travels to the Soviet Union, breaking the magic circle. Vadim is insane, his love and madness far-fetched, unlike the love and madness of Nabokov's other ever-present delusional, unreliable narrators. It is as if the sane writer and his schizoid persona are trapped within the closed, fictional universe of the novel, "the constellation of my tears and asterisks." Here, the negation of reality leads, ironically, to the total negation of the writer.

4

By all outward measures, Sebastian Knight does not resemble his creator at all. Yet it is in *The Real Life of Sebastian Knight* where we can find one of the keys to Nabokov's fictional universe. It is the novel that completes the other two, *The Gift* and *Look at the Harlequins!* The secret of the structure, though, resides in the style of Sebastian's novels. The novel is full of allusions to everything that can be filed under the thematic category of "reality." The parodic doppelgänger in Vadim's bibliography for *The Real Life of Sebastian Knight* is titled: *See Under Real.*

The Real Life of Sebastian Knight is Nabokov's first novel written in

English. For Nabokov, language is no mere instrument of expression but something tangible, material. In the way that exile turns what is objective into subjective memories, so Nabokov shapes the abstraction of language into something subjective, an individual form of expression that becomes a stand-in for what was lost, for his "private tragedy." When speaking of language, Nabokov visualizes the words literally; the graphic morphology of words, the manipulation of letter patterns. In his poem "An Evening of Russian Poetry," he writes

> Beyond the seas where I have lost a sceptre,
> I hear the neighing of my dappled nouns,
> soft participles coming down the steps,
> treading on leaves, trailing their rustling gowns,
> and liquid verbs in *ahla* and in *ili*,
> Aonian grottoes, nights in the Altai,
> black pools of sound with "I"s for water lilies.

It was not difficult for Nabokov to begin to write in English; he mastered everything he needed very quickly. The challenge in fact was how to transform the loss and pain of exile into the miracle of a new language that truly belonged to him? How could he brand it with his own individual style of creative estrangement, and turn common words into private, specific ones? It would call for a level of originality and a distinctiveness that would not betray him, but would stay with him all his life like the warmth of first love, like a butterfly wrapped in its cocoon dreaming, hidden deep in the fabric of the books he writes. Nabokov is caught in the void between the two languages at first. English offers the allure of a warm hotel to a guest out on a dark, stormy (and eternal) night, but it also devastates him. In the end his achievement is nothing less than miraculous. Vadim says: "In the world of athletic games there has never been, I think, a World Champion of Lawn Tennis *and* Ski; yet in two Literatures, as dissimilar as grass and snow, I have been the first to achieve that kind of feat."[40]

In *The Gift*, Fyodor becomes exultant when he suddenly remembers the books that he has yet to produce. In fact, *The Gift* is the novel he plans on writing in the future. *The Real Life of Sebastian Knight,* which presents itself as an appraisal of Sebastian's published works, surveys the life of Sebastian Knight. The novel poses the question Who is the real Sebastian Knight? The conflict and resulting tension are found in the space between the question and answer. The book is supposed to be a biography, and from the opening we find the standard range of styles expected of the genre. Yet other questions eventually emerge, such as "can we ever discover the fundamental truths of humankind?" and "can anyone truly know another human being?"

After Sebastian Knight's death, his younger half-brother, identified only as V, embarks on research to compose his biography. He relies on memory, interviews, his brother's books, and a fair amount of conjecture and sleuthing. The general details of his older brother's life are relatively simple. Sebastian Knight is a British writer who was born in St. Petersburg in 1899, the first son of a Russian father and a British mother. When Sebastian was four, his mother decided to leave the family, and his father, calmer and more self-possessed, eventually remarried. V was born of this second marriage, in 1906. Sebastian's mother reappeared in their lives briefly, but the event drew their father into a duel to defend her honor, which resulted in his death. Far from home and her loved ones, his mother died in a boardinghouse in France. Sebastian, meanwhile, had been writing poetry since he was a boy. He never signed the poems with his name, instead drawing a chess figure: a black knight. In fact, he adopted his mother's last name, Knight. Sebastian fled revolutionary Russia for Western Europe, accompanied by his stepmother and younger half-brother. He pursued his studies at Cambridge University, while the others remained in France. Sebastian, whose life distanced him from his family, became a notable writer. He met Clare Bishop, and their relationship grew into love, friendship, and cooperation. Later, Sebastian's heart condition worsened just as he became involved with a mysterious Russian woman. The relationship consumed his time and sapped his energy over the last years of his life. He severed ties with Clare, and died a lonely death in a remote hospital in France, in 1936. Is knowing the facts of Sebastian Knight's life enough to truly know him? We are acquainted with the details of his life, but who was he really? His true self eludes us completely.

In *Lectures on Russian Literature* Nabokov touches on Gogol's decline: "He was in the worst plight that a writer can be in: he had lost the gift of imagining facts and believed that facts may exist by themselves. The trouble is that bare facts do not exist in a state of nature, for they are never really quite bare: the white trace of a wrist watch, a curled piece of sticking plaster on a bruised heel, these cannot be discarded by the most ardent nudist. A mere string of figures will disclose the identity of the stringer as neatly as tame ciphers yielded their treasure to Poe."[41] And finally he writes: "I doubt whether you can even give your telephone number without giving something of yourself."[42]

V gathers the details, but they are not enough. He is curious. Sebastian's life has always been distant and alluring, like a lighthouse. Now that he is gone, he poignantly longs to understand more about that life, and this yearning is what spurs him to seek out the people who knew his brother well: their governess, Sebastian's close friends, his secretary, Mr. Goodman. Each one of the people he interviews gives his or her own version of Sebastian, and each account seems to give more away about the speaker than about the subject. The reader comes to see the characters in this novel as more volatile than those in *The Gift* and *Look at the Harlequins!*, also variations on the biography theme. In effect, it's not the details of Sebastian's biography that matter, but the manner in which the biography is being narrated. What V says about one of Sebastian's novels, *The Prismatic Bezel*, is also true of the book he is writing: "The heroes of the book are what can be loosely called 'methods of composition.' It is as if a painter said: look, here I'm going to show you not the painting of a landscape, but the painting of different ways of painting a certain landscape, and I trust their harmonious fusion will disclose the landscape as I intend you to see it."[43] The key to the novel is the style of Sebastian's books. And the characters represent various points of view, while they are, of course, themselves too.

V journeys to Lausanne to interview Mademoiselle, their governess, now deaf and confused. She recalls minutiae from the boys' childhood that he finds either distorted or displaced, particularly how much she claims Sebastian adored her. But what aggravates V is that Mademoiselle never asks about Sebastian's later life or how he died. V also fails to talk to Clare. Sebastian's closest college friend, now a prominent Cambridge scholar, has forgotten many of the details of their shared experience and admits that his "reminiscences are getting shallower and sillier." Nina, the mysterious woman who entered Sebastian's life in the years before his death, seems to prefer playing a game of cat and mouse with V to helping him solve anything. And finally there is Goodman, Sebastian's secretary, who has written a quick and dismissive biography titled *The Tragedy of Sebastian Knight*. V's motivation for his book is partly a response to Goodman's, since the secretary's carelessness and lack of curiosity (even regarding the subject of his research) characterize everything that Sebastian despises. Before casually running into V in Cambridge, for example, Goodman had no idea Sebastian even had a stepmother and half-brother. To Nabokov, not being curious constituted a cardinal sin. Like *Alice's Adventures in Wonderland,* the protagonists of Nabokov's novels travel to the far corners of unknown worlds in pursuit of their white rabbits. Curiosity is a consequence of intellectual passion, the absolute dedication to discovering the details. But Goodman hides whatever he does not know behind a smokescreen of generalizations and falsely authoritative statements. Instead of describing Sebastian's unique personality, he concocts a fictitious and generic character for him, calling to mind Nabokov's words in his *Lectures on Russian Literature:* "The difference between the comic side of things, and their cosmic side, depends upon one sibilant."[44]

Goodman's book, which paints "poor Knight" as the product and victim of the vagaries of what he calls "our time," is highly successful, of course. Goodman's reductive perspective recalls the realities of "Post-war Unrest" and the "Post-war Generation" and the challenges facing a sensitive youth in the cold, cruel world. This version of Sebastian (a character created and shaped entirely by Goodman) becomes a churlish, reclusive young man. If we substitute Sebastian's name in Goodman's book with that of any other writer of his generation, there would be no need to modify a thing. The self-importance and bantering tone of Goodman's "thick flow of philosophical treacle" in fact appeals commercially to the establishment: the book offers the type of ideas that attract mediocre minds, regardless of how vacuous and lacking in content; it is written for a preexisting consensus.

Yet Goodman's scheme is ambitious. To prove he was Sebastian's friend and associate, he tells a few anecdotes he swears were told to him (and only him) by Sebastian himself, about his student years in England. The first two are old college jokes that anyone from Cambridge would know, and they prove that Sebastian must have been pulling Mr. Goodman's leg. The third story Sebastian tells Goodman is the plot of his first novel, which had never been published: "A fat young student . . . travels home to find his mother married to his uncle; this uncle, an ear-specialist, had murdered the student's father. Goodman misses the joke." In the fourth, Goodman says that Sebastian was overworked and suffering from hallucinations, and "used to see a kind of optical ghost—a black-robed monk moving swiftly towards him from the sky."[45] Which comes from a Chekhov story. It is almost as if Sebastian had an inkling that Goodman was planning on writing a biography and forging stories after his death, so he exacted a sort of anticipatory revenge. Later V finds that Goodman had taken advantage of Sebastian's forgetfulness about money to cheat him. Goodman is finally dismissed when Sebastian finds out by chance that he had changed an epithet in one of his books.[46] What greater offense is there than writing without knowledge or creativity? For Nabokov, creativity is not separate from morality.

There is only one useful characteristic of Goodman's biography; it shows us how deeply Sebastian reviled his former secretary and, like his creator, how delightful a sense of humor he had. Nevertheless, the question remains: is it really possible to know someone who is no longer alive? What else is there to do besides gearing up and chasing after whatever clues can be found? It takes V some time to figure this out and consciously accept the limitation: the only way to truly discern and appreciate the truth about Sebastian is to be Sebastian. Toward the end of the quest, he finds Nina, unaware at first that she is the mysterious woman. Not only does she fail to introduce herself, but she immediately begins to toy with him, teasing him like a chess master frolicking with a novice (as she had with Sebastian, perhaps?). Once V realizes her identity, he departs without a word, despite her fundamental role as a witness to Sebastian's last years of his life. Why? Because he has found what he had been looking for.

While on the trail of Sebastian's last love, Nina Rechnoy, V encounters "by a chance conjuncture of circumstances" one of Sebastian's schoolmates, whose sister, Natasha Rosanov, had been Sebastian's first love. The whole quest seems to be following a strange harmony by placing Sebastian's first adolescent romance "in such close proximity to the echoes of his last dark love."[47] What does this continuity mean? The novel's plot seeks to find witnesses who could give first-person testimony to Sebastian's life. But in a quest of this nature, whatever truth is found largely depends on the method(s) employed. The approach of the person investigating is what lends significance to the results. In fact, we slowly come to realize that Sebastian has planted clues for each person who wants to find the truth about him. For example, he left Goodman a series of absurd stories. And when V begins sorting through the remaining belongings in his brother's flat, he comes across an envelope full of newspaper clippings and a set of photographs. Sebastian had intended to write a fictitious biography, V discovers; was it an autobiography? As the story moves forward, more hints and clues emerge. Could it be that Sebastian wanted V to complete his unfinished work? When V chances upon Sebastian's first girlfriend, he writes of the new pages: "A more systematic mind than mine would have placed them at the beginning of this book, but my quest had developed its own magic and logic and though I sometimes cannot help believing that it had gradually grown into a dream, that quest, using the pattern of reality for the weaving of its own fancies, I am forced to recognize that I was being led right, and that in striving to render Sebastian's life I must now follow the same rhythmical interlacements."[48] So now his brother's first love sits beside the last, as if by their closeness they enter into a conversation, question each other in counterpoint, and the answer they give is the stuff of life itself and the closest possible approach to human truth.

This leads us to an important technical device Nabokov employs in *The Real Life of Sebastian Knight:* the juxtaposition of different, even contradictory aspects of a life, to create a synthesis. V deploys this device, even if he often does so unwittingly. Not only does he juxtapose the miscellaneous versions of Sebastian's life as they are relayed by the different people with whom he engages, but he takes the same approach with the individuals themselves and with the literary versions of Sebastian. So each narrator challenges the other narrators and each account challenges the veracity of every other version. Toward the end, he reveals the parallels between Sebastian's first and second homelands, and between his literary and real lives.

The scene of Sebastian and his first love, Natasha Rosanov, opens with them in a boat at a bend in a river, "lustily rowing." But the picture morphs, and they're suddenly at another bend in the river.[49] In the final scene, the girl confesses that she has fallen in love with someone else. (Brian Boyd points to a link between the name of Natasha Rosanov and Nina Rechnoy, noting that *rechnoy* is the Russian adjective from *reka,* meaning river in Russian.)[50] Both his romantic interests prove unfaithful. Natasha is a kindhearted sixteen-year-old girl, and Nina Rechnoy is a glib femme fatale who has many lovers and is unable to appreciate Sebastian's true worth. What brings Sebastian to Nina when he is on the verge of death is not just the memory of his first love but also that of his other, stifled love, Russia. Sebastian adores the memory of his mother even though she was largely absent. He also loves his motherland. He tries very hard to become an Englishman, even adopts his mother's last name. He embraces the language and writes his books in English. But now as death looms, he remembers his neglected brother and writes him the last letter of his life, in Russian. When V arrives at the hospital as the novel closes, he asks after the English gentleman. But the hospital staff knows Sebastian only as the Russian gentleman. It is as if there have always been two Sebastians with two different dispositions and two different nationalities. It is only in this biography that these two restless souls find a single homeland. Returning to the two lifestyles, each, according to V, calling the other into question, we can now query how time informs this counterpoint of questions and answers. It adds a further juxtaposition: not merely what is real and what is unreal, but also what is past and what is present, creating a timeless state where both past and present are expressed.

Following Sebastian's instructions, V burns not only Clare's letters but Nina's too. And when he eventually recognizes Nina, he never asks her anything about Sebastian.[51] Yet the truth seems now to have come into focus. How is that? In the first place, V's research has allowed him to approximate Sebastian in a new way. First, just because of his curiosity and search he feels closer to Sebastian. Second, upon meeting Nina he falls into the same snare that had trapped Sebastian, and for the same reason: he does not recognize her. As a result, he loses his desire, his need, to speak to Nina, because obviously he is now walking in Sebastian's shoes. Although V's search has allowed him to begin channeling Sebastian's life, Sebastian's real life remains elusive. Reality is volatile, especially when we pursue it retroactively. And, more important, returning to the past is an impossible feat. Yet there is a still a way to identify the real life of Sebastian Knight; perhaps it's the only way.

5

As V is walking away from Sebastian's old college friend's porch in Cambridge, carefully skirting the puddles, the friend calls out to him, just as Goodman's secretary, Clare's friend, called V back at the end of his meeting with Goodman. Something had just occurred to him. Suddenly, a "voice in the mist" can be heard, asking: "Who is speaking of Sebastian Knight?" And the chapter ends on this question. But in the following chapter, V regrets that his book is not of the "well-oiled" type, with the easy, comfortable swing to a resolution. No cheery old don with "long downy ear-lobes" who, like a welcome passerby, "had also known my hero, but from a different angle" had appeared. In fact, that "Voice in the Mist rang out in the dimmest passage of my mind. It was but the echo of some possible truth, a timely reminder: don't be too certain of learning the past from the lips of the present. . . . Remember that what you are told is really threefold: shaped by the teller, reshaped by the listener, concealed from both by the dead man of the tale." So if we ask the question: "Who is speaking of Sebastian Knight?" Right now it's his best college friend, and his half-brother. So who is the third? The third is Sebastian himself, "rotting peacefully in the cemetery of St. Damier." But he's also laughingly alive in his books, "peering unseen over my shoulder as I write this (although I dare say he mistrusted too strongly the commonplace of eternity to believe even now in his own ghost)."[52]

So let's begin from the end. Sebastian's ghost guides his brother along in his research and writing of the biography. Why? The answer is veiled at the end of the pursuit. But the following clues ought to suffice. The person narrating and the person listening shape the stories that are told in the novel, while the dead hero, Sebastian, has concealed the truth. So we aspire to a territory that is devoid of the past and of death, a place where the passage of time is rendered meaningless. A place where time is always fixed at "year one."[53] In short, we must find a place where our protagonist, Sebastian, never dies, but is more alive than any other living creature. The only place where time is immortal is in Sebastian's novels.

Sebastian narrates a story from his own life in *Lost Property,* when he takes a trip to the Continent after leaving Cambridge, and spends a fortnight in Monte Carlo. One day he goes for a long walk and ends up in a place called Roquebrune. He realizes that this is where his mother had spent the last days of her life, thirteen years earlier, in a boardinghouse called Les Violettes. He finds the place and asks permission to rest for a few minutes on a blue bench in the garden, under a large eucalyptus. He is so engrossed in the memory of his mother that he sees her specter slowly walking up the stairs. The scene is both excruciating and trivial at once. The thump of an orange that slips from the bag on his knees rouses him back from the reverie. A few months later in London, a relative of his mother's corrects his mistake: she had died in the other Roquebrune in France: "the one in the Var." Goodman recalls this scene in his book in an effort to prove that Sebastian is never serious, but always poking fun at everything. We find rooted in this episode an important clue about Sebastian's style, and Nabokov's, in the way Sebastian, and his creator, confront the world. V explains it for us, Sebastian Knight "used parody as a kind of springboard for leaping into the highest region of serious emotion."[54] Parody, like juxtaposition (or paradox), begins with something serious, then calls its seriousness into question. V goes on to explain that Sebastian "was ever hunting out the things which had once been fresh and bright but which were now worn to a thread, dead things among living ones; dead things shamming life, painted and repainted, continuing to be accepted by lazy minds serenely unaware of the fraud."[55] Sebastian (like his creator) never consents to secondhand concepts.

The Roquebrune episode makes it clear that, in Sebastian's life, reality often turns out to be more ironic than any fiction. And by the same token, reality is more anarchic and confused than art. V offers an explanation: he is not trying to describe Sebastian's childhood with methodical continuity, as if he were a character in a novel. The result of that would have been one of those *biographies romancées* he deems "by far the worst kind of literature yet invented."[56] So reality can take the guise of a story in the same way that a story has an element of reality. In a sense, *The Real Life of Sebastian Knight* is about the marvels of reality. And if we find the reality of Sebastian's life disordered and volatile, Sebastian's stories are our recompense, being the essence of their creator's reality, offering the best solution to the puzzle of his personality. Clearly information about Sebastian is not scarce. But what bestow life on these scattered realities and reveal his sentiments are his novels. When we reach a point where information appears uncooperative and adds nothing, the novels, if assessed attentively, come to our aid with a smile.

Sebastian's first novel, *The Prismatic Bezel,* spoofs certain well-worn literary devices and is a "rollicking parody" of the detective story. V is quick to explain that Sebastian isn't aiming his cannons at "penny dreadfuls" or other lowbrow forms. What "annoyed him invariably was the second rate, not the third or N-th rate, because here, at the readable stage, the shamming began, and this was, in an *artistic* sense, immoral."[57] Throughout Nabokov's novels, there are endless references to other literary works and genres. In his fiction, the novel as form is constructed using the building blocks of reality, making literature a point of reference that takes on a life of its own, free from history or from everyday life. Nabokov also employs a number of different literary forms in each of his novels. So it follows that Sebastian's novel *The Prismatic Bezel* is hyperbolically "Nabokovian." There is a murder; everyone is trying to find who did it as they wait for the detective to arrive from London, and he falls prey to the most far-fetched series of mishaps. But the story begins to shift and the characters gradually take human shape under the long shadow of their collective distrust. By the time the detective arrives, a policeman enters to announce that the cadaver has disappeared. They come to find out that the victim was never really dead, just

disguised in a gray wig, fake beard, and dark glasses in his role as a minor
character in the novel, because, you see, "one dislikes being murdered."[58]
The novel, of course, alludes to events in Sebastian's own biography. And
we, too, pursue the narrator in our search for the real identity of a dead
man. Is this meant to foreshadow the idea that perhaps in the end we too
will discover that Sebastian is not really dead? Is the investigator himself
being pursued?

Sebastian's first novel has a linear plot and proceeds in an apparently conventional way. But just when the reader is lulled into feeling safe
and secure, we arrive at an abyss, its surprise ending, where the dead is in
fact undead. The void is not merely a figment of the author's imagination
or something that belongs to him alone. The reader, too, should feel that
gaping chasm, assuming that the exercise of reading is to experience life
and art, or perhaps life through art. His mental well-being, which is often
a euphemism for a lazy mind, needs to be disturbed, given a good shake.
Here, Sebastian disrupts convention by employing parody or otherwise ma-
nipulating a familiar genre to create something new. And as V explains, if
the heroes of the first novel are "methods of composition," then the second
novel, *Success,* deals primarily with "methods of human fate."[59] *Success* describes how "two lines of life were made to come into contact." Boy meets
girl in an encounter that seems like a happy accident: "Both happen to use
the same car belonging to an amiable stranger on a day the buses went on
strike." The writer begins looking into the origins of the accident. What
circumstances had to align for this to happen? What caused this specific
person to pass this particular point, at this given time? When that line of inquiry reaches a dead end, Sebastian begins looking into the girl's life, trac-
ing her line of fate. He does the same with the man, Percival Q, a commercial traveler. It becomes clear that fate has, repeatedly and insistently, been
secretly preparing their encounter. "I shall not go into further details of this
clever and delightful novel," V tells us. Suffice it to say that the novel deals
with how fate works to turn coincidence into an essential and even logical
force, how it delicately schemes and toys with the magic of love and art to
spin the silken threads of life.

Before describing Sebastian's last novel, it seems right to consider a portrait of him by one of his painter friends, Roy Carswell. More exactly, it is a painting of Sebastian's face reflected in a pool of clear water. There's a "slight ripple on the hollow cheek" and a "withered leaf has settled on the reflected brow."[60] Sebastian is peering into the pool, mirrored Narcissus-like: Sebastian facing Sebastian. The painting was made in 1933. Sebastian dies in early 1936. Sebastian's poet friend P. G. Sheldon thinks that the world of Sebastian's last novel, *The Doubtful Asphodel,* was casting a shadow over the rest of Sebastian's life. He says the novels and stories were but "sly tempters under the pretense of artistic adventure leading him unerringly towards a certain imminent goal."[61]

Sebastian's last novel is about a man on his deathbed. His reflections and reminiscences fill the entire book, "like the swell and fall of uneven breathing." The dying man is the hero of the tale. The other characters involved are depicted realistically, but we never know the real identity of the dying man. "The man is the book; the book itself is heaving and dying, and drawing up a ghostly knee." The characters go on with their lives, but the center of the book is filled with the continuous procession of "thought-images." He expresses in detail the agony of the physical process of dying, and leads the reader to a point where we believe we are on the brink of an absolute truth, an answer to "all questions of life and death, 'the absolute solution' was written all over the world he had known." The reader has the idea that he knows the mystery of death. But the author pauses to ask himself: is telling the truth a wise act? "Shall we follow him to the end? Shall we whisper the word which will shatter the snug silence of our brains?" The answer is yes, and as we turn back to the dying man, we find it is too late. "That minute of doubt was fatal: the man is dead. The man is dead and we do not know. . . . We hold a dead book in our hands." But V keeps faith and believes that if he reads the book again, this time more attentively, the secret will be revealed. The "absolute solution" is there, somewhere, "concealed in some passage." This is Sebastian's last novel. The hidden secret, we shall see, is fixed in the way the plot advances, a process V follows unwittingly. To discover the truth of Sebastian's life, we have to figure out what is motiving V onward in his quest.[62]

In *The Doubtful Asphodel,* Sebastian refers to the act of reading. He also shapes the outline of his own biography. Why do we read? Why is V on this quest? We read because we are curious, and because we like to know things. Does it mean that we get closer to reality the farther along we are in the book, and the less there is to read? There is no simple answer. Obviously we approximate reality, but we never actually attain it. A moment of hesitation suffices for the secret to remain forever undeciphered, hidden in the book. But there is no secret: the reality of the book resides in the experience of reading it. If V sometimes feels that Sebastian's "shade" is standing beside him and helping him along on his quest, or that he is channeling Sebastian's soul, or walking in his shoes, it is because like any sleuth/reader, he is experiencing the reality of his pursuit, albeit intuitively. An ideal reader searches out the truth of a book not because there is a meaning to be derived, but for the very act of reading. And this is how the ideal reader discovers its truth.[63] V arrives at the truth about Sebastian's life when he dissolves into Sebastian's spirit. Sebastian's shade stands beside V, but there is an even greater conjuror standing beside Sebastian. As Brian Boyd points out when he describes the novel as a philosophical puzzle, "V. may be none other than Sebastian talking about himself, or the 'someone whom neither of us knows' may be the author talking about himself in a way that disguises his personal disclosures."[64] V writes about Sebastian's "queer habit of endowing even his most grotesque characters with this or that idea, or impression, or desire which he himself might have toyed with."[65] And so by lending these parts of himself to the characters in his works, Sebastian allows them to live on in those characters. Genuine writers are truly alive only in their books.

There's another consideration for readers who prefer a more straightforward approach; it's due not only to the compositional twists and turns in Sebastian's stories that V discovers the path for his quest. For example, one of the central themes of *The Real Life of Sebastian Knight* is how art influences real life. In Sebastian's short story "The Back of the Moon," we come across Mr. Siller, considered by V as one of Sebastian's most lifelike characters. Siller is perhaps the best physical embodiment of a theme that had first appeared in Sebastian's earliest works: the search for the truth of another person's life. V finds the character so delightful that he quotes Sebastian's meticulous description of him: "It is as though a certain idea steadily growing through two books has now burst into real physical existence."[66] A few chapters farther along, this particular line of enquiry meets a dead end. The last lead V has to follow up on is the identity of the mysterious woman (Nina) Sebastian met at the hotel. But V is unable to procure from the hotel administrator the list of guests at the hotel on the dates in question. Despairing, he takes a train out of town. At the next station, a slight man boards. For the sharp reader, his physique is familiar. He speaks with a heavy accent in mistake-ridden, broken English, and behaves in a very peculiar fashion. Though V is not in the mood to socialize, the newly arrived passenger introduces himself as Silbermann. We find that Silbermann deals in "hound-muzzles" and has been in "de police." There's a scene in the next chapter reminiscent of *Alice's Adventures in Wonderland,* in which Silbermann delivers a guest list to V and disappears, without charging for his services or leaving an address or phone number. Silbermann gives V a notebook as a gift on this first encounter, which is what V uses to write *The Real Life of Sebastian Knight.* Obviously, Silbermann and Siller are the same character in different iterations. Silbermann even refers to the title of Sebastian's short story; "You can't see de odder side of de moon. Please donnt search de woman." This raises the question of whether trying to find the truth about someone's life might be like trying to see the dark side of the moon.[67]

6

Sebastian wrote a new novel, *Lost Property,* after leaving Clare. V considers it "a kind of halt in his literary journey of discovery: a summing up, a counting of the things and souls lost on the way, a setting of bearings."[68] There is a short chapter on an airplane crash with a sole survivor. A half-dozen letters were found scattered in a field, among the belongings of the deceased passengers. One of them was in an envelope addressed to a woman, though the formal letter inside read "Dear Mr. Mortimer, in reply to yours of the 6th."[69] Another one in a business envelope contained a breakup letter from a man to his erstwhile sweetheart, a mixture of apologies, explanations about the other woman, with whom he is terribly unhappy, and expressions of despair and kindness. There is much in it that could have been what Sebastian wanted to express to Clare. V is amazed to see a man who is at once committing to paper the things in his life that were causing him personal anxiety, while building a fictitious and faintly absurd story, the whole time remaining aloof. This has always been Nabokov's method or style.

Nina is depicted as a stock character. Her former husband says he sometimes feels as though she never actually existed. He says she is a type, a type that you can find in any cheap novel. In other words, she does not seem to be real. Again we run into the phenomenon of unreal reality (or real unreality).[70] Imagination is a magical force with two opposing roles: it creates a false perception that makes us think we are witnessing reality, but it is the only path that can lead to the true essence of what is real. Magic and reality are constantly at odds with each other and as a result, they reveal each other's shortcomings. Yet they coexist to such an extent that you cannot describe one without describing the other. That is how Nina begins duping V in the first place. Initially, she pretends to be the French acquaintance of Sebastian's mysterious inamorata. But just as she thinks she's got V hoodwinked, just as he feels the pull of being attracted to her, the truth about her identity is suddenly revealed. At last, we encounter Nina, the last witness to Sebastian's life. Why, then, does he leave without further clarifications? We must return to the narrator for the story's resolution.

There is no witness to V but V himself. Shortly before Sebastian's death, in January 1936, V receives a letter from him. Sebastian was seldom in touch over the years, so it is odd for him to receive word from his half-brother out of the blue. But the truly surprising detail is that Sebastian writes to him in Russian. Sebastian writes that he's "fed up [*osskomina*] with a number of tortuous things and especially with the patterns of my shed snake-skins [*vypolziny*] so that now I find a poetic solace in the obvious and the ordinary."[71] He also asks after V. V is unaware that his brother is ill, and the letter makes it clear that in the last days of his life, Sebastian was in the process of recovering his heritage, and taking stock of everything he had once tried so hard to forget. He was preparing himself, and his brother, for a future task. The past cannot be imposed upon the present, but neither can it be forgotten. Without its Russian component, Sebastian Knight's real life would have been imperfect and as a result, rendered meaningless.

The need to find "poetic solace in the obvious and the ordinary," which Sebastian expresses in his letter, brings us back to *The Gift*, and Fyodor's effort to find the poem that resides in the depth of the novel's prose. Sebastian's brief statement expands, almost immediately, when V describes his dream after reading the letter. He writes: "I know that the common pebble you find in your fist after having thrust your arm shoulder deep into water, where a jewel seemed to gleam on pale sand, is really the coveted gem though it looks like a pebble as it dries in the sun of every-day."[72] What else could be expected from the creator of *Lolita?* Nabokov sets himself a harder task than more lyrical writers like Virginia Woolf, who moves her prose in the direction of poetry; he seeks the poetry hidden in the pool of his prose. This procedure is not limited to his prose alone; it is something he applies even in his everyday life. Nabokov used to astonish his friends and acquaintances in America with his relish for pedestrian writing (especially events covered by sensational newspapers). The origins of many of Nabokov's best characters can be found in this habit—*Lolita*'s Charlotte, for example.[73] Or we could say it is a way of discovering the poetry in everyday life and saving it from being commonplace and tedious. Isn't it true, after all, that poetry, in the broad sense of the word, removes what is opaque to expose the precise essence of things? Sebastian eventually realizes that one of his sins has been his indifference toward his apparently normal brother; a brother who is his heir and who blossoms after Sebastian's death.

Let us return to Sebastian's letter and the unpleasant dream it provokes in V, which he recounts in meticulous detail: V and his mother are waiting uneasily for Sebastian to arrive. When he finally shows up, he brings tragedy with him—something unbearable for V. He disappears, but V hears him call out and knows that what he has to say is something important. But he dares not approach. Eventually, when he summons his courage, the voice rings out "laden with such absolute moment, with such an unfailing intent to solve for me a monstrous riddle, that I would have run to Sebastian after all, had I not been half out of my dream already."[74] This is evocative of how Sebastian's last novel ends. V is at once curious and eager to know the secret but lacking in the courage or the determination to make the discovery. So even awake, V follows the pattern of the dream, probably against his own wishes. Even though Sebastian asks him to come and see him, he delays the trip until he finally receives a telegram from the Russian family doctor. The telegram is written in French, but the doctor spells Sebastian in Russian, with a "v" rather than a "b," reminding us that his name is of Russian origin: Sevastian. And it also reveals the fact that V is rooted in Sebastian. So the nearer we get to the end of the novel, the clearer the brothers' similarities become. V must hurry now, but before setting out, and without knowing why, he gazes at his own image in the looking glass for a moment.

V's nightmarish journey starts from this point. He is in a rush, but suffers setbacks. First, he has to get to Paris as soon as possible. As the train begins to move, he realizes that he left Sebastian's letter in his desk and does not remember the address. Once in Paris he finds a telephone booth with scribbles and sketches on the wall around him, which catch his eye. "Who were those idle idiots who wrote on the wall 'Death to the Jews' or '*Vive le front populaire*'?" he asks himself. Some anonymous artist had begun blacking squares, and it reminds V of a chessboard, and the words "*ein Schachbrett, un damier*" come to mind. In a flash, he remembers that the hospital is in St. Damier. Mishaps and hitches continue to thwart his journey. "Would I ever get to Sebastian?" he asks himself. "Would I find him alive if I did ever reach St. Damier?" Late that evening he makes it to the hospital, where he runs into yet another snag: the attendant at the desk does not recognize Sebastian's name. But he does know the Englishman is still alive, and he brings V to room 36. (Sebastian died at thirty-six years of age, in 1936. His house number is also thirty-six. And as V said, the year 1936 "seems the reflection of that name in a pool of rippling water. There is something about the curves of the last three numerals that recalls the sinuous outlines of Sebastian's personality.")[75]

V sits on the couch outside the door of the English gentleman's bed. He can hear his soft, quick breathing. He is no longer worried now about the secret he is waiting for Sebastian to disclose. He feels a warm flow of "simpler, more human emotion." V simply wants to be with his brother now, talk to him about his books, which he knows by heart. He knows them so well they could be his own. But after he gets up and tiptoes out into the corridor, the patient's mistaken identity is revealed; this English gentleman is not Sebastian. The Russian gentleman who was Sebastian passed away the night before. In death, Sebastian became Russian again. Now V has to don Sebastian's English mask. Two months after Sebastian's death, V embarks on writing *The Real Life of Sebastian Knight* in English. Now it is V who steps into an unknown world to search out Sebastian's secrets. He has to live out his brother's life: the voyage of discovery comes to an end and the two halves become one whole. The two halves make up whom?

The end of the story takes place in a peculiar environment: between sleeping and wakefulness, as if the process of conclusion is vague but very pleasant. V explains that he was never able to see Sebastian again (not alive, at least). But his life had completely transformed after hearing the breathing of the dying man he had thought was Sebastian, as if he were listening to Sebastian speaking for those few minutes he was there. He never discovers Sebastian's secret, but he learns another: "that the soul is but a manner of being — not a constant state — that any soul may be yours, if you find and follow its undulations." And he goes on to say, "Thus — I am Sebastian Knight." V sees himself on a lighted stage, impersonating Sebastian. All the characters in Sebastian's life are coming and going around him: his few friends, his lovers, even Mr. Goodman, "the flat-footed buffoon." And "the old conjuror waits in the wings with his hidden rabbit." But finally the masquerade comes to an end and everybody returns to daily life, Clare to her grave. But our hero remains. For try as he may, he cannot escape his part: "Sebastian's mask clings to my face," he says, "the likeness will not be washed off." And this leads us to the book's final sentence: "I am Sebastian, or Sebastian is I, or perhaps we both are someone whom neither of us knows."[76]

It is in the light of *The Real Life of Sebastian Knight* that two other novels acquire greater clarity, the earlier Russian novel *The Gift* and his last, *Look at the Harlequins!* There is a threefold similarity: first, in the author's link to the characters in his novel, second, in the characters' links to the reader, and finally, in the author's link to the reader. These three relationships intermingle and form a single entity somewhere in the recesses of the author's mind. At the end of *The Gift*, Vadim's suspicion is not baseless: Vadim, the character, as created by the author, is in fact the handiwork of another writer's imagination. These interrelationships spring from Nabokov's approach to the art of storytelling. He writes in *Lectures on Russian Literature:*

> The admirable reader does not seek information about Russia in a Russian novel, for he knows that the Russia of Tolstoy or Chekhov is not the average Russia of history but a specific world imagined and created by individual genius. The admirable reader is not concerned with general ideas: he is interested in the particular vision. He likes the novel not because it helps him to get along with the group (to use a diabolical progressive-school cliché); he likes the novel because he imbibes and understands every detail of the text, enjoys what the author meant to be enjoyed, beams inwardly and all over, is thrilled by the magic imageries of the master-forger, the fancy-forger, the conjuror, the artist. Indeed, of all the characters the great artist creates, his readers are the best.[77]

The writer is the magician or conjurer standing outside of the scene. He is dead Sebastian guiding V, and V is his best reader, because he is the one who reads all the novels with a keen eye, and who re-creates them. V's quest is the same as the quest of the reader. Every reader seeking truth steps into an unfamiliar world, a world created and shaped by the writer. Fyodor wants to write other people's biographies, Vadim wants to write his own biography, and V wants to write his brother's biography, providing at once the image of the writer, and also that of the reader. The reader is the writer's twin. And for Nabokov, an ideal reader is one who likes to travel. The ideal reader leaves his or her own reality behind in order to travel to the writer's imaginary world, traveling without a backpack full of prejudices. The ideal reader is nourished along the way by the breadcrumbs the writer leaves along the trail. At the end of this voyage of discovery, the ideal reader finds an unknown self. What the reader gains is the direct result of his or her vision and the encounter with the art of the novel.

7

The above serves as an introduction to the idea of the void. Another novel on this subject comes to mind, one that is the closest to *The Real Life of Sebastian Knight,* and probably one of the best examples of the void: *Alice's Adventures in Wonderland.* Nabokov, the great magician, always professed deep esteem for Lewis Carroll, and translated *Alice* into Russian when he was young. There are two scenes of particular interest; one is at the beginning of the first volume, the second at the end of the sequel (which Nabokov did not translate), *Through the Looking-Glass.* The first work opens with a bored Alice sitting beside her sister, who is reading a tedious book: there are no pictures or conversations. Suddenly a white rabbit with pink eyes rushes in front of her. The rabbit, wearing a waistcoat, pulls out a pocket watch and says to himself: "Oh dear! Oh dear! I shall be too late!"[78] A normal child watching the scene would probably have been petrified with fear. But Alice has a curious nature and she takes off, running after the rabbit. When the rabbit disappears down the hole, Alice, without considering the consequences, jumps after it. This is how the adventure begins. Alice is a creative reader, unafraid of stepping into a world created by someone else. Though she feels helpless and confused several times throughout the journey to Wonderland, she is never discouraged. On the contrary, at every turn she tries to decipher the language of this new world, and to work out its logic.

In *Through the Looking-Glass,* Alice climbs past the surface of the mirror and into the world that exists beyond it. The characters move like chess pieces, and Alice wants to become queen, which is no easy task. Having begun as a pawn, she must play the game out to the end if she wishes to achieve her objective. She finds a peculiar creature in each of the squares, and as a result they become "squires." She learns that there is no set of instructions, so at every new stage the player is faced with a new set of rules. It is easy to see why critics compare *The Real Life of Sebastian Knight* to

Lewis Carroll's novels. If Alice had not flouted danger at the outset, there would have been no story.

In *The Real Life of Sebastian Knight,* when V's search comes to an end, we are not given the "absolute solution." The only "absolute solution" is death, and the only weapon is art: the one faces the other. The themes we encounter in this novel are repeated frequently in Nabokov's oeuvre. The central theme deals with how to fill the void that lies between two sets of nothingness. This is evoked in the first line of *Speak, Memory:* "The cradle rocks above an abyss, and common sense tells us that our existence is but a brief crack of light between two eternities of darkness."[79] In every novel, however, the void is portrayed in a different way, and filled in a different way. *The Real Life of Sebastian Knight* is about a void, a deep void that is filled by art and an even deeper one that is created by art. And of course it is also about how the creative mind works. As V explains in connection with Sebastian's first novel, all the characters serve as "methods of composition." There is a void between a creative mind and the world surrounding it, between the inner feeling that needs to be expressed and what is actually expressed, between the writer and the reader or the critic, between imagination and reality. Every aspect of this void interferes with every other one, and disrupts it. Through parody, through critiques of common things by way of what is uncommon, through countless digressions, the reader is ousted from familiar spaces or settings into strange, unfamiliar ones. The aim of the void is to continually upset the reader's familiar habits, as well as to unsettle reality itself.

Sebastian is a lonely character. The image of his adolescence, given by his younger brother V, describes him exactly at the time of his death. His evasive and volatile nature is reminiscent of his mother's elusiveness, and it gives Sebastian an attractive, mysterious air, just as this same characteristic made his mother more enchanting in Sebastian's eyes. Sebastian's loneliness is, at the same time, the loneliness of a creative mind, since such minds do not see what is familiar in the world the same way as others do. After he learns the truth about his heart disease, and that he is facing the void of death, Sebastian becomes even more aloof, distancing himself even from those who are closest to him. In fact, the void of death carries Sebastian farther back into the past—back to the forgotten country, its language and love.

Reconsidering the chessboard motif, we know that Sebastian adopts his mother's last name. The word "knight" means, among other things, a mounted soldier in armor. But here the meaning originates in chess. Sebastian is, like a chess knight, the most evasive piece in the game. The knight's unique ability is that it can jump over any other piece. Hyde cites H. Golombeck in *America's Russian Novelist,* interpreting this unique property to mean that the knight "leaves the board intermittently, in order to attack or (more often) defend, and in doing so enters momentarily some obscure dimension outside the planometric conventions of the game."[80] In art, there are no restrictions. The chess movements in the novel are not restricted to Sebastian alone. As in chess, if Sebastian's knight is to have any logic in the story, there must be an opposing piece. So the reader is invited to find the other (hidden) pieces. Clare is the most obvious one: Clare Bishop marries five years after Sebastian leaves her, then dies in childbirth. Clare's husband's last name is Bishop. We encounter other "bishops" in the novel, too, like the Bishop of Gloucester. A chess bishop cannot change the color of its squares, and plays a less flexible role by comparison with the knight. By the end (or endgame) of the novel, the question remains: which has proved to be the better piece, the knight or the bishop?

On a simpler level, the relative independence of the knight evokes Sebastian's isolation. As a result of his loneliness, Sebastian is able to relate to the surrounding world only through his works of fiction: the worlds he creates and the treasures hidden within. He wants the reader to be tempted into chasing the white rabbit and taking a blind leap into the abyss. Sebastian's reality assumes the form of his imagination.[81] V explains that Sebastian's life, though far from being dull, lacks the "terrific vigor" of his literary style. He relates that reading Sebastian's novels always conjures this or that childhood memory, causing the impression of "suddenly soaring up from the floor," moving dangerously close to the dangling crystal chandelier. It reminds him that his father used to fling open the door, pounce upon him, throw him into the air, and finally "bump me down as suddenly as he snatched me up," much the same way that Sebastian's prose "sweeps the reader off his feet, to let him drop with a shock into the gleeful bathos of the next wild paragraph."[82] The joy of flight blends with the anxiety of the widening space below. Elsewhere, V explains that the "manner of [Sebastian's] prose was the manner of his thinking and that was a dazzling succession of gaps; and you cannot ape a gap because you are bound to fill it in somehow or other—and blot it out in the process."[83]

Elsewhere, V speaks of Sebastian's painful struggle with words. One of the reasons was his need to bridge the abyss between expression and thought. In other words, to fill a void: "the maddening feeling that the right words, the only words are awaiting you on the opposite bank in the misty distance, and the shudderings of the still unclothed thought clamouring for them on this side of the abyss."[84] Sebastian was not interested in ready-made phrases, V argues, because his thoughts were of an exceptional build, and "no real idea can be said to exist without the words made to measure." V invokes another metaphor, that "naked" thought begs to be clothed in order to become visible. In *The Real Life of Sebastian Knight,* more than in any other of Nabokov's novels, it is not only the creative mind that is revealed, but also the process by which it is shaped and the way it works. We get a clear picture of how an artist like Sebastian (and his creator) incorporates voids into his work more than other writers. In fact, what brings Nabokov closer to Kafka or to Beckett is not any direct influence of theirs, or his deep understanding of their writing. There is a greater immediacy: the proximity to a void and the attempt to describe it.

Nabokov's views on Gogol probably offer the best explanation of this aspect of Nabokov himself. In one of his lectures, he speaks of the strangeness of Gogol's creative genius. He says that every literary masterpiece depends on the irrational, the absurd. Even "steady Pushkin, matter-of-fact Tolstoy, [and] restrained Chekhov," Nabokov writes, "have all had their moments of irrational insight which simultaneously blurred the sentence and disclosed a secret meaning worth the sudden focal shift." Every writer, in some way, shifts the rational plane in one way or the other. He describes Gogol's shift in two movements: a jerk and a glide, "a lyrical gust that sweeps you up and then lets you fall with a bump into the next traphole."[85]

And so we return to the beginning of Alice's story and the unknown void that suddenly opens in front of her: the beginning of all wonders. And in the second example, from *Through the Looking-Glass,* we find Alice together with Tweedledum and Tweedledee, observing the Red King fast asleep in the woods. The brothers tell Alice the king is dreaming, and she is a character in his dream. Alice objects to this logic, since she has created everything and everyone, including the king, in her own dream. But they insist, saying that if the king were to wake up, she'd "go out—bang!—just like a candle!"[86] This paradox distresses Alice, even after she wakes up. The story ends with a question to the reader: "Which do *you* think it was?" At the end of *The Real Life of Sebastian Knight,* when V/Sebastian alludes to "someone whom neither of us knows," we are facing a repetition of the question posed by the narrator of *Through the Looking-Glass.* Who has created whom? In an infinite regression of two mirrors facing each other, there is a circular paradox in which the creator of the dream confronts the one created by the dream. Is reality the creator of imagination? Or is it the other way around?[87]

THREE

The Oppressor and the Oppressed

Invitation to a Beheading, Bend Sinister

1

In the fourth chapter of *The Real Life of Sebastian Knight*, V visits his brother's apartment in London for the first time, a few months after his death. V peruses his belongings, and catches sight of two framed photographs. They're placed side by side, "in the dim shadows above the bookshelves." One is the conventional picture of a curly-haired child playing with a puppy, the type of happy photograph one might see on a cereal box. It conveys a sense of beauty similar to that of plastic flowers or painted toys, playing to the sentiments conjured by a collective memory but only on a shallow, superficial level. It is the type of picture that appeals to a sensitive personality, a "person of the arts" who writes about supposedly eternal human suffering. The second photograph has a contrary impact and appears to negate its partner. It is an enlarged photograph of a Chinese man, "stripped to the waist, in the act of being vigorously beheaded."[1] V questions their juxtaposition, thinking it in poor taste, but he presumes that Sebastian must have had a reason for placing them there that way, and he continues about his business. For a close reader of Nabokov, however, this incongruous pairing is obviously meaningful, a key theme. Here we find an association between cruelty (which has somehow managed to acquire a sort of justification for itself) and what is commonplace, banal, run-of-the-mill. (Nabokov used a special Russian term for this, *poshlust*, to describe a form of complacent mediocrity or philistinism: "not only the obviously trashy but also the falsely important, the falsely beautiful, the falsely clever, the falsely attractive.")² What are the elements that create a link between the two spectacles, the cruel and the commonplace? The answer to this question is central to Nabokov's two "political" novels: *Invitation to a Beheading* and *Bend Sinister*. He rails against the cruel and banal aspects of *poshlust* in his lectures and articles, but in these novels Nabokov specifically focuses on them as the main components of the totalitarian mentality.

It is important to keep in mind the significance for Nabokov of the historical events that took place during the relatively short period of time during which he wrote *Invitation to a Beheading*. In 1934, Nabokov interrupted work on *The Gift* to feverishly compose *Invitation to a Beheading*, completing the first draft within "one fortnight of wonderful excitement and sustained inspiration."³ In the introduction to the English translation of the novel (1959), he explains that he wrote it some fifteen years after escaping the Bolshevist regime, and just before the Nazis reached the apex of their power: "The question whether or not my seeing both in terms of one dull beastly farce had any effect on this book should concern the good reader as little as it does me."⁴ With this in mind, and in line with Brian Boyd's assertions in *The Russian Years*, it appears as though the embryonic source of *Invitation to a Beheading*, and the ghastly charade that lurks in the background, can be found in *The Gift*.⁵

Between the first draft of *Invitation to a Beheading* and its first revision, Nabokov continued researching and writing the Chernyshevski biography for *The Gift*, and in the process made an interesting discovery. Although Fyodor is dedicated to writing Chernyshevski's biography, he is not the least bit fond of him. Yet when he sees that Chernyshevski, the enemy of capital punishment, risked his own life when mocking the poet Zhukovski, he is genuine in his admiration. Zhukovski made an "infamously benign and meanly sublime proposal to surround executions with a mystic secrecy (since, in public, he said, the condemned man brazenly puts on a bold face, thus bringing the law into disrepute) so that those attending the hanging would not see but would only hear solemn church hymns from behind a curtain, for an execution should be moving." Fyodor also talks about his father, who used to think that every man knows deep down that there is something abnormal about the death penalty, because it is like "the uncanny reversal of action in a looking glass that makes everyone left-handed." He goes on to cite the Swabian code of medieval Germany, under which an actor who was insulted had the right to seek satisfaction by striking the perpetrator's shadow. And in China it was an actor — a shadow — who performed the duties of executioner, "all responsibility being as it were lifted from the world of men and transformed into the inside-out one of mirrors."[6]

The domain of *Invitation to a Beheading* is an example of this type of inside-out world. We learn from the first sentence that the novel's fragile hero has been sentenced to death. The story takes place in an unspecified utopia, and he is opaque when all citizens are required to be transparent. His crime is that of "gnostical turpitude."[7] Although he manages to hide this vice for a long time, his secret is eventually revealed, and he is tried and found guilty. Yet the executioners withhold the date of his execution, turning every day into possibly his last. He has no idea how long he has left: A day? A week? More than a week? Less? And his only comfort in this strange atmosphere is writing. As the story unfolds, the reader discovers with increasing discomfort its artificial texture. However, "artificial" in this context does not imply weakness in the novel; it is, rather, a description of the novel's structure. The reader gradually notices that the setting and ambiance have clearly been fashioned into a slapdash imitation of a stage set, shabbily arranged and in poor taste. And as a result, the story unfolds on a number of levels at the same time. It depicts the resistance of a creative mind to being confined by a totalitarian mentality where uniformity is not only the norm but the law. Yet the novel does not stop at merely denouncing the reality of totalitarianism in praise of artistic creativity, it goes much farther. It also illustrates the totalitarian mind-set and a particular type of vulgar, philistine art as codependent, each necessitating the other. Art possesses its own truth and civilizing ideas, but in the utopia characterized by *Invitation to a Beheading,* the true nature of art parades as its own vulgar parodic double.

This charade is, of course, narrated from the point of view of the story's main character. Cincinnatus sees everything as a hackneyed, nightmarish spectacle from which he cannot escape. Even the moon he sees through the jail window is a fake, not more than a painting on the set's backdrop. According to convention, the spider that lives in a corner of the jail weaving its web and being fed flies by the jailer should become Cincinnatus's faithful companion. At the close of the story, however, we find that the spider is made of springs, plush, and elastic. The hoary judge who murmurs the death sentence in Cincinnatus's ear puts his mouth so close that he "panted for a moment, made the announcement and slowly moved away, as though ungluing himself."[8] The jailer, Rodion, the defense counsel, and the prosecutor make themselves up so grotesquely that they look garish to everyone else. The narrator provides a detailed description of Rodion's appearance when he comes to visit Cincinnatus. He is wearing a jet-black toupee smoothed over his head, his eyes are bulging, and his "thick sallow cheeks" are covered in a "somewhat obsolete system of wrinkles." The narrator describes his face as having been "selected without love."[9] Yet despite Rodion's "majestic solidity," he has a way of dissolving into thin air, and then reappearing again through the cell's door, like the unforgettable Cheshire cat in *Alice's Adventures in Wonderland.* The lawyer and jailer swap places. When they first introduce the executioner to Cincinnatus, it is in the guise of a fellow prisoner. They introduce him as M'sieur Pierre (in the world of this novel, what is chic is always conveyed in a mock French fashion). M'sieur Pierre says that he receives the same room and board as the prisoner. Cincinnatus calls them "specters, werewolves, parodies."[10] In these scenes, though, the device of the double is not meant merely as satire or parody. Cincinnatus also has a double, a twin self who is more intelligent and braver than the ordinary, everyday Cincinnatus. A double who represents his creative imaginative self. "The double, the gangrel, that accompanies each of us—you, and me, and him over there—. . ."[11]

The jail resembles a budget hotel. Since the jailers pretend the jail doesn't exist in reality, the prisoner is treated as if he were a guest. His confinement and eventual execution are seen not as punishments but as acts of compassion. On one wall of Cincinnatus's little cell is a list of the eight rules for inmates, like a hotel's standard regulation notice. "1. Leaving the prison building is positively forbidden. 2. A prisoner's meekness is a prison's pride. . . . 5. Singing, dancing and joking with the guards is permitted only by mutual consent and on certain days. . . . 8. The management shall in no case be responsible for the loss of property or of the inmate himself."[12] There is another rule that is central to the story itself, the sixth: "It is desirable that the inmate should not have at all, or if he does, should immediately himself suppress nocturnal dreams whose content might be incompatible with the condition and status of the prisoner, such as: resplendent landscapes, outings with friends, family dinners, as well as sexual intercourse with persons who in real life and in the waking state would not suffer said individual to come near, which individual will therefore be considered by the law to be guilty of rape." This is a species of logic that brings to mind the Queen's famous line in the trial scene of *Alice's Adventures in Wonderland:* "Sentence first—verdict afterwards."[13]

To act as a totalitarian ruler is to adhere to a set of fake values and a particular mind-set, *poshlust.* The photograph of the child in *The Real Life of Sebastian Knight* offers one striking example, and we find additional explanation in Nabokov's essay "Philistines and Philistinism" in *Lectures on Russian Literature,* in which he goes into detail on this mentality's distinguishing features. *Poshlust* "is not only an esthetic judgment but also a moral indictment. The genuine, the guileless, the good is never *poshlust.*"[14] It turns the sincere into something banal, and at the same time reveals the vulgarity of things that try to hide behind a veneer of civilization. "*Genteel* implies the lace-curtain refined vulgarity which is worse than simple coarseness," Nabokov explains in the essay and offers the example that "to burp in company may be rude, but to say 'excuse me' after a burp is *genteel* and thus worse than vulgar."[15] A lie that tries to hide a banal reality under the cover of gracefulness is the worst kind. In the characterization of M'sieur Pierre, all these facets are portrayed with precision and an eye for the telling detail.

In his definition of what distinguishes the vulgar, Nabokov refers to the terms "genteel" and "bourgeois." He clarifies that he follows not Marx's usage of "bourgeois" but Flaubert's: a "state of mind, not a state of pocket." A bourgeois does not belong to any particular class. "A *bourgeois* is a smug philistine, a dignified vulgarian." A philistine is both an international phenomenon and one that spans all classes, from an English Duke to an American Shriner to a Soviet worker or a French diplomat. "A laborer or a coal miner can be just as bourgeois as a banker or a housewife or a Hollywood Star," Nabokov writes. The "genteel bourgeois," the full-blown philistine, is a product of triteness and mediocrity, a conformist, someone who seeks personal identity in the collective. Somebody who can be typified as "a pseudo-idealist, . . . pseudo-compassionate, . . . pseudo-wise." Someone who throws around such grand words as "Beauty," "Love," "Nature," and "Truth," which become "masks and dupes when the smug vulgarian employs them."[16] Such a person does not care about art or literature—his essential nature is "antiartistic"—but a philistine wants information, and so reads glossy magazines and identifies with the sparkling people splashed over the pages and ads. In his analysis of Gogol, Nabokov refers to this collective as "bloated dead souls."[17]

What identifies a group is, naturally, the uniformity of its members. For Nabokov, the radical critics who fought despotism and the absolute monarchy of the tsars were not themselves immune to philistinism and *poshlust,* eventually evolving a new form of despotism that puts art at the service of the state and considers it good only when it is of practical benefit to the people. So the equation works that if for the tsars writers were the servants of the state, under communism writers became the servants of the masses, and in both scenarios the individual is duty-bound to show absolute obedience to the group. By the same token, in dealing with two particular regimes in 1930s Europe—fascism and communism—in his "political novels," Nabokov tries to reach beyond the surface action of these regimes to exhibit a particular material point of view. Obviously, it can be argued that the best—meaning the cruelest—examples of this particular way of systematizing life are depicted in the acts of the regimes. But illustrations of this same approach to life can be found in any human habitat, and at any time—for example, the Ku Klux Klan in the United States. In his *Lectures on Russian Literature,* Nabokov demonstrates the similarity between what Western fascists wanted from literature with the demands of Bolsheviks by citing two representatives of those groups. First he quotes a prominent Nazi, Alfred Rosenberg, who was the minister of education: "The personality of the artist should develop freely and without any restraint. One thing, however, we demand: acknowledgement of our creed."

Then he quotes Lenin: "Every artist has the right to create freely; but we, Communists, must guide him according to plan."[18] The proximity of these modes of thinking, Nabokov remarks, would be diverting if it were not so sad, and one can see this in the concluding ceremonies of both *Invitation to a Beheading* and *Bend Sinister.* Two assumptions lurk behind both declarations: an agreement in their worldview and fundamental opposition to individuality, a stalwart negation of the right to be different, and, taken to its logical conclusion, disapproval of any form of creative force that would consolidate this individuality in works of the imagination. This negation calls into question all that a despotic frame of mind would have us accept blindly.

According to Nabokov, criminals generally lack imagination. Since they are unable to imagine, they are not capable of perceiving the obvious consequences of their crimes. If only they could use their imaginations, they would be able to call storytelling to their aid and not bungle in their real lives what imagined characters do in fiction. From Nabokov's point of view, the writer's role is not to show that crime is a "sorry farce." Nor is it his or her job to maintain the moral compass of the country. "The twinkle in the author's eye as he notes the imbecile drooping of a murderer's underlip, or watches the stumpy forefinger of a professional tyrant exploring a profitable nostril in the solitude of his sumptuous bedroom, this twinkle is what punishes your man more surely than the pistol of a tiptoeing conspirator. And inversely, there is nothing dictators hate so much as that unassailable, eternally elusive, eternally provoking gleam."[19] In this way, for Nabokov, an opposition that is usually confined within the boundaries of a sociopolitical resistance transforms into a full-scale struggle for the purpose of upholding the individual "self." Though this struggle appears to be full of obscurities, it is, in reality and in the realm of one's soul, more vivid than any political resistance.

2

In *Invitation to a Beheading,* Nabokov posits an example of the world of the murderer and the despot. It is a world in which *poshlust* rules, together with an insistence on uniformity and conventionality, reminiscent of another type of world, that of Eugène Ionesco's *Rhinoceros,* or yet another, of Kafka's *The Trial.*[20] Obedience alone is not enough in a world that denies imagination. Only complete obliteration of individual thought will suffice; the executioner's lamentable need is not for conformity but for the confirmation of his words and actions on the part of his victim. In Nabokov's novel, the banal oppressors stand behind the door and peek through the keyhole, scrutinizing every movement Cincinnatus makes. They strip him of all private space. He will be pardoned only if he becomes like them, which can only mean death. After all, isn't death the termination of an individual's imagination, one's particular viewpoint and unique identity? Remaining true to one's origins and principles, making use of individual creativity— these are acts that defy the bourgeois tenets of *poshlust.* The world of *Invitation to a Beheading* is not genuine but is governed by conformist rituals repeated in detail, even though they have long been stripped of meaning. It runs parallel to the world of art, but it is devoid of creative imagination. The people who uphold and promulgate the ideas of this world pay tribute only to themselves, tirelessly, puffing the feathers of their own respectability. Both at the novel's beginning and its end, the warden expects the prisoner to confess and thereby confirm how well the warden is treating him, doing him a favor. In this collective danse macabre it is not the death penalty that signifies, because execution is not enough. What is important is the spectacle of participation in collective rituals, where the beleaguered victim surrenders his distinctiveness and his independence to the collective group.

If everything in the world that Cincinnatus inhabits is a cheap fabrication, if what is termed "real" actually means "unreal," then the only possible way to describe and apprehend "reality" is to make good use of allegory and the expository form. Hence the sensation one has as a reader of walking on clouds, or a sense of weightlessness, accompanied by a form of timelessness. (Cincinnatus details for his mother the fake nature of the hands of a clock.)[21] Time loses its usual day-to-day meaning. For Cincinnatus, time can be measured only from the moment his execution date is announced. Part of this weightlessness and timelessness is rooted in the unpredictability of the despotic mentality. Cincinnatus is tormented by the fact that he cannot devise even the simplest of plans for anything; he lives in a world devoid of logic, where nothing can be trusted. He has been sentenced to death, but the event remains unscheduled, rendering each morning his last. The jailers promise Cincinnatus that he can see his mother and wife, and force him into complying with the preparatory minutiae for their visits, but they never materialize. And when finally he is in no mood to see his mother or his wife, they are admitted to see him. Once his execution date is finally announced, the jailers hold a full valedictory gathering. But when morning arrives, we find that the executioner is indisposed, having eaten something that did not agree with him, and the execution is postponed until further notice. The execution finally takes place unexpectedly, as if impromptu, and Cincinnatus has no time to prepare himself.

In *Invitation to a Beheading,* the word "unexpected" is meant to connote not something "surprising" or "new" but an absurd situation in which nothing follows the rules of logic. Cincinnatus asks several times: "Is there in the so-called order of so-called things of which your so-called world consists even one thing that might be considered an assurance that you will keep a promise?" And then he rephrases his question: "Is there in this world, can there be, any kind of security at all, any pledge of anything, or is the very idea of guarantee unknown here?"[22] He gets no answer. The reason is that one of the principal determinants of a tyrannical mentality is the refusal of responsibility. It is demonstrative of a mentality whereby a person considers others duty-bound to fulfill their wishes, but reneges even the slightest gesture of reciprocity toward others. A conscientious society is founded upon the respect of one human for the individual imagination of all others, which is what makes society hold itself accountable to each of its constituents. The mode of society described in *Invitation to a Beheading* rejects the idiosyncratic, the particular, the other. "The law" does not abide difference. For this reason, the framework of mutual responsibility under the law, allowing members of the society to benefit from both collective and individual security, is rendered meaningless here. No single person has a specific identity. No one can, within the bounds of specified privileges, benefit from any guarantee of security. The form of democracy Nabokov cherished stems from his belief in individuality. In a totalitarian society, by contrast, no one can plant his or her feet firmly on the ground because "the law" reflects the wishes of a certain individual or a certain group, and what terrorizes people most is not a fear of lawlessness, but the law itself.

The law controlling the world of *Invitation to a Beheading* distorts and disrupts not only the day-to-day logic but language too. After all, language is what constructs the atmosphere of the novel. For here, as in many of Nabokov's other stories, language is used as a subversive element. Although the novel's phrasing sounds routine and ordinary, in practice it never stops warping the conventional nature of language. Nabokov achieves this effect by placing familiar words and expressions in unfamiliar locations or situations. As a result, language is no longer a means for conveying information; rather, it becomes primarily a tool for distorting whatever information might be conveyed. This forces the reader to experience the world of *Invitation to a Beheading* directly and without explanation. The prisoner's language differs from that of the jailer's. If Cincinnatus tries to write in what could be called a poetic language, the other characters speak in cliché or a prefabricated form of language that ends up satirizing itself. The novel's use of language becomes like a mirror revealing the jailer and his farcical world at the same time, wedded to each other.

Here we arrive at one of Nabokov's defining concerns. Nabokov's father set the precedent for and deeply shaped many of his son's ideas, though Nabokov continued to refine and polish them throughout his long literary career. One such concern is the role of culture as a civilizing force, and the use of language as a key part of this process. The characters in *Invitation to a Beheading* are crafted not only by their speech and behavior, together with the narrator's explanations, but also by their use of language. The jailer's and the executioner's use of language accurately exposes their hidden *poshlust* as they luxuriate in clichés, trite observations, and tired opinions. The scaffolding of their vocabulary is rickety and besmirched from overuse and strained application, and we begin to recognize the major contrast and tension between their language and that used by Cincinnatus. Denounced for opacity as a child, Cincinnatus has since tried to learn how to be transparent like everyone around him, who are able to understand each other at the outset "since they had no words that would end in an unexpected way, perhaps in some archaic letter, an upsilamba, becoming a bird or a catapult with wondrous consequences."[23] The world cannot abide such unpredictability, and in Nabokov's view, this mind-set defines public enemy number one: *poshlust*. This attitude should come as no surprise on the part of a son whose father entered politics with the idea of changing the world fundamentally; both father and son were fiercely aware of the particular brand of philistine vulgarity that *poshlust* defines.

Nabokov does not focus on language alone. The form of art preferred by the characters in the novel is also representative of their level of culture. Here the mode of perception or interpretation of art (which in Nabokov's novels is also generally indicative of the perception of life) constitutes a central axis in the narrative structure. *Invitation to a Beheading* satirizes a particular class of imitative art, which claims to be realistic. In depicting the totalitarian mind-set, Nabokov also presents the totalitarian nature of the imitative types of language and artistic genres born of it, a mind-set that believes it simply, and exclusively, holding a monopoly on reality. Naturally, such a mind-set believes that it can easily impose its version of reality on others. There are many examples. What M'sieur Pierre likes best is photography. He has filled an album with photographs of Emmie, the prison director's young daughter. But he has retouched the images of Emmie's face such that they become biographical, a "photohoroscope" in Nabokov's term: images of her "present face were supplemented by shots of other people—for the sake of costume, furniture and surroundings—so as to create the entire décor and stage properties of her future life."[24] The most famous novel in this imitational or photohoroscopic field is titled *Quercus,* and Cincinnatus has already read a third of it by the time the novel opens, nearly one thousand pages. The main character is an oak tree and the novel a biography of that oak. "Employing the gradual development of the tree (growing lone and mighty at the edge of a canyon at whose bottom the waters never ceased to din), the author unfolded all the historic events—or shadows of events—of which the oak could have been a witness."[25] This form of transparent art acts as a mirror for the citizens of the land.[26]

Nabokov's own novel, of course, is the polar opposite of *Quercus.* It overflows with various games and is filled with bends moving in different directions. This is not because Nabokov opposes reality but, on the contrary, because he respects reality. He sees reality as something complex and opaque. The apparent movement away from surface reality observed in the structure of his novels is, at root, an attempt to approximate the true density and opaque essence of existence. It calls to mind Iris Murdoch's idea that "our current picture of freedom encourages a dream-like facility; whereas what we require is a renewed sense of the difficulty and complexity of the moral life and the opacity of persons. . . . We need a new vocabulary of attention."[27]

This gives rise to two questions: *to what extent can fiction be true? And assuming that stories can be true, what happens to their fictional nature?* In an article on Pushkin written in 1937, Nabokov tries to find an answer to these questions. He asks whether it is possible to imagine in its full reality the life of another, "to relive it oneself and transfer it intact onto paper?" He doubts that one can, as one is "tempted to believe that thought itself, in fixing its beam on the life history of a person, inevitably deforms it. Thus, it can only be the verisimilar, and not the veritable truth, that the mind perceives. . . . And yet what rapture for a daydreaming Russian to depart into Pushkin's world! These visions are probably fraudulent and the real Pushkin would not recognize himself in them, but if I invest in them a bit of that same love I experience in reading his poems, won't what I make of this imaginary life be something resembling the poet's works, if not himself?. . . Thus one would like to think that what we call art is, in essence, truth's picture window; one has to know how to frame it, that's all."[28]

3

When, without explanation, Cincinnatus narrates an event that occurred during his childhood, we do not know whether it truly happened or was a dream, like everything else in the novel. Once when he was a child, on an excursion with schoolmates, he got separated from the others. It happened in a little town "so drowsy that when a man who had been dozing on a bench beneath a bright whitewashed wall at last got up to help me find my way, his blue shadow on the wall did not immediately follow him." Cincinnatus believes that in his carelessness, he mistook what he saw. Crucially, however, in Cincinnatus's mind, time is reduced to a moment separating the man's sluggish movement from his immobile shadow: "the pause, the hiatus, when the heart is like a feather." Cincinnatus lives in this rare kind of interim time. And he declares, "Part of my thoughts is always crowding around the invisible umbilical cord that joins this world to something—to what I shall not say yet."[29]

Nabokov is always looking for that "pause" in order to instantaneously pierce and reveal a second level of reality. The skeleton key that unlocks Cincinnatus's personality is his search for this other reality. The secret he is trying to uncover is akin to the invisible coiled umbilical cord attaching him to this world. He recognizes what it is. He truly recognizes it, but he doesn't want to utter its name. *Invitation to a Beheading* is not only about what can be touched and put on show for everyone to see. It is also about this secret and this pause. A totalitarian mind-set takes on the role of a cruel sorcerer who wishes to lock away the novel's protagonist, the hero, in a magic castle and prevent him from divulging his secret. Nabokov gives the role of sorcerer to politics in its most essential form (like *poshlust*). But art defies the sorcerer. Politics belongs to the collective. It has a language that is apparently simple and accessible but is in reality unable to convey the meaning of anything genuine. Even so, politics claims to be seeking to achieve great human ideals. Art, by contrast, deals with every human being privately. It has a labyrinthine, storied language that deals with ostensibly insignificant details in its celebration of individuality.

The confrontation between art and politics does not come out of the blue. It did not begin with *Invitation to a Beheading* or end with *Bend Sinister*. Fresh from Washington, Mildred McAfee Horton became the president of Wellesley College when Nabokov was teaching there. She was not happy with Nabokov's anti-Soviet stance (the Soviet Union was an ally of the United States at the time). In a letter to Horton in 1946, Nabokov writes that "governments come and go but the imprint of genius remains and it is this imperishable pattern that I should like my students (if any) to discern and admire."[30] This stance against the interference of politics did not originate with Nabokov. In fact, his views are quite similar to those of two of his beloved Russian writers. Chekhov believed that if great writers participate in the political process, they should do so only "to put up a defense against politics." He said, "There are enough prosecutors and gendarmes already, without adding to the number."[31] For Pushkin (whose life and works are attacked by the right and the left alike), according to Nabokov, "discomfort and oppression can be engendered not only by the police regulations of a tyrannical government, but . . . by a group of civic-minded, politically enlightened radical minds."[32] From the outset, Nabokov's works are involved in this confrontation between politics and the arts, demonstrating the destructive role of totalitarianism.

In *Invitation to a Beheading,* the topic of politics provokes ontological tension. The novel is more about a political state of mind than about any particular government or specific stance; apart from Cincinnatus, the characters are meant to be not personalities but examples of totalitarian mind-sets. Who is Cincinnatus? He is the son of an unknown drifter who spent his childhood in a large institution. He teaches children in a kindergarten in division F. All of this is insignificant: what matters is Cincinnatus's basic illegality, an uncontrollable, unalterable fact.[33] As a result, Cincinnatus is alone. Even when his wife comes to pay him a visit with her extended family and their furniture, filling the prison cell with disruptive noise, he is still alone. Throughout the last chapter, he repeats "by myself" over and over again.[34] Nabokov's emphasis on individuality is manifest in this novel more than in any other. However, though Cincinnatus is the most isolated of Nabokov's characters, he is never depicted in a simplistic way.

Cincinnatus is a peculiar type of hero or character. At the beginning of the novel, we learn his unheroic weaknesses; he fears death. When he returns to his cell after he is sentenced, his legs shake so badly that he cannot stand or walk unaided. He has never wanted to stand out, appear different to other people. On the contrary, throughout his life, he has tried to hide his otherness. Cincinnatus has otherworldly troubles too. He feels a close bond to a different world, a better world, Antiterra. Yet he also remains attached to the everyday world. So on one level, *Invitation to a Beheading* is about the lengthy process by which Cincinnatus must extract himself from his terrestrial relationships. And though he is locked away throughout the novel, held by his enemies in a little room in a castle, his adventures are not unlike those of legendary heroes who brave danger in their quest for the Holy Grail. What is Cincinnatus to do? It appears as though he has no other choice but to undergo trials by fire and flood to gain access to his coveted treasure, that holy secret. The only difference is that the age of heroism is over. There is nothing holy awaiting the quester at the end of the road.

Cincinnatus's engagement with the world that holds him captive is not limited to an understandable fear of death. He is married to a common, ignorant woman, with whom he once fell madly in love, despite her serial and unconcealed love affairs. Marthe talks about every infidelity with a cruel and insensitive coyness. She bears two children, neither fathered by Cincinnatus; the son is lame and evil-tempered and the daughter dull, obese, and nearly blind. When she comes to visit Cincinnatus in jail, her entire family in tow, a hilariously comic scene, despite its dark and bitter resonance worthy of a Marx Brothers film, ensues. Marthe lumbers in, accompanied by a new, very proper young man who is forever coddling her lest she catch cold. Marthe's father enters and settles into a leather armchair, shaking his head angrily, his gaze fixed on Cincinnatus. Marthe's maternal grandparents sit side by side on identical high-backed chairs: "The grandfather tightly clutched in his small hirsute hands a bulky portrait, in a gilt frame, of his mother, a misty young woman, in turn holding a portrait."[35] Marthe's twin brothers show up too; one holds a sheet music scroll and the other, "in sky-blue plus-fours, a dandy and a wit, . . . had also fixed a crepe arm band on his sleeve and kept indicating it with his finger as he tried to catch Cincinnatus's eye."[36] Pieces of furniture are carted in with the family, as are household utensils, even sections of walls. A mirrored wardrobe carries its own private reflection, "namely, a corner of the connubial bedroom with a stripe of sunlight across the floor, a dropped glove, and an open door in the distance."[37] Finally, Marthe's two children, lame Diomedon and obese Pauline, reminders of her infidelity, arrive.

Cincinnatus is a captive of this world. In the first chapter, after he is led to jail, Rodion the jailer comes in and offers to dance a waltz, and Cincinnatus agrees. The narrator offers a detailed description of both characters. We learn that the jailer smells of sweat, tobacco, and garlic. And the prisoner is much smaller than Rodion and light as a leaf. They dance their way out of the cell; a guard stands at a bend in the corridor. They trace a circle and glide back into the enclosure.[38] The waltz displays the circular nature of Cincinnatus's actions. Every maneuver is circular in motion; at the end of each route, he returns to the starting point. He easily leaves the cell and the castle on the first night and heads home, but when he gets there, he finds that in fact he has gone full circle and returned to his cell. Cincinnatus is a captive of these circles, at the center of which is lodged his temperament. The castle jail is described in a way that makes everything appear unreal, fantastical; the jail staff, described as Cincinnatus sees them, do not appear to have human faces. They are "some sort of wretched specters. . . . They torment me as can torment only senseless visions, bad dreams, dregs of delirium, the drivel of nightmares and everything that passes down here for real life."[39] Naturally, Cincinnatus yearns to wake up, but he cannot do so without help from outside, help that he fears. His soul has grown lazy, his mind riddled with contradictions. Although quite familiar with the nonhuman and, more important, unreal nature of his guards, he cannot escape the talons of captivity.

Cincinnatus believes that everything around him is imitation, no more than a parody, and that he has been deceived. In the beginning, M'sieur Pierre is introduced to him as a fellow prisoner and probably a fellow activist. Cincinnatus hears a tapping, a scratching from behind his cell wall that sounds like a message in Morse code. It spurs hope in him for some unknown prisoner tunneling through a subterranean corridor. At the end of a long, excruciating wait, Rodrig Ivanovich appears, accompanied by M'sieur Pierre. The director's young daughter, Emmie, who has suddenly become very affectionate with Cincinnatus, promises to rescue him. In reality, theirs is a flight of fancy, they move in a circle and end up in her father's dining room. Having lived among ghosts and shadows for so long, he has been hiding from them the fact that he is a real, living person. He makes this confession to his "lawyer," who is, of course, not real. How can Cincinnatus be so simple-hearted, a condition sometimes not so different from simpleminded?

Cincinnatus is not merely gullible, he is timid too, and lacks courage. He accepts that he was born transparent and that his nature is reclusive. In a word, Cincinnatus is a victim. And he accepts his condition as a victim. The novel is narrated from Cincinnatus's point of view. However, Nabokov uses this perspective not only to generate sympathy for the victim in the face of the cruel and inhuman behavior of his oppressors and his executioner but also to ensure that we experience how the victim deals with the situation before him, and at the same time that we constantly witness the mentality of the executioner and oppressors. Sustaining overwhelming pressure from all sides, Cincinnatus inevitably retreats to find refuge in the solitary space of his own mind. He tries to dwell there, by himself, in the depths of his own soul, at as far a remove as possible from the unpredictable and uncontrollable nature of the truth outside him. The truth outside him is devoid of logic, which renders it unreal. As a result, he is left alone, in solitude, by himself and with only his innate creativity.

Yet the only way to escape this false world is through experience. Sometimes, the need to break free from the cocoon of loneliness and tackle reality is so strong that it overshadows everything else. There are moments when Cincinnatus's need for freedom "the most ordinary, physical, physically feasible kind of freedom" is so powerful and sweet an urge "that everything seemed better than it really was."[40] But these are only fleeting moments. Cincinnatus knows that he has to seek this freedom not in this world but elsewhere. But how? And where? As Cincinnatus sees things, the reality outside him is not reality; reality is lurking somewhere in the depths of his dreams and his imagination. And these dreams relate to a different world that is, as we have seen, hiding behind those short "pauses." Alongside the timid and cowardly Cincinnatus who surrenders to the jailer stands a different Cincinnatus, and from the very beginning of the book it is this double who disrupts things, this double who tramples on the jailer's head: it is he who refuses to surrender. And, in the end, it is this double who leads Cincinnatus's other "self" (his real "self"?) to that "other world."[41]

Through his writing, Cincinnatus makes his double victorious. In the first few minutes alone in the prison cell, he notices a sharpened pencil and a sheet of blank paper awaiting him on the table. From that moment on, Cincinnatus writes all the time. Initially, he cannot express what he has in mind or even complete his sentences. As time goes by, however, his language acquires more transparency and more clarity. It appears that the mere exercise of writing is what leads the writer (any writer?) into another dimension. Cincinnatus's last attempt at writing coincides with a peculiar event that would seem to be a sort of prophecy. Immediately after being informed that the execution rituals have been postponed again due to M'sieur Pierre's ill health, and before M'sieur Pierre suddenly reappears to sweep Cincinnatus off with him, the jailer walks into the cell carrying a delicious lepidopteran victim rolled in a towel to offer the voracious spider. But the moth escapes the jailer's clutches and disappears, and the jailer, who is frightened of the moth, leaves Cincinnatus alone. Cincinnatus, knowing where the moth is hiding, begins to write. Butterflies and moths, in whatever form they appear, play an essential role in Nabokov's works. Here it appears that the moth brings Cincinnatus's double to mind and heralds the good news that freedom is imminent. Cincinnatus, who has been held captive by his jailers, approaches death (and freedom): it is under these conditions that he writes. He confesses that he has been duped by everything: "all of this theatrical, pathetic stuff." He has been deceived by many: "a volatile maiden, a mother's moist gaze." But now, that life has come to an end. He "should not have sought salvation within its confines," he writes. He has, however, discovered the rift between reality and that other world, and he can now explain everything.[42]

The text is left unfinished. The moth seems to have fallen asleep, and Cincinnatus caresses its wings. There is no more waiting now: they come to fetch him. Although he has been waiting for this moment all along, M'sieur Pierre's arrival is unexpected, and he is not fully prepared to go. He still feels fear. He is led by the executioner into an old, damaged carriage, and they pass through the streets and the crowds before eventually arriving at the plaza. There is a vermilion platform in the center, "no, not quite in the centre, that precisely was the dreadful part." Cincinnatus keeps saying "by myself."[43] M'sieur Pierre, wearing a white apron, expects him to cooperate, no excitement, no fuss, please. Cincinnatus repeats "by myself." M'sieur Pierre shows Cincinnatus how to place his head on the block and count to ten. The shadow of the executioner's swing is already visible. Cincinnatus begins the count, but another Cincinnatus asks: "Why am I here?"

In answer, he gets up and looks around. The moment of clarity arrives, at first almost painful, frightening. He investigates and finds that everything is coming apart, everything is collapsing. The platform in the middle of the plaza has crumpled into a cloud of reddish dust. The last few rows of spectators are just painted masks. The remaining trees are two-dimensional. A woman rushes past wearing a black shawl, carrying "the tiny executioner like a larva in her arms." A spinning wind picks up. Cincinnatus makes his way to where "to judge by the voices, stood beings akin to him." And the novel ends. Cincinnatus has successfully abolished the vicious circles, accessing instead a new spiral—within the magic world of death (and art).[44]

1

Invitation to a Beheading has a happy ending. A happy ending conditional on the presupposition that Nabokov is trying to explore the world of totalitarianism through the context of a creative mind. It is also conditional on our accepting that Nabokov prefers to consider how creative minds perceive and assess the totalitarian mind-set and how to resist its onslaught, rather than to depict the horrific reality of totalitarianism. The novel unfolds within the confines of Cincinnatus's mind. It is from there that the world outside is revealed to be a farce: he is released from the hold of this farce only when his mind fully rejects the spectacle. The main thing is not the oppressor's power; it is the hidden power of the oppressed. When Cincinnatus rejects the farce, the farce does not merely come to an end: it disintegrates. I repeat: it disintegrates. The happy ending of *Invitation to a Beheading* depends on these assumptions. Otherwise, we have to accept that a totalitarian state (of mind), in fact, heralds such horror that death becomes the only means of salvation.

Nabokov described *Invitation to a Beheading* as a "violin in a void" in his introduction to the English translation.[45] A strange definition perhaps, but easily recognizable for the reader. It is the same impression one has when reading *Bend Sinister*. One reason for this is that each of the protagonists is utterly alone. It is particularly true of Cincinnatus. He complains that he would have to desist if writing with a contemporary reader in mind, but "as there is in the world not a single human who can speak my language; or, more simply, not a single human who can speak; or, even more simply, not a single human; I must think only of myself, of that force which urges me to express myself."[46] This is the familiar lament of a writer who has something to say but who knows that no one in his country or among his compatriots wants to listen. Unlike Cincinnatus, Krug, the main character of *Bend Sinister,* is sentimentally attached to his family and a few of his friends.[47] As the story unfolds, however, Krug is forcibly and cruelly separated from the people who are close to him. In the end, he is completely alone. In the moments that follow, it is as if the gentle but insistent sound of a violin increases in resonance a hundredfold in such absolute emptiness. Even though apparently no one is listening, the sound of the solo fills the void. Similarly, lean and diminutive Cincinnatus's writing resembles that of Krug, who is neither small nor thin but is, like Cincinnatus, childlike; Krug, too, suffers the same profound loneliness as Cincinnatus.

The protagonists of both *Bend Sinister* and *Invitation to a Beheading* struggle against bitterness and cruelty in a deep void characterized by the sociopolitical pressures of worlds more or less familiar to them. Unlike most of Nabokov's protagonists, neither is living in exile but instead in his respective homeland, though both confront the same difficulties that usually befall exiles. For example, social assimilation is impossible, because each thinks differently from the people around him. Undoubtedly, their isolation affects their language. But it is precisely because of their isolation that language can be best applied. In *Invitation to a Beheading,* Nabokov creates a fundamental difference between Cincinnatus's poetic expressions and the cliché-ridden speech of the jailers. In *Bend Sinister,* too, language is a vital tool. Nabokov describes Krug's compatriots as indistinguishable: "Everybody is merely an anagram of everybody else." From this perspective there is no difference whatsoever among human beings. "Paronomasia is a kind of verbal plague, a contagious sickness in the world of words" that heralds a bigger social malaise.[48] It can be argued that these two characters and their jailers do not understand each other's languages, not even the literal meanings of the words they use, and this informs the tragedy and reveals the reason both books feature the idea of individual freedom within society more than do any others of Nabokov's novels. The reader will find a kind of victory at the end of each novel that serves at the same time as a kind of defeat. Victory comes because neither prisoner yields to the designs of his executioners, and defeat because in these totalitarian worlds, escape (salvation) is impossible. If Nabokov eventually shows some mercy to Cincinnatus and Krug, paradise can be regained only beyond death, in the kingdom of art.

Bend Sinister (1947) abounds with many of the themes, telltale pauses, tricks, and narrative devices found in *Invitation to a Beheading*. It acts as a sort of bridge connecting one of Nabokov's best earlier works, *Invitation to a Beheading* (1935–1936) to the works produced when he was at the height of his powers. A close examination of *Bend Sinister* offers valuable insight into certain components of Nabokov's later literary worlds, though it lacks the maturity of *Lolita* and *Pnin*. Spectacular in part, the whole falls short of the miraculous dazzle and grandeur of these two subsequent works. In seeking to clarify the relationship between *Invitation to a Beheading* and *Bend Sinister*, we can also see how the latter announces certain aspects of Nabokov's later works. The two novels resemble each other in a variety of different ways, both in context and structure. The main theme is that of opposing frames of consciousness: creativity versus totalitarianism. In both novels, the ambiance is intentionally dystopian. *Invitation to a Beheading* takes place during the period of German fascism and Russian communism, while *Bend Sinister* occurs soon after the Second World War. Nabokov admits that without these "infamous models" he could not have "interlarded this fantasy with bits of Lenin's speeches, and a chunk of the Soviet constitution, and gobs of Nazist pseudo-efficiency." In the introduction that he later added to *Bend Sinister* (in 1963), he writes that the "influence of my epoch on my present book is as negligible as the influence of my books or, at least of this book, on my epoch."[49] Nevertheless, the object in writing these two novels goes beyond political arguments. His point of view is best explained in *Lectures on Russian Literature:* "At this superhigh level of art, literature is of course not concerned with pitying the underdog or cursing the upperdog. It appeals to that secret depth of the human soul where the shadows of other worlds pass like the shadows of nameless and soundless ships."[50]

Bend Sinister tells the story of Adam Krug, world-famous philosopher and sole celebrity of international renown in his Central European country, which is now in the grip of a dictator named Paduk. The two characters have known each other for a long time—were, in fact, schoolmates. Krug, who used to call his peculiar friend Toad, was a bit of a bully and used to trip Paduk and then sit on his face. The totalitarian regime operates on the principle that only the group matters, not the individual. "'Alone' is the vilest word in the language. Nobody is alone." In Paduk's words (in Krug's imagination), "when a cell in an organism says 'leave me alone,' the result is cancer." All Krug wants is to be alone with his work and with his friends.[51]

The novel opens with the death of Krug's wife, Olga. Thereafter, the only thing besides his work that brings Krug happiness is his eight-year-old son, David. Krug's name bestows honor and respect on his town, and what Paduk wants is his name, to legitimize the regime. They deploy all sorts of maneuvers and threats to make him capitulate. They look for his weakness and they find it: his son. Soon David is arrested and, after a series of mishaps, sent by mistake to the Institute for Abnormal Children. Although Krug had finally agreed to cooperate in order to get his son back, it is already too late. Efficiency and meritocracy are not inherent to totalitarian regimes. In this utopia, as in Nazi Germany, they experiment on little human creatures, and they film these experiments. In one of these sessions, "Orphans" occasionally serve as a "release instrument" for the benefit of murderous criminals.[52] David is killed in this process, even though he is of use to the state only while alive. Krug, who is thrown in jail, sees the heartrending film of his son being torn to pieces. The narrator, however, unable to endure witnessing so much cruelty, finds himself compelled to intervene: he frees Krug from his hold on reason. The novel ends in a tragicomic scene: Krug's friends have been rounded up and now face execution as a means of breaking Krug's resistance. Paduk comes along to watch. The firing squad is ready. But Krug, now mad, thinks he is back at school. Returning to the habits of childhood, he reaches for one of his playmates' hat, a "sissy sealskin bonnet," and throws it to another. He then wants to make fun of Toad. As he runs toward Paduk, a bullet grazes his ear, and then another better-aimed bullet hits him. Paduk is crouching, shaking with fear and "protecting his dimming face with his transparent arm."[53] The narrator gets up to investigate the sudden twang on the wire netting of his window. A big moth with furry feet is clinging there. Is it a message from Krug? The narrator is no longer worried about him; the very last lap of his life had been happy, "and it had been proven to him that death was but a question of style." He closes by noting that it is a good night for mothing.[54]

In addition to these familiar themes and literary devices in *Bend Sinister*, Nabokov also introduces a new element, which he progressively develops to excellence in *Pnin, Lolita,* and *Ada*. It concerns the pain or despair that accompanies any binding human relationship. In these later novels, we encounter images that reflect our bonds with people who are dear to us, the sorrow that results when these are lost, and the truth that the catastrophe of loss can never be remedied or erased, even when Nabokov considers the alternative worlds of art and death as places that offer benevolent, compassionate refuge. In his introduction to *Bend Sinister*, he reminds us that the system of holding people hostage is as old as the oldest war, though "a fresher note is introduced when a tyrannic state is at war with its own subjects and may hold any citizen in hostage with no law to restrain it."[55] He observes that the trope has an even more recent configuration in what he calls "the lever of love" by which a rebel is helplessly tied to his "wretched country by his own twisted heartstrings." Nabokov adds that this method has been applied successfully by the Soviets. In the same introduction, Nabokov explains that *Bend Sinister* is not about life and death in a "grotesque police state" and that the characters are not "types" or carriers of ideas. Paduk and Doctor Alexander, Hustave and Crystalen, the soldiers—all are "only absurd mirages, illusions oppressive to Krug during his brief spell of being, but harmlessly fading away when I dismiss the cast." Nabokov reveals what is key to *Bend Sinister:* "the beating of Krug's loving heart."[56] He claimed to have written the whole book for the pages concerning David and his father.

This is one of the vital differences between *Invitation to a Beheading* and *Bend Sinister*. Even those closest to Cincinnatus deceive him. As a result, he is truly on his own, without close bonds to any other character in the novel. Even his one-sided, hopeless love for Marthe is without depth as a relationship. It is, therefore, Cincinnatus's solitude that informs him and causes him finally to sever the ties that bind him to the totalitarian world. This is not a dilemma that Krug has to confront. Like Nabokov, and unlike Cincinnatus, Krug is deeply in love with his wife and his son. In the first few pages of the novel, the reader is provided with a detailed description of Krug. First, the narrator describes his visual appearance, but then he ventures beneath the visible surface: there is a shirt that is depicted with precision, as is his underwear. Underneath is white skin, and under this layer, there is a dead wife and a sleeping child. Krug is constantly asked what his weakness is. The "lever of love" in Krug's life is David, who is killed by thugs (mistakenly, and with the mindlessness shared by all executioners and thugs throughout history). It is a form of loss that Nabokov knew well. After all, two fascists killed his father by chance, and his brother perished in a Nazi concentration camp. This element, the "lever of love" displayed in the most unvarnished way in *Bend Sinister,* was then refined and perfected in his subsequent novels, particularly *Pnin.* How to endure, to somehow fill the sudden void that follows the death of a loved one? How is it possible to do that in the wider, more grotesque void of an intellectually barren society? A totalitarian state in which mere curiosity is regarded as the purest form of defiance? For Nabokov, remember, curiosity is a magical force that bestows a charmed quality on imagination. Were it not for curiosity, Alice would never have experienced her journey down the rabbit hole. And were it not for curiosity, few books would have found readers.

Along with the lever of Krug's love for his son, Nabokov brings two other notions of control into *Bend Sinister.* The first is a mistaken assumption arising from the cruelty of the despot's thought processes and, by extension, the thoughts of his political allies. Since Paduk is willing to commit any crime necessary, he immediately assumes that he has perfect control over the lives of his citizens, and perpetuates that assumption in the others. As a result, qualities of cunning or guile, which are the hallmark of mediocre minds, are misconstrued as intelligence, just as espionage, when used as a measure for gaining control, might be misconceived as inquisitiveness. Essentially, though, the oppressor's absolute cruelty is rooted in two different forms of weakness. One is a lack of imagination. Imagination is the faculty by which a human being is able to place himself in the shoes of another and feel empathy. The absence of empathy prevents Nabokov's tyrant from successfully subjugating the minds of his victims or, at least, the minds of victims such as Krug, and that's why all Paduk's attempts to control rebellious minds, the sources of defiance and insurgency, are proven to be futile and impracticable. The second weakness lies in a deep-rooted insecurity or a lack of self-confidence. This manifests itself as a lust for power that can never be satiated through leadership alone. The tyrant wishes to destroy creative minds, yet at the same time he requires validation from these very minds. In fact, it is only through this endorsement that he will achieve absolute victory. Craving praise from his former schoolmate (the indifferent Krug), Paduk is portrayed not only as cruel, but also pitiable. There is no need for further explanation: "levers" can be applied to tyrants too.

Another difference between the two novels is the relationship that exists in each between the writer-narrator of the work and the protagonist, and between the writer-narrator and rest of the characters.[57] (The structural relationship between author, narrator, and main characters reaches a pinnacle in *Pnin,* where thematically, the use of points of view and characterization shows an astonishing display of contradictions.) In *Bend Sinister,* the writer-narrator comes to Krug's aid as a deus ex machina on two separate occasions. Krug's madness is a direct result of the relationship the writer-narrator establishes with the character, in his role as "someone in the know," or "a mysterious intruder," as Nabokov says in the introduction, an "anthropomorphic deity impersonated by me."[58] Moreover, the writer-narrator is constantly disrupting the narrative flow.[59] According to several critics, this device is meant to illustrate the novel's artifice (as Nabokov himself confirms in the introduction). In so self-conscious a novel, where the writer-narrator is such a pronounced metaleptical presence, and in contrast with a more conventionally realistic style, the reader is reminded that what the characters say is not real, as they are no more than figments of the writer's imagination, "my whims and megrims," as Nabokov also volunteers in the introduction.[60] An interesting and overlooked aspect to the peculiar relationship between the writer-narrator and the protagonist involves its

effect of making the characters seem more real, more lifelike. What happens
when a character, no more than artifice, a mere vessel of language, assumes
such a lifelike personality, is that its creator's imagination takes on skin and
flesh, a body, and the faculty of the imagination is charged with significance
within the context of everyday life. And when the writer-narrator feels such
a profound depth of empathy with his creation Krug that he cannot abide
his suffering, it inevitably means that the writer-narrator, too, perceives his
Krug as a living, breathing personality. The reader, then, is not alone in
perceiving authorial presence behind the text; the novel's protagonist does
too. (There's a good reason why Nabokov repeatedly breaks into the realm
of his novels with a real or assumed identity.) As Nabokov himself points
out in *Bend Sinister,* Krug is vaguely aware of his creator's presence, and
this is also a central device in *Look at the Harlequins!* Similarly, *Invitation
to a Beheading* opens with a quote from a French thinker, Pierre Delalande,
who is in fact another figment of Nabokov's imagination; "Comme un fou
se croit Dieu, nous nous croyons mortels."[61] Nevertheless, we should keep
in mind that to Nabokov this imaginary world is as real as "reality" gets. Just
as the characters in a novel need an author in order to exist, so the reader,
by observing the writer's imaginary worlds, is offered a glimpse of his real
identity, recalling an earlier question: *Is Alice the Red King's creator or his
creation?*

When we examine the plot, it becomes clear that the real world is
derived from the magical one. Krug means circle in Russian, and his first
name is Adam.[62] Nabokov and Krug are linked further by plot. In Nabokov's words, "the plot starts to breed in the bright broth of a rain puddle."
The novel opens with Krug observing a puddle from a window of the hospital where his wife is dying. "The oblong pool, shaped like a cell that is about
to divide, reappears subthematically throughout the novel," Nabokov ad-
vises, proceeding to list a series of references that allude to the puddle as if
he were giving a table of contents: "an ink blot in Chapter Four, an inkstain
in Chapter Five, spilled milk in Chapter Eleven, the infusoria-like image of
ciliated thought in Chapter Twelve, the footprint of a phosphorescent is-
lander in Chapter Eighteen, and the imprint a soul leaves in the intimate
texture of space in the closing paragraph." He goes into even greater detail

on the significance of the novel's opening chapter, pointing out that "the puddle thus kindled and rekindled in Krug's mind remains linked up with the image of his wife not only because he had contemplated the inset sunset from her death-bedside, but also because this little puddle vaguely evokes in him my link with him: a rent in his world leading to another world of tenderness, brightness and beauty."[63] This theme, his idea of "tenderness, brightness and beauty" is repeated in a variety of different ways throughout his oeuvre, and it is what represents the best of *Bend Sinister*'s characters, the sparks of youthfulness, of courage, and, of course, love.

5

Edmund Wilson and Nabokov maintained a healthy correspondence over the course of their friendship. In one of his letters, in 1947, Wilson has this to say about *Bend Sinister:*

> You aren't good at this kind of subject, which involves questions of politics and social change, because you are totally uninterested in these matters and have never taken the trouble to understand them. For you, a dictator like the Toad is simply a vulgar and odious person who bullies serious and superior people like Krug. You have no idea why or how the Toad was able to put himself over, or what his revolution implies. And this makes your picture of such happenings rather unsatisfactory. Now don't tell me that the real artist has nothing to do with the issues of politics. An artist may not take politics seriously, but, if he deals with such matters at all, he ought to know what it is all about. . . . As it is, what you are left with on your hands is a satire on events so terrible that they really can't be satirized—because in order to satirize anything you have to make it worse than it is.[64]

Nabokov replied: "Someday you will read it again."[65]

At the heart of Wilson's criticism (and at the center of the two "political" novels produced by Nabokov) lies the important question, the eternal polarity — reality versus fiction. Contrary to what Wilson asserts, Nabokov does not lack an understanding of, or familiarity with, the issues he raises in *Invitation to a Beheading* and *Bend Sinister*. Furthermore, his ideas on these subjects reside exclusively within the boundaries of the problems they raise. An example of an author unfamiliar with these issues is Wilson himself: he receives his information from theoretical studies rather than practical experience. Nabokov observed the Russian Revolution firsthand, faced Nazi Germany with a Jewish wife and son, suffered numerous involuntary displacements, and lost many of his relatives and loved ones to the political turmoil of the times. Nabokov's problems are personal ones, but they also fall within the realm of arts and letters. His personal anguish, especially in relation to his father's death, is so deeply entrenched in him that it does not surface in his novels in a facile way. Though he distances himself from political stances, he nevertheless critiques, in his writings as well as in his speeches and interviews, the tyranny of totalitarian regimes better than most political commentators. Nabokov's criticism is not dependent on current affairs or daily news cycles, and since his work is more focused on an analysis of the mind-set that propels these regimes, his observations are wide-ranging — and always new. Wilson explains the artistic challenge clearly: the truth about these regimes, especially Russian communism and German fascism, is too horrific to invite satire. A further complication: any artistic encounter with the unpalatable realities of life, whether approached in a serious way or through satire, forces the artist to confront this problem. The naked truth alone does not only appear to lack a sense of reality, it appears to be *counter* to reality. The reason for the success of great realistic novels such as *Anna Karenina* (loved by Nabokov) is not that they include the naked truth in their narratives: what it comes down to is a question of style.

But what are we to do with a novel that resides in a void? Or a novel whose reality constitutes a small void enclosed within a bigger "nothing"? In Anna Karenina's life, there is a superficial circuit of appearances, together with a kind of continuity and a kind of guarantee or reassurance built in to that reality. In fact, one of the difficulties characters might face in realistic novels is that the external truth does not lend itself to much change. Tension and unforeseen developments occur mainly in the characters' consciousnesses. By contrast, the world of totalitarianism, as Cincinnatus and Krug find out, is a world overflowing with the unexpected, based on the absence of continuity. The external truth, being artificial or forged and, in the final analysis, unreal, constantly tries to impose itself on all aspects of personal life and thereby to disrupt the internal order of every human being. Such totalitarian worlds rely upon constant connections and disconnections (a particular type of freedom from time and space) and on an "unreal reality." Although Nabokov rightly depicts the oppressors and the executioners in *Invitation to a Beheading* and *Bend Sinister* as stupid clowns, nothing detracts from the horror of what occurs, the transgression of the individual's mental and physical boundaries. If some readers such as Wilson think that this alone is not so horrible, the reason is simply that they have not experienced such horror.

Here we are confronted with another dilemma: can what is horrifying and unbearable in real life translate into a bearable and even pleasant form in certain works of art? We only have to look at the success of horror fiction, movies, and TV dramas. When we read about the most heartrending, heinous crimes in the peace and comfort of our homes, are we truly able to grasp the depth of the tragedy? To put it another way: what is the use of reconstructing what has happened more completely and "more realistically" in the real world? In this way, the presentation of tragedy is either so refined that it gives aesthetic pleasure to the reader, or so real that it paralyzes the reader's thought processes. For instance, how do we deal with the question of torture in works of art? Is it not the case that a detailed description of how torture is applied, together with that of the victim's reaction to it, eclipses any exploration of the torturer's consciousness and indeed everything else? On many occasions, this type of description automatically determines how the reader will react. For example, descriptions of the despotic nature of Russian communism have their own particular type of reader, and—for those who have experienced it firsthand—are not such descriptions a renewed affirmation of the nature of a tyrannical regime? The answer to these questions is beyond the scope of this chapter and this book. Nevertheless, it is essential to pose them, even though they remain unanswered. Raising these questions helps us to remember the obstacles confronting the critics (and other readers) of Nabokov's two political novels.

When we are dealing with such subjects, the only form of work that allows for potential explanation is the kind that comes from the empathic imagination, which by reaching beyond reality still affords the reader a little room to breathe. It is the only way a reader can truly reflect on situations that are sentimental or emotional in nature, and Nabokov's two novels have these qualities. If we satirize reality, we reshape that reality: For example, Cincinnatus's jail cell appears to parody a hotel room. What is familiar about the jail cell is not portrayed as something distorted within the framework of the novel, but the truth about the prison is revealed in another way. By uncovering the hidden relationship between two apparently unrelated objects, the reader is able to view the object in question in a different light, from a different angle. This literary device (which I refer to as metaphor and will address further in subsequent chapters) is a constant in *Invitation to a Beheading* and *Bend Sinister*. Objects are described obliquely or with a little twist, slightly askew, or out of kilter with their uniform value. The tone of voice the jailer uses when he speaks is one such example. What is familiar becomes slightly distorted, and so too is the manner in which things are described: the location or setting we thought of as normal undergoes a fundamental change. Just as you get to the comic moment, a trapdoor opens beneath your feet absurdly and without warning. This recalls Nabokov's description of Gogol's style: "a combination of two movements: a jerk and a glide." This device has two important characteristics: the first is that the reader becomes involved in the unfolding process of the narrative, and the second is that the reader keeps his or her distance from the narrative as a result of the apparently unreal experience. In this way, the real experience is conveyed to the reader and, at the same time, the work imposes an aesthetic distance; this is an essential element for any work of art.

Throughout *Invitation to a Beheading* and *Bend Sinister*, Nabokov tries to render the familiar unfamiliar through a process of estrangement. Each novel's structure houses an aesthetic and a moral judgment; for Nabokov, morality and art always go hand in hand. From the very first pages

of each novel, it is clear that we have entered a world where the protagonist is the victim of bullying and ridicule, where dreams and actions are
both called into question. It is as though the novel at once means to mirror
the reader's feelings and to mock them. Orwell, in *1984,* tries to turn the
novel's artificial, unreal world (or science fiction) into something commonplace; Nabokov, in these novels, moves in the opposite direction. As a result, he ends up with a paradox: the reader is asked to believe in the reality
of a world that is constantly contradicting itself. Both Nabokov's novels are
based on two types of negation. One is the negation of the protagonist's
expectations, and the other, more subtly, is the negation of the reader's expectations. But the question arises: what is it that absorbs the reader into
the novel and makes a relationship possible? In *1984,* the writer wants us to
believe in the world of the novel, to enter this world, and to imagine ourselves as its hero.[66] Nabokov's novels do not expect the reader to follow this
process. Obviously, the reader would not wish to identify with characters
such as Humbert Humbert or Kinbote, but even with Pnin or Cincinnatus
the way the narrative is presented and progresses is too incongruous for
the reader to relate fully to the protagonist, or to identify with his position.
Nabokov's trick or device is not to engage the reader in mere confrontation.
Rather, he pulls the reader out of the lethargy that confrontation inevitably
inspires.

Two threads run through *Invitation to a Beheading* and *Bend Sinister:* "compassion" and "parody." The thematic combination is simple in
form. In later novels, however, it becomes more complex (and it reaches the
pinnacle of complexity in *Lolita*). Here, we encounter the oppressor and
his proxies through parody and observe the protagonist with compassion.
The two themes advance in harmony, moving in parallel lines. It is only in
later work that we find the two themes combined in one character and the
two spaces fused together. The external space in *Invitation to a Beheading* and *Bend Sinister* belongs to the negative characters and the internal
psychological space to the positive. Cincinnatus and Krug remain prisoners
of the circlelike spaces of their jailers, although the external space, with all
it contains, exists for only as long as they think of it as real. As soon as Cincinnatus, who is about to be put to death, stands up, the executioner loses

his aura of invincibility and the negative external world crumbles away. The singularity of these works lies not in their unexpected happy endings but in the coexistence of two heterogeneous worlds for such a long time, throughout the narratives.[67] How, then, have our heroes been able to endure these unreal worlds? Have we not always asked this question after a totalitarian regime has collapsed?

6

Invitation to a Beheading and *Bend Sinister* oblige the reader to confront the art of storytelling in a fundamentally different way. Both treat notions of authenticity by way of a technique that the Russian formalists considered central to artistic expression: defamiliarization or *ostranenie*. The formalists argued that all art, including literature, should depict or describe things by transforming the familiar into the unknown or alien, deflecting new attention onto things that have become mundane or taken for granted. The effect is produced, in formalist thought, because a work of art at once shows what is real, but also distinguishes it from its everyday reality through aesthetics. Russian formalists believed that this distinction was intrinsic to the goal of any true work of art. The defamiliarization technique is more pronounced in certain art forms, and is not limited to notions of what is real.[68] For example, narrative art, rich in tradition, follows a series of tropes that have become familiar over time and through repetition, making them trite and ineffective. New fictions react against these familiar motifs and repetitive structures and techniques. Every new novel disrupts or subverts depleted literary conventions by "laying them bare," or by using satire, caricature, or parody, for example. These subversive fictions disturb what has become customary and familiar to the reader. Occasionally, this strategy can lead to jolting readers out of their comfort zone, defamiliarizing them, "disturbing the peace," in James Baldwin's expression.

The critic Victor Shklovsky, one of the founders of Russian Formalism, coined the term in 1917.[69] Shklovsky believed that our lives, and thus our perceptions, become habitual, automated. Instead of relying on the process of thinking and imagination, he argued, our perception retreats into the unconscious, fading without even leaving an impression. According to Shklovsky, habit prevents us from seeing the real presence or existence of things. Reactions become routine and reflexive from prior assumptions. Art, on the other hand, bestows personality on objects that have become merely unimagined outlines, by making use of unfamiliar details, opening our eyes to what we have hitherto failed to see. Art makes us see our environment anew.[70] Defamiliarization reveals and, at the same time, distorts reality. This applies in the real world just as in art. The reason is that every work of art, whether created consciously or otherwise, is, among other things, a response to previous works of art; defamiliarization occurs within the arrangements or structures of art. We see this clearly in the structures of *Invitation to a Beheading* and *Bend Sinister*. The building blocks of these two novels (and the way they are combined and presented) are such that they simultaneously take their place as new novels and satirize earlier novels, whether utopian, gothic, or romantic, or even realistic or socialist. Through defamiliarization, storytelling is transformed into a critique of storytelling within the layers of both novels.

The work of the Russian Formalists calls to mind the idea of consciousness at the center of Nabokov's novels. All that we fail to see in a conscious way, as well as all the things that have become automatic for us, follow a formula and in a way cease to exist. In *Invitation to a Beheading*, Cincinnatus, the only consciousness in the world of the novel, discovers the fabricated nature of everything that surrounds him. It is precisely for this reason that the beheading ritual is transformed into a liberation ritual, because no lies or false relationships can trick him any longer. For Cincinnatus, writing is the only method for seeing things differently. If habit makes the mind lazy and dull and prepares it to accept all past premises, the language of this mind-set, similarly, espouses meaningless clichés. A vivid example is the language of the oppressors and the executioners in *Invitation to a Beheading* and *Bend Sinister*. It is a language attached to repetitive, meaningless beliefs and customs, overused language that is exhausted and ineffective. Such expression, having been cast away from its origins and rendered impotent and unable to describe the phenomena that surround us, is no longer fit for purpose. It is only through the remedy of imagination, and by using the language of creative thought, that we can rediscover and express, once again, the true power of so many different things.

By now, the relationship between the two adjacent photographs in Sebastian's study should have become clearer. The myth of *poshlust* is the same as that of totalitarianism; the image of the innocent child is not accidental: the totalitarian mind-set is in need of such tricks. It appeals to the deepest human sentiments with a view to creating there a refuge for totalitarianism and enabling it to proliferate while shielded, hiding in plain sight. It makes use of parental love, patriotism, love of one's language, commitment to human values, and, of course, art in an effort to inculcate a single idea and effect a single demand. In this way, individual creativity is overshadowed by the collective mentality, and everything is reduced to banality.[71] The two photographs displayed in Sebastian's study connect directly to Vasily Zhukovsky, Pushkin's friend and literary executor, who suggested that execution rituals should be refined and beautified. The same ornamental interest can be observed in *Invitation to a Beheading*. Both the executioner in *Invitation to a Beheading* and the oppressor Toad in *Bend Sinister* do their utmost to gain their prisoner's approval and validation. This is how they seek to prettify their behavior. As an adverse result, they are depicted as not only grotesque but also miserable. We observe the ugly aspect of the torturer in any novel that deals with this subject. However, in Nabokov, we discover the antagonists' false nature through their wretched and lamentable deeds. Lest we presume that the wish to destroy a prisoner's body and soul is too serious a subject to make the reader laugh, it is in *Invitation to a Beheading* and *Bend Sinister* that we learn that laughter, this particular form of laughter prompted by the grotesque and the miserable, is essential, and how important it is to familiarize ourselves with the false sweetness of the crust that covers ugly things and bitter truths.

Generally, the way a writer approaches her work creates a constellation. It is in this limited realm that the relationship between the reader and the work takes form. From the opening sentences of these two novels, we find ourselves within some sort of game. Moreover, this game has nothing to do with the subject matter. There are two players: the prisoner and the jailer. The prisoner—whether Cincinnatus or Krug—remains the same throughout the novel, while his opponents are played by different characters: the jailer, the executioner, the despot. The game, of course, is a representation of reality. It is true that what we see always looks unreal, as it is just a game; but at the same time it also looks real, because it is the reality as presented within the game. For the theatergoer, the actor or actress on stage is at once a face the spectator recognizes and (the personification of) the role he or she is representing. The audience at a play is familiar with this duality, even if only unconsciously. By contrast, the reader of a novel that makes use of this device will discern complexity in the structure of the novel, as notions of verisimilitude are destabilized. Such novels disrupt and agitate the reader's mind as well as the reality that is being presented in them.

The obstacles that the author places in the reader's path are first linguistic and then structural. These obstacles hinder or alter comprehension of the text, which is what the Russian formalists encouraged. How do readers react to these difficulties? They either put the novel aside, exiting the novel by the same door that led them in, or continue to read, thanks to their interest and their curiosity. However, they will have to pause repeatedly as each obstacle prevents them from being absorbed into the world of the novel, and also because each hurdle forces them to deliberate and reconsider. In these two novels, it is not only the totalitarian mentality that is being questioned and examined; it is also our particular way of seeing the form of the novel. The reader is pulled out of a secure world. Her or his reading habits and preconceptions are revealed. It is not only M'sieur Pierre who wants everybody to think like him; the Toad is not the sole despot. In these novels, as David Rampton writes, Nabokov does not just fabricate fictions as objects; he creates an organic discourse.[72]

This is how the perception that underpins the discussion of totalitarianism reaches beyond the boundaries of the novel. The novel extends this perception to the reader, who expects the novel to follow a structure that is compatible with his or her habits and customs, which will provide a simple literary exercise full of familiar concepts together with a message and anticipated guidelines. *Invitation to a Beheading* and *Bend Sinister*, however, neither guide the reader in the right direction nor provide a new set of instructions. In fact, a reader who has accepted the "invitation" extended by one of these novels can hardly guess the outcome; neither reaches any particular judgment or significant verdict. What is important is the reading process. Nevertheless, isn't it true that most of us prefer the simple, untroubled world of M'sieur Pierre or the Toad to the lonely, perilous worlds of Cincinnatus or Krug? Do any of us feel, like Cincinnatus, that an invisible umbilical cord connects us to another world? It is not an easy question to answer. But these two novels are with us now, and we can go back to them and read them again, think about them anew. Cincinnatus's mother says: "It always seems to me that a marvelous tale is being repeated over and over again, and I either don't have the time to, or am unable to grasp it, and still somebody keeps repeating it to me, with such patience!"[73]

Cruelty

Pnin

1

In *Invitation to a Beheading*, Cincinnatus's mother recalls toy grotesques from her childhood. They are peculiar objects, not just crooked and misshapen, but completely distorted. The monstrous things, called *nonnons*, are absurd and perplexing objects, sold together with a mirror that deforms everything, providing a flawed image of whatever they reflect. But with a *nonnon* placed in front of it, "the shapeless speckledness became in the mirror a wonderful, sensible image; flowers, a ship, a person, a landscape."[1] A number of critics consider these mirrors to represent the apparently upside-down world that is, in fact, the magical world of art, trompe l'oeil.[2] The world of *Pnin* (1955) is just such a world. The most significant dimension of the novel is the relationship between the author, the novel's narrator, and the characters: Nabokov/the narrator/Pnin. We have seen the initial outlines of this link or relationship in earlier novels: in *Invitation to a Beheading*, Cincinnatus eventually succeeds in freeing himself from the bonds of his nightmarish world, entering a world that undoubtedly belongs to its creator. In *Bend Sinister*, the writer-narrator rescues Krug more overtly. It is in *Pnin* that this device of liberation reaches its high point, however. Cincinnatus and Krug, along with other of Nabokov's characters, eventually travel to a world whose particular characteristic, in Nabokov's words, is "beauty plus pity," which he considers "the closest we can get to a definition of art,"[3] a terrestrial twin of or substitute for the paradise lost. However, *Pnin*, narrated in the third person, ends unexpectedly and astonishingly, because of the tension between the narrator and the protagonist.

Pnin belongs to a particular narrative lineage whose most famous and arguably best example is *Don Quixote*. These types of narrative have two conflicting or contradictory characteristics. First, their authors' conscious (or unconscious) devices and innovations render them popular with many literary theorists, enabling them to draw on a wide variety of theories to respond to them, and thereby discover or develop new ones. Second, such narratives are organized around protagonists who tend immediately to stray beyond their books (and are further projected by critics, artists, and illustrators). They settle in the minds of the wider public, people who have not even read the narratives. These are figures such as Hamlet or Don Quixote, who live for centuries, forever, in the minds and cultural framework of readers and nonreaders alike. This is particularly so because many a reader or critic is certain that his or her interpretation of, for example, *Hamlet* is the right one. In other words, protagonist and reader exist in a new relation, as the character constantly breaks free of the book's narrative itself to tell the story unimpeded, in the language and the style of a new narrator. As the critic works to contain *Hamlet* intellectually, Hamlet himself exists outside the critical realm and beyond containment.[4]

In the spring of the academic year 1951–1952, Nabokov, who was never fond of *Don Quixote,* taught a class on Cervantes's novel at Harvard. *Don Quixote* was one of the university's favorite course subjects. The well-known critic Harry Levin usually taught the class. In his absence, a critic like I. A. Richards would step in, or a writer such as Thornton Wilder. Nabokov returned the breakaway *Don Quixote* to Cervantes's text, giving a detailed, minutely accurate, and fresh analysis. As a result, Nabokov's lectures on *Don Quixote* provided answers to many of the commentaries that were prevalent at the time. As Guy Davenport explains in his foreword to Nabokov's lectures, when Don Quixote is brought up in any discussion, the problem of *whose* Quixote inevitably arises: Jules Michelet's? Miguel Unamuno's? Joseph Wood Krutch's? By contrast, Nabokov not only assumes a contradictory stance with his revisionist interpretation, swimming against the tide, but provides an exceptional analysis that is uniquely his own.[5]

I begin this reading of *Pnin* with Nabokov's interpretation of *Don Quixote* because it reveals the main structural elements of *Pnin,* though there is little similarity between the two novels. I allude here not to how one novel may be referenced in another, particularly for similarities in subject matter, or what Nabokov often conjures deliberately in his novels by indicating correspondences or antitheses, such as the counterpoint with *Anna Karenina* at the beginning of *Ada*. A deeper relationship links *Pnin* to *Don Quixote* (and Kafka's *The Metamorphosis* and Gogol's *The Overcoat*); undoubtedly, the naïve knight created by Cervantes and Nabokov's idealistic professor belong to the same family of protagonists, a relationship that transcends time and space. As Boyd notes, *Pnin* is Nabokov's reply to *Don Quixote*.[6]

Don Quixote is the kind of book whose plot is hard to remember. Instead, one recalls individual episodes, certain successions of events, as when our hero tilts at windmills, imagining giants. The plot of *Don Quixote* is by and large determined by the formation of character: it is Quixote himself who creates the novel's plot and at the same time conceals it through his unique personality, which is at once transparent and opaque. The same can be said about the personality of Pnin. We can also say that *Pnin*, like *Don Quixote*, negates the predominant definition of a traditional novel, depending, of course, on the critics with whom we agree: those who consider *Don Quixote* to be the first modern novel (in the course of its transformation from a romance) or those who classify it purely as a novel. If we question what the plot of *Pnin* is, my answer would be: an account of the events that took place over a period of time in the life of Timofey Pnin, a university professor of Russian origin in an American university. Beyond this, Pnin (like Quixote) belongs to the group of protagonists who evade and transcend the bounds of their narrative frames, forever escaping. Nabokov writes of Quixote's personality as a "stroke of genius on the part of Cervantes, [which] looms so wonderfully above the skyline of literature, a gaunt giant on a lean nag, that the book lives and will live through the sheer vitality that Cervantes has injected into the main character."[7] It is a long, amorphous shadow cast upon receptive posterity. Nabokov's caveat is that *Don Quixote* is not even one of the great novels of the world by way of plot: it offers "a very patchy haphazard tale." This is one of Nabokov's principal arguments: Quixote's personality or perceived character acquires greatness beyond that of *Don Quixote* and somehow escapes Cervantes's grasp (and the presumed proprietorship of subsequent reader-narrators who consider themselves his creator and owner). It is, in fact, thanks to the never-ending, ever-evolving personality of Quixote that *Don Quixote* achieves timelessness.

Nabokov raises the issue of cruelty in Don Quixote's world, "hideous cruelty," a degree of viciousness that seems justified in the eyes of the characters in the novel (and even in the eyes of the author himself). The history of the period, especially Spanish history in Cervantes's lifetime, contextualizes the depiction of this level of brutality as inevitable; Cervantes is merely following the norms of his time. However, the protagonist, comic by design, somehow generates compassion along with laughter. Quixote appears, in his vitality, his sincerity, and his spontaneous acts of kindness, to possess a remarkable autonomy of character. Nabokov attacks those critics who described Cervantes's book as the greatest novel ever written, or "the Bible of Humanity," as Sainte-Beuve called it, or said that it was humorous and humane, full of "sensitive, keen-witted folks."[8] In Nabokov's words, if the critics set ideology aside and reread the novel with greater attention, they too would reach the conclusion that *Don Quixote* is an "encyclopedia of cruelty," and "one of the most bitter and barbarous books ever penned," although, he allows, "its cruelty is artistic."[9] Nabokov offers a detailed list of the physical cruelties and mental abuses in the novel, noting that "the symphony of mental and physical pain presented in *Don Quixote* is a composition that could be played only on musical instruments of the remote past. Nor should anyone suppose that those strings of pain are twanged nowadays only in remote tyrannies behind iron curtains. Pain is still with us, around us, among us."[10] It is located in the everyday, Nabokov tells us, for example, when prodigies are bullied, in police treatment of vagrants, in the malpractice inherent in even the best governments. We find all these things in *Pnin,* too.

Having considered these central points in Nabokov's interpretation of *Don Quixote* (its timelessness and its cruelty), we return to the question of connections and relations. While Nabokov's views unfold in his lectures, he explores only vaguely and indirectly the relationship between the novel's narrator and its protagonist. Is the narrator of *Don Quixote* laughing at Quixote alongside the other characters in the novel? If so (and Nabokov believes this to be the case), what is the nature of the relationship between the narrator and the protagonist? Nabokov infers that the ridicule of Quixote eventually prompts the reader to feel empathy for him, and that the satire that at first had Quixote in its sights transfers to the narrator and the reader: as a result of their empathy, the narrator and reader are satirized. From Nabokov's point of view, Quixote gradually detaches himself from the book that made him. He leaves his homeland and his author's desk, "roaming space after roaming Spain." This is why today we find Quixote even greater and more popular than he was at the time of Cervantes. As Nabokov puts it, "he has ridden for three hundred and fifty years through the jungles and tundras of human thought—and he has gained in vitality and stature. We do not laugh at him any longer. His blazon is pity, his banner is beauty. He stands for everything that is gentle, forlorn, pure, unselfish, and gallant. The parody has become a paragon."[11]

2

In *Pnin*, too, a parody becomes a paragon. Pnin and Quixote are similar enough that Pnin could be considered a literary descendent of Quixote, yet there remains a fundamental difference between the two. The world of imagination is, for Pnin (but not for Quixote), the ideal refuge and place of appeal.[12] Pnin is the most pleasant and likable character in all of Nabokov's novels and certainly the funniest. From the very beginning, when the novel was serialized in the *New Yorker,* it has enjoyed popular appeal, something still true today. Nabokov himself once said that of the thousands of characters he had created, Pnin was his favorite (followed by Lolita).[13] Pnin seems ready from page one to sever ties with what is taking place within the novel, and go his own way. The sheer force of his personality overshadows the traditional structural devices such as plot, setting, or atmosphere. The plot is arguably rather flimsy, even predictable. In fact, the events or the episodes in the novel are linked by theme, and by how other characters are presented and portrayed. If we look for the subject or overriding motif in *Pnin,* we find almost nothing but Pnin's personality, which raises the question: how does this parody of character occur? And how is Pnin transformed into a paragon?

In the novel's opening chapter, Timofey Pavlovich Pnin, a Russian-born professor at Waindell College, travels to the city of Cremona to deliver a lecture, invited by the Cremona Women's Club. He imagines that he has boarded a train to Cremona, but in fact he is on the wrong train. The narrator offers a detailed, memorable image to describe the middle-aged Pnin that seems deceptively realistic — "Ideally bald, sun-tanned, and clean-shaven, he began rather impressively with that great brown dome of his, tortoise-shell glasses (masking an infantile absence of eyebrows)"[14] — and we are told about the colors and patterns on his socks, the prudish long white underpants he used to wear in postimperial Russia and that he no longer wears in the heady, brazen atmosphere of the New World. As the story unfolds, we become more and more aware of the importance of the initial description.[15] Apart from the fact that Nabokov likes to focus on details of character and place, the reason why Pnin is depicted with so much attention is to highlight his personality, which emerges as the novel's central topic. Pnin feels good about himself, he thinks that he has avoided boarding the slow train that he was asked to take because he has found another train that departs later but that arrives at his destination at almost the same time. He is unaware of having consulted a train timetable many years out of date. Gradually, the reader will see that whenever Pnin feels self-satisfied and, more important, secure, it is a sign that he is all at sea (as in this case, where the narrator reminds the reader that Pnin is on a train heading elsewhere). As the novel progresses, the problems that Pnin faces in exile become more familiar: his apparently never-ending conflict with a foreign environment, his so-called second homeland, and his struggles with all manner of objects, with language, and with alien customs and practices.

Pnin discovers his mistake, the first in a series of mishaps, and the starting point of several episodes that are at once sad and funny. We find Pnin wandering about in a place that is new and unknown to him. He doesn't feel very well, "porous and pregnable," he says.[16] He sits on a stone bench under some laurels to regroup. Is the seizure he experiences a heart attack? (The narrator reassures us that it is not.) Pnin's nausea is accompanied by a sequence of despairing memories from his past. He remembers having a high fever when he was a child. The memory is full of the detail of being cared for by doctors, and the profound kindness of his family. Now in his fifties, sitting on the stone bench, he recalls the four-section screen of polished wood bearing a pyrographic design from his childhood bedroom. The image was of an old man hunched up on a bench and a squirrel holding a reddish object. When Pnin finally begins to feel better, sitting on his bench under the laurels, he notices a gray squirrel on the ground before him, nibbling at a peach stone. (Throughout the novel, squirrels will play the role of a magical symbol connecting Pnin to his past.) Here, the narrator explains that he hates happy endings, as they make him feel cheated. "Harm is the norm. Doom should not jam."[17] Despite the narrator's predisposition toward cruelty, Pnin's adventure ends happily: he arrives at the meeting, in time and in good health, and once again, laughter and applause alternate. This reminds us of Nabokov's description of Gogol's technique of articulating how a strange character navigates a strange reality. A lady accompanies Pnin to the rostrum in order to introduce him to the audience; *poshlust* enters the space of the novel with her. Aside from the fact that she talks more about former speakers and future speakers than about Pnin himself, when she finally comes to introduce him, she describes an imaginary Pnin instead of the real one, a generic Russian-born professor. Pnin, however, is musing on his past. He sees lost loved ones among the audience in the lecture hall: his family, his friends, and a dead former sweetheart. In the narrator's words, he remembers all those who were "murdered, forgotten, unrevenged, incorrupt, immortal";[18] they are still alive in his heart. These memories unfurl until he takes his place at the podium.

In the final chapter, we will return to this lecture. What is presented at the beginning of the novel as an event in Pnin's life in the end becomes anecdotal and parodic. Jack Cockerell, the head of Waindell's English Department, has specialized in impersonating Pnin.[19] The novel ends with his recounting one of Pnin's adventures for the narrator: Pnin rises to address the Cremona Women's Club and notices that he brought the wrong lecture.[20] There are important points regarding Pnin's personality and the novel's structure in this juxtaposition of the beginning and the ending. Cockerell represents a world where Pnin is locked in a never-ending conflict with the simplest of its elements. Just as Pnin is unfamiliar with this world (repeatedly boarding the wrong train or bus), neither does this world know Pnin, misconstruing his behavior and the reason why he is even there. The novel's tension arises from the clash between the character and the world around him, and this confrontation lends an air of irrationality not only to Pnin, but to his surroundings too.

In chapter 25 (volume 1) of *Don Quixote,* as related by Nabokov, Quixote says to his servant, Sancho Panza: "How is it possible for you to have accompanied me all this time without coming to perceive that all the things that have to do with knight-errantry appear to be mad, foolish, and fantastic. . . . Not that they are so in reality: it is simply that there are always a lot of enchanters going about among us, changing things and giving them a deceitful appearance, directing them as suits their fancy, depending upon whether they wish to favor or destroy us."[21] Reality and illusion are interwoven in the pattern of life. From Cockerell's point of view, Pnin is a fantastical creature, just as the enchanters surrounding Pnin constantly distort the appearance and the truth of everything or so Pnin imagines; these are the same enchanters from Don Quixote's world. For example, Cockerell's skit at the end of the novel distorts the reality of the lecture at Cremona Women's Club. In any case, both Cockerell's version and the narrator's prior telling display the tension between Pnin and the world of enchanters around him. It seems as though we are constantly advancing as far as the edge of this world and then retreating (just as Pnin's heart attacks take him to the brink of death and then back). If this world should tilt on its axis just a bit farther (or if Pnin truly loses his foothold), he will certainly be ejected. However, guardian angels support Pnin against the enchanters, and an uncertain equilibrium is maintained. To explain the angels' role in supporting Pnin first requires further exploration of the world of the enchanters, since Pnin's suffering, brought about by his incompatibility with the real world of the novel is the work's central theme.

Like most of Nabokov's other protagonists, Pnin is an innocent; he remains alone and vulnerable throughout the novel. In *Invitation to a Behead-*

ing and *Bend Sinister,* however, the world of bullies and the executioners appears farcical, whereas in *Pnin,* it is the protagonist himself who is depicted as being foolish within a familiar world. Nevertheless, Pnin seems to be more likable than Cincinnatus and even Krug because he is a much more lifelike character, who engages our emotions. Moreover, since he's been created in a realistic world (not a theatrical one), he inspires greater empathy. When the narrator compares Pnin and his fellow scholar Laurence Clements, he explains that "there are human solids and there are human surds,"[22] and he says that both Clements and Pnin belongs to the latter category. Pnin himself might not welcome the comparison; there is a reason why Pnin does not like Charlie Chaplin films, which is "unnamed but vividly evoked" in a scene in the third chapter.[23] As G. M. Hyde observed, "Pnin, a nonpareil, has no use for rivals."[24] Similarly, Pnin, who was so often regarded as an eccentric, even a failure, in the eyes of others in the novel, with their conventional ideas of success, is, as a result, very fond of those likewise branded. For example, he frequents a new yet poorly received restaurant called "The Egg and We,"[25] because he sympathizes with its owner, all of which recalls something Nabokov wrote in his *Lectures on Russian Literature:* "Akaki Akakievich, the hero of *The Overcoat,* is absurd *because* he is pathetic, *because* he is human and *because* he has been engendered by those very forces which seem to be in such contrast to him."[26] Nabokov's definition of human absurdity, of being stuck in a strange world, is strangely similar to Pnin's plight, and the duplicitous world of enchanters he must confront. In his description of Akaki Akakievich, Nabokov writes: "He is not merely human and pathetic. He is something more, just as the background is not mere burlesque. Somewhere behind the obvious contrast there is a subtle genetic link. His being discloses the same quiver and shimmer as does the dream world to which he belongs."[27] Nabokov's fictions, then, are not absurd as a result of an absurd character; the worlds of these novels are already absurd, and as a result, the protagonist, who questions the prevailing logic, is considered absurd (and portrayed accordingly).

Exile is not the same for everyone. Pnin is ready to take his place in a new world, but his new compatriots insist on imposing their own reality on him. What torments Pnin in exile is not only his separation and distance from his heritage, aspects of which are impossible to express, but how trivial and unimportant this separation and distance is from any perspective other than his own. We understand this better when we compare Pnin with other immigrants who treat the process of exile as a profession, trading in a false nostalgia. What more horrifying betrayal is there than taking undue advantage of a collective pain? The narrator describes immigrants who invoke Russia with "Mother Volga songs, red caviar, and tea."[28] What is genuine appears more vulnerable precisely because its truth is under threat. And what could be more painful to witness than the manipulation of everything that is so significant and so vibrant for Pnin? This second homeland is not such a bad place considering that it has provided a place of refuge for Pnin, but the enemy is the same as ever: ignorance, compounded by arrogance and the smug self-satisfaction that such ignorance breeds. A student enrolls in Pnin's class because she thought that once she had mastered the Russian alphabet, she would be able to read "Anna Karamazov" in the original Russian. And it is from the confines of this world that Cockerell ridicules Pnin. In fact, Cockerell is the extreme example of the mocking mind-set shared by many of the novel's characters.

Pnin's endless battle with the world around him extends to objects as well as people. Arguably, Nabokov never dealt so thoroughly with the tension between the inner world of a protagonist and the world outside: "His life was a constant war with insensate objects that fell apart, or attacked him, or refused to function, or viciously got themselves lost as soon as they entered the sphere of his existence."[29] Despite this, Pnin loves all manner of gadgets; electric devices mesmerize him. As the narrator observes, "he had a passionate intrigue with Joan's washing machine. Although forbidden to come near it, he would be caught trespassing again and again."[30] He has the same relationship of simultaneous repulsion and attraction with his ex-wife (who soon enters the novel), with his second homeland (America), and, eventually, with *poshlust*. He finds it all vulgar and compelling at once, a combination that appeals to Pnin and distresses him at the same time. Depending on the reader's point of view, this is the kind of distress that renders Pnin either a hero or a pathetic antihero. Joan and Laurence Clements immediately discern the distress in Pnin's fixation with the enchanting and incomprehensible. Joan, who the narrator warns us uses the word "pathetic" perhaps a little too often, tells her husband that she wants to invite "that pathetic savant" for a drink, along with other guests.[31] Her husband replies that should she do so, he, who is also a pathetic savant, would go straight to the movies. Laurence and Joan have just met Pnin, and are as yet unfamiliar with his mood and his temperament: Pnin does not accept their invitation.

3

The setting for the second chapter of the novel is the Clements' house. The couple soon makes friends with Pnin, appreciating his "Pninian worth." Laurence is a professor at Waindell. His only popular class is called the Philosophy of Gesture. His greatest success, a course in which twelve students enrolled, was called the Evolution of Sense. His lectures on the subject begin and end with the phrase: "The evolution of sense is, in a sense, the evolution of nonsense."[32] It is a sentence that, inevitably, brings *Alice's Adventures in Wonderland* and *Through the Looking-Glass* to mind. Joan and Laurence's only daughter has recently gotten married, and they want to rent her room. Pnin, who is constantly moving, makes a telephone call upon the recommendation of the librarian at Waindell. A comedy of errors ensues — textbook Pnin. The librarian's name is Mrs. Thayer. Pnin mispronounces her name as Fire, and Joan hears it as Feuer or Fayer. His visit to the property unfolds in the same ill-starred manner. By the time they have reached an agreement and Pnin has become their new lodger, and Joan wishes to invite Pnin to her party, she can justify using her favorite adjective "pathetic."

Liza, Pnin's ex-wife, comes to visit. Pnin is still desperately in love with her. They met in Paris among émigré Russians when Pnin had nothing to offer her but love. When they met, Liza was still a student, but eventually she became a psychoanalyst. She wrote "ovipositing" verse "mainly in halting anapaest," imitating Anna Akhmatova and using techniques already exhausted by "other rhyming rabbits."[33] When they met, she was just recovering from an unsuccessful love affair (and an unsuccessful attempt at suicide). So when Pnin writes her a "tremendous love letter" (in the narrator's words), five of her close analyst friends advise: "Pnin — and a baby at once."[34] But their marriage was fueled only by Pnin's blind love, despite Liza's repeated cases of infidelity. Liza telephones one day from Meudon to say that she is going to Montpellier with a man who understands her "organic ego" and that she would never see Timofey again. Later, the psychoanalyst Dr. Eric Wind writes a letter of apology, assuring Pnin that he is eager to marry "the woman who has come out of your life into mine."[35] Pnin is incapable of denying Liza anything, not even a divorce, but we gradually learn that Dr. Wind's wife is in no hurry to oblige him similarly.

Along with other Russian émigrés looking to escape Paris (and Europe), Pnin manages to acquire an American visa after a friend's intercession. One day soon after, his doorbell rings vigorously, and Liza returns as his "faithful and lawful wife, ready to follow him wherever he went — even beyond the ocean if need be."[36] She is seven months pregnant. These days are the happiest in Pnin's life: he accepts Liza back, welcomes the unborn child passionately, and eagerly plans for the future. On the ship, a stranger appears. Pnin is playing chess. The stranger interferes on behalf of his opponent to such an extent that Pnin ends up losing the game. The stranger then invites Pnin to drink a couple of beers with him at the bar, and introduces himself: he is Dr. Eric Wind. Liza couldn't find a way into America; her only route was as Pnin's wife. Would Pnin permit Dr. Wind to pay "at least one-half of the lady's passage"? Pnin declines. The "nightmare conversation" continues as Dr. Wind insists that he should at least be allowed to pay for the beer. In America, Liza and Timofey part and she marries Dr. Wind. She gives birth to a boy, whom she names Victor.

Now, many years later, Pnin looks forward to seeing Liza again, but when they meet Pnin has the feeling that the day he had been waiting for so long is slipping through his fingers all too quickly. He longs to know what Liza wants (he has no doubt that she wants something) so that they can enjoy the rest of their time together. Liza spoils everything immediately by reciting her latest poem about her new love. Eventually, she divulges the reason for her visit. She no longer loves Dr. Wind at all, is deeply involved with another man, George, and has sent Victor to an expensive school, for which Eric now refuses to pay the fees. She asks whether Pnin would be willing to pay a part of the money needed for Victor's education. She adds, incidentally, that she does not approve of Pnin's brown suit (funded by the Cremona lecture): "A gentleman does not wear brown."[37]

After Liza's departure, Pnin walks home through the park, thinking of her. He longs to embrace her, keep her by his side, Liza, "with her cruelty, with her vulgarity, with her blinding blue eyes, with her miserable poetry, with her fat feet, with her impure, dry, sordid, infantile soul." He reasons: "If people are reunited in Heaven (I don't believe it, but suppose), then how shall I stop it from creeping upon me, over me, that shriveled, helpless, lame thing, her soul? But this is the earth, and I am, curiously enough, alive, and there is something in me and in life — He seemed to be quite unexpectedly (for human despair seldom leads to great truths) on the verge of a simple solution of the universe."[38] He is distracted by the sight of a squirrel at a drinking fountain; the squirrel is obviously thirsty. Pnin eventually figures out which button to press in order to provide water for the squirrel, which takes a long time to drink the water and eyes Pnin coldly. Pnin weeps "quietly and freely," imagining that the squirrel must have a fever, but once its thirst is quenched, the animal departs without the least sign of gratitude. Later, when Joan returns home, she encounters a broken Pnin, sad and funny to behold, his shoulders shaking and hands trembling as he tries to muffle his sobs, his distress causing his accent to thicken markedly: "I haf nofing left, nofing, nofing!"[39]

Liza is a focal point for Pnin's pain and suffering. Pnin struggles with enchanters both in human and object form, and they have numerous, dissimilar layers or surfaces. One of these seemingly illegible layers takes the form of personal relationships. Liza deeply resembles the woman who introduces Pnin at the Cremona lecture: neither of them intentionally wishes to irritate or torment Pnin (in contrast to, for example, Cockerell), but their attitudes toward him are more horrifying even than Cockerell's. For them, Pnin is not a victim to torment; they simply do not see him, to them he is invisible. Such treatment denotes their mediocrity and self-absorption. They are one-dimensional, and the narrator enjoys poking fun at them, albeit indirectly, but it's not enough for Nabokov to simply ridicule their egocentric behavior. The subject of egocentricity in Nabokov's work, in fact, requires further explanation. The American philosopher Richard

Rorty, in a book largely devoted to the subject of pain, *Contingency, Irony, and Solidarity* (1989), describes utopia as a world in which human solidarity is achieved not by inquiry but by imagination. It is the power of imagination that enables us to empathize with strangers and to see them as "fellow sufferers." Rorty argues that solidarity "is not discovered by reflection but created."[40] Rorty's approach recalls the importance of curiosity in Nabokov's fiction. Curiosity is the overriding theme. It is directly related to the power of imagination, to the power that enables human beings to empathize. In his epilogue to *Lolita,* Nabokov himself explains the world of art (somehow, somewhere, connected with other states of being) in only four words: "curiosity, tenderness, kindness, ecstasy."[41] Liza is a bad poet in part because she is self-indulgent, devoid of empathy.

Egocentricity quells any instinct for curiosity; when we live only in our own world and think only of our own interests, we have no capacity truly to visualize other people's problems. In Jane Austen's novels, egocentric characters are one-dimensional and comical but also unaware of the pleasures of discovery and deprived of personal development. Nabokov treats self-centered characters the same way. The difference is that in Nabokov's world (and perhaps in the twentieth century, and maybe all the more after the Second World War), egocentricity has acquired a previously unforeseen level of cruelty. In Nabokov's novels, we find these cruel characters in various guises: consider Goodman in *The Real Life of Sebastian Knight,* or the government agents in *Invitation to a Beheading* and *Bend Sinister.* In Nabokov's later novels egocentric characters are drawn more intricately. Rorty sees *Lolita*'s Humbert Humbert and Kinbote in *Pale Fire* as champions of total self-regard, "exquisitely sensitive to everything which affects or provides expression for their own obsession, and entirely incurious about anything that affects anyone else."[42] These two characters are by no means one-dimensional; on the contrary, they are multifaceted and complex vessels, their complexity in part due to the fact that they are not presented as comical or one-dimensional. In fact, the opposing features of the oppressor and the oppressed in totalitarian worlds are exhibited simultaneously as parts of the same character in Nabokov's later novels. These complex figures end up sacrificing not only other people but themselves too.

Pnin focuses on the pain experienced by the protagonist. Liza and Eric make no space in their interactions with Pnin for his emotional life; he is invisible in the relationship, his words unheard, his pain unacknowledged. Their cruelty comprises both large-scale and trivial abuse or misuse and extends to their own child, Victor. Nabokov had a low opinion of psychology and psychoanalysis. He also deeply resisted totalitarianism. At first, the two phenomena seem unrelated, but one can imagine Nabokov's wry smile as his writing successfully juxtaposes the two. Instead of being curious, Liza and Eric interfere in other people's lives. Moreover, they place themselves in a position of judgment toward other human beings (as a collective, not as individuals). Where is the totalitarianism? In the appropriation of the private space. Pnin writes about Liza and Eric in a letter in his haphazard, peculiar English: "It is nothing but a kind of microcosmos of communism—all that psychiatry. . . . Why not leave their private sorrows to people? Is sorrow not, one asks, the only thing in the world people really possess?"[43]

Like all those who live in the world only through prescribed conventions, Liza and Eric lack creative faculties, especially in their encounters with other people. When psychoanalysis or any other school of thought takes a totalitarian approach, or imprisons the world within the limited agenda of one individual, it eradicates the sense of pleasure that comes with discovery. It means that everything is preordained and prepackaged. This is the nature of the relationship Liza and Eric have with both Pnin and their son Victor. The narrator explains derisively, "Both parents, in their capacity of psychotherapists, did their best to impersonate Laius and Jocasta, but the boy proved to be a very mediocre little Oedipus. In order not to complicate the modish triangle of Freudian romance (father, mother, child), Liza's first husband had never been mentioned."[44] Until, that is, their marriage begins to disintegrate and they need Pnin's money. Their aloofness and lack of interest in other people's feelings and sentiments reduces their relationships to utilitarian exercises. The only human beings they notice are the ones they need. But even then, it is not the person helping them who becomes their primary focus; the central concern is still their need. Liza only comes to visit Pnin when she wants something. When she is with him, she cannot pay attention to anything but herself and her problems.

Enchanters do not differentiate one individual from another. They make fun of Pnin because he does not conform to the principles and beliefs of the group. He is not prepared to replicate the stereotypical image the Americans have of émigré Russians. A human being unlike others, who doesn't follow conventions, is always an unwelcome presence in the group and inevitably meets with indifference, mockery, or even harassment. Pnin preserves his individuality by protecting his private space. Liza's blindness (and that of other enchanters) leads to her constant interferences in Pnin's life. Totalitarianism isolates people like Pnin, forcing him to emigrate. However, not even in exile do the enchanters tolerate Pnin's being different. They ridicule his personality and cruelly reduce him to caricature. Pnin's salvation, even in his relationship with Liza, is his difference, and their physical distance. The narrator notes: "I do not know if it has ever been noted before that one of the main characteristics of life is discreteness. Unless a film of flesh envelops us, we die. Man exists only insofar as he is separated from his surroundings. The cranium is a space-traveller's helmet. Stay inside or you perish. Death is divestment, death is communion."[45]

4

What most closely ties *Pnin* to *Don Quixote* is one of the enchanters, who torments Timofey Pnin with constant intrusion and tries to lead him astray. This enchanter is none other than the narrator. Nabokov describes the relationship between narrator and protagonist with exceptional intensity in this novel. With many centuries separating Cervantes from Nabokov, the latter acts in a much more self-conscious manner than the former. In *Pnin,* the narrator has a dual role: on the one hand, his neutral voice narrates the story; and on the other, he occasionally appears within the novel in a minor role. Gradually, as we observe this narrator-character from Pnin's point of view, it seems as if we are dealing with the cruelest of all enchanters. This unnamed character appears whenever Pnin has been suffering, and he has been directly involved in causing the suffering. (It is principally the narrator's role here that illustrates Nabokov's perception of the relationship between Cervantes and Quixote, and of the relationship between every subsequent reader-narrator and Quixote.) If, at the outset, we consider Pnin's opinion of the narrator to be exaggerated, the deeper we delve into his life, the more we begin to agree with him, and so the plot thickens.

What is the traditional relationship between a narrator and a protagonist, when they are not one and the same? The narrator generally adopts a personality and a point of view more or less similar to that of the author. Often the narrator serves as savior, sympathizer, fellow-sufferer, or sometimes the protagonist's devotee (and, similarly, he can also function as the antagonist or antihero or rogue). In some works the narrator is no more than a mask for the writer. Nabokov tends to wander around the worlds he creates. He is so committed to these imaginary worlds that the reader might get the impression that even the author is a character in the book. In *Bend Sinister,* Nabokov — the narrator — intervenes directly and saves his main character. In *Pnin,* there are hints and allusions that make us believe that the narrator is Nabokov himself, and that he is in fact one of the malevolent enchanters in Pnin's world. Although the narrator respects Pnin and considers himself a friend, he is also the source of many of his woes and displays enchanter-like cruelty. The narrator not only inveigles his way into the most private corners of Pnin's life but also discloses Pnin's secrets with no regard for privacy. Pnin says: "The history of man is the history of pain!"[46] In *Pnin,* we encounter not only a history of pain but a history of the way pain is given testimony.

What do we know about the narrator of *Pnin?* First of all, we realize that the narrator, like Pnin, is a Russian émigré, and that St. Petersburg looms large in his background. He lives in Paris during Pnin's time there, and when Pnin arrives in America, so too does the narrator. The narrator seems to be a man of letters, and a successful academic figure (unlike Pnin). In fact, when Pnin is eventually politely dismissed, it is the narrator who is appointed to the academic chair in his stead. The narrator, who apparently respects Pnin and appreciates his academic credentials, writes him a letter to request that he stay on at the university to collaborate with him. Pnin declines. He even refuses to meet the narrator. Furthermore, he tries to escape the narrator, and he succeeds. Pnin, known to us for his nobility of character throughout the novel, reacts coarsely to the narrator's polite behavior and greets his kindness with hostility. Why? How is it that now we suddenly see Pnin as the offending party?

In the novel's first six chapters, we come across signs and suggestions pointing to the narrator, but not until the last chapter does he disclose his relation to Pnin. The narrator remembers Pnin's father, an ophthalmologist, at whose office he first saw Pnin as a child. He also recalls when Pnin and his young friends staged a play. He refers to having met Liza in Paris. Although he is not explicit, we realize that he has had a relationship with Liza; it was after this affair that Liza attempted suicide. The narrator goes on to explain that he owns Pnin's love letter to Liza and has read the contents: "I am not handsome, I am not interesting, I am not talented. I am not even rich. But, Lise, I offer you everything I have, to the last blood corpuscle, to the last tear, everything."[47] Via these memories (and, of course, indirectly), the theme of the cuckolded husband manifests itself. In the waiting room of Dr. Pavel Pnin, Timofey's father, the twelve-year-old narrator saw a lady wearing a plumed hat offer her hand to be kissed by a cavalry officer, who leaned toward her the moment her husband was called into the doctor's office.[48] When Pnin staged a summer play with friends, the narrator is almost sure it was Pnin who performed, behind the costume, the small role of irate Gentleman. And years after the affair, when Liza and the narrator met again in Paris, Liza revealed that she had "told Timofey everything" but that he was a "saint" and had "pardoned" her. What is Pnin's reaction to the narrator's own recollections? Whenever the narrator tries to reference past events, Pnin accuses him of making everything up. "He is a dreadful inventor."[49]

The narrator/Pnin rapport also sheds light on the author/narrator relationship. At first, the reader is duped into thinking that Nabokov is the narrator, only to realize that this narrator's account is not entirely trustworthy. Soon the reader noticed that the narrator is another character who bullies Pnin covertly and sometimes even openly. Moreover, Nabokov does not confine himself to describing the situation but actually makes the reader experience the cruelty directly. It is not only cruel enchanters who are bullying Pnin, some of whom—enemies operating through kind friends—he may not be aware of. Our protagonist is held captive by an overpowering, omniscient narrator present everywhere, even in Pnin's own mind. And how can a character resist a narrator's cruelty (and the author's account of this cruelty)? Pnin decides to flee, on his birthday and in the closing pages of the novel.[50] The reader, unable to trust the narrator, becomes compassionate toward Pnin, understanding Pnin's declaration that private sorrows are the only thing in the world that individuals truly possess. Pnin spoke these words in a specific context, with a specific meaning, but their resonance can be heard throughout the novel. If the narrator and the author compound their cruelties toward Pnin, is Pnin's flight a final defense of his private sorrows, even from the reader, who feels for him?

Nabokov and Pnin appear to have little in common; they are from very different family backgrounds, and in character and appearance they are dissimilar. Any closeness between them seems unlikely, given Nabokov's hoax of appearing twice as both narrator and the author who creates that narrator as an injurious enchanter. Yet Nabokov and Pnin do in fact share certain things, as is revealed when the novel plumbs the deepest levels of consciousness: both have experienced a type of pain profound and formless, disempowering and inarticulable, where feelings escape words. This experience is characterized by grief over the death of loved ones who escaped Bolshevism only to be killed in exile by the Nazis, by being forced to forfeit one's past and mother tongue, by being locked in eternal battle with a foreign language, and by losing completely the safe space of childhood to embark instead on life in a nightmarish world that belongs to bullies and executioners.

Unlike Cincinnatus or Krug, however, Pnin does not reside in a more or less abstract dystopia; the totalitarian menace does not even have the excuse of an unreal environment to fall back on. Like his creator, Pnin lives in a world that is tantalizingly "real" (and in a democratic country) but is also full of memories and people strengthened by the despair or failure of others. Nabokov placement of his protagonist in this workaday world makes Pnin's pain and sorrow an unbearable burden. His pain is individualized; but his world is the world we all share, and his pain can therefore become ours too. This is why the narrator's cruelty, a reminder of the totalitarian mind-set, is so unexpected and so horrifying.

In *Invitation to a Beheading,* the narrator's world, or the world on whose behalf the narrator speaks, heralds emancipation (and salvation). In *The Real Life of Sebastian Knight,* the relationship between the author, the narrator, and the protagonist is so close by the end of the book that they merge into one body. In *Bend Sinister,* the writer-narrator, hinting at deliverance, becomes such a tangible presence that he eventually comes to Krug's aid. But in *Look at the Harlequins!,* the narrator Vadim considers the author to be the enemy. By comparing these three works with *Look at the Harlequins!,* Nabokov's last novel, we can see how the traditionally passive figure of the mere narrator gradually morphs into an agitator. In an imaginary curve charting the evolution of the narrators of Nabokov's novels, the narrator of *Pnin* would be located at the halfway point: in *Pnin,* the narrator belongs to the material world of ours, whereas Pnin himself belongs to that other world beloved by Nabokov; still, the usual authority of the narrator has not been diminished: he is integral to the novel's plot, not merely a force lying beyond it. This narrator will no longer play the role of deliverer, however. Pnin refuses to meet the narrator or talk to him when he calls. Finally, poor Pnin, driving a sedan crammed with bundles and suitcases, is clearly running away from the narrator (and the limiting enclosure of time). On the last page, the narrator is left alone with Cockerell, together with Pnin's impersonator (or Pnin's double), who starts spouting gossip about him.

5

In chapter 6, Pnin finally finds a house he can call home. Life on his own in a "discrete building" proves amazingly satisfying to a "a weary old want of his innermost self, battered and stunned by thirty-five years of homelessness."[51] One of the "sweetest things" about this new place is the silence that surrounds him now, "in blissful contrast to the persistent cacophonies that had surrounded him from six sides in the rented rooms of his former habitations." Pnin thinks to himself that had there never been a Russian Revolution or had all the events that followed never happened, "no exodus, no expatriation in France, no naturalization in America, everything—at the

best, at the best, Timofey!" everything would be more or less the same as
it is now: "a professorship in Kharkov or Kazan, a suburban house such as
this, old books within, late blooms without."[52] Resettled, he is a different
Pnin: heroic, independent, brimming with self-confidence, a robust Pnin
with enviable privacy. He still loves his homeland, but he realizes his homeland can be anywhere: Pnin's homeland is, in fact, Pnin himself.

Pnin throws a modest housewarming party. He invites his friends,
including the Clements. However, we know that whenever Pnin begins to
feel comfortable and, in particular, self-confident, fate (for want of a better
term) is lying in wait to disrupt this longing for happiness. The party is a
success, but Pnin discovers at the end of the evening that his academic
future is in jeopardy, that there is no next term for him, and that peace and
quiet have, once again, abandoned him. Before he finds out, Pnin describes
the courses he had prepared for the following year with much enthusiasm:
"On Tyranny. On the Boot. On Nicholas the First. On all the precursors
of modern atrocity." And he goes on to say, "When we speak of injustice,
we forget Armenian massacres, tortures which Tibet invented, colonists
in Africa." This is when he declares: "The history of man is the history of
pain!"[53] This is the central theme of the novel revealed by Pnin in an un-
biased manner, despite his long-standing (and, from Nabokov's point of
view, fully justified) hatred of the Bolsheviks. Pnin condemns any type of
cruelty, unconditionally, no matter who is the perpetrator, what race or nationality, or what the aim is. In this, too, he resembles Nabokov. Nicholas
I's position at the top of the list of his courses is not accidental or meaningless: Pnin starts from the same point as professional revolutionaries, gradually opening up and giving breadth and depth to what started as a sound-
bite. We hear all of this, of course, from Pnin himself, and what we hear is
part and parcel of Pnin's own personal story. His story is that of pain. It is
not confined to persecution by a totalitarian regime but encompasses the
cruelty of human beings toward one another when at their most intimate.
Is there an irony in the fact that Pnin's academic expression of pain is, despite his experience, something his professional life in academia ultimately
prohibits? Here, too, is cruelty.

Pnin's relationship with Liza moves in opposite directions. The worlds of totalitarianism and *poshlust* are revealed through their relationship, yet this relationship leads the reader to other secret connections: for example, Pnin's bond with his past. Pnin's past does not fade into the present: the Revolution abruptly and brutally breaks his link to his past, irreversibly, leaving it forever incomplete. Pnin's present in exile is not a continuation of his past even if his past is still present within him, bringing pain, recalling death, and prompting silence. His occasional cardiac arrests transport him from the "real" world to that other world, a world that is otherwise apparently inaccessible. In fact, the acceptance of pain and these occasional encounters with the past give *Pnin* a certain eloquence. The past brings with it guardian angels who confront the oppressor enchanters of this world of mundane, repetitive events. In chapter 5, which precedes the party and the impending doom for Pnin's academic position, we come to meet the guardian angels. In this chapter, the confrontation between past and present and between angels and enchanters is complete, and the reader travels to the epicenter of Pnin's troubles: to that intoxicating black abyss in the depths of which golden stars revolve around an invisible point: pain.

In this chapter, Pnin is invited to the country house of Al Cook (the Americanized name of Aleksandr Petrovich Kukolnikov). Every summer, Al invites a number of his émigré friends to this retreat, a large, hospitable place. Pnin has recently purchased a humble, secondhand (or an umpteenth-hand) car from one of his students, a "pale blue, egg-shaped two-door sedan, of uncertain age and in mediocre condition."[54] The theme of Pnin's endless battles with appliances endures, prompted now by the vehicle. He has taken driving classes at Waindell Driving School but has learned little, so he spends his time while laid up with a sore back reading the forty-page driver's manual with attentive relish. Now he is on his way to the country estate. He stops at a filling station, where "an inscrutable white sky hung over a clover field, and from a pile of firewood near a shack came a rooster's cry, jagged and gaudy—a vocal coxcomb. Some chance intonation on the part of this slightly hoarse bird, combined with the warm wind pressing itself against Pnin in search of attention, recognition, anything, briefly reminded him of a dim dead day when he, a Petrograd University freshman, had arrived at the small station of a Baltic summer resort, and the sounds, and the smells, and the sadness—"[55] These recollections characterize his entry into the domain that encompasses homesickness and nostalgia over a lost, scenic past. Besides the helpless Pnin, the homeless Pnin, and the farcical Pnin, there is yet another Pnin, shrouded in the sudden haze of unanticipated recollections that emerge from the world within.

Cook's retreat is like a little piece of Russia in the heart of a vast America. It is a secluded, dreamlike bubble. Though the house is as real as the surrounding hedges, this little Russia exists in reality only in émigré dreams. As soon as an émigré visitor sets foot on the terrain, the atmosphere begins to morph. Movements become slower and voices milder. There is no longer any conflict between Pnin and the world around him. The estate is more the handiwork of nature than human effort, reminiscent of the images of Vyra that Nabokov evokes in *Speak, Memory*. The longer a person stays there, the more the atmosphere assumes the colors and fragrances of the past. The green landscape is rejuvenated by rain, seen from behind the milky-white curtains of the window of a bright, cheerful room. The images seem obscure. The language is soft, punctuated by long silences as articulate as words.

This miniature Russia receives émigré Russians with open arms. This applies particularly to "liberals and intellectuals who had left Russia around 1920." They swarm about the estate, lounge on rustic benches in the shade, loaf in hammocks, and discuss "émigré writers—Bunin, Aldanov, Sirin."[56] You do remember Sirin? Here, anyway, is the sort of place where the émigrés regain their lost (or concealed) identities. Younger generations may think of themselves as American and remain at a remove from the traditions and etiquette of their parents' backgrounds and past. Here, on the estate, the way others interact with Pnin is completely different from how people like Cockerell treat him. Now we get to know his strengths, not his weaknesses, or realize that Pnin's weaknesses are, from a different point of view, his strengths. Pnin, who is sometimes outwitted by his alarm clock, takes part in a debate on *Anna Karenina* and puts forward views that could rival the most proficient critics. Nabokov lends his protagonist some of his own ideas (as he does in *The Real Life of Sebastian Knight*). Pnin counters the (apparent) temporal confusion in *Anna Karenina* and offers detailed explanations as to the difference between "Lyovin's spiritual time and Vron-ski's physical one."[57]

Pnin and his friend Chateau walk through a meadow for a dip in the river, where they encounter a cluster of small butterflies. Chateau says it's a pity that Vladimir Vladimirovich (Nabokov) is not with them to see it. Pnin responds that he feels Vladimir Vladimirovich's entomology is merely an affectation.[58] His friend contests the point. Pnin wants to swim and re-moves a cross from his neck to hang on a twig, his friend warning him that he may someday lose it. "Perhaps I would not mind losing it," Pnin retorts. "I wear it merely from sentimental reasons. And the sentiment is becoming burdensome. After all, there is too much of the physical about this attempt to keep a particle of one's childhood in contact with one's breast bone." To which Chateau responds, "You are not the first to reduce faith to a sense of touch."[59] This episode is meant as a portal to the world they left behind, the world about which, as we have seen, Pnin almost never speaks. Yet for Pnin, as for the author who created him, the past is entirely material, tangible (as it is in Nabokov's letters to his mother and his private notes), and that carries a charge of pain. After dinner, Pnin suffers another mild seizure and sits down on a bench to rest. Roza Shpolyanski notices him sitting alone and joins him, talking about their mutual friends until tea is served. Pnin tells her he will follow her in shortly, then remains alone for a little while. From this evening tea, we are carried to another dinner and evening tea. The narrator does not tell us that Pnin is daydreaming or remi-niscing about the past. He simply describes Dr. Pnin (Timofey's father) and his friend Dr. Belochkin so deeply absorbed in their game of chess that Mrs. Belochkin has the maid serve them tea where they are seated (which is minutely detailed), at a corner of the veranda of a country house, cozily illuminated by kerosene lamps. "Timofey Pnin was again the clumsy, shy, obstinate, eighteen-year-old boy, waiting in the dark for Mira," the Beloch-kins' daughter.[60]

This is how the importance of Pnin's memory of Mira is revealed, and its centrality in the development of his personality. The reader realizes the delicate link between Pnin's heartache and his lost past. Pnin gets up before long and makes his way back through the pine trees. In the background, a number of young people are listening to music on the radio. Pnin (like his creator) doesn't care for jazz, but while complaining about the youngsters and their jazz, he remembers the fads of his own youth, and, eventually, Mira's story is told—Mira's passion for photography, her amateur dramatics, what happened during the Revolution, and the last time they met: "The Civil War of 1918–22 separated them: history broke their engagement." The last time he saw her was sometime in the early thirties in a Berlin restaurant. They were both married by then. Mira retained her unforgettable smile: "The contour of her prominent cheekbones, and the elongated eyes, and the slenderness of arm and ankle were unchanged, were immortal." The pang of tenderness remains, "akin to the vibrating outline of verses you know you know but cannot recall." Gradually, not only is a different world revealed, but a different Pnin is disclosed, a Pnin loved not by Liza but by the charming, delicate Mira. The memory of young love is naturally sweet and its loss naturally sad, but Pnin has trained himself never to remember Mira. For, according to the narrator, "if one were quite sincere with oneself, no conscience, and hence no consciousness, could be expected to subsist in a world where such things as Mira's death were possible."[61]

Mira escaped Russia, only to be exterminated by the Nazis. She was taken to Buchenwald in a cattle car and killed. The narrator reminds us that only an hour's walk separates Buchenwald from Weimar, home to Goethe, Herder, and Schiller. The tragedy does not end there, though. In one of the most poignant sections of the novel, the narrator explains that as the exact cause of her death is not known, in Pnin's mind Mira is forever dying, "undergoing a great number of resurrections, only to die again and again."[62] Each time he imagines a new way for her to have died, Pnin himself dies over and over again, silently, without a word about his most intimate grief. The pain and sorrow hang round his neck, like his cross. He does not make his sorrow public, nor does he adopt the role of a victim (or hero). He lives an honest life, with the memory of all those who have been "murdered, forgotten, unrevenged, incorrupt, immortal, many old friends" who are alive, unscathed, in his mind.[63] It is now that we better understand the questions he has raised earlier: "Why not leave their private sorrows to people? Is sorrow not, one asks, the only thing in the world people really possess?"[64]

Pnin returns to the house slowly, walking through the pine trees. "The sky was dying." The chapter closes with the image of two dark figures in profile, on a distant crest, silhouetted against an ember-red sky. "They stood there closely, facing each other. One could not make out from the road whether it was the Poroshin girl and her beau, or Nina Bolotov and young Poroshin, or merely an emblematic couple placed with easy art on the last page of Pnin's fading day."[65] But nothing is one-dimensional in this chapter or in this novel or at this moment of Pnin in despair, which nevertheless affords the narrator an opportunity for creative satire. As Pnin watches this "emblematic" image and contemplates the short distance between Buchenwald and Weimar, the narrator quotes Dr. Hagen, the director of Waindell College, referring to Germany as "that nation of universities." Dr. Hagen once more pays a compliment to "another torture house, Russia — the country of Tolstoy, Stanislavski, Raskolnikov, and other great and good men."

6

Liza's fourteen-year-old son, Victor, is scheduled to visit Pnin and to stay with him for a few days. We have seen that Liza has bullied Pnin into paying for Victor's education; now she talks to Victor about Pnin as the former husband she had kept a secret from him. Although the narrator remains silent on the issue, we detect that Liza is again using Pnin to help solve her problems; she is now separated from Victor's father and on the verge of yet another marriage. *Poshlust* personified, Liza is simultaneously successful and unsuccessful in using Pnin. Seeing him confronted by the malevolent enchanters, the guardian angels of Nabokov's other world are active. Pnin and Victor do not have a lot in common; the age gap is considerable, and they come from very different worlds. Before long, however, we discover that Victor is not an ordinary child: he shows rare artistic talent as a painter. The fourth chapter is dedicated to Victor's acquaintance with Pnin. Nothing remarkable happens: Pnin arranges their meeting; the narrator gives us the details of Victor's background; we read about their first encounter; and this chapter ends with Pnin and Victor sleeping in separate rooms. What consequence does Victor have on Pnin's life and on the structure of the book if he appears only in this part of the novel?

Pnin goes to a sports shop to buy Victor, whom he has yet to meet, a present. The salesperson brings him the wrong kind of ball. "'No, no,' said Pnin, 'I do not wish an egg or, for example, a torpedo. I want a simple football ball. Round!'" He uses his hands to outline "a portable world." The narrator continues to describe the situation: "It was the same gesture he used in class when speaking of the 'harmonical wholeness' of Pushkin."[66] The salesman realizes that what he wants is a soccer ball, and Pnin buys the ball he wants. Before long, Pnin finds out that Victor doesn't like sports at all, and gives him some money and a book instead. Pnin had looked for a novel by Jack London, so popular in Pnin's Russia but not as widely read in this country. Unable to find *Martin Eden,* he does manage to find another of London's novels, *The Son of the Wolf.* Victor's gratitude at the gift derives from a misunderstanding; he thinks it is a translation from Russian. "Last summer I read *Crime and* . . . A young yawn distended his staunchly smiling mouth," and he never finishes his sentence. Pnin muses back (with "sympathy, with approval, with heartache") to seeing Liza yawning fifteen, twenty, twenty-five years ago in Paris, and says goodnight.[67]

In the brief scene when he is buying the ball, we encounter a complete image of Pnin, his personality, his bond with Russian culture (including, of course, Pushkin), his alienation from the culture of his place of exile, and the comic bent of his culture clashes, the outcome of the types of misunderstanding to which Pnin has become accustomed. Pnin has developed the habit of keeping his portable world close by as he navigates this new, alien terrain. This scene is a microcosm of the novel: from the narrator's duplicitous tone, to the presence of cruel enchanters, to the double blow that involves his thwarted plans and his experiences of some form of misunderstanding at every turn. There is a hidden layer beneath every one of the mix-ups; there are guardian angels on hand too. Pnin, still the ideal character in spite of everything, is given to dreams. He is a dreamer and a wanderer, as if he has not been allowed to take root; he roams from one university to another, from one house to another, from one town to another, and from one world to another. His dreams reveal his rich inner world. Pnin's roots are in this other world. It is here that we recognize the strength of his character and the key to his self-sufficiency. Oblivious to the enchanters, he moves from a familiar culture to an unknown one. He moves from one book to another (we will meet him again in *Pale Fire*). What emerges from his encounter with Victor, despite their misunderstandings, is that Pnin can give voice to a reality that lies beyond the destructiveness of Liza's world. He establishes a rapport with Victor that is much deeper than the one Victor has with his real parents. Pnin's world finds continuity in Victor.

Victor, too, is a dreamer. Chapter 4 begins with one of his dreams: Victor's father, the king of an imaginary Russia, is sitting at his capacious desk. A revolution has broken out, "decapitations and folk dances had already started," but Victor's father will not abdicate, "the answer is no. I prefer the unknown quantity of exile."[68] Victor has never much liked his real father and does not sleep well, descending into dreams every night. They are usually incoherent mixtures of an "Italian film made in Berlin for American consumption"; of adventures like "*The Scarlet Pimpernel*, recently staged at St. Martha's, the nearest girls' school; an anonymous Kafkaesque story in a *ci-devant* avant-garde magazine read aloud in class by Mr. Pennant"; and versions of family stories about the flight of Russian intellectuals from "Lenin's regime." In Victor's favorite scene from the dream, the solitary father king, or *solus rex,* to use a Latin coinage that according to the narrator is how "chess problem makers term royal solitude," walks along the beach of the Bohemian Sea, waiting for an American adventurer with a high-powered motorboat.[69] This is one of the instances where the present predicts or facilitates the future: before long, Victor's dream in this book turns into Charles Kinbote's reality in another, in the form of the paranoid protagonist-critic of *Pale Fire.*[70] Like many of Nabokov's characters, Victor can create a dreamworld and remain faithful to his dreams. Although the ingredients of Victor's dreams are a mixture of the most banal stereotypes, he succeeds in creating a world that embraces Pnin indirectly in the form of an ideal father who, despite appearing lonely and atypical, is not willing to capitulate. (At the end of the chapter, when Pnin and Victor are both asleep, Pnin's dream, in which he waits for a boat by which he is to escape the Bolsheviks' talons, is an extension of Victor's dream; Victor has for once fallen asleep exceptionally quickly).[71] The nucleus of Victor's way of thinking is a result of the actions of Liza, who has not only tried to impose Victor on Pnin but at the same time has tried to prepare Victor to accept Pnin as she perceives him. As a result, in Victor's dreamworld, Pnin is an extraordinary hero, "the great Timofey Pnin, scholar and gentleman, teaching a practically dead language at the famous Waindell College."[72]

In chapter 4, the narrator provides details of Victor's past. Victor has been exceptional from a young age. He does not reflect the stereotypes his parents have learned and promulgated. As the narrator puts it, "Genius is non-conformity. At two, Victor did not make little spiral scribbles to express buttons or port-holes, as a million tots do. . . . He made his circles perfectly round and perfectly closed." At three, he is asked by his father to draw a portrait of his mother and he responds with "a lovely undulation, which he said was her shadow on the new refrigerator." At five he uses perspective; at six he already recognizes something many people never distinguish: the colors of shadows, "the difference in tint between the shadow of an orange and that of a plum or of an avocado pear."[73] Psychological studies and research carried out by Papa (Dr. Eric Wind) and Mama (Dr. Liza Wind) get them nowhere. Eventually, they have no choice but to leave their "little patient" to his own devices (though not before Nabokov takes a few good swipes at therapists and in defense of genius).

At school, Victor is a distinguished pupil. He is lucky to have an extraordinary art teacher, Mr. Lake, whom he reveres, though he is less respectful of other teachers (another opportunity for Nabokov to offer an assortment of his own theories). Victor's teacher lacks genius but has a profound knowledge of technique; he is also indifferent to schools and trends and eschews the idea that contemporary art is better art, arguing that "Dali is really Norman Rockwell's twin brother kidnapped by gypsies in babyhood." He considers Van Gogh "second-rate" and Picasso "supreme, despite his commercial foibles." He also asks: "If Degas could immortalize a *calèche*, why could not Victor Wind do the same to a motor car?"[74]

Victor's teacher, Lake, tells his students that the solar spectrum is not a closed circle but a "spiral of tints from cadmium red and oranges through a strontian yellow and a pale paradisal green to cobalt blues and violets, at which point the sequence does not grade into red again but passes into another spiral, which starts with a kind of lavender grey and goes on to Cinderella shades transcending human perception."[75] Here what is at stake, even before the talk of Cinderella shades or the idea of painting a motorcar, is primarily Nabokov's writing style rather than Victor's artwork. He writes in *Speak, Memory,* "In the spiral form, the circle, uncoiled, unwound, has ceased to be vicious; it has been set free."[76] The narrator describes this ideal painting, which, according to Lake's ideas, Victor is able to paint, and by describing it in such detail makes it appear before the reader's eyes. This inevitably recalls *The Real Life of Sebastian Knight* and Sebastian's portrait by his friend Roy Carswell, in which his face is reflected in a pool of clear water.[77] In *Pnin,* we see a polished black sedan parked at the intersection of a tree-lined street. "Now break the body of the car into separate curves and panels; then put it together in terms of reflections." This way, the surrounding scenery is mirrored, and the images of the heavy spring sky, the outline of a building, an inverted tree, and even the painter himself, are collected over the reflective surface: everything is there in a microcosmic version. The narrator refers to it as a mimetic and integrative process, which Lake calls the necessary "naturalization of man-made things."[78]

This "naturalization" approach is the style Nabokov uses in *Pnin.* There is obviously nothing new in the idea of reality being reflected in the mirror of art. What is new is the manner by which Nabokov merges the mirror with the reflection of reality, creating an irrefutable though invisible nexus between reality and art. As Nabokov writes on Gogol in elaborating his assertion that Gogol was not a realist: "Gogol, of course, never drew portraits—he used looking glasses and as a writer lived in his own looking glass world."[79] In *Pnin,* this realm of mirrors is not marginal in the everyday world (as in *Invitation to a Beheading* and *Bend Sinister*) but is more like what V says in *The Real Life of Sebastian Knight* about the pebble that appears like jewel in water: "I know that the common pebble you find in your fist after having thrust your arm shoulder deep into water, where a jewel seemed to gleam on pale sand, is really the coveted gem though it looks like a pebble as it dries in the sun of everyday."[80] In *Pnin,* too, this dream-world remains hidden at the substratum of the everyday world (at least the enchanters cannot see it). Does this mean that Quixote and Pnin are mad? Or is it the world around them that is mad and, for that reason, collectively perceives these two protagonists as mad? The answer is clear. What remains is the question of the young genius: what is Victor's role? We have seen that Pnin's world continues and expands in Victor's. Conversely, as we will see, Victor is placed at the center of Pnin's universe, just as Victor gathers the scattered fragments of this universe and transforms them into a single object, the gift he later gives to Pnin.

7

Pnin appears to be luckier than Quixote. *Don Quixote*'s narrator is not quite as sympathetic toward the hero of his story; there is nothing to indicate or imply that his dreamworld is real. Quixote's dreams are figments of his imagination, and when he eventually discovers the nature of reality, when he becomes wise, the only option open to him is regret and death. *Pnin*'s narrator both torments Pnin and appreciates his value. Moreover, Pnin's life is not entirely at the narrator's mercy: though the narrator impishly derides happy endings, the novel he narrates ends happily. Despite the many misfortunes that befall Pnin, which in any case is nothing new in his life, he eventually manages to flee his narrator. Throughout the novel, too, there are subjects and themes that even from the depths of Pnin's solitude and despair will transport him (and the reader) to a different place, including, for example, the world of Cinderella and her glass slippers.

Pnin is not plot driven; instead it is composed of several different leitmotifs and patterns. This becomes particularly significant when the assortment of motifs and patterns incorporates characters and even words that weave together to form a metatheme. Pnin's magical world is constructed with the bricks and mortar of these devices, and though they may not initially appear significant, they are in fact an integral component of the novel's infrastructure. We can find one example in Nabokov's repetition of numbers, specifically the number three and its derivatives: Pnin's birthday falls on February 3 (according to the pre-Revolution calendar); the Pushkin poem that Pnin recites to his students is identified by not only the date but also the hour it was composed: three minutes past three; he has unsuccess-ful relationships with three women (the last is one of his students, Betty Bliss, who tries hard to attract Pnin's attention); the narrator's third meeting with Pnin takes place at a location called Three Fountains; and finally, we have the connection between three characters and three squirrels.[81]

One of the novel's prevalent motifs is the repeated appearance of the squirrels: links in a daisy chain connecting Pnin's two worlds. Pnin returns to events of his lost childhood in chapter 1 after a slight heart epi-sode on a park bench. He remembers his room, which contained a four-section screen of polished wood decorated with a pyrographic design. The screen's image is of an old man hunched up on a bench and a squirrel hold-ing a reddish object. Pnin cannot figure out what the red object is. Age eleven, he imagines that he will have the opportunity to solve this problem while sick in bed, but a fever prevents him. Now in his fifties and sitting on a park bench in an unfamiliar town, Pnin merges with his eleven-year-old self for a few seconds. Again it appears that he holds the key to solving the puzzle. But the wind picks up and distracts him. This happens just as a gray squirrel is in front of him, nibbling a peach stone. After meeting Liza, too, he feels as though he is on the verge of solving "a simple solution of the universe" when a squirrel disturbs his thoughts.[82] Pnin, sitting on the bench and facing a squirrel, is not merely recalling the image on the screen of his childhood but reiterating or re-creating it as well. This is reminiscent of Martin (the main character in *Glory*), who eventually disappears into the painting he had seen as a child. The past and present, together with reality and dream, are reflections of each other (like the car and the scenery around it in Victor's painting).[83]

It becomes clear that whenever a squirrel appears, whatever prob-lem Pnin is facing at that moment is within reach of being resolved. He loses his suitcase in one scene, and in another he loses his way, and in both cases things end well. Gradually, we encounter this association of ideas at a deeper level. In one scene, the imagery evokes the squirrel. Pnin is occupied by research as well as by teaching; he intends to write a book on Russian culture, and he is studying to that end. The book is meant as a *"Petite His-toire* of Russian culture, in which a choice of Russian Curiosities, Customs,

Literary Anecdotes, and so forth would be presented in such a way as to reflect in miniature *la Grande Histoire*—Major Concatenations of Events." According to the narrator, Pnin was still at the "blissful stage of collecting his material," describing in detail Pnin the scholar, carrying lists and notes, pulling out a catalogue drawer "like a big nut, to a secluded corner and there make a quiet mental meal of it, now moving his lips in soundless comment, critical, satisfied, perplexed, and now lifting his rudimentary eyebrows and forgetting them there, left high upon his spacious brow where they remained long after all trace of displeasure or doubt had gone."[84] The image is depicted from the point of view of Pnin's students, who, according to the narrator, enjoy watching these scenes and consider it both a treat and an honor. The narrator, of course, avoids using the word "squirrel" in this connection, but leaves no room for doubt.

The squirrel motif also has other, more complex implications. The reader encounters three inanimate squirrels in the course of the novel; these squirrels represent different themes. They are different from the living squirrels that merge with Pnin, whose own habits and actions often appear to be squirrel-like—the narrator uses words to describe Pnin that immediately call squirrels to mind. The first of the three inanimate squirrels is a stuffed toy that the narrator sees as a child when visiting Dr. Pnin's house.[85] The door of the schoolroom is open and he glimpses it there. Dr. Pnin, Pnin's father, was a close friend of Dr. Beluchkin, Mira's father. Brian Boyd explains that *Beluchka* is a diminutive of *Belka,* which means "squirrel" in Russian.[86] The second is the gray squirrel on a picture postcard that Pnin sends to Victor. Pnin has not yet met Victor in person; the postcard belongs to an educational series that Pnin selects especially for the purpose of their correspondence. An explanation on the card, saying that the word "squirrel" comes from the Greek word meaning "shadow-tail," alludes to the link between Pnin and Victor and needs no further explanation, especially given that Pnin invites Victor to visit him during the next vacation.[87] These two images suffice to demonstrate how Pnin's world expands by way of squirrels. The third squirrel collects all the thematic nuts together, and is an even more complex animal.

During the party at Pnin's house, Margaret Thayer, the university librarian, looks at the glass bowl and says that its color reminds her of what she always imagined was the greenish-blue tint of Cinderella's glass slippers. Pnin the scholar explains that the French word *vair* (meaning hide) gradually transformed into the French word *verre* (meaning glass). As he concludes, he recalls that Cinderella's slippers were made not of glass but of Russian squirrel fur. (Mira's father was a fur merchant, we have earlier learned.)[88] The subject of this conversation is the glass bowl described in detail at the beginning of the party, whose beauty and green sheen now enchant the guests. It is Victor's gift to Pnin (and the guests are quick to draw Pnin's attention to its value). A few sentences describe the Cinderella-like shades of the bowl as well as the magical past (Mira's) and the magical future (Victor's) reflected in the bowl. This is a good example of the way a theme (in its capacity as substitute for plot) develops the scene and shapes the novel. The party, as we know, ends disastrously for Pnin: he learns that he will lose his post at Waindell College. Pnin is tidying up, washing the dishes. Victor's magic bowl, covered in soapsuds, is in the sink with the rest of the plates and cutlery. As he is drying a nutcracker, it falls out of Pnin's hand and into the soapy water, and he hears the sound of breaking glass. Pnin turns away for a moment, "staring at the blackness beyond the threshold of the open back door." A green lacy-winged insect is circling the lamp. A butterfly? If so, there is no cause for concern. Pnin goes over to the sink and puts his hand in the water. A wine glass is broken; "the beautiful bowl was intact."[89] The guardian angels are keeping watch. The squirrels, aided by the glass slippers, disclose Cinderella's identity to the prince. Love for Mira preserves the magic of the past not only for Pnin's present but also for Victor's future. The pebble is, in fact, a jewel after all.

8

I have elaborated on Pnin's magical world. But what about Pnin himself? It is generally assumed (or it might reasonably be assumed) that a character who is able to find her way into a magical world is entirely different from the rest of us. Alice, for example, has curiosity, courage, and, consequently, a personality beyond that of ordinary girls. Another example is Cinderella, a character who recalls Pnin. Looking from a different angle, we can say that a person who manages to find a way into a magical realm must remain connected to and dependent on the everyday world at the same time. In practice, such characters are the only ones capable of finding a magic wand because it would be impossible for them to live without it. So besides the question of the uniqueness of Pnin's personality, there is another question to consider: how does a magic wand come to Pnin's rescue? It is particularly relevant in *Pnin* because the narrator openly admits that he hates happy endings; unlike the narrators of *Invitation to a Beheading* and *Bend Sinister,* he says that he has no intention of answering any cry for help or intervening in the denouement.

Again, we find the narrator, a suspicious persona at best, combining aspects of both angel and enchanter. He acts against the protagonist and at the same time serves as his protector. We have to accompany this persona in order to enjoy the novel, and we have to oppose him in order to properly appreciate Pnin's character. The narrator thus becomes a foil, created to give clarity to the protagonist's personality. Pnin is the most magical element in the novel; what Nabokov wrote about Quixote applies to Pnin too. The whole novel revolves around Pnin's personality, and all other characters are colorless by comparison. It is only in their dealings with Pnin that they gain hue and relevance; it is Pnin's imagination, like Quixote's, and his prism of dreams, that saves the other characters from the banality of everyday life. The imagined, artificial dreamscapes of Pnin and Quixote are signs of the power and charm of imagination. The secondary characters are not depicted as complex or multidimensional, functioning only in an adjunct capacity to Pnin's personality. Many of Nabokov's novels are structured as explorations of how the pendulum veers from reality to dreams, from life to death, from the present to the past, or vice versa. *Pnin* is built on this foundation. *Pnin* charms and fascinates the reader in the same way that Pnin fascinates his students. According to the narrator, Pnin is beloved by his students "not for any essential ability but for those unforgettable digressions of his, when he would remove his glasses to beam at the past while massaging the lenses of the present."[90]

In a brilliant chapter of his book on Nabokov, *America's Russian Nov-*

elist, G. M. Hyde, when dealing with Pnin, recalls the tradition of *skaz.* The word, a cognate of *skazka* (which means a popular or vulgar story in Russian), refers to a narrative that the author introduces indirectly, through the intercession of an imagined narrator. *Skaz,* having its origins in popular oral storytelling, refers to myriad tricks and methods deployed by the storyteller—diversions, parenthetical points, and habitual or repetitive phrases—in order to stop the narrative and divert the audience's attention from the story back to the storyteller. In this way, the improbability of the story is concealed and further excitement generated, exactly as we see in *Pnin.*[91] Naturally, the Russian formalists immediately subjected *skaz* to literary criticism. Shklovsky explains Sterne's *Tristram Shandy* with the aid of *skaz.* In an article published in 1919, entitled "How Gogol's 'Overcoat' Was Made," the formalist scholar Boris Eikhenbaum references *skaz* repeatedly. Eikhenbaum argues that if we recover the elements of *skaz,* it would enable us to make a richer critical approach to any literary text, and although a popular/oral story falls within the realm of improvisation, and there is no room for improvisation in a realist novel, Eikhenbaum still believes that the most interesting contemporary novelists maintain the "illusion of improvisation" wherever they inevitably find themselves in contact with colloquial language. Eikhenbaum notices this characteristic even in Tolstoy. Gogol, he maintains, does not narrate at all, but merely plays about, utilizing allusion and mime and, in this way, embarks on a sort of solo performance (with author as protagonist).[92]

Nabokov wrote extensively on Gogol, whose work he enjoyed and respected. Among other works, we can refer to his 1944 book *Nikolai Gogol,* which Hyde believes was influenced by Eikhenbaum. *Pnin* can be considered Nabokov's best gift to Gogol. According to Hyde, Nabokov succeeds, in *Pnin,* in creating his own critical "pattern" following his search for the sources of the methods or devices employed by Gogol. He then incorporates this pattern in the structure of his own novel. Hyde quotes Eikhenbaum as saying that in novels where the plot alone is important, narrative tricks or devices are used merely as formal links between events, but when *skaz* has a fundamental role to play in a novel, the narrator somehow appears in the foreground, as if the "pattern" is being used only for combining and connecting the various tricks of the *skaz* style. In such a novel, the emphasis is on elegance of diction and wordplay, and various kinds of pun. In such a narrative, not only does the narrator interrupt in order to address the reader directly, but the narrator's use of language transforms to become the sort of language in which audio allusions acquire an importance far greater than the straightforward meaning of individual words. These are elements that are at the service of the comedy in Gogol's novels, as they are in *Pnin*.[93]

Hyde points several times to the obvious humor in Nabokov's works by way of Henri Bergson's famous 1900 treatise *Laughter*. In the case of *Pnin*, he quotes this passage from Bergson: "To prevent our taking a serious action seriously, in short, in order to prepare us for laughter, comedy utilizes a method, the formula of which may be given as follows: *instead of concentrating our attention on actions, comedy directs it rather to gestures.* By *gestures* we here mean the attitudes, the movements, and even the language by which a mental state expresses itself outwardly without any aim or profit, from no other cause than a kind of inner itching. Gesture, thus defined, is profoundly different from action. Action is intentional, or, at any rate, conscious: gesture slips out unawares, it is automatic. . . . Action is in exact proportion to the feeling that inspires it. . . . About gesture, however, there is something explosive."[94] There are numerous puns and plays on Pnin's name that exemplify this (even in *Pale Fire*).[95] The first time Pnin introduces himself by telephone, the narrator tells us that it sounds like a "preposterous little explosion," and Joan, to whom he is speaking, calls it "a cracked ping-pong ball, Russian."[96] On the most superficial level possible, Pnin's name counts as an audio allusion that constantly attracts the reader's attention. Quoting Eikhenbaum on Gogol, Hyde applies the same logic to Nabokov's *Pnin:* "His narratives are bound together in part by the logic of mime: the sonic properties of words, their rhythms and harmonies, create the illusion of a complementary semiotic system parallel to the sense."[97]

What Hyde leaves out is that Pnin's personality and the novel itself within its specific genre have tragic as well as comic characteristics, a metaphoric vision. Hyde is correct to note in his explanation of the senseless world surrounding Pnin the proximity of an impending abyss that is ready to swallow man and his devices. Hyde also states with accuracy that it is

Pnin's comic sense, and the alternation of pathos and clowning, of laughter, that rescue the novel from the clutches of automatism.[98] But he does not consider that the feeling of pain swells around the void and around the laughter. For Pnin (and, of course, for Nabokov), the cruelty of Mira's death can never be considered an ordinary act in an acceptable world. *Pnin* is Nabokov the novelist's response to this question. Pnin's own response is laughter. How do the readers respond? Nabokov, the academic, writes, in the introduction to his lecture on Kafka's *Metamorphosis:*

> A poor man is robbed of his overcoat (Gogol's "The Greatcoat,"
> or more correctly "The Carrick"); another poor fellow is turned
> into a beetle (Kafka's "The Metamorphosis") — so what? There
> is no rational answer to "so what." We can take the story apart,
> we can find out how the bits fit, how one part of the pattern
> responds to the other; but you have to have in you some cell,
> some gene, some germ that will vibrate in answer to sensations
> that you can neither define, nor dismiss. *Beauty plus pity* —
> that is the closest we can get to a definition of art. Where there
> is beauty there is pity for the simple reason that beauty must
> die: beauty always dies, the manner dies with the matter, the
> world dies with the individual. If Kafka's "The Metamorpho-
> sis" strikes anyone as something more than an entomological
> fantasy, then I congratulate him on having joined the ranks of
> good and great readers.[99]

Genius and Madness

Pale Fire

1

Victor's chapter of *Pnin*, chapter 4, begins with the description of an imaginary father: "The King, his father, wearing a very white sports shirt open at the throat and a very black blazer, sat at a spacious desk whose highly polished surface twinned his upper half in reverse, making of him a kind of court card."[1] He stands in an isolated palace, contemplating forced abdication and exile. Before long, we see Victor's imaginary father pacing a Bohemian shore, ready to make his escape. An American adventurer is to meet him with a powerful motorboat to take him to safety. Pnin, too, in his corresponding dream, sees himself on shore, having escaped the Bolsheviks. He, too, is waiting for a boat to arrive from the other side of the "hopeless sea" to rescue him.[2] The hero figure of Victor's imaginings is a king who is left alone on a chessboard: *solus rex*. According to the narrator of *Pnin*, this is a term used by chess problem creators, known as composers. Five years after the publication of *Pnin*, we come across the same expression in *Pale Fire* (1962), with the same meaning and in similar circumstances (here, too, a powerful motorboat is awaiting the fugitive hero).[3] Could it be that the chess king in *Pale Fire* first appeared in Pnin's and Victor's dreams even before *Pale Fire* was written? Or has the lone king of Victor's dreams escaped *Pnin* only to reemerge in *Pale Fire* as the central figure? (This would be like Pnin himself escaping the grasp of the narrator of *Pnin* to resurface in *Pale Fire* as head of the Russian Department at Wordsmith College.)[4] This curious reappearance is not a habitual question for critics alone: within the novel, one of the two protagonists, Charles Kinbote, insists that the other, the poet John Shade, should call his latest opus "Solus Rex" instead of "Pale Fire," the significance of which, as we shall see, is totally lost on Kinbote.[5]

Is this yet another Nabokovian sleight of hand? Is he doing it solely for the purpose of referring the reader to another of his novels (Nabokov advertising Nabokov)? The pale light of this fire flickers in Nabokov's work even before he migrated to America, long before *Pale Fire* and *Pnin* were written: Nabokov planned on writing a sequel to *The Gift,* and in a folder marked "*The Gift* Part II," he had mapped out part of this second volume, in which Fyodor and Zina settle in Paris, having successfully escaped Nazi Germany.[6] But in the last chapter, Zina is killed in a senseless accident. Although Nabokov put the book aside, the notion of a sequel persisted. Meanwhile, he wrote *The Enchanter,* the manuscript of which he thought was lost, only to find it many years later; this novel was a prototype of *Lolita.*[7] The last novel he was at work on before arriving in America is *Solus Rex;* he left it incomplete. The first and second chapters were published as short stories: "Ultima Thule" and "Solus Rex." This unfinished novel of 1939–1940 was revived in 1960–1961 with a totally different structure, in a different language, and under a different title: *Pale Fire.* In our everyday lives, past experiences that happened so long ago that we have almost forgotten them suddenly recur. In Nabokov's novels this game of hide-and-seek unfolds in a variety of ways.[8]

Both chapters of the unfinished novel of 1939–1940 were translated into English years later (largely by Nabokov and his son) and published in 1973 in a collection of short stories titled *A Russian Beauty and Other Stories.* In the first chapter of the unfinished novel, Sineusov, a Russian émigré, writes a letter to his dead wife. He tells her that he is shortly to meet up with Adam Falter, his boyhood mathematics tutor in St. Petersburg. Sineusov runs into Falter on the Riviera, where Falter claims that he has accidentally solved the riddle of the universe, but that he is not prepared to disclose the solution to Sineusov. When he reveals it by mistake to an Italian psychiatrist, the latter's heart stops beating from the shock. Sineusov, in mourning for his deceased wife and desperate to find a way to revive her, convinces himself that Falter is not mad, but a true seer. He tries to get his old tutor to reveal the secret to him, but Falter refuses. Eventually, Falter explains that he has inadvertently disclosed the key to the secret during their conversations but that, fortunately, Sineusov has not noticed. We also become acquainted with a Nordic poet who asks Sineusov to illustrate his poems with images and drawings. In the hope of alleviating his sorrow, Sineusov agrees. The poem concerns an imaginary island called Ultima Thule. Addressing his departed wife, Sineusov writes: "Ultima Thule, that island born in the desolate, gray sea of my heartache for you, now attracted me as the home of my least expressible thoughts."[9] In his introduction to the English translation of the story, Nabokov writes that in "the course of evolving an imaginary country (which at first merely diverted him from his grief, but then grew into a self-contained artistic obsession), the widower becomes so engrossed in Thule that the latter starts to develop its own reality."[10] Sineusov declares that he will return from the Riviera to the apartment he has in Paris. Instead, Sineusov moves into a bleak palace on a remote northern island. Again, the creation of a dreamworld acts as an antidote to the painful realities of everyday life.[11]

Nabokov's protagonists are often solitary individuals. They can neither return to the dreamworld of the past nor live in the world in which they are trapped. They are left with no choice other than to dwell in memory and to summon creativity to their rescue. They create worlds that serve as refuges against the cruelty of everyday life. In this context, all these characters are in exile. Both Cincinnatus and Krug are in exile even in their homelands because of the totalitarian systems, fascism and communism, in operation. Nabokov can save them only because of the seemingly unlimited power of a creative writer. The exiled Pnin is also a lone king on the chessboard, unable to bypass the other chess pieces. Eventually, Pnin frees himself from the narrator's clutches to take refuge in another novel. If all these characters, from Fyodor to Pnin, experience the type of mental isolation that is considered creative and even good despite being held captive within overwhelmingly banal worlds, Kinbote, the protagonist of *Pale Fire*, is of a different breed. Kinbote has neither a past nor a future; he lacks even a present. He is the lone king of an imaginary territory that does not belong to him even in the realm of imagination. Kinbote lives in a no-return exile—separate from his dreamland (where Nabokov generally places his protagonists)—which for Kinbote lies in the distant future. This dynamic is established either in a footnote or somewhere beyond the last page of the novel. Like Humbert in *Lolita,* Kinbote fails to reach his dreamland. While Humbert is able to experience a lost paradise at least in the past, Kinbote never has the chance to do so except in his colorful, boundless imagination. He refers to himself, obliquely, as the *Solus Rex.*[12]

Lolita and *Pale Fire* (and sometimes *Ada*) are considered by most to be Nabokov's masterpieces. Some critics believe that the miracle of these novels lies in their dazzling, intricate structures that are, at the same time, comprehensible. These are the novels where all the principal elements and themes of Nabokov's fictions attain perfection. Moreover, according to Richard Rorty (who dislikes *Ada*) in *Contingency, Irony, and Solidarity,* what is so noteworthy in *Lolita* and *Pale Fire* is the sheer originality of their two protagonists, Humbert and Kinbote. "No one before had thought of asking what it would be like to be a Skimpole who was also a genius—one who did not simply toss the word 'poetry' about but who actually *knew* what poetry was."[13] Rorty believes that the reason Nabokov became so much more revered than other first-rate writers of his time is the ascription of the "genius-monster—the monster of incuriosity—to Nabokov's contribution to our knowledge of human possibilities."[14] The innovative structure of *Pale Fire* also attracted critical attention. From the beginning, *Pale Fire* caused a stir among the literary establishment. It is the type of novel that enables critics to fashion and invent all manner of new theories, itself a diversion from perhaps one of the most astonishing characteristics of *Pale Fire.*[15] Although *Pale Fire* broke fictional conventions and challenged traditional ideas of the novel, it nevertheless, against all odds, remains a novel. Its three main characters and their three story lines shape the novel's plot. The novel reaches its denouement when the three movements converge. This point is often overlooked, so let us not focus our attention on the Nabokov of allusions and tangential remarks, but rather concentrate in detail on Nabokov the storyteller.

2

Pale Fire, which was published in 1962, is divided into four sections: the foreword written by Dr. Charles Kinbote, a man from a country called Zembla;[16] the 999-line poem "Pale Fire," written in heroic couplets by John Shade, a prominent American poet who has passed away; Kinbote's commentary on Shade's poem; and Kinbote's index. Despite such a structure, *Pale Fire* is emphatically a novel.

Dr. Samuel Johnson is famous not only for being one of the great literary figures of eighteenth-century Britain but also because his young friend and disciple James Boswell wrote his biography. *The Life of Samuel Johnson* (1791) is considered one of the most brilliant biographies in English-language literature. At a certain level, the picture Kinbote paints of his relationship with Shade reminds us of Samuel Johnson and Boswell, his indefatigable biographer.[17] Kinbote himself suggests this comparison from the beginning, as he quotes Boswell on Johnson in the book's epigraph.[18] Thus the first theme emerges: the complex relationship between a biographer and his subject. The biographer is not only an adoring disciple; he's also a nuisance. He is constantly interpreting his subject (and refashioning him too?). In many cases, a published biography even displays the biographer's personality more than that of his or her subject. (Nabokov had firsthand experience of this: the first biography written about him, Andrew Field's *Nabokov: His Life in Part* [1967], was published during his lifetime, and all these problems then became all the more evident to him).[19]

The title of Shade's long poem, which is also the title of the novel, *Pale Fire,* has its origin in Shakespeare's *Timon of Athens.* The play is about a generous nobleman who squanders his wealth by lavishing gifts on friends who do not reciprocate later, when his creditors arrive. Timon curses the Athenians and takes refuge in a cave near the seashore. In the cave, he finds a trove of gold by luck, and he ends up giving it all away, this time in bitterness. He grows old, a recluse and an itinerant, and dies alone. Dr. Johnson described the play as "a very powerful warning against that ostentatious liberality, which scatters bounty, but confers no benefits, and buys flattery, but not friendship."[20] Shade's relationship with the play is apparently a simple one: he is looking for a title for his poem. With the aid of a few

Shakespearean lines, he arrives at "Pale Fire" and mentions this circumstance within the poem itself.[21] Kinbote's relationship with the play is more complex, however. All he has with him is the Zemblan translation of *Timon of Athens,* and he tangentially compares himself with the exiled Timon. He comments on Shade's quotation of Shakespeare but writes his footnotes without reference to the original work. This gives us one of the most beautiful (and brutal) jokes in the novel: The phrase "pale fire" comes from a moment when Timon is suspicious toward everybody and everything, even the sun, the moon, the sea, and the earth. Kinbote takes lines from the play that reads

> The sun's a thief, and with his great attraction
> Robs the vast sea: the moon's an arrant thief,
> And her pale fire she snatches from the sun:
> The sea's a thief, whose liquid surge resolves
> The moon into salt tears. (act IV, scene 3)

and retranslates them back into English from the Zemblan:

> The sun is a thief: she lures the sea
> and robs it. The moon is a thief:
> he steals his silvery light from the sun.
> The sea is a thief: it dissolves the moon.[22]

Because Kinbote does not bother to check the original Shakespeare, the title words are lost and the phrase "pale fire" means nothing to him.

Pale Fire thus posits two sides of a complex relationship and a preliminary framework of confrontation. There is also from the outset the theme of stealing (or borrowing life-giving light), though at the most obvious level, this refers to the light that the biographer obtains from his subject. Without Johnson, there would be no biographer named Boswell. Similarly, without Shade, there is no Kinbote. Nonetheless, as we shall soon see, Kinbote lays claim to something else. From the beginning of the book, we encounter not only the peculiarities of Kinbote's personality but his curious assertions too. He ends his foreword with these words: "Let me state that without my notes Shade's text simply has no human reality at all since the human reality of such a poem as his (being too skittish and reticent for an autobiographical work), with the omission of many pithy lines carelessly rejected by him, has to depend entirely on the reality of its author and his surroundings, attachments and so forth, a reality that only my notes can provide. To this statement my dear poet would probably not have subscribed, but, for better or worse, it is the commentator who has the last word."[23] It is clear from the very start that the overall comic atmosphere of *Pale Fire* derives from the mistakes and misunderstandings of Kinbote the commentator, who most certainly does not have the last word, if indeed there is any last word to be had. What becomes gradually apparent, contrary to what Kinbote contends, is that Shade's long poem comprises a complete autobiography. Furthermore, the information that Kinbote gives the reader is not about Shade but about Kinbote himself. His commentary is really a corollary to an imaginary poem that he would have liked Shade to write about Kinbote's own past. Here is the moon, stealing light from the sun.

The eponymous poem in "Pale Fire" has a thoroughly traditional form, and an air of Alexander Pope, the eighteenth-century English poet.[24] Composed of heroic couplets, it runs to 999 lines, divided into four cantos. As we learn from Kinbote's commentary, John Shade (1898–1959) wrote the poem in his native New Wye in the Appalachian region of the United States.[25] Some critics claim that the poem is unfinished. Kinbote insists, however, that there is only one missing line in the poem: a nicely rounded one thousand lines is the intended tally. The poem is not incomplete, he nevertheless maintains, because the first line is to be repeated as the last, as becomes evident when we note that the nine-hundred-ninety-ninth line does in fact rhyme with the first. Kinbote's hypothesis sounds plausible. The spiral structure of the poem, he submits, is compatible with the general tone. In fact, "Pale Fire" is a metaphysical poem, shaped around the poet's life and feelings, especially on the question of death. However, while Shade ruminates poetically, he details his private life, despite the fact that he does not intend to tell a story. As a result, "Pale Fire" is, at the same time, transformed into a complete autobiography, giving us an intricate account of the poet's life. John Shade's wife, Sybil, is central to the poem. They were childhood sweethearts, and their loving relationship lasted a lifetime. But they shared deep sorrows too: John and Sybil's only child, Hazel, committed suicide at the age of twenty-three. Hazel, who was not beautiful, could not endure her lot and drowned herself in a lake. Following the loss of their daughter, the poet and his wife sought out every conceivable, credible, or magical source to try to find out what prompted the girl to act as she did, to no avail.

The idea of another world that accompanies the concept of death does not depend solely on the memory of Hazel. Shade recalls that "playful death," always present since childhood, pulled at his sleeve every now and then. He remembers that one day when he was eleven years old, he felt a sudden "sunburst" in his head, "And then black night. That blackness was sublime. / I felt distributed through space and time."[26] He recollects that as a young man, one day he began to doubt man's sanity: "How could he live without / Knowing for sure what dawn, what death what doom / Awaited consciousness beyond the tomb?" Eventually, during a sleepless night, he decides to explore this "inadmissible abyss, / Devoting all my twisted life to this / One task. Today I'm sixty-one. Waxwings / Are berry-pecking. A cicada sings."[27] The structure of the poem is dependent on the theme of death, but Shade manages to present his living world at the same time, with all the details that make life meaningful. For example, Sybil, busy with everyday tasks, brightens the poem with her presence. This is a confrontation with death rather than an exploration of the void. Shade's work in fact glorifies a loving marriage and everything that happens every day even though it might appear small and insignificant. Shade's life passes within the context of the democratic order of a cultured society, beside a dearly beloved wife: a shining context that will persist, even after death. At the same time, Shade's life unspools at the edge of an unknown abyss. Toward the end of the poem, Shade ventures:

> I'm reasonably sure that we survive
> And that my darling somewhere is alive,
> As I am reasonably sure that I

> Shall wake at six tomorrow, on July
> The twenty-second, nineteen fifty-nine,
> And that the day will probably be fine.[28]

But he will not wake up tomorrow, because this is the last night of his life. Death comes to Shade in the most unexpected way — life still thrives at the extremes of the illogical, proving the futility of any form of logic.

Kinbote's notes include a skillful satire of what constitutes a typical critical commentary. In effect, they are a parody of the form. This gives Nabokov the opportunity to deal with many of his main concerns. But the more we read the commentary, the more we notice that following the inclination set by the foreword, Kinbote has a peculiar understanding of poetry. Apparently, Kinbote is not only critiquing the world portrayed in Shade's poem: he is commenting on, and crafting, a different world, one that is richer and more fantastical than Shade's. At first, Kinbote's life seems to be a simple one, if enigmatic and lonely; he is a homosexual, a vegetarian, an exile, and very tall. He is the exact opposite of Shade. Kinbote explains that he opts for a teaching post at Wordsmith College out of his love for Shade's poetry. He rents a house next to the Shades', hoping to become better acquainted with them. From this point on, Kinbote perpetually stalks the Shades, peeping through his window, observing them from the garden, ready to seize any opportunity to speak to the poet. As a result, according to Kinbote, Shade becomes more and more interested in the stories that Kinbote shares with him about his own past. Kinbote tries to pique his interest, hoping that these memories will find their way into the long poem that Shade is composing, thus immortalizing the memories and Kinbote himself. This prompts Kinbote's question: how can the reader understand the human reality of the poem without being familiar with the author's reality and his surroundings? "A reality that only my notes can provide."[29]

Kinbote's autobiography is narrated through the notes attached to the book's third chapter, titled "Commentary." Kinbote ostensibly has no intention of telling his own life story. He maintains that he is merely contextualizing, giving background to the contents of Shade's poem. Nonetheless, his extraordinary story begins to emerge. Dr. Charles Kinbote is, in fact,

Charles II or "Charles the Beloved," the last king of Zembla, a northern European country. In the wake of an Extremist revolution, he has no option but to escape and to live in exile. Although Kinbote pretends, throughout the novel, that he is an ordinary Zemblan refugee, we gradually come to realize that the opposite is true, and he in fact wants the reader to realize that Beloved Charles is none other than himself. In the footnotes to Shade's poem, Kinbote paints a fascinating picture of his cherished country with surprising lyrical grace: a dreamlike palace, a young king, and a beautiful but sad queen. Disa is deeply in love with her husband, yet the king never seems remotely interested in her and lives only for his adored young male pages. The story continues. The revolutionaries imprison Charles in his palace, but he is able to escape. A fad has spread among his supporters of replicating his attire, which permits him to foil the revolutionary police, and Charles flees Zembla and eventually Europe. Once in the United States, he adopts a pseudonym and takes a teaching post at Wordsmith. But the story does not end there. A number of Zemblan Extremists decide to assassinate Charles; Jakob Gradus is tasked with finding Charles and killing him. One of Kinbote's theories is that Gradus set out from Zembla almost on the same day that Shade began writing his poem. Thus, as Shade's long poem moves forward in the main text, and as Kinbote tells the story of Shade's life in his commentary, so Gradus approaches his target. It is as if the poem develops in meter tapped out by Gradus's advancing footsteps (keeping in mind that the central theme of the poem and the novel is death). Kinbote claims that he later sees Gradus in prison and that the source of his theory is Gradus himself.[30]

Shade almost completes "Pale Fire," mentioning the next day's date in the body of the poem itself.[31] According to Kinbote, he pays a visit to Shade on the evening of July 21, 1959, taking advantage of Sybil's absence, as he considers her an enemy and a rival. When he finds out that the work is near completion, he suggests that they celebrate by having a drink at his house. They set out together walking. Gradus, recently arrived in America, shows up in New Wye that same day. He does not have Charles's address and frantically goes about trying to find him. Kinbote has provided a detailed account of Gradus's movements just before this, to the extent of describing what he ate and the "intestinal internecine war" afterward.[32] We follow Gradus as he looks for Kinbote at the university. Though he does not name our old friend Professor Pnin outright, it appears that Gradus encounters him.[33] Eventually, he secures the address. The arrival of Gradus at Kinbote's house coincides with the moment when Kinbote and Shade are walking through the garden (and when a butterfly lands on Shade's sleeve).[34] Gradus shoots and kills Shade in error. Kinbote's gardener delivers a severe blow to Gradus's head with a spade. Kinbote runs into the house to call the police, but before doing so he hides the envelope containing the poem in a closet under his shoes, having retrieved it from Shade's side. (Charles has always wanted to be immortalized in Shade's poem, as we know.) In the chaos and confusion of the ensuing hours, he even manages to acquire Sybil's permission to edit and publish the poem. No one can stop him now: Kinbote considers himself the rightful owner of "Pale Fire."[35]

If Kinbote's fantasy autobiography is shaped between the lines of his footnotes on Shade's poem, there is yet another narrative set in motion by Kinbote's adventures. Each story clarifies itself as another story unfolds. The way the assassination scene is portrayed is a good example of this: the narrator insists we accept his account, that Gradus's true intention was to assassinate Kinbote. But the narrator's version allows for a completely different interpretation of Shade's murder: Kinbote's landlord, the strict Judge Goldsworth, is on a European sabbatical at the time, and the assassin, Jakob Gradus—aka Jack Degree, or Jack Grey, or Jacques de Grey, or James de Grey—is a mad criminal on the run wishing to exact revenge on the judge. In this telling, Kinbote is neither the target nor the central figure. But then what is the version offered by Gradus/Grey? There is none: Gradus/Grey commits suicide in jail ("I was forced to leave New Wye soon after my last interview with the jailed killer").[36] The main question, however, concerns not the assassin but the truth behind Kinbote's story. If Kinbote is not the *solus rex* as he claims, then who is he? There are nearly as many answers to this question as there are critical responses to *Pale Fire*.[37] We also have access to Nabokov's notes. Brian Boyd cites one of them: "I wonder if any reader will notice the following details: 1) that the nasty commentator is not an ex-king and not even Dr. Kinbote, but Prof. Vseslav

Botkin, a Russian and a madman."[38] In the world of make-believe he hides behind Kinbote's mask and invents the story of "Charles." There is a casual reference to Botkin when Professor Pardon speaks to him: "I was under the impression that you were born in Russia, and that your name was a kind of anagram of Botkin or Botkine?" Kinbote explains that he has mistaken him for another refugee professor.[39] In his 1962 diary entry, Nabokov also writes: "He commits suicide before completing his Index, leaving the last entry without p[age] ref[erences]." (This last entry reads: "*Zembla,* a distant northern land.")[40] The first point may not escape the attention of the good reader familiar with Nabokov and his narrative art, but how carefully has the text to be read in order not to miss the second point?

In *Pale Fire,* the plot takes shape on the basis of the actual, intellectual, and imaginary movements of three principal characters: the poet, the poet's interpreter, and the poet's killer. In his role as commentator, Kinbote finds a second meaning for Shade's poem and second identities for himself and for the assassin. The plot's complexity springs from the fact that the two central characters of the novel are, in fact, the protagonists of two different stories, each of whom is presented in two distinctive ways (in Shade's poem and in Kinbote's commentary). The two subsidiary story lines run in parallel at times, occasionally intersect, and finally meet. From these two narrations, Gradus emerges. At the same time, another story line is taking shape beneath the surface: the so-called "real" version of events, involving the cruel judge and the mad Jacques de Grey. Again, the question arises of what is "real" or "unreal." But the good reader of Nabokov knows not to look for the reality of the text; reality is inlaid in the storytelling. In an interview, Nabokov said, "You can get nearer and nearer, so to speak, to reality; but you never get near enough because reality is an infinite succession of steps, levels of perception, false bottoms, and hence unquenchable, unattainable."[41]

Armies of critics have pronounced on *Pale Fire,* but few have paid attention to Nabokov's art of storytelling. To me, it appears that the genius of *Pale Fire* lies in its author's extraordinary use of traditional elements of fiction. In fact, the most traditional elements of novel writing (plot, setting, characterization) are all integral to *Pale Fire;* the only difference here is that these elements have come to the party in disguise. The distinction lies in the difference between a writer who hides his inadequacy by deploying tricks or devices, and the author whose techniques are inseparable from the story. What critic can avoid being enchanted by the devices in *Pale Fire* or disregard the allusions to Nabokov's other works, and other literary sources?[42] For example, in "The Mechanics of *Pale Fire*" (1970), Nina Berberova examines the relationship between *Pale Fire* and *Timon of Athens* and demonstrates that Timon is at the root of Kinbote's character.[43] Similarly, G. M Hyde and Robert Alter consider the contrasting worlds of Kinbote and Shade.[44] Robert Frost and, of course, Alexander Pope are influences on Shade (who has written a book about Pope). The serene, stable, discreet (and "Augustan")[45] mien of John Shade lies in stark contrast to the chaos and madness of Kinbote: a spectacular, magnificent, Shakespearean world brimming with poetry and fervor.[46] Critics surmise so many allusions to other works that it would seem as though there is a reference or a hint hiding behind every word of *Pale Fire*. But the importance of a literary work can never be measured in its concentration of devices or the number of its references or allusions. And what great literary work does not encourage commentaries as numerous as commentators?[47]

3

John Shade is another of Nabokov's positive characters. Mirrors, as we have seen, play an important role in Nabokov's work.[48] For Nabokov, the world of art is the world of mirrors, the type of mirrors that we encounter in *Alice's Adventures in Wonderland* and *Through the Looking-Glass*. But the world of *Pale Fire* is not one of symbols: here, mirrors serve a different purpose. The structure of the novel is based on borrowed or stolen reflections, replicas either of reality or imagination. For example, Kinbote's commentary, along with the foreword and the notes, constitutes a mirror that is held to Shade's poem. At the same time, Shade's work is itself a mirror in which one can observe the reflection of Shade's inner world. Similarly, the mirror held by Kinbote to Shade's poetry reveals Kinbote's inner world. The two mirrors, Shade's and Kinbote's, face each other, and in the reflection of one mind we can therefore perceive the reflection of the other. The novel's tension arises from the fact that these two confronting mirrors are not of the same construction. Nor are they *nonnon* mirrors. The two worlds are located at two opposite poles, yet they intersect at a certain point and reflect one another.

In connection with Shade's poem, much critical attention has been paid to the various meanings that the word "shade" invokes, such as "shadow," "phantom," and so on. The first line of Shade's poem includes the word "shadow": "I was the shadow of the waxwing slain."[49] The first stanza comprises twelve lines, or six rhyming couplets. At the beginning of the first stanza, we encounter the image of a waxwing that mistook the reflection of the sky in the window for the real sky, which has cost it its life. In the first note of his commentary, Kinbote posits the idea of the poet and the dead bird as one and the same, making use of this confluence to veer into a series of digressions and diverse interpretations: "We can visualize John Shade in his early boyhood, a physically unattractive but otherwise beautifully developed lad, experiencing his first eschatological shock."[50] Shade touches the dead bird and becomes familiar with death for the first time. When in the last year of Shade's life, Kinbote "had the fortune of being his neighbor," he often saw waxwings feeding nearby. He also identified in New Wye, with the help of the gardener, a number of "tropical-looking little strangers and their comical calls," and observed that a crested bird called in Zemblan *sampel* ("silktail") resembles the waxwing "in shape and shade, is the model of one of the three heraldic creatures . . . in the armorial bearings of the Zemblan King, Charles the Beloved (born 1915)."[51] Finally, he gives the date when the first lines of the poem were written, a few minutes after midnight on July 1, which synchronizes with the date of Gradus's departure from the Zemblan capital on July 5.[52] Kinbote's digressions notwithstanding, the images embedded in the opening four lines of the poem are quite different from the commentary's interpretation. Shade identifies with the shadow of the bird, not the bird itself, and in the third and fourth lines, we see that the shadow of the bird lives on in the reflection of the sky. Kinbote construes Shade's imaginary world as his real one. By contrast, Shade's soul, like the bird's shadow—the artist living and working—continues to soar in this world of imagination and reflections.

In the following lines, the repeated imagery evokes the theme of a shadow or a reflection. Shade, who is now in his bedroom, sees his reflection beside a lamp and an apple on a plate, in the glass of the window, the darkness outside serving as a background. The room and all its furniture appear to be suspended above the lawn. In his notes, Kinbote remains silent about these lines. In the last lines of the first stanza, snow, still falling, has covered the lawn. The reflections of the chair and the bed appear to be standing in the snow "in that crystal land."[53] In his commentary, Kinbote offers only two notes about the twelve lines of the first stanza entitled "Lines 1–4: I was the shadow of the waxwing slain" and "Line 12: that crystal land." He opens this second note with the claim that this is probably an allusion to "Zembla, my dear country."[54] Among Shade's early draft pages of the poem, Kinbote finds two lines that were later removed: "Ah, I must not forget to say something / That my friend told me of a certain king."[55] The two lines are clearly juvenile and not of the caliber of the rest of the poem. Are they forgeries by Kinbote? Would Kinbote go this far to prove that "Pale Fire" concerns Zembla? Is the reader aware of Nabokov's irony? Much farther on (in the note to line 550), Kinbote suffers from a guilty conscience, confessing, albeit indirectly, that these two lines are "distorted and tainted by wistful thinking."[56] Mad or otherwise, Kinbote truly admires Shade's genius. Following the two possibly forged lines, Kinbote digresses once more to detail how he would often rebuke the poet, saying "You really should promise to use all that wonderful stuff, you bad gray poet, you!"[57] He refers to his own stories of Zembla and the reign of Charles the Beloved; when he was still in Zembla, Charles taught in disguise like an ordinary teacher simply because he loved literature. There is also an implicit allusion here to the similarity between Charles and Kinbote.

In the poem's first canto, we become acquainted with Shade the poet. In the realm of imagination, he is able serenely to cast his dead body aside and carry on flying like the shadow of a bird. Moreover, poetry allows him to re-create everyday life in the magical world of art. This is a strange form of creativity that seems deceptively simple, though reminiscent of Robert Frost, himself a devotee of Alexander Pope. It is no accident that in the poem, Shade writes that all colors, even a simple gray, make him happy: "My eyes were such that literally they / Took photographs."[58] He says that he was brought up by his aunt Maud, a bizarre but lovable character: "A poet and a painter with a taste / For realistic objects interlaced / With grotesque growths and images of doom." Her room was preserved, unchanged since the day she died, like "A still life in her style: the paperweight / Of convex glass enclosing a lagoon."[59] With this paperweight Shade offers us another image: that of the numerous echoes of this canto, the multitude of reflections of everyday life in the mirror of art.[60] His imagined self, released from normal routines, finds life to be something like a crystal cage, a cage that, according to him, has been constructed "artistically."[61] Shade discerns a "beautiful and strange" phenomenon: the reflection of the rainbow of a thunderstorm in a distant "opal cloudlet."[62] This is another transparent circle that retains, within it, the reflections of both living phenomena and crystal cages. But we are not dealing with mere reflection: with every object, its core purpose or "the time of the object" finds itself imprisoned within the crystal cage too, and thus becomes eternal, timeless.

The second canto is a description of life's joys and sorrows. It opens with the idea of death—Shade's obsession—though it is also in this canto that he elaborates his love for a young woman who eventually becomes his wife. At the time of writing, they have been married for forty years. Shade addresses her just as Nabokov addresses his own wife, Vera, and as Vadim in *Look at the Harlequins!* addresses his true love: "You."[63] Shade also writes, in even greater detail, of his love for another girl: the daughter he lost. Both are very Nabokovian reflections: a celebration of life, love, and marriage and the simultaneous constant awareness of death and fear of loss. Beside a seemingly safe and stable family life, an "abyss" suddenly appears. The cruel and the absurd lurk around every corner, not just in totalitarian societies or under exceptional circumstances, but on the margins of everyday life, where we feel safest and most secure.[64] Death takes his beloved daughter away. Reality may seem simple and straightforward, but he does not find the reality of death easy to accept. Like his creator, John Shade spends his life searching for proof that death is not the end. Like Nabokov, he wants to convince himself that ghosts of our dearly departed remain in contact with us somehow. John Shade is too intelligent to accept just any myths or notions, but he never gives up trying to find something that would enable him to believe. Shade's belief system lies, in fact, outside the realm of religion, unlike that of Kinbote, who carries on an almost endless argument with the poet with respect to faith. Yet in this search for an afterlife, the road ahead appears treacherous and the destination always an enigma. What remains readily comprehensible is ordinary life—but what moment in any life can reasonably be labeled "ordinary" or "normal"? Crucial for Shade are his love for his wife and the grief they share over losing their daughter. He recognizes them as distinct emotions, yet they are inseparable. He also ponders dichotomies like death after life and life after death. The most common phenomena (birth, love, death) fuel his most abstract thoughts.

In the third canto, Shade engages directly with the theme of death. One of the characteristics that distinguish Shade from Kinbote (and on a different level, from Gradus) is the way the poet arrives at his abstract thoughts (not merely the ideas themselves). Every one of Shade's thoughts arises from his own life experience: the outcome of feeling love and sorrow and manifold other emotions. Compared to Kinbote's life (real or imagined), Shade's seems dull, but only Shade dares to travel to the depths of every experience, both to love and mourn deeply. Kinbote, meanwhile, changes his "friends" all the time but remains alone, never genuinely experiencing love or loss, never investing in life profoundly. If Shade considers death to be an enormous void, for Kinbote it is life that is empty. Another difference between poet and critic is that Shade is naturally curious; the process of his thoughts is based on his desire to know. Kinbote, like all of Nabokov's fictional monsters, is cursed with a lack of curiosity, and therefore a lack of empathy. While Shade wants to know, Kinbote wants to impose what he already knows, or thinks he knows, on the world, including his interpretation of a dead man's poem. Even before his daughter's death, Shade explores a number of ways better to understand life after death, visiting the "Institute (I) of Preparation (P) / For the Hereafter (H)."[65] (This recalls a similar institute in *The Gift*.) He finds that this lay institute is of no use to him, and the tasteless venture helps him to know what "to ignore in my survey / Of death's abyss." He also agrees with his wife, observing as they drive by the institute, "I really could not tell / The difference between this place and Hell."[66] Eventually, the poet suffers an attack or fit, and his heart stops briefly. He comes back to life from this seizure, feeling he had "crossed / The border," returning with the memory of seeing a tall white fountain ("The tale I told provoked my doctor's mirth"). To the poet, the fountain is, naturally, real, and when he reads in a magazine about a woman who has had a similar experience and also saw a white fountain, he hastens to meet her. Eventually, he finds out that there was a misprint: the woman had seen the image of a mountain, not a fountain. "Life Everlasting—based on a misprint!"[67] From this Shade learns that "texture" is what is significant, not "text," and "topsy-turvical coincidence" is more important than dream: "Some kind of link-and-bobolink, some kind / Of correlated pattern in the game, / Plexed artistry, and something of the same / Pleasure in it as they who played it found."[68]

In life, then, as well as in art, Shade seeks the magical coincidence that implies a hidden pattern. Only through art can he find answers to the questions unanswered by life. The fourth and last canto is about poetry and the ways poems are made. Shade describes two methods of composing: in method A a poem takes form solely in the poet's mind and in method B on a sheet of paper. Naturally, each method has its advantages and disadvantages.

> In method B the hand supports the thought,
> The abstract battle is concretely fought.
> The pen stops in mid-air, then swoops to bar
> A canceled sunset or restore a star,
> And thus it physically guides the phrase
> Toward faint daylight through the inky maze.
> But method A is agony! The brain
> Is soon enclosed in a steel cap of pain,
> A muse in overalls directs the drill
> Which grinds and which no effort of the will
> Can interrupt, while the automaton
> Is taking off what he has just put on
> Or walking briskly to the corner store
> To buy the paper he has read before.[69]

Shade then lists the things he likes, and—as our author is Nabokov—he also recounts the things abhors. *Poshlust* makes an appearance here:

> Now I shall speak of evil as none has
> Spoken before. I loathe such things as jazz;
> The white-hosed moron torturing a black
> Bull, rayed with red; abstractist bric-a-brac;
> Primitivist folk-masks; progressive schools;
> Music in supermarkets; swimming pools;
> Brutes, bores, class-conscious Philistines, Freud, Marx,
> Fake thinkers, puffed-up poets, frauds and sharks.[70]

Every search leads to art, art being the apparently figurative sky. The bird with a body is killed so that its shadow can fly in infinite space. In addition to this juxtaposition of the real and the reflected, a number of circular or mirror images recur through the poem, reminiscent of the landscapes enclosed in Aunt Maud's glass cage. Glass, crystal, and snow link various parts of the poem, functioning as symbolic mirrors: moons that steal light as well as suns that give light. The poet leaves his poem incomplete. Kinbote's contention that the poem completes itself when the first line is reread as the last seems feasible, because instead of closing, the circle of images continues forever in the form of a spiral, and there's a magical gravitational force pulling all the elements of the novel inexorably toward a central originating point of contact between the bird and the windowpane, the site where art takes flight.

4

Let us return to Charles Kinbote himself, the novel's apparent antagonist. In the fourth canto, Shade refers to *"Man's life as commentary to abstruse | Unfinished poem,"* adding "Note for further use."[71] In his commentary on these lines, Kinbote, uncharacteristically avoids digression. He simply writes: "If I correctly understand the sense of this succinct observation, our poet suggests here that human life is but a series of footnotes to a vast obscure unfinished masterpiece."[72] The thought expressed here reflects the relationship between Shade and Kinbote. If Shade's life can be seen as a commentary on his art, it follows that Kinbote's life can be assessed through his commentary. Kinbote's personality has two principal characteristics: like most of Nabokov's protagonists, he is an exiled immigrant, and like most exiles in Nabokov's fiction, he struggles with the problem of identity. Most of these exiles are busy rebuilding their pasts in pursuit of a lost dream but Kinbote's problem is not merely living in the void of exile. The reader will not find even an iota of reliable information about Kinbote's past, because his imaginary world and his inner void preclude a past. If Kinbote is a tragic character, this is why; Nabokov's perennial exile has here reached a point where he no longer has a past or a present. He has nothing. This is what fuels Kinbote's abject dependence on Shade.

In most of Nabokov's works, the protagonists are creative and therefore unique—in contrast with the antagonists, who are neither individual nor endowed with creative faculties. Recalling Richard Rorty's remarks on creativity and the imagination, in *Lolita* and in *Pale Fire* we come across a new form of central character: Humbert and Kinbote are at once creative and destructive "genius-monsters." Humbert falls in love with a young and defenseless girl, and Kinbote is in love with a poet or, in fact, with an unfinished poem (itself defenseless because Shade is dead). In other words, each manages to create a world around his object of desire, capitalizing upon Nabokov's astonishing expressive power at its height. Yet their creativity also involves destruction, because despite their passion, they see nothing outside of themselves; love breeds hatred and knowledge spreads ignorance. Kinbote, as an example of Rorty's "monster of incuriosity," exposes in his own personality the dangers of solipsism in creative people.[73] Some of Kinbote's personality is conveyed through the eyes of Sybil, Shade's wife, who has always disliked him. She describes him as "an elephantine tick; a king-sized botfly; a macaco worm; the monstrous parasite of a genius."[74] He is a "parasite" as he has no life of his own and feeds off of Shade's poetry, and he is a monster because he attaches no value to other people's lives as he relentlessly plunders from them in order to construct his own imaginary identity. If in tales and fables monsters cruelly murder the innocent, Kinbote's "murder" of Shade is symbolic because in stealing Shade's poem, he also steals his life.

Still, in a distorted way, Kinbote and Shade are cut from the same cloth. Kinbote claims that he has gradually provided Shade with the King of Zembla's life story, hoping that he would immortalize Charles in his poem. When the poet is killed, Kinbote discovers that the poem is not about Charles at all but is a poetic autobiography, whose protagonist is the exact opposite of Kinbote. Then Kinbote rereads the poem and arrives at a different conclusion: although Shade has betrayed him by not mentioning Kinbote's Zembla whatsoever, "Pale Fire" on reflection appears imbued with aspects of his stories. He claims that in his commentary and prose style he is "borrowing a kind of opalescent light from my poet's fiery orb, and unconsciously aping the prose style of his own critical essays."[75] To call Shade and Kinbote "polar opposites" is therefore both accurate and insufficient. The similarities that arise between Shade's poetic autobiography and Kinbote's Zemblan life story cannot be simply ignored; these proximities complicate the relationship between Shade and Kinbote but also provide an essential key to understanding the novel.

Kinbote describes an encounter with a visiting German professor, Professor Pardon, who claims to have been to Zembla and who notices the resemblance between Kinbote and Charles. As there are other lecturers present when they meet, Kinbote is forced to deny any connection. An argument about similarities ensues, and Kinbote, who has not shaved for about a year (presumably to disguise himself), seeks to deflect attention from himself with a joke: "All bearded Zemblans resembled one another." He continues: "the name Zembla is a corruption not of the Russian *zemlya*, but of Semberland, a land of reflections, of 'resemblers.'"[76] Linguistic shenanigans aside, the central notion is unambiguous: Zembla is the land of resemblances, of reflections, as between the sun and moon, recalling the light the moon takes from the sun, likewise evoking the first lines of Shade's poem: a windowpane, mirroring the sky, steals its reflection. This evocation also mirrors the relationship between art and reality, and between Kinbote and Shade in both the different ways they approach the power of imagination and their shared identity as artists. Shade reconstructs the reality of his

life in a poem, and Kinbote re-creates his own life as allegory in his commentary on the same poem. Zembla resembles Aunt Maud's crystal paperweight in Shade's poem, "convex glass enclosing a lagoon."[77] In Kinbote's
commentary, he cites his Uncle Conmal's description of the Zemblan language as "the tongue of the mirror."[78] An imaginary land dependent on the
so-called real world, Zembla becomes a metaphor for the novel's principal
theme, the distorted reflection of one world in the mirror of another.

This theme is writ large in Uncle Conmal's life story. Conmal is the
half-brother of the queen, Charles's mother. He learns English by himself,
simply by memorizing a dictionary, and works for roughly half a century
translating Shakespeare, subsequently focusing on poets who emerged in
the Bard's wake. On his only trip to London, he finds the city shrouded
in fog and the language incomprehensible. While translating Kipling, he
falls ill; his dying words ask in French what the English word for death is:
"Comment dit-on 'mourir' en anglais?"[79] The Zemblan edition of *Timon
of Athens,* owned by Kinbote, is, in fact, Conmal's translation. Kinbote retranslates into English an extract from the play. This is a futile endeavor, as
the key quotation (Shakespeare's reference to "pale fire") is lost in translation. Kinbote is fully aware of the farce: Shakespeare translated by someone with no knowledge of English. What he fails to register is the ironic extent to which his own commentary on Shade's poem resembles his uncle's
translation of Shakespeare. Nonetheless, Conmal, though foolish and un-
hinged, is treated respectfully; Quixote, at his most ridiculous, remains likable. Conmal, referring to Zemblan as the "tongue of the mirror," identifies
that distorted and stolen resemblances are not limited to ideas or memories,
but apply to language itself, and Conmal's definition of Zemblan can apply
equally to Shade's poetry and to Kinbote's commentary. Kinbote, then, is a
creator, however warped his approach, and he shares certain similarities of
situation with Pnin. As with Pnin, known or unknown enemies surround
him; like Pnin, he is in exile and far from home; and, like Pnin, Kinbote
pines for a lost culture, an imaginary world.

Kinbote and Shade share an artistic mentality. Like Shade, and Nabokov himself, Kinbote is smitten with the magical nature of art. In his foreword he writes that his admiration for Shade was a sort of "alpine cure" and

that whenever he looked at him he "experienced a grand sense of wonder," especially in the presence "of other people, inferior people." He believes that others took the poet for granted and failed to discern "the romance of his presence." Kinbote very much exemplifies Nabokov's enchanted reader when he writes, "I am witnessing a unique physiological phenomenon: John Shade perceiving and transforming the world, taking it in and taking it apart, re-combining its elements in the very process of storing them up so as to produce at some unspecified date an organic miracle, a fusion of image and music, a line of verse." Kinbote associates this phenomenon with a childhood memory of his uncle's castle and watching a magician eating vanilla ice cream after a fantastic performance. "I stared at his powdered cheeks, at the magical flower in his buttonhole where it had passed through a succession of different colors and had now become fixed as a white carnation, and especially at his marvelous fluid-looking fingers which could if he chose make his spoon dissolve into a sunbeam by twiddling it, or turn his plate into a dove by tossing it up in the air."[80] This, of course, is symptomatic of the relation between art and magic in Nabokov's work. In his fascination Kinbote reminds us of V in *The Real Life of Sebastian Knight*, who although very different from him, is similarly enthralled by his brother's creative genius. When V observes Sebastian looking at pigeons that will be fictionalized later (in Sebastian's third book, *Lost Property*), he witnesses the writer constantly using his eyes, likened to a camera by Shade, to record what Nabokov calls the "divine details."[81] Kinbote, like Sebastian, is also drawing on his artistry to subvert and reinvent the realities around him. The magic of art lies in the artist's unconscious and transformative practice of alchemy, producing his interpretation of the world as he sees it. Kinbote's description of Shade thus applies equally to himself. Increasingly, after Nabokov's migration to the United States in 1940, he relinquished his last links to Russia, and what emerged was a revised focus not only on the writer-conjurer but also on the reader, a gifted but limited reader, fascinated by creative genius.

When similarities between Charles and Kinbote are discussed, Shade defends Kinbote (according to the latter), saying that they do not really resemble each other: "Resemblances are the shadows of differences. Differ-

ent people see different similarities and similar differences."[82] Though it
may appear that it is Kinbote who interprets and explains Shade, perhaps
it is really Shade who gives substance to Kinbote. We are familiar with their
similarities, but what are their differences? Shade, with his apparently constant and stable values, has been raised in a democracy and epitomizes a
particular form of artistic conviction: he has lived in one country his entire
life, in the same state, and even in the same house; he has ever loved only
one woman and has remained faithful to her. Moreover, his standing in society is stable, as is his link to his past; he is able to preserve Aunt Maud's
room just as it was in her lifetime, filled with her eccentric possessions.
This basic sense of security and his loving personal relationships enable
him to empathize and sympathize, and likewise to distinguish between past
and present and between reality and fancy. By contrast, Kinbote, whose
life is defined by instability and homelessness, is unable to make these dis-
tinctions. Like Shade, he is gifted with a creative mind, but unlike him,
Kinbote lacks the curiosity and empathy necessary to give shape and substance to his creative urges. It follows that if Sebastian confronts Goodman,
Cincinnatus confronts M'sieur Pierre, and Krug confronts Paduk, the confrontation between Shade and Kinbote is subtler because of their affinities.
In *Pale Fire,* lines of demarcation between protagonist and antagonist are
blurred. Gradus has the task of representing *poshlust* and showing blind
obedience to the group. It is in Gradus, the murderer, that we find traces
of Paduk and other villains. In contrast, monsters like Kinbote and Humbert enjoy a complexity (and a complicity with their victim) that is missing
in other villains.

     The differences between Shade and Kinbote thus originate with Kin-
bote's instability. Losing one's homeland, culture, and language is obviously not unique to Kinbote; it happens also to Pnin, who eventually stands
on his own two feet. Pnin learns to remember his past and, more important, to forget his past. Pnin also learns how to reconstruct both the past
and the present. Kinbote's instability transcends his statelessness, however.
He lacks an inner homeland, the sort of home and culture that no one can
take away. This is the principal difference between Shade and Kinbote (and
Nabokov cleverly conceals this difference in the way he renders his char-

acters): Shade possesses an inner anchor, the portable home central to a creative mind, while Kinbote, deprived of that anchor and its related sense of self to locate him both in reality and in imagination, is in essence without both; all he owns is an infinite void. Cincinnatus finds his appetite for survival in his other rebellious creative self, Krug locates his in his love for his family, and Pnin draws sustenance from his passion for his work and his memories. But for Kinbote, the past is a blank canvas on which he can draw whatever he likes. Thus Kinbote, unlike Shade, conceals his true ego in a self-made fantasy world and loses track of that ego. Unlike Krug, nourished by his love for his family, and unlike Pnin, nourished by his lost love, Kinbote can only feed on this imaginary past and Shade's present (real and imaginary), because he has no real past or present of his own. Kinbote's character combines the positive traits associable with, for example, Pnin, yet also calls to mind the executioners of *Invitation to a Beheading* and *Bend Sinister.* What links Kinbote in an intricate and circuitous way to M'sieur Pierre and his ilk is Kinbote's interference in Shade's life. But M'sieur Pierre, who has no creative faculties whatsoever, can only destroy. Kinbote is struggling to re-create himself and is so obsessed with seeking to define this unstable self that he is able to communicate with others only through the similarities (and, of course, differences) that he finds between himself and them, or seeks to impose on these relationships.

The parasitic quality of his relationships stems from Kinbote's inability to construct a world that will transcend and outlast the tyrannies of time and man. The figure of Charles, concocted by Kinbote, acquires aspects of Shade's life and art to such an extent that Kinbote steals Shade's description of his adored wife in the first few lines of the second canto for his own purposes. (Kinbote says that Sybil is only a few months older than her husband; she must be sixty-one in the summer when Shade writes "Pale Fire.")[83] The poet describes Sybil's profile when she was in high school and states that it has not changed. He details her glistening teeth, "the shade beneath / The eye from the long lashes; the peach down / Rimming the cheekbone," silky brown hair and bare neck, "the Persian shape / Of nose and eyebrow."[84] It is an idealistic version of her real self: he sees in her today the young girl she used to be. Kinbote claims that Queen Disa, Charles's wife,

looks similar: "Disa at thirty, when last seen in September 1958, bore a singular resemblance not, of course, to Mrs. Shade as she was when I met her,
but to the idealized and stylized picture painted by the poet in those lines
of *Pale Fire*."[85] Is Sybil's image in Shade's poem idealistic because he finds
Sybil herself ideal? Conversely, the image of idealized Disa (whom Kinbote
considers to be real) is contingent upon Shade's poem. Kinbote writes in
his commentary that he hopes the reader will "appreciate[] the strangeness
of this, because if he does not, there is no sense in writing poems, or notes
to poems, or anything at all."[86]

One of the central themes of *Pale Fire* is the similarity between art
and reality. At first glance this seems like a highly improbable similarity
(like the resemblance between Sybil and Disa or between Shade's poetry
and Kinbote's commentary), but the essence of the likeness is defined by
way of strangeness. Every trace of real life that finds its way into a work of
art is transformed into a new reality — any comparison between the realities
of life and those of art are, by definition, accompanied by wonder. Hence
the distinction Shade draws when he says, "Resemblances are the shadows
of differences. Different people see different similarities and similar differences."[87] This theme can be found throughout Nabokov's fiction. In *The
Gift,* for example, we come across a familiar address written countless times
until one day it makes us hesitate — it looks unfamiliar. Or we encounter a
familiar word such as "ceiling" spelled "sealing" or "sea-ling." We keep
persisting with trusted forms until we end up with a "completely wild and
unfamiliar" word such as "ice-ling" or "inglice."[88] What is especially concerning is that this may happen across our entire life. After all, this is what
every work of art does with every object. Kinbote maintains that Shade has
constructed "Pale Fire" on the basis of Kinbote's own accounts and, as a result, he has the right to extract his true version from Shade's poem. Toward
the end of his commentary, he explains in a note that following his disap-
pointment on first reading the poem, he reread it, this time more attentively.
Expecting less, he liked the poem better, and he writes, "My commentary
to this poem, now in the hands of my readers, represents an attempt to sort
out those echoes and wavelets of fire, and pale phosphorescent hints, and
all the many subliminal debts to me." With these notes, Kinbote exacts, as
he puts it, his "little revenge."[89]

On one occasion, when Kinbote is alone with Shade and has related another part of Charles's story (concerning Charles and Disa's relationship), Shade raises two questions: "How can you know that all this intimate stuff about your rather appalling king is true? And if true, how can one hope to print such personal things about people who, presumably, are still alive?"[90] Kinbote tells him not to worry about such trifles; the good news is that once the poem is complete, Kinbote will divulge an "ultimate truth, an extraordinary secret, that will put your mind completely at rest."[91] This apparently is when he will share the secret that Charles the Beloved is none other than himself. In the meantime, Kinbote reveals something more interesting for the reader: as soon as the poem is transmuted into poetry by Shade, "the stuff *will* be true, and the people *will* come alive. A poet's purified truth can cause no pain, no offense. True art is above false honor."[92] Kinbote is right to say that art will resurrect and redeem the reality it shapes. The problem is that in requiring him to recount his Zemblan narrative, Kinbote demands that Shade build an imaginary world for his truth, one that will provide an identity for Kinbote, and allow him to become real. Everyday reality provides the ingredients for imagination in Shade's case, but for Kinbote the opposite is true: he replaces an object with the reflection of that object. Even in magic, as Alice and her travels to Wonderland demonstrate, there should be some association with reality to permit imagination to become meaningful. For Shade, the world of art is the world of magical reflections, a very traditional notion (Shade writes a traditional poem). Is it possible for a person whose reflection we see in a mirror to walk away and leave her reflection behind to live on without her? Though Kinbote (unlike Nabokov) holds no unconventional ideas of art, he successfully, and profoundly, alters Shade's image. But Kinbote, having discarded his own identity, has become a captive reflection. Imprisoned in a mirror, it can attain salvation and reality only with the help of a creator. The elegant balance of *Pale Fire* comes from beyond the conflict between Kinbote and Shade, where Nabokov's adored "new art" shimmers, free from dependence on either reality or its reflection.

When Professor Pardon, the German professor, questions Kinbote's real identity, saying that he was under the impression that he was born in Russia, Shade asks: "Didn't you tell me, Charles, that *kinbote* means regi-

cide in your language?" To which Kinbote responds, "Yes, a king's de-
stroyer." Professor Pardon replies too, telling Shade that he must be mistaking Kinbote for a refugee from Nova Zembla. Kinbote adds, in brackets,
that he longed "to explain that a king who sinks his identity in the mirror
of exile is in a sense just that."[93] Thus, at its most profound level, the mirror theme is embedded not only in the structure of the novel but also in its
very language. Kinbote is a vessel of language. Language is our only way of
articulating and thereby possessing our reality; it is our portable home. The
only asset owned by émigré Russians was the Russian language, written in
the form they brought with them (the Bolsheviks altered even the Russian
alphabet, removing letters they considered superfluous). In the third canto,
we encounter the image of a decrepit old man, a refugee not related to Kinbote's story, whose last gasps are voiced in "two tongues" at the moment of
his death. Kinbote offers an apparently nonsensical, but beautiful, analysis
of these two tongues, in a simple list, without any explanation: "English
and Zemblan, English and Russian, English and Lettish, English and Esto-
nian, English and Lithuanian, English and Russian, English and Ukrainian, English and Polish, English and Czech, English and Russian, English
and Hungarian, English and Rumanian, English and Albanian, English and
Bulgarian, English and Serbo-Croatian, English and Russian, American
and European."[94] This more or less rhythmic list gains a certain form of poignancy, especially because the pairing of "English and Russian" is repeated
four times. It is probably more expressive than any detailed description or
poetic imagery in its evocation of the helplessness of exile and the bitterness
of lacking language. How can we simply write Kinbote off as a lunatic? And
how can we possibly laugh at him?

5

Jakob Gradus is the murderer in *Pale Fire,* the third central character in the
novel, and, according to Kinbote, Shade's killer by accident, his intended
victim having been Kinbote. Gradus is a completely negative character, depicted through his links to the world of glass and mirrors. In the novel's
index, we come across the name "Sudarg." In a brief note, Kinbote mentions "*Sudarg of Bokay,* a mirror maker of genius, the patron saint of Bokay

in the mountains of Zembla . . . life span not known."[95] In Kinbote's commentary, too, we find that Sudarg of Bokay is the maker of one of Zembla's astonishing magical mirrors.[96] Obviously, "Sudarg" is "Gradus" read from right to left, as in a mirror, as Bokay is Yakob, recalling Jakob. Shade imprisons reality in the glass cage of his poem, and Kinbote is able to drown himself in a world of mirrors of his own invention. Each is a prison created by the association of ideas facilitated by the power of imagination. Sudarg is an artful sorcerer who works with the world of light, color, and reflection. The negative reflection of Sudarg, Gradus, lacks imagination though he deals in glass. The significance of Gradus (even though he is no more than a figment of Kinbote's imagination within the framework of the novel) becomes evident through his relationship with Kinbote. If Kinbote senses his inner void and seeks to fill it, Gradus feels nothing. He used to work in a glass factory but had no talent for it. He likes crystal objects, but when he sees a small crystal giraffe in a souvenir shop in Geneva, and later a little hippopotamus made of violet glass, all he does is ask the price, before purchasing other things.[97] Gradus prefers to see objects as monochromatic, gray; his aim is to bleach fancy of its colors.

There is a reason why the Zemblan revolution begins in an annex of the glass works and why Gradus, a grotesque figure, "a cross between bat and crab," is tasked with regicide. An especially devout group of Extremists calling themselves the Shadows draws up the plot. They are "the shadow twins of the Karlists and indeed several had cousins or even brothers among the followers of the King."[98] For example, if Odon helps Charles to escape, it is his brother Nodo who sends Gradus after him. Kinbote (and ultimately Nabokov) relishes every chance to describe Gradus: "Mere springs and coils produced the inward movements of our clockwork man. He might be termed a Puritan. One essential dislike, formidable in its simplicity, pervaded his dull soul: he disliked injustice and deception. He disliked their union—they were always together—with a wooden passion that neither had, nor needed, words to express itself."[99] This might even be praiseworthy in another, Kinbote finds, but in this case is "a by-product of the man's hopeless stupidity." Anything that surpasses Gradus's understanding is considered suspect; he worships general ideas "with pedantic aplomb. The generality was godly, the specific diabolical. If one person was poor and the other wealthy it did not matter what precisely had ruined one or made the other rich; the difference itself was unfair, and the poor man who did not denounce it was as wicked as the rich one who ignored it."[100]

In Nabokov's fiction, we often encounter characters like Gradus, by different names and in different guises. Such characters tend to have always one particular role such as executioner or murderer. Like Gradus, they dislike and mistrust "people who knew too much, scientists, writers, mathematicians, crystalographers and so forth."[101] If life is hollow and meaningless without light and color playing their parts, without fancy and the fire of imagination, this does not concern Gradus, who can neither relate to the world of others, as Shade does, nor be sufficiently indifferent to others to create his own world, like Kinbote. It is only a character like Gradus, an upholder of generalizations and uniformity, who can, readily and in cold blood, kill a human being—even if it is the wrong one; because for Gradus one person is indistinguishable from another. In Nabokov's earlier novels, *Invitation to a Beheading* and *Bend Sinister,* this type of character, the main enemy of creativity and compassion, is also the antagonist. However, in the complex and intricate *Pale Fire,* we encounter two creative minds in conflict. In other words, in *Pale Fire,* the combination of creative genius (Shade) and his murderer (Gradus/Gray) is complicated by Kinbote, who has Shade's imagination but like Gradus lacks empathy—if Jacques Gray/Gradus kills Shade in reality, Kinbote plans an assault on Shade's imagination, through the theft and reinvention of his poem. Accordingly, death casts not one shadow over Shade's life but two. As if to emphasize this twofold shadow, Kinbote is insistent in his commentary on the simultaneity of different stages in Gradus's journey and the dates of composition of the four cantos of Shade's poem. In the same way that he brings his fabulous Zembla to a little university town in America, Kinbote imposes Gradus on the novel's playful workings of light and shadow. Gradus draws closer and closer: the farther the poem and its commentary advance, the louder the steps become, as though Kinbote alone can hear the echo of death's footfalls in the real or imaginary landscapes of life.

Holding a French passport, Gradus flies from Onhava, the Zemblan capital, to Copenhagen, and then on to Paris, Geneva, and Nice. These flights coincide with Shade's composition of the opening lines of canto 2.

Kinbote draws attention to these chronological coincidences throughout his commentary in order to justify an ongoing account of Gradus's life story. Gradus's first mission is to provide the Shadows with Charles's assumed name and whereabouts, which he bungles but eventually discovers after a plethora of mix-ups and errors. Gradus then flies to New York and finally on to New Wye, where he kills Shade instead of Kinbote. Gradus's fundamental characteristic is his lack of success; he fails at every undertaking—in his career, in his private life, and in his political activities. If Pnin is perceived as unsuccessful, it is only in the eyes of the mediocre characters of the novel. Pnin's failure is indicative of the banality of what surrounds him. Gradus, by contrast, is banality incarnate, and has no other redeeming world.[102] Even when he finally succeeds in his homicidal mission, he murders the wrong man.

Gradus is a figment of Kinbote's imagination, and Kinbote is an imaginary character in a novel by Vladimir Nabokov. Nonetheless, life outside the novel, the weight of reality, is not without significance: the Gradus episode recalls Trotsky's assassination. For Nabokov, however, there is a more important association, and the reader can find hints that lead to Nabokov's biography; as Brian Boyd reminds us, Shade's murder occurs on July 21, Nabokov's father's birthday.[103] Once again, a seemingly irrelevant detail discloses something that torments Nabokov on a deeply personal level. Sebastian Knight, too, maintains a distance while writing about feelings that are intensely private. How can we not be reminded of Vladimir Dmitrievich Nabokov when we read *Pale Fire*? Gradus brings to mind the two Gradus-like fascists who mistakenly murdered Vladimir Dmitrievich. Personal feelings and emotions color Nabokov's fiction: the catastrophe of his beloved father's death had a profound effect on him. He could hide his sorrow, but he could never forget it, and the only way he could take his revenge was through fiction. Beyond the at first apparently farcical nature of Gradus's dark, ponderous personality, and behind Kinbote's madness in envisioning a nightmare featuring this grotesque scarecrow, we glimpse the memory of an unforgotten sorrow. Yet curiously, it is the flippant tone of the novel that keeps the bitterness of the real tragedy alive.[104]

The simple way that Nabokov presents Jakob Gradus does not detract from his symbolic importance. Gradus is the only character in the novel who does not dream (unless of blood occasionally, according to Kinbote).[105] Instead, he has only ideology, objective, and means. Kinbote explains his mean-mindedness, describing him eating a "small, softish, nearham sandwich, vaguely associated with the train journey from Nice to Paris last Saturday night,"[106] even though he has plenty of money. It is not only stupidity that makes him lick his thumb before turning a page of the newspaper, gaping at the pictures, his lips moving "like wrestling worms" as he works down the columns of printed matter. He sleeps "lying belly up *on* the bedclothes, in striped pajamas," without removing his socks, and begins his "blurry daily existence by blowing his nose." He washes his hands scrupulously, "with the nice, modern liquid soap" and this made him feel neat and clean. He had shaved yesterday, so that it was "out of the way."[107] In Gradus's world, colors have become so manipulated that they have faded completely. Noise does not bother him, and can even be a pleasant surprise as it takes his mind off things. It is of note that if Jakob Gradus exists only in Kinbote's imagination, then Jack Grey, the mad criminal who escapes from jail in order to kill a judge and who eventually commits suicide in another prison, belongs to the so-called real world. But there is no difference between Jakob Gradus and Jack Grey; they are of the same stock. Unlike Shade's world of light and crystal or Kinbote's world of mirrors, the world of Gradus/Grey consists only of dark, opaque glass that rejects light and color. Nevertheless, a fact of both Shade's and Kinbote's realities is the certainty of a Grey/Gradus—in Zembla or in America, there is always an assassin who can pass through walls of mirrors and glass; a would-be murderer is always with us, and his bullets always kill, even if only unintended targets.

6

At the end of his commentary, Kinbote considers what his future holds. "God will help me, I trust, to rid myself of any desire to follow the example of two other characters in this work. I shall continue to exist."[108] He realizes he will have to adapt, relocate, find another campus to prowl, another guise, perhaps as an "old, happy, healthy, heterosexual Russian, a writer in exile, sans fame, sans future, sans audience, sans anything but his art."[109]

This overt reference to his ever-playful creator, Nabokov, implies a certain authorial kinship with Kinbote—and the quartet of "sans," a clear echo of the end of Jaques's "seven ages of man" speech in *As You Like It,* invokes Shakespeare. Nabokov's presence in his own fiction is nothing new; he has made an appearance in many other books, but in *Pale Fire,* he both appears in relation to the adored protagonist, John Shade, and emerges from behind Kinbote's mask. The very possibility that a Kinbote could have become a Nabokov gives credence to the suspicion that Kinbote is no ordinary monster, no Gradus, but one who implicates us, because he reminds us that we could be he—he could be our demonic double. Kinbote goes on to weigh more alternatives for what he could do now: perhaps he will make a motion picture—*Escape from Zembla,* for instance—or forge a new theatrical career, "pander to the simple tastes of theatrical critics and cook up a stage play, an old-fashioned melodrama with three principals: a lunatic who intends to kill an imaginary king, another lunatic who imagines himself to be that king, and a distinguished old poet who stumbles by chance into the line of fire, and perishes in the clash between the two figments." The possibilities seem endless to Kinbote. "History permitting, I may sail back to my recovered kingdom, and with a great sob greet the gray coastline and the gleam of a roof in the rain. I may huddle and groan in the madhouse. But whatever happens, wherever the scene is laid, somebody, somewhere, will quietly set out—somebody has already set out, somebody still rather far away is buying a ticket, is boarding a bus, a ship, a plane, has landed, is walking towards a million photographers, and presently he will ring at my door—a bigger, more respectable, more competent Gradus."[110] These are the closing lines of the novel, apart from the index.

The essential components of Kinbote's personality are laid bare in the final sentences of the novel. The dreamer Kinbote cannot be separated from the lunatic Kinbote; the Kinbote who sees himself as a king and the Kinbote who thinks of himself as a lunatic are two sides of the same coin. The self-portrait gains complexity when Kinbote imagines staging a play. First, the theme of creativity versus reality is expressed with clarity; the poet, who is the creator of imaginary worlds (even though Shade fashions an autobiography with his poem), loses his reality in the fictitious confrontation between two make-believe characters. Conversely, another creator (the mad Kinbote) bestows reality on his imaginary Zembla as a result of his desire to return home. It is a long way since *The Real Life of Sebastian Knight,* and here there is no mistaking jewels for common pebbles. Second, Kinbote does not refer to two characters (Shade and Gradus) but to three (Shade, Gradus, and Kinbote). In the plot of the play described, it is Shade who is "real" to Kinbote: Kinbote considers himself to be an "imaginary" character, one of two figments. Glimmering in the depths of Kinbote's imaginary world, like a jewel in the water, lies the character of a writer in exile; Kinbote even claims that he may reappear in the guise of an exiled Russian writer, and this writer is surprisingly reminiscent of Nabokov. Nabokov, the character who frees Krug yet torments Pnin, the author of *Pnin* and *Pale Fire,* emerges from behind Kinbote's mask and not Shade's, which means, in the final assessment, that Nabokov sympathizes with Kinbote, or, to put it another way, Nabokov gives the novel's last word to Kinbote but sympathizes with both Shade and Kinbote, and leaves implicit that it is Shade's poem that will ultimately endure.

As detailed, Richard Rorty analyzes how cruelty is portrayed in Nabokov's oeuvre. For Rorty, Nabokov concentrates not on "the 'beastly farce' common to Lenin, Hitler, Gradus, and Paduk," or of torturers, executioners, and agents of fascist or communist totalitarianism, but on "the *special* sort of cruelty of which those capable of bliss are also capable." He also focuses on the possibility that there can be "sensitive killers, cruel aesthetes, pitiless poets — masters of imagery who are content to turn the lives of other human beings into images on a screen, while simply not noticing that these other people are suffering."[111] From Nabokov's standpoint, cruelty that stems from incuriosity is the worst possible sin; Rorty draws our attention to the comment in Nabokov's afterword to *Lolita,* where he associates "aesthetic bliss" with "curiosity, tenderness, kindness, ecstasy."[112] Curiosity, as Rorty notes, comes first. Nabokov the theorist, he argues, considers the creation of works of art to be the only duty of an artist, and, although he does not believe the artist or the author should have any social or moral responsibility toward society, Nabokov the author, especially as we find him in *Speak, Memory,* is horrified and repulsed by cruelty of any kind, not only

other people's but also his own. According to Rorty, it is in the belief that
creativity is his sole duty *and* out of a fear of cruelty that Nabokov crafts his
masterpieces. Nabokov the theorist and Nabokov the novelist are thus distinct. Nabokov's concern is that it may not be possible to combine the joy
of creating a work of art with tenderness and kindness. Rorty perceives two
contrasting literary types in Shade and Kinbote: while Shade is curious,
tender, and kind, the final component for reaching "aesthetic bliss," the
quality of ecstasy, belongs entirely to Kinbote because Kinbote is the greater
aesthete; Shade remains subjected to sentimentality and to the fantasies of
other people, while Shade's poem exists independently of either him or
Kinbote. Kinbote may be self-obsessed, and incurious as to the plight of
others, a "genius-monster," but he nonetheless creates ecstasy. Yet this Kin-
botean ecstasy is insufficient, solitary and insubstantial, it lacks curiosity,
tenderness, kindness. Kinbote, hoping to immortalize Zembla by way of the
glory of Shade's poem, does not register that the art of poetry cannot be
borrowed and that the written word cannot be separated from the person
who originates it; the moon can take only so much from the sun. As with
Humbert, Van, and Ada, the other "genius-monsters" in Nabokov's fiction,
sheer passion alone is insufficient in life or in art, because in both of them
we need to observe and to connect, even with those we dislike, and such
passion as Kinbote's is blind. Rorty concludes that the creation of a character like Kinbote is tantamount to a self-critique of Nabokov the theorist,
and in the end, finds Nabokov the novelist a man of high moral principles.
Nabokov fears that there is potentially no synthesis of ecstasy and kindness, so "he creates characters who are both ecstatic and cruel, noticing
and heartless, poets who are only selectively curious, obsessives who are as
sensitive as they are callous."[113]

Kinbote and Shade debate the question of sin in the novel. Shade expresses his belief that man is born good. Kinbote asks Shade in response
whether he denies that sin exists. Shade answers that he can name but two,
"murder, and the deliberate infliction of pain." Kinbote queries whether
"a man spending his life in absolute solitude could not be a sinner?" Shade
replies that he still could be; he could "torture animals. He could poison
the springs on his island. He could denounce an innocent man in a posthu-

mous manifesto." (Which perhaps has its equivalent in arbitrarily adding a commentary to a stolen work of poetry.) Kinbote asks for the password to goodness and Shade replies, "pity." Their conversation segues into the question of "Who is the Judge of life, and the Designer of death?"[114] Shade replies: "Life is a great surprise. I do not see why death should not be an even greater one." Quoting St. Augustine, Kinbote says, "One can know what God is not; one cannot know what He is." Kinbote adds that he knows God is not despair. "He is not terror."[115] Just before Shade's murder, Kinbote invites Shade to his house for dinner and a drink, eager to see the "finished product," promising to divulge *why* he gave him the theme, or rather *who* gave it to him, willing to reveal his identity if Shade shows him the poem. Shade replies that he had already guessed his secret a while ago, but Kinbote, self-absorbed as ever, does not register his response.

There are evidently several stages to knowing who Kinbote is and becoming able to judge him. The reader's sense of his identity migrates from Kinbote the commentator describing the poem, to Kinbote the imaginer who relays his own life story instead of offering a commentary, to Kinbote the madman who lives in his own make-believe world, to, finally, Kinbote the desperate figure who can command our sympathy. The examples I have mentioned serve to explain why Shade eventually treats the solipsistic Kinbote with tenderness and kindness. The contrast in character is clear. Shade has all the characteristics of an Enlightenment poet, like Pope, as we glean from his discussions with Kinbote on the dubious existence of God, his civilized ideas of art and the humanities, and his notion that pity is the password. Kinbote, meanwhile, is helpless and so lonely despite his flamboyant imagination that he suppliantly clings to a creator he perceives as superior. Shade accepts everything and accommodates Kinbote's idiosyncrasies, his way of making a nuisance of himself, and even his lunacy; Shade considers compassion to be a true test of humanity. The fundamental difference, then, lies in Kinbote's lack of both curiosity and compassion. Furthermore, it is important to note that while Shade understands Kinbote's sense of desperation, he does not indulge Kinbote's demand to write a poem about the Zemblan King Charles and thus bring him to life. Could it be because he does not fully realize what Kinbote wants? Or is he simply not prepared to rework the great poem of his life for the sake of his mad neighbor? Would he have immortalized Kinbote and his fantasies in his poem had he been, like his own creator, a greater poet?[116] Would he have transcended his own aesthetic limitations if he had, like his creator, immortalized Kinbote and his mad fantasy in the poem?

When Kinbote eventually faces the reality of Shade's poem, he "cannot express the agony!" because though beautifully written, it is "void of my magic, of that special rich streak of magical madness which I was sure would run through it and make it transcend its time."[117] This magical madness is what makes Kinbote so attractive to the reader; critical appraisals of *Pale Fire* often perceive, behind Kinbote's magical madness, the kind of sensitivity to art that is the polar opposite of Shade's. If Shade represents the serene, logical, and orderly world of Pope (though a great poet like Pope is not devoid of his own particular madness or love for madness), Kinbote stands for Shakespeare's restlessness, disorder, and glorious mania: magical madness. While these two worlds are obviously very different, Shade and Kinbote nevertheless share the same attitude toward the commonplace and the mediocre. They both share the same attitude in their confrontation with people like Gradus, "for whom romance, remoteness, sealskin-lined scarlet skies, the darkening dunes of a fabulous kingdom, simply do not exist."[118] Before such people, Shade and Kinbote are allies, and this alliance applies to readers too. In conversation, Shade and Kinbote discuss teaching Shakespeare's works at college. Shade says one must set aside the ideas and the social background behind the plays and instead "train the freshman to shiver, to get drunk on the poetry of *Hamlet* or *Lear,* to read with his spine and not with his skull." This of course recalls Nabokov's approach as a teacher of literature. Kinbote asks whether he is able to appreciate Shakespeare's purple passages, and Shade answers, "Yes, my dear Charles, I roll upon them as a grateful mongrel on a spot of turf fouled by a Great Dane."[119] Here, perhaps, Nabokov defends himself before critics who object to the playfulness and pomposity of his own prose, oblivious to or unable to recognize "magical madness."

Although he commands sympathy, we cannot completely absolve Kinbote, for he steals Shade's poem. What is it about Kinbote that causes us to pity him and even at times like him? The answer is that unlike Gradus, Kinbote is aware of his inner void and suffers as a result. He cannot be the good, loving man in reality that he can be in his dreams. Gradus, of course, does not dream. Sometimes, however, even taking refuge in a dream is not enough, as even dreams do not always compensate for personal short-comings or resolve inner conflicts. Consider Kinbote's relationship with his imaginary Queen, Disa, whose name is clearly derived from "paradise" (*paradisa* in Zemblan), in this case a marital/sexual paradise that Kinbote has never had and will never have.[120] To Kinbote, Disa is nothing like Shade's Sybil, though she does resemble the poetic portrait of Sybil as a young woman. The connection between Charles and Disa inverts that between Shade and Sybil: Kinbote claims that Shade does not love his wife and that his invented King Charles is a homosexual with whom Disa is in love, and married for reasons of contingency. Kinbote summarizes the sentiments Charles entertained toward Queen Disa in a short phrase: "friendly indifference and bleak respect."[121] Yet Disa continues to love her husband, though aware of his numerous dalliances and despite all the pain and suffering he causes her.

The emotional upheaval begins with dreams. Kinbote explains at the outset that despite all his cruelty and callousness, Charles constantly seeks to make amends for the suffering he causes Disa by dreaming about her. In these dreams his love for Disa drives him to helplessness. "These heartrending dreams transformed the drab prose of his feelings for her into strong and strange poetry, subsiding undulations of which would flash and disturb him throughout the day, bringing back the pang and the richness— and then only the pang, and then only its glancing reflection—but not af-fecting at all his attitude towards the real Disa." Although these dreams in no way alter his behavior toward the unhappy queen, the "gist, rather than the actual plot of the dream, was a constant refutation of his not loving her. His dream-love for her exceeded in emotional tone, in spiritual tone, in spiritual passion and depth, anything he had experienced in his surface existence. This love was like an endless wringing of hands, like a blunder-ing of the soul through an infinite maze of hopelessness and remorse."[122] This utter and desperate dependence on dreams best contextualizes Kinbote's complete exile from reality. The dreams serve to elucidate Kinbote's character and mind-set. How can one not sympathize with and feel sorry for a character who seeks love so eagerly? Similarly, how can one not pity every exile who can summon his past, his language, and his homeland only in dreams? When we see him thus, Kinbote breaks free from the egoistic enclave of his mind (and from the world of mirrors) and becomes a wholly tragic figure. Toward the end of the novel, he describes a sad, sunny Sunday morning: "There was no cloud in the wistful sky, and the very earth seemed to be sighing after our Lord Jesus Christ." In this moment he experiences hope "that there is a chance yet of my not being excluded from Heaven, and that salvation may be granted to me despite the frozen mud and horror in my heart."[123]

If the principal flaw in a character like Kinbote is his lack of curiosity, the fact that, according to Sybil, he is on the level of "an elephantine tick; a king-sized botfly; a macaco worm; the monstrous parasite of a genius," salvation depends on that very combination of mad ignorance and self-awareness. Of course, salvation can also be attained through the kindness of a character such as Shade (or indeed his creator); after all, the Shade-Kinbote relationship lies at the very center of *Pale Fire*. In a note on "The madman's fate," Kinbote explains that he personally has never known any lunatics, but he has heard of several amusing cases, including one at a university cocktail party. The hostess, noticing Kinbote's arrival, explains that they had been talking about an old man at a railway station "who thought he was God and began redirecting the trains." The hostess considers the old man "technically a loony" but Shade calls him a "fellow poet." Kinbote responds: "We all are, in a sense, poets," and the scene comes to a close.[124] Shade expresses the notion that lunacy should not be attributed to "a person who deliberately peels off a drab and unhappy past and replaces it with a brilliant invention."[125] Such a person is instead a poet. This assertion illuminates the personality of John Shade, the poet, as well as of Charles Kinbote, the commentator, and, most important, the relationship between the two (without the slightest reference to the insignificance of Gradus, the assassin). Kinbote's madness (and his genius) is appraised, and, in the final judgment, situated in the realm of poetry.

Love

Lolita

1

In *Pale Fire,* "shade" is a key word that appears throughout the novel as a kind of leitmotif. It is the poet's name, it is in the first line of his poem, and it is the tag of a group of Zemblan Extremists, the Shadows, who, according to Kinbote, are responsible for murdering Shade. In fact, the word explains not only one of the novel's central themes but also its two-part structure. Shade's poem and Kinbote's commentary are at once independent sources of light and shadows of each other. However, this contrast is not restricted to *Pale Fire;* it recurs throughout Nabokov's body of work. In *Lolita,* particularly, shades are exceptionally subtle. Alfred Appel, in his annotations to *Lolita,* observes that the French word *ombre,* meaning shade or shadow, is apparent in the protagonist's name (or pseudonym), Humbert Humbert; he is of partly French origin, which makes the connection even clearer.[1] The other main character, Lolita, will eventually die in a town called Gray Star, which Nabokov called "the capital town of the book."[2] In a *Playboy* interview, Nabokov mentioned Lolita's surname, Haze, as a place where "Irish mists blend with a German bunny — I mean, a small German hare."[3] A gray star is one veiled by haze.

We can best examine the interplay of shadow and light in *Lolita* through the twists and turns of Nabokov's prose. Anthony Burgess celebrated Lolita's name tenderly in a poem he wrote for *Triquarterly* to celebrate Nabokov's seventieth birthday (January 1964): "That nymphet's beauty lay less on her bones / Than in her name's proclaimed two allophones. / A boned veracity slow to be found / In all the channels of recorded sound."[4] Nabokov wrote in his epilogue to the novel that it records his love affair with the English language.[5] Arguably, no other name in the history of English-language fiction has come so imaginatively to life, become so evocative of the protagonist herself, embodying her different attitudes, and perhaps in no other novel does Nabokov rely so utterly on the magical and illusory power of words, revealing their reach as well as their limitations, the ecstasy as well as the suffering they cause those who, like Humbert, "have only words to play with."[6] Words in *Lolita* become shades that do not conceal reality but instead illuminate it. The name Lolita is that of a twelve-year-old girl and the heroine of the novel: Nabokov explained that he needed a "diminutive with a lyrical lilt to it" for his character's name, and that the letter L is "one of the most limpid and luminous" in the alphabet. He combines this with the suffix -ita, which adds "a lot of Latin tenderness." The origin of the name is Dolores, recalling *dolor* in English and *douleur* in French, and "pains" in the plural in Spanish, which, according to Nabokov, bring "roses and tears" to mind. "My little girl's heartrending fate had to be taken into account together with the cuteness and limpidity," he wrote, and "another, plainer, more familiar and infantile diminutive: Dolly, which went nicely with the surname 'Haze.' "[7]

Yet Lolita is not a symbolic title or name with a moral or a message in tow. It is more of an invocation, in the very sound, sight, and corporality of the name. With "Lolita," Nabokov brings the reader closer to actually experiencing the character's personality, her impudent beauty, fragility, youth, and defenselessness. "Lolita" even succeeds in creating an image of the character's fate: it conveys a sense of ambiguity, and also of transgression, that directly invokes the innocent, carefree existence that will be denied the young girl. This is also true of the novel's prose, whose texture is close to that of real experience, language that does not merely denote but also evokes. In a note to Alfred Appel while he was preparing the *Annotated Lolita,* Nabokov writes: "There exist novelists and poets, and ecclesiastic writers, who deliberately use color terms, or numbers, in a strictly symbolic sense. The type of writer I am, half-painter, half-naturalist, finds the use of symbols hateful because it substitutes a dead general idea for a live specific impression."[8] Within this context the importance of shades and shadows in *Lolita* becomes clearer. Appel quotes the great French symbolist poet Stéphane Mallarmé, who refers to one of his own sonnets as *allégorique de lui-même*—which is a fitting description of Nabokov's best fiction, especially *Lolita*.[9] This context gives the melody of Lolita's name the charm and the mischief of childhood even as it exudes suspicion and sadness. For that reason, we find a list of her names and nicknames and how to pronounce them from the very first paragraph: "She was Lo, plain Lo, in the morning, standing four feet ten in one sock. She was Lola in slacks. She was Dolly at school. She was Dolores on the dotted line. But in my arms, she was always Lolita."[10] Is there anything a critic can add that will better imply the innocence that will be betrayed, the childish imp that will become prey to transgression and despair, and wrenched away from her happy-go-lucky youth?

"Lolita" also recalls the name of another little girl: Annabel. Humbert himself says that in a certain magical and fateful way, the lure of Lolita began with Annabel, a girl he fell in love with as an adolescent, one distant summer.[11] Annabel, too, is a name not without significant interrelated combinations: Annabel and the syllable "li" in Lolita's name echo a poem by Edgar Allan Poe: *Annabel Lee* (1849).[12] Both Annabel Lee and the "I" in Poe's poem are children who live beside the sea and whose passion for one another is "a love that was more than love."[13] But envious winged seraphs steal Annabel from her lover when she falls ill and dies. The "I" in the poem claims that even death cannot destroy their love and that no power—heavenly angels or demons down under the sea—can separate his soul from Annabel's. *Lolita* alludes to the poem, but also to Poe himself, who considered the death of a beautiful woman "the most poetical topic in the world"; Poe's own wife, whom he married at the tender age of thirteen, died at twenty-four.[14] In Poe's story *Ligeia* (1838), the narrator summons his beloved dead wife to return to take the place of his current wife as she is on her deathbed.

Before the narrative actually begins, we are introduced to Dr. John Ray in the foreword, who is the editor of a manuscript entitled "Lolita, or the Confession of a White Widowed Male."[15] John Ray informs us that the manuscript was written by Humbert Humbert, the assumed name of a middle-aged European scholar imprisoned for killing the playwright Clare Quilty. Humbert wished for his "confessions" to be published only after Lolita's death. Lolita, we are informed, has since died in childbirth, and Humbert himself succumbed to "coronary thrombosis" while in jail a few days before his trial.

Humbert Humbert's manuscript details his sordid relationship with Lolita, a twelve-year-old American girl whose widowed mother, Charlotte, has taken him in as a lodger. Charlotte becomes infatuated with her dark, handsome European tenant, while Humbert lusts after the beautiful Lolita. He marries Charlotte to be closer to her daughter, but Charlotte then dies in a freak accident partly caused by her discovery of Humbert's diary, where he confesses his secret passion. Humbert thus takes possession of little Lo, not only as her guardian but also in a literal, physical sense. They drift from motel to motel for two years until she finally escapes with Clare Quilty, the man Humbert is accused of killing. Humbert *has* committed a crime, but we discover its true nature only at the end of the novel.

Yet Annabel, a character who is absent from the start, shapes this narrative. She was the thirteen-year-old Humbert's first love, with whom he experienced the awakening of sexual desire. But four months after their summer parting, the little girl fell ill and died. The memory of this star-crossed love casts a shadow over every one of Humbert's subsequent relationships, and his life thereafter is shaped by an insatiable desire to resurrect his lost love, hence his attraction to very young girls rather than to women his own age. However, he is not attracted to just any little girl, but to those whom he calls "nymphets," a diminutive derived from "nymph," of Greek origin. In Greek and Roman mythologies, nymphs are goddesses of mountains, rivers, and trees who manifest as fairies. Nabokov's coinage found its way into the English language and is still used to signify a sexually precocious girl. Humbert, too, creatively refers to himself as a "nympholept," a person overwhelmed by and obsessed with a desire for something elusive and inaccessible.[16]

Butterflies flutter and alight through most of Nabokov's fictional world, especially in *Lolita,* where they become integral to its central theme. Another definition of "nymph" is the larva of the caterpillar, which in turn becomes a butterfly when it breaks free of its cocoon, and we know that one of the butterfly subspecies discovered by Nabokov belongs to the *Nymphalidae* family, called Nabokov's Wood-Nymph. Appel refers to butterflies when reminding us that transformation is one of the novel's central concerns, crucial to understanding "some sense of the various but simultaneous metamorphoses undergone by Lolita, H.H., the book, the author, and the reader."[17] The reader, deeply absorbed in the novel, is gradually transformed into one of Nabokov's characters, an experience that inevitably changes that reader. "Just as the nymph undergoes a metamorphosis in becoming the butterfly, so everything in *Lolita* is constantly in the process of metamorphosis."[18] Lolita becomes a fully grown woman when she escapes Humbert's oppression. Humbert's lustful passion is transformed into love. And eventually, Humbert's notes are transformed into a novel.

There is also an unsuccessful metamorphosis at the novel's heart: Humbert's attempt to transform Lolita into Annabel, Annabel who, in Poe's poem, is in love with "I," and the Annabel who reciprocated Humbert's love as a child. One of Nabokov's recurring themes in his fiction is that of paradise lost: if Humbert remains a failed lover recounting a private tragedy, he is at the same time a successful man of letters who creates *Lolita*. In fact, this metamorphosis is the only means by which Nabokov allows his protagonists to regain their lost pasts.

When Humbert visits Charlotte Haze's house, he catches sight of Lolita in the garden and finds in her his lost Annabel. She has the same shoulders, the same hair, and even the same beauty spot. He rents the room only to get closer to Lolita, titillated by her presence, by everything about her, and by the temptation of possessing her.[19] Lolita gets caught in Humbert's web when Charlotte dies; he whisks her away on a road trip during which they wander relentlessly, keeping their distance from others because Humbert is apprehensive that their secret may be discovered, unaware that the playwright Clare Quilty is already following their every move. Lolita is captive for about two years. Humbert, in the guise of stepfather, not only takes sexual advantage of Lolita but also effectively steals her childhood. Lolita prefers Quilty to Humbert and eventually runs away with him. Some years later, Humbert receives a letter from Lolita, asking him for financial assistance. Humbert goes to visit Lolita and discovers that he still loves her, even though she is no longer a "nymphet" but a married and heavily pregnant seventeen-year-old living on the edge of poverty. He has been transformed, but still she will not reciprocate his feelings. She will forever remain his unrequited, inaccessible love. The only way he can truly possess *his* Lolita, live with her forever, is to write about her. The most important metamorphosis, the one Humbert had pinned his hopes on, was to transform Lolita into Annabel and once again possess his childhood love. He fails. Instead something else happens; his notes become a novel; his triumph must be creative: what is lost in reality is captured in art.

Humbert obsesses over his revenge on Quilty, the man who steals Lolita from him, who does not really care for her, and then dumps her despite her infatuation. Humbert kills Quilty in a lengthy, farcical scene, and the novel ends after Humbert details the manuscript he has written in "fifty-six days." In his last will and testament he stipulates that the book is to be published only after Lolita's death, which he, naturally, supposes will postdate his own.[20] Until Humbert met the adult Lolita, despite his obsessive passion for her, he never really saw the real her; she was ever only a figment of his imagination—Annabel in Lolita's body. During their last encounter, however, he acknowledges that he loves her as she is, accepting her independent reality. He can write his book only once that occurs. True art can never exist without reality. The greatest artists are those who experience reality deeply enough to turn it into fiction; the most important factors in metamorphosis are love and art, only within the pages of the novel is it possible for Humbert to remain by Lolita's side. Humbert addresses Lolita directly in the last few lines, telling her to forgo pity for Quilty, because "one had to choose between him and H.H., and one wanted H.H. to exist at least a couple of months longer, so as to have him make you live in the minds of later generations."[21] And he concludes, "I am thinking of aurochs and angels, the secret of durable pigments, prophetic sonnets, the refuge of art. And this is the only immortality you and I may share, my Lolita."[22] The novel begins and ends with Lolita's name, illustrating Nabokov's overarching theme: the link between reality and art, how a cruel and intolerable reality can be transformed through the magic of art into something timeless and overflowing with tenderness. Among all other metamorphoses in *Lolita,* the transformation of Humbert into a writer is the most important event, especially considering that this could not occur without Humbert seeing himself as he really is through discovering his real feelings for the real Lolita.

In *Lolita,* as in every other Nabokov novel, the narrative tension lies in the space between reality and fiction. The characters become real not only through the divine details that Nabokov borrows from life but also through their literary sources. Appel reminds us that Lolita's given name, Dolores (Latin, *dolor,* pain, sorrow) originally referred to the Virgin Mary or "Our Lady of Sorrows," and also to "The Seven Sorrows" of the life of Jesus Christ. Algernon Charles Swinburne, the nineteenth-century English poet, wrote a poem entitled "Dolores" in 1866, which although not concerned with psychological pain, was subtitled "Notre Dame des Sept Douleurs."[23] Dolores is also a toponym: for a river, a valley, and a small town in Colorado, where Nabokov once caught a rare butterfly. Some of the novel's key scenes are set precisely in this valley. When Humbert finally confronts Quilty just before killing him, he asks, "Do you recall a little girl called Dolores Haze, Dolly Haze?" He adds, "Dolly called 'Dolores, Colo.?' "[24] Appel gives clues to the various layers embedded in the name of Dolores Haze and its abbreviations. Amazing the many feelings and emotions a name can evoke. When we examine how Nabokov plays with Lolita's name (and the names of other characters), every allusion points in the direction of a different theme and adds depth and scope to the novel. Brian Boyd writes that Nabokov once observed that Pushkin's major theme was the threefold formula of human life: the irretrievability of the past, the insatiability of the present, and the unpredictability of the future. Boyd concludes: "This might be the only formula one could apply to such an unformulaic novel as *Lolita.*"[25]

2

Mallarmé's notion of work that is allegorical of itself recalls the process of involution that recurs throughout Nabokov's fiction; authorial intrusions and seemingly active participation in the narrative lend the work a level of self-consciousness, an awareness of its status as fiction. Nonetheless, *Lolita* is no mere allegory or symbolist novel. In the note to Appel I cited earlier, Nabokov prefers a more multifaceted approach: "When the intellect limits itself to the general notion, or primitive notion, of a certain color it deprives the senses of its shades. . . . I think your students, your readers, should be taught to see things, to discriminate between visual shades as the author does, and not to lump them under such arbitrary labels such as 'red.' . . . Only cartoonists, having three colors at their disposal, use red for hair, cheek and blood."[26]

In *Lolita,* words that are given the task of describing images and experiences often suggest multiple interpretations. As a result, they enrich the novel with unexpected dimensions that can sometimes seem contradictory. This method is inspired by Nabokov's definition of art. Art for Nabokov means magic, dreams, enchantment, and, of course, reality. The first three words belong more or less to the same semantic cluster, but "reality" does not seem to belong to that cluster: most of Nabokov's novels are built atop this precise contradiction. *Lolita*'s plot, unlike that of *Pale Fire,* remains within the bounds of a traditional novel, and the flow of the narrative takes the reader from one event to the next, along the axis of time. But in fact, the plot of *Lolita* is riddled with deliberate contradictions that complement and parse each other like light and shade, like the different resonances in the music of Lolita's name.

Lolita has a distinctive personality, but nothing truly distinguishes her from the multitude; she thinks, behaves, and inhabits the world like any other normal American teenager. The magic (not benevolent) arrives with Humbert: it is he who sees Lolita as an angel, and it is in his mind that she becomes a magical being. Humbert's Lolita is not an everyday girl with an everyday life. Whatever is created for and around Lolita (like a nickname) and whatever they experience together (the motels, for example, like the Enchanted Hunters) have the qualities of a fairy tale, such is the charmed web of deception that entangles Humbert, even when he is the fantasist. In every fairy tale, despite the prospect of a happy ending, there is always a wicked enchanter or a monster that stands in the way of dreams coming true. Astonishingly, Nabokov presents side by side what is attractive and what is *poshlust* in his image of American society. Similarly, the reader feels conflicted in her reaction to Humbert, disgusted *and* compassionate. Humbert best articulates the contradiction: "I am trying to describe these things not to relive them in my present boundless misery, but to sort out the portion of hell and the portion of heaven in that strange, awful, maddening world—nymphet love." He goes on: "The beastly and beautiful merged at one point, and it is that borderline I would like to fix, and I feel I fail to do so utterly." Then he asks: "Why?"[27] This, of course, is one of the novel's crucial themes: how the bliss of the past can become the misery of the present. The beastly and the beautiful, the portion of hell and of heaven, that neither reality nor art can differentiate so easily.[28]

The enchantment of Lolita stems from Humbert's past: something lost that seems to have been imbued with magic. This past carries forward a paramount obsession for what can no longer be attained. Desire for something irretrievable is a powerful motivating force, but it has a brutal side to it: although in reality it is unattainable and evasive, in our mind it seems as real and close, just like the skin touching the flesh. Furthermore, since Lolita and her world are linguistic constructions, the past comprises a literary past as well. Humbert is in need of Poe's assistance to make sense of his loss, while at the same time imbuing Poe's work with new significance. *Lolita* is shaped not only by the physical and moral present but by past literary experiences, too. So the present always remains indebted to the past; through art and memory Nabokov's characters face the present and retrieve the past. Memory is what saves Pnin from banality; imagination is what saves Cincinnatus from totalitarianism; in the world of *Bend Sinister*, where to imagine is as if to commit a crime, daydreaming charts a course to salvation; and in *The Gift, The Real Life of Sebastian Knight,* or *Look at the Harlequins!,* art is what saves life from the mundanity of routine. However, in *Lolita,* as mentioned in the context of *Pale Fire,* we face a much more complex scenario as Humbert's aesthetic sense confronts his inner cruelty. If we can dissolve and obliterate the present in the past, if we can transform Lolita into Annabel, and if we can evaporate reality in our imagination, what is the outcome? In most of Nabokov's novels, imagination struggles in the clutches of reality. In *Lolita,* on the contrary, reality is captive to fantasy, giving the novel its tragic, at times unbearable beauty.[29]

Shaped through this interplay between heaven and hell, past and present, reality and art, *Lolita* explores these contrasts through character (Humbert's two personalities), juxtaposition (Humbert/Lolita or Humbert/ Quilty), the novel's themes, and the temporal aspect (real and imaginary), as well as on a structural level, which it is at once tragic and parodic. Annabel's death is tragic, and while Humbert's relationship with Annabel was serious, his liaison with Lolita burlesques that relationship. Similarly, the novel as a whole mocks the confessional genre of fiction, and the final scene is a parody of Poe's horror stories, especially *The Fall of the House of Usher* (1839).[30] G. M. Hyde even claims that Quilty's mansion is like a Disneyland version of the Ushers' house. Humbert tells Quilty everything he wants him to know in verse form, a poem that clearly parodies T. S. Eliot's *Ash Wednesday* (1930).[31] Readers who consider murder the worst of all crimes, like members of the invisible jury invoked in the novel, will be shocked to discover that the scene in which Humbert kills Quilty is probably the funniest and most farcical in the book.[32] Why? Because the tragedy lies elsewhere; Humbert has committed a greater crime. After killing Quilty, while sitting in his car awaiting the police, he recalls that after Lolita's escape, he was "on the ghost of an old mountain road." He describes the peaceful day and the scenery in detail. Walking toward a "friendly abyss," he "grew aware of a melodious unity of sounds rising like vapor from a small mining town that lay at my feet, in a fold of the valley." After detailing the images and sounds, he says: "Reader! What I heard was but the melody of children at play, nothing but that." He gives us here one of the keys to understanding the novel: "I knew that the hopelessly poignant thing was not Lolita's absence from my side, but the absence of her voice from that concord."[33] This reminds us of when Humbert sees the pregnant Lolita and knows that he truly loves her, not the image of Annabel in her but "*this* Lolita." He knows this as clearly as he knows he will die one day: "I loved her more than anything I had ever seen or imagined on earth, or hoped for anywhere else." He thanks God: "It was not that echo alone that I worshipped." At this point, few readers can resist feeling sorry for Humbert, for here lies the contrast or the contradiction, the lust and the "tangled vines" of his heart. He ends the novel with the unrequited sadness of an affectionate love, having eventually attained self-awareness.[34]

Losing Annabel is not the only tragedy; her death alludes to the human condition, in a line from a poem in *Bend Sinister* that "looks forward" to *Lolita:* "All loveliness is anguish."[35] It is possible neither to prevent Annabel's death nor to preserve Lolita's youth: loveliness is transient. Humbert, who wants to stop the flow of time, is both a tragic and comic character. To sacrifice the present at the altar of the past is a form of crime, akin to the sacrifice of Lolita's reality at the altar of Annabel's memory. Humbert refers to a period before his acquaintance with Lolita when "I would be misled by a jewel-bright window opposite wherein my lurking eye, the ever alert periscope of my shameful vice, would make out from afar a half-naked nymphet stilled in the act of combing her Alice-in-Wonderland hair. There was in the fiery phantasm a perfection which made my wild delight also perfect, just because the vision was out of reach, with no possibility of attainment to spoil it."[36] A vision, a reflection, is inaccessible. Humbert goes on to admit that "the very attraction immaturity has for me lies not so much in the limpidity of pure young forbidden fairy child beauty as in the security of a situation where infinite perfections fill the gap between the little given and the great promised."[37] The transient reality of Lolita is imprisoned in the frozen world of Humbert's abhorrent inducement. He wants Lolita to remain, much like a butterfly, pinned and motionless, her beauty forever guarded. The miraculous aspect of the narrative is that Humbert simultaneously presents Lolita to us in motion, throwing pebbles, riding a bicycle, playing tennis, at the same time that he wants her to become a frozen image, a still photograph. An artist immortalizes the transient moments and temporal beauty of life, but Humbert's objective is not to create art but to capture and freeze the life of a real person. Art freezes fleeting moments; it has the paradoxical role of fixing motion while capturing the essence of that motion. But to turn a living person into an object of art is both fatal and criminal.

Humbert longs to be "on that intangible island of entranced time where Lolita plays with her likes."[38] He pleads, "Ah, leave me alone in my pubescent park, in my mossy garden. Let them play around me forever. Never grow up."[39] Later Humbert documents "that mimosa grove—the haze of stars, the tingle, the flame, the honey-dew, and the ache remained with me, and that little girl with her seaside limbs and ardent tongue haunted me ever since—until at last, twenty-four years later, I broke her spell by incarnating her in another."[40] The characteristic Nabokovian elements of art (memory, imagination, magic) are present in the realm of Humbert's relationship with Annabel/Lolita. There is only one element missing: what John Shade calls "pity," which is what Nabokov defines at the end of *Lolita* as integral to art: "For me a work of fiction exists only insofar as it affords me what I shall bluntly call aesthetic bliss, that is a sense of being somehow, somewhere, connected with other states of being where art (curiosity, tenderness, kindness, ecstasy) is the norm."[41] Humbert's is a totalitarian mentality that imposes its own image upon the reality of another individual; he is a solipsist. But Humbert, to a greater extent than Kinbote, has a creative mind and at some point becomes aware of his own monstrous nature. Yet he remains a captive of his dreams; he imagines awakening to be the same as dying. What would have happened if Alice had remained imprisoned in Wonderland? Humbert is stuck in the wonderland of his temptation. What awakens him is writing.

Lolita does not exalt only art and the artist; the magical beauty of the novel lies in the way it presents everyday reality. Humbert is a creative, highly cultivated narrator, and much of what he considers vulgar is similar to Nabokov's own ideas of *poshlust*. Yet in no other novel does Nabokov celebrate the unique beauty of ordinary life to such a great degree. In *Lolita,* the inner beauty of ordinary people is visible even in their *poshlust,* and it is Humbert, the monster, who remains blind: the character with the creative mind in Lolita is also the villain. The statement of discovery in *The Real Life of Sebastian Knight* rings particularly true in this novel in so many ways: "I know that the common pebble you find in your fist after having thrust your arm shoulder deep into water, where a jewel seemed to gleam on pale sand, is really the coveted gem though it looks like a pebble as it dries in the sun of everyday."[42] For Nabokov, art in essence is a celebration of life whose primary role it is to discover that the pebble camouflages a gem. The morality at the heart of *Lolita* concerns the sanctity of individuals. Unlike his more political novels, here even those characters representing *poshlust* deserve our compassion. The image of Lolita's mother, Charlotte, is perhaps the best example of this, the embodiment of "not only the obviously trashy but also the falsely important, the falsely beautiful, the falsely clever, the falsely attractive." Jealous of Lolita's youth, Charlotte treats her daughter harshly at times, making her an unsympathetic character, too. If she were a character in *Invitation to a Beheading* or *Bend Sinister,* she would probably be a spiteful one-dimensional character. The sophisticated nature of Charlotte's personality makes judgment difficult, however: Charlotte had a son who died when he was only two, and she had loved the boy deeply. Humbert mocks Charlotte's behavior and her feelings, but the reader perceives something different, even though she is *poshlust* incarnate; Charlotte draws on the reader's empathy. No one has the right to destroy this character's life, though of course Humbert gives himself that right. Charlotte may not command our esteem, but she treats Humbert kindly, because she loves him. Humbert, however, manipulates her feelings only as a means to possessing Lolita, and with her mother's death Lolita loses her home, her family life, and above all her childhood. We are reminded at the end of the first part of the novel that, because of his cruelty, Humbert is Lolita's only refuge; she has no one else and nowhere else to go.

Humbert sees Lolita as a silly girl who lacks the finesse to understand the beauty and transcendence of life, but who is nonetheless a siren. Yet there are instances that depict Lolita's deep loneliness and distress and afford a glimpse of her inner beauty in spite of Humbert (who, let us not forget, is the narrator). He references her inadvertent sighs in class,[43] the sobbing in the night "every night, every night — the moment I feigned sleep."[44] When Humbert sees her reflection in a mirror without her noticing, he describes the look on her face as "an expression of helplessness so perfect," so pure in aspect that it restrained him "from falling at her dear feet and dissolving in human tears."[45] And when Lolita's chubby friend Avis is picked up from school by her father, Humbert notes that Avis has "a wonderful fat pink dad and a small chubby brother, and a brand-new baby sister, and a home, and two grinning dogs, and Lolita had nothing."[46] On another occasion, Humbert overhears Lolita say to a friend, "You know, what's so dreadful about dying is that you are completely on your own." Humbert is "struck . . . that I simply did not know a thing about my darling's mind and that quite possibly, behind the awful juvenile clichés, there was in her a garden and a twilight, and a palace gate — dim and adorable regions which happened to be lucidly and absolutely forbidden to me, in my polluted rags and miserable convulsions."[47] Lolita has all the aspirations, albeit conventional ones, of girls her own age, like her veritable passion for the cinema. At first she finds Humbert interesting because he cuts the figure of and has the look of a film star. But that is not all, and Humbert eventually does find out, too late, that indeed there is a lot in Lolita's rebellious mind to which he is not privy.

Sebastian's style in *The Real Life of Sebastian Knight* uses "parody as a kind of springboard for leaping into the highest region of serious emotion."[48] *Lolita*, too, uses parody, when serious matters are called into question and subverted by comedy. Humbert wants to kill Charlotte but never acts on that desire, though the ultimate responsibility for Charlotte's death (and Lolita's) is his. Conversely, although he premeditates Quilty's murder and carries it out to plan, by the end of its enactment he feels somehow as though it was Quilty's plan that had been implemented. If the scene of Quilty's murder is represented farcically, the scene of Charlotte's accidental death is heartrending, especially in retrospect, when we see Lolita remember her in Humbert's presence. Humbert's moral turpitude is his greatest vice, greater even than murder (or, in fact, murders, direct or indirect). It cannot be justified by his inability to control his obsession. From Nabokov's point of view, failure to see others or a failure to be curious deprives us of our humanity. Nabokov's negative characters are portrayed without exception as selfish and self-centered. Humbert, however, has the possibility of writing as an outlet, and the prospect of self-awareness through the exercise of creativity; he gradually begins to feel empathy, and, eventually, feels pity and compassion toward other people.

3

Humbert is by far one of Nabokov's most creative characters, along with others of his writerly persuasion, such as Fyodor, Sebastian (and V), Vadim, and Kinbote. Yet in *Lolita,* thematic emphasis is placed on the notion that creativity alone is not enough. In *Pale Fire,* creativity itself is central to the novel. *Lolita,* however, combines the intricate problem of love with ideas of creativity and cruelty. In his afterword to *Lolita,* Nabokov recalls an American critic who referred to the work as his love affair with the romantic novel. Nabokov does not object, but suggests instead that the love affair is with "the English language."[49] Undoubtedly, *Lolita* is a love story, as it is the parody of a love story (an often overlooked fact). Following convention, lovers ought to be "good" characters, content that they have each other even when they are helpless in the face of the cruelty of the outside world. For them, love is enough. In *Lolita,* all the rules are broken. Lolita is a fairy-tale character, a girl who willingly enters the monster's palace. But behind the monster's mask there is no charmed prince to be set free by her. Humbert may look like Prince Charming, but the similarities end there. If he arrives on the scene seeming sorrowful or eager, he wishes not to save the girl, or to free her, but to enslave her. The elements of romance change into a nightmare. The monster takes the girl away in a car and drags her from motel to motel to conceal her even in her enslavement.

Humbert is indeed a monster.[50] However we construe Lolita's complex personality (she initially finds Humbert attractive and is mischievous in rivalry with her mother), nothing lessens the depths of her tragedy. Humbert's love is no more than a brutal seduction; all the grace and tenderness of a loving relationship is nonexistent. M'sieur Pierre is not alone in personifying the cruelty of the totalitarian mind-set in Nabokov's fiction. Humbert, this refined European who belies the idea that a poet cannot commit a crime, behaves infinitely more cruelly than M'sieur Pierre: possession of the body is not enough for him; he wants to possess the soul, too; he wants to subjugate Lolita's mind. The horror Nabokov reveals is that the "political" cruelty of totalitarianism can be located even in our most intimate relationships. In fact, the relationship between Humbert and Lolita is much more real and more tangible than the dynamic between M'sieur Pierre and Cincinnatus (and, of course, much harsher). In *Invitation to a Beheading* and *Bend Sinister,* their creator helps Cincinnatus and Krug to find a way out of their predicaments. But how can one escape someone like Humbert, a creator himself? His debased dreams have now replaced reality, and the tragedy in *Lolita* is that the aim is not to recognize and reveal reality, or to create an alternative world, but to enslave and reconstruct reality. Lolita loses her own reality under Humbert's gaze. Every lover usually reconstructs his beloved to fit an ideal. But Nabokov's parody reveals the terrible truth of how such an attempt can turn into a totalitarian impulse. At the beginning of the affair, Humbert writes: "What I had madly possessed was not she, but my own creation, another, fanciful Lolita—perhaps, more real than Lolita; overlapping, encasing her; floating between me and her, and having no will, no consciousness—indeed no life of her own."[51]

At the end of the novel, Humbert declares that he is against capital punishment ("for reasons that may appear more obvious than they really are"). He says if he were the judge, "I would have given Humbert at least thirty-five years for rape, and dismissed the rest of the charges."[52] The impact of this rape ripples through the novel, and becomes central to the reader's interpretation of the book. But the notion of rape is not circumscribed by the act alone, since it is not Humbert's only crime. The question of individuality, the respect it should be given, and infringement of personal liberty are subjects that appear and reappear in a variety of different ways in Nabokov's novels, especially in *Pnin*. In *Lolita*, the concept is expanded to allude to other, more figurative forms of imposition or appropriation, as, for instance, in art when we impose our opinion and our words—more simply, our ideology—on a novel. Humbert himself regrets that nothing can expunge from his memory the acts of "foul lust" he has inflicted on Lolita, which unfold themselves into "limbless monsters of pain." He declares that unless someone can prove to him that "it does not matter a jot that a North American girl-child named Dolores Haze had been deprived of her childhood by a maniac, unless this can be proven (and if it can, then life is a joke), I see nothing for the treatment of my misery but the melancholy and very local palliative of articulate art."[53] Love, like art, is no more than selfishness and violence when it is devoid of the pity that leads to empathy; the violation of another person's individuality, which deprives her of what she can be or what she wants to be, is unforgivable.

Empathy, in life and even in art, is what enables us to step beyond our self-interest and vanity and find a way into a different world to see how other people live. This is what Humbert is eventually forced to do. He accepts Lolita as an independent person and not merely as an object of his lust; "this Lolita," whatever shape or form she might have in the future, is who she really is. He realizes that he is in love with this "real" Lolita. For Humbert, as for most of Nabokov's protagonists, art is the one road to salvation; this remains the case despite his admission that art is "melancholy" and a "local palliative." Yet by the time he realizes the depth of the tragedy he has caused, he has distanced himself from it in order to write about it. Narrative art comes to his rescue. Can it be that a story that is properly told purifies? As narrator, Humbert is not entirely masterful; he is another one of Nabokov's inadequate narrators, unaware of how much they are revealing to the reader. As a result, the reader accesses information in spite of the narrator rather than because of him. Kinbote, of course, is the least competent and most exaggerated narrator of all. In *Lolita,* Humbert is not entirely reliable, but neither is he entirely unreliable. Only when the novel is taken as a whole does it reveal its different aspects to the reader: the many faces of Lolita, Charlotte, Quilty, and even Humbert.

Writing about one's experience creates a distance between the writer and the experience. However, writing is the reconstruction (and retrieval) of an experience that belongs no longer to the writer's present but to her past. By writing, Humbert retrieves from his memory not only Annabel but Lolita too. Recovering or retrieving the past (in the case of Annabel) disrupts his perceived reality in the present. Humbert thus learns that he cannot treat Lolita (a human being with her own free will and a specific individuality) like a toy and play with her as he pleases. For this reason, he employs language to come to his aid: "Oh, my Lolita, I have only words to play with!"[54] Linguistic dexterity can reconstruct reality with words; like Kinbote, Humbert borrows this ability from Nabokov, facilitating with distance and in time an account of his experiences or the lust that burns in his soul. The very act of writing about the experiences of one's life thus serves as a form of purification. Humbert claims that he initially had the intention of using these notes "in toto at my trial, to save not my head, of course, but my soul. In mid-composition, however, I realized that I could not parade living Lolita."

He later reschedules publication: "I wish this memoir to be published only when Lolita is no longer alive."[55] He then dies in jail; there is no trial for him in a court of law. Nonetheless, it is clear that the horrendous reality of his relationship with Lolita becomes bearable (and ponderable) only when narrative distance permits him to write it down in the form of a story.

No other novel stands so far away from (or is so dissimilar to) Nabokov's known personality, unless we claim that Nabokov had the same obsession as Humbert! Yet at the same time, *Lolita* is trademark Nabokov in its familiar themes of cruelty, the lack of empathy or pity, and the long shadow of memory. Distinct here, though, is *Lolita*'s portrait of Nabokov's love affair with the English language. Nabokov brought two things out of Russia, as is widely commented: memory and language, what Pnin refers to as the "portable world."[56] The loss of Russia and the loss of the Russian language were equally painful; he writes about it in the afterword to *Lolita,* calling it his "private tragedy."[57] In a sense, the Russian language, childhood joy, and adolescent love are all, in fact, like an Annabel that he can never forget: a limitless temptation that, in most of his stories, often leads to destruction and death. As *Lolita* reveals, it is by no means possible to recover the past in one's everyday life. In a letter to Vera in 1942, Nabokov writes of a lightning bolt of undefined inspiration: "a terrible desire to write, and write in Russian—but it is impossible." He goes on to say, "I don't think anyone who hasn't experienced these feelings can properly appreciate them, the torment, the tragedy." And, finally, he laments that "English in this case is an illusion, ersatz."[58] Lolita's personality has a strong relationship with the English language. The temptation to see Annabel in Lolita and transform her into Annabel becomes comprehensible.

Nabokov writes to fill the void of exile. He loves the English language and uses it to perfection. *Lolita* is his crowning accomplishment, recreating his own idiosyncratic prose style in English. Unlike Humbert, he does not seek to revive his lost love in another; he makes use of Russian's range of possibilities to enrich his English. He may seemingly never possess Jane Austen's flawless register or the deceptively simple, graceful ease of Henry James, but Nabokov's portmanteau English is beautifully distinctive, incorporating everything he has lost in life—his memory of Russia and the Russian language. There is a Russian scintilla behind the prose style in *Lolita,* strange and unfamiliar. Even readers unfamiliar with Russian find some unknown twist or unpredictable turn of phrase on every page of the novel. The sentences are full of colorful spaces. The author romanticizes English even as he writes; we watch the love affair unfold. Nabokov's major novels were written in English, yet Russian is an essential presence—sometimes clearly in the plot (as in *Pnin*), sometimes behind the mask of the novel's subject (as in *Pale Fire*), and sometimes at the subtextual linguistic level (as in *Lolita*). With Russian at the novels' core, Nabokov regains what he has lost and gains the upper hand over the Bolsheviks, exile, and destiny, too. He even conquers time in *Ada.* Maturity means internalizing and transforming experience; it also means accepting pain and suffering. Maturity depends on the courage to deeply experience things, and at the same time, the ability to distance oneself from the experience. *Lolita,* Nabokov's best novel, apparently the one farthest from the writer himself, distils all his core themes and concerns: the bitterness of loss and the difficulty of recovery.

Nabokov said that one of his aims in writing *Speak, Memory* was to prove that "[my] childhood contained, on a much reduced scale, the main components of [my] creative maturity."[59] This is certainly the case for Humbert, the difference being that Nabokov makes use of his past, unlike Humbert, who remains imprisoned by his childhood memories. At the end of *The Gift,* Fyodor shows no qualms about drawing from his own life, saying, "I so shuffle, twist, mix, rechew and rebelch everything, add such spices of my own and impregnate things so much with myself that nothing remains of the autobiography but dust—the kind of dust, of course, which makes the most orange of skies."[60] In *Lolita,* we observe this orange mist on every page of the novel and its magical reverberation in the novel's prose. In fact, only the mist of art remains to us: art and love. Humbert quotes an ancient (and innovative poet): "The moral sense in mortals is the duty / We have to pay on mortal sense of beauty."[61] Lolita eventually escapes, and as Humbert puts it, he "los[es] contact with reality." This concept is quite familiar to Nabokov's readers. Humbert writes a poem about life whose last line about himself reads: "And the rest is rust and stardust."[62]

4: Plot

In *Speak, Memory,* Nabokov presents how a creative mind operates "from the charting of dangerous seas to the writing of one of those incredible novels where the author, in a fit of lucid madness, has set himself certain unique rules that he observes, certain nightmare obstacles that he surmounts, with the zest of a deity building a live world from the most unlikely ingredients—rocks, and carbon, and blind throbbings."[63] *Lolita* is just such a novel. If, for Nabokov, "a great writer is always a great enchanter," it follows that "great novels are above all great fairy tales." Nabokov's emphasis on magic and enchantment is, in fact, his reaction to various schools of thought that consider an ideal novel to mirror reality or to function in the service of ideology, or those who think novels are for solving sociopolitical problems. His reflection on fairy tales, however, is crucial: what links "Cinderella" and "Sleeping Beauty" on the one hand and *Tom Jones, Pride and Prejudice, Madame Bovary, Ulysses,* and *Lolita* on the other? Is it the presence of the brave, handsome prince whose white horse with its flowing mane brightens a corner of our dreams? Or is it the heroine awaiting her Prince Charming? What attracts us to this flowing mane and that attendant beauty is their evasion of reality, the possibilities they evoke that hide in the life of the imagination. These adventures have never taken place, and never will, but every fairy tale reminds us of the unexpected things that might occur if we were not bound by banality and the rules of everyday life. In its simplest definition, a fairy tale transforms limitations into limitless possibilities. The limitations of the usual have no place beside the white horse's glistening mane. A second attraction of a fairy tale: our eagerness to tell stories and our need to hear them.

Does the shadow of a young girl and that of a Prince Charming cast itself over most novels? Can *Lolita* be regarded as a fairy tale? *Lolita* lacks a happy ending, and in the foreword the "editor" tells us that the protagonists are all dead and that "no ghosts walk."[64] In fact, the death of these characters is a precondition of our reading, per Humbert's will. Nonetheless, the book is the story of a dreamlike quest, and Humbert appears like a prince out of a fairy tale. Humbert explores the "kingdom by the sea" of Edgar Allan Poe's poem "Annabel Lee." He, like the "prince" in Poe, is searching for his ideal but lost darling. He encounters many obstacles, overcomes many perilous situations, and eventually finds and possesses his beloved. But though all the elements of a fairy tale are present in *Lolita,* they exist in nightmare form, anathema to a fairy tale. The innocence, wisdom, and occasional mischief of fairy tales can be observed here too, warped and recast in Lolita's complex personality. It is as though, enslaved as Lolita is, these pure fairy-tale ingredients lose their magic luster, the pixie dust tainted with the mature sorrow of self-awareness. The pervading ambience of a fairy tale cannot make the story more bearable but can only intensify the melancholy.

If the adventure of the plot does not have a happy ending, the same cannot quite be said for the novel itself. Nabokov artfully employs the fairy-tale elements as Humbert indicates in the novel's last few lines: "I am thinking of aurochs and angels, the secret of durable pigments, prophetic sonnets, the refuge of art."[65] Magic lies not in the adventures themselves, then, but in the way these adventures are propounded. The fairy-tale nature of the novel has been transferred from its subject(s) to the structure of the novel. In real life, death is the inevitable end of every story, but the limitless possibilities of an enchanting fairy tale remain available. Art overflows with possibilities; only art can challenge the absolute restriction of death. If the novel has a happy ending, it is because Humbert succeeds in immortalizing himself and his Lolita in his text; this is their reunion of sorts. The boundless possibilities of human imagination can create an exalted poem out of any banality or find happiness in every sorrow; in acknowledging the human condition, imagination circumvents endless despair. How? Fairy tales aestheticize the victory of the imagination over the sorrows of real life. Following the initial euphoria of reading *Lolita,* parsing the principal themes and the structure helps to reveal how Nabokov's masterpiece is at once so real and so elusive.

Addressing the jury, Humbert says: "I am trying to describe these things not to relive them in my present boundless misery, but to sort out the portion of hell and the portion of heaven in that strange, awful, maddening world—nymphet love. The beastly and beautiful merged at one point, and it is that borderline I would like to fix, and I feel I fail to do so utterly. Why?"[66] These words constitute the central theme of *Lolita,* and make up one of its structural elements: Humbert seeks to cut away the portion of hell from that of heaven only to discover that such a separation is impossible. The novel's plot begins here and ends at the same point. As we have seen, and unlike a host of other contemporary novels (including many of Nabokov's own, like *Invitation to a Beheading* and *Pale Fire*), *Lolita* apparently assumes a more traditional novelistic form. Chronologically coherent, *Lolita* has the appearance of a realistic novel, in the tradition of Turgenev, Tolstoy, and Chekhov, but — parallel to the tradition of realism — there exists another tradition of darkly satirical, picaresque novels by great writers such as Laurence Sterne in Britain, Denis Diderot in France, and Nikolai Gogol in Russia. Nabokov has an even greater respect for this tradition.

Nabokov has described Gogol's narrative method as a shift in two movements, a jerk and a glide, "a lyrical gust that sweeps you up and then lets you fall with a bump into the next traphole."[67] In his book dedicated to Gogol, Nabokov refers to the writer as a strange creature, because "genius is always strange," because great literature "skirts the irrational"; he describes how "steady Pushkin, matter-of-fact Tolstoy, [and] restrained Chekhov" experienced moments of "irrational insight which simultaneously blurred the sentence and disclosed a secret meaning worth the sudden focal shift." For Nabokov, Gogol is at his best when "potter[ing] happily on the brink of his private abyss." The absurd was Gogol's muse, though not the "quaint or the comic" or something that provokes "a chuckle or a shrug": Gogol's "abyss" is more or less tragic (as in *Dead Souls*), and his use of the absurd is "linked up with the loftiest aspirations, the deepest sufferings, the strongest passions."[68] In fact, this abyss is what lies at the heart of life, and Nabokov's void thus derives from the Gogolian tradition of nineteenth-century Russian literature. There are a number of tears or apertures in the textural surface of Gogol's works that are absent from the prevailing conventions of realism. These fissures give rise to peculiar structures; in Gogol's novels what disrupts the structure of the story is primarily the story itself (or, in other words, the style of storytelling), as is the case in Nabokov's oeuvre too. As a result, this narrative style disrupts not only the reality of the novel but the reality of the outside world too. Or, to be more accurate, it disrupts our perception of the facts of everyday life, and shatters the story's traditional world. More important, it destabilizes the reader familiar only with everyday life and its faithful reproduction in fiction.

Lolita's plot combines aspects of Tolstoy's realism with elements of Gogol's profound sense of the absurd and Nabokov's particular passion for demonstrating the creative process. *Lolita,* like most of Nabokov's novels, combines tragedy with a parody of tragedy, so the plot moves, inevitably, along these two different lines. There are other complications too: *Lolita* bears the style of a confessional novel and also the appearance of a detective story, complete with chase scenes and getaways. Events are related chronologically, yet this linear narrative is constantly being disrupted. The springboard plot submerges the reader in a nonlinear and uneven world. The movements of Humbert's mind and his constant digressions into the past advance askew to the linear (and material) movements of characters from one point to another. Although the voids of the present are filled with (and explained by) the past, the past repeatedly halts the apparent forward movement of the novel. Every scene of the novel teems with contrasting shades of light and dark, or the interruption of a chronological sequence that gives the general impression of nostalgic or sentimental reflection. The linearity of the action gives way to Nabokov's choice spiral, and the simple plot of *Lolita* enfolds two storytelling traditions, the duality of two tones (serious / satirical), and, finally, the duality of two different stories: Humbert tells his story primarily for the purpose of explaining (and, of course, justifying) his murder of Quilty; the real story being told, in fact, is that of his love for Lolita. The novel's plot allows for a real story to show itself beyond the self-evident one (Quilty's murder). The plot sheds light on the principal theme: Humbert's real crime is not Quilty's murder but the nature of his relationship with Lolita.

As Humbert and Lolita constantly move from one motel to the next, making "getaways" because Quilty is pursuing them (although in these chapters Humbert is not yet acquainted with Quilty), the suspense in this section of the novel (as happens in any genre novel of pursuit) hangs on the question of who will prevail, Humbert or Quilty? Quilty is successful and, effectively, steals Lolita away from Humbert. But this outcome does not comprise a finale. Why? Again, because there are two stories running alongside each other, moving forward on (at least) two levels. Quilty enters the frame at the beginning of the novel, exactly as a substitute for Humbert; Quilty, Humbert's twin, is obviously guilty of a relationship with Lolita. It is in Quilty's mirror that Humbert is eventually brought face to face with his sin (the name Quilty obviously evokes the word "guilty").[69] From the moment Lolita is gone, Humbert pursues her. Though he knows why he has lost her, he does not know how; the cycle of pursuit and getaway continues. But now that Quilty carries the burden of guilt, Humbert is a truly "selfless" lover. When Humbert eventually does find Lolita, there is still no denouement. Lolita rejects Humbert, as she does not wish to share her life with him, so the question changes: what else can a devoted lover do but to take his revenge on the guilty monster? This is another pursuit without an exact ending. Having read the editor's foreword, the reader already knows how the novel ends. The murder scene is primarily comic in tone, but Quilty's murder at Humbert's hand is tantamount to Humbert himself being killed. A novel is not composed of plot alone.

5: Point of View

In *Lolita* the issues dealing with point of view, like the plot, are complex and can be misleading. The novel opens with a foreword by Dr. John Ray, Ph.D., a purported specialist in psychology. He explains that following Humbert's death in captivity, Ray was asked by his cousin, Humbert's lawyer, to edit the manuscript of *Lolita*. He was probably chosen by his eminent cousin, he explains, because he had just been awarded "the Poling Prize for a modest work ('Do the Senses make Sense?') wherein certain morbid states and perversions had been discussed. My task proved simpler than either of us had anticipated."[70] Thus we initially view the plot through Dr. Ray's so-called "scientific" lens. Dr. Ray mixes jargon and flavorless language with a sudden poetic and emotional outburst. The point of the foreword, though, is not limited to sarcasm and Nabokov's familiar sendups of psychology. Dr. Ray provides further explanation for what he calls the "old-fashioned readers who wish to follow the destinies of the 'real' people [the quotation marks are Dr. Ray's] beyond the 'true' story."[71] So here "reality" — from Nabokov's point of view, always, and only, "reality" as seen by the writer — is seen from behind two different screens. Dr. Ray effectively discloses the novel's ending, something that "old-fashioned readers" would probably prefer not to know as they begin to read. These are all snares set by Nabokov: the only thing the reader finds out is that the "demented" Humbert has committed murder. And, with the aid of some pointers, the reader can intuit that Lolita is no longer alive. That is all. The reader has to reach the end of the book to discover that Humbert is not (and is) Lolita's killer.

Among the names of the characters that Dr. Ray introduces in his foreword is that of a colleague of Quilty's, Mrs. Vivian Darkbloom. Dr. Ray explains that Mrs. Darkbloom has written a biography, *My Cue.*[72] The point is that this author's name is, in fact, an anagram of the name of a certain writer who published his autobiography just before the publication of *Lolita:* Vladimir Nabokov. The permutation of Nabokov's name is not without precedent: we encounter Mr. Vivian Badlook in *King, Queen, Knave,* and Vivian Bloodmark, whose field is philosophy, in *Speak, Memory.* Vivian Darkbloom also provides footnotes to *Ada.* In the title of Vivian Darkbloom's book, *My Cue,* the word "cue," apart from being an obvious allusion to the first letter in Quilty's name, leads us directly back to Nabokov. Again, we are dealing with the writer's moniker, perhaps because he initially intended to publish *Lolita* under a pseudonym. Nabokov is again hiding behind a mask within the text of his novel. Although the views expressed in the foreword are Dr. Ray's, we occasionally encounter references that evoke the novel's author, and Dr. Ray's creator.

Dr. Ray explains that "a great work of art is of course always original, and thus by its very nature should come as a more or less shocking surprise." Dr. Ray has "no intention to glorify" Humbert. He admits that Humbert is "horrible," that he is an exemplar of "moral leprosy" and a mixture of "ferocity and jocularity," which betrays a sort of "supreme misery perhaps, but is not conducive to attractiveness." He is "ponderously capricious." His casual opinions on America, its landscape and people, are "ludicrous." The "desperate honesty that throbs through his confession does not absolve him from sins of diabolical cunning." But "how magically his singing violin can conjure up a tendresse, a compassion for Lolita that makes us entranced with the book while abhorring its author!" So Dr. Ray—who up to this point has appeared interested only in psychological questions and whose waggish opinions would seem rather funny to a reader familiar with Nabokov's skepticism of psychology—concludes his foreword with this "case history" embedded in Humbert's confessions and with an essay on the educational benefits of the book.[73] This provides Nabokov with an ideal opportunity for satire. Dr. Ray's perspective fulfils two objectives before the novel even begins: first, readers are given a sketch of Humbert as the protagonist, and second, we are introduced to the key question of contrast (the beauty *and* the turpitude of Humbert's character). Who can introduce the novel's unreliable narrator better than the unreliable narrator of the foreword? Nonetheless, Dr. Ray's slant succinctly summarizes the overall tone of the novel in the best possible way: the combination of Humbert's "ferocity and jocularity" denoting his "supreme misery," for example.

Lolita is narrated in the first person singular. The narrator, however, is more than singular. He has a multilayered character, as does his narrative. Humbert, like the narrator of any novel, creates the atmosphere of the novel. But the portion of hell in Humbert cannot be separated from the portion of heaven. He is a lover as well as a murderer. He creates tragedies, but he is also tormented by tragedies. The narrator of *Lolita* enchants the reader and keeps the reader at a sufficient distance so that they can arrive at conclusions different from Humbert's. The expression "unreliable narrator" refers exactly to this type of narrator. Humbert experiences an all-encompassing, obsessive passion; the entire story is told from that very angle. This angle, or perspective, is drawn in such a way that the reader, while absorbed by Humbert's passion, does not disregard the tragedy he creates. This resembles the reader's situation in *Pnin,* where we become privy to Pnin's pain and anguish despite the narrator's callousness in describing them; the reader sees beyond the narrator's solipsism. It is also reminiscent of *Pale Fire,* where despite the impositions of Kinbote, the narrator, we come to learn how Shade thinks. In *Lolita,* the narrator's representations function more delicately, allowing us even to observe Humbert's own character against what Humbert himself divulges as narrator. For example, Humbert is not only European, he is also highly refined and his views are by no means insignificant or unworthy of attention. Despite Dr. Ray's opinion, Humbert's criticism of the *poshlust* that dominates the lives of Americans like Charlotte is relevant and beautiful, even if his critical views lack empathy and sympathy. However, structural perspective enables the reader to see whatever Humbert sees, and more besides.

In *Lolita*, windows that remain closed to Humbert open up and familiarize the reader to the complexity of Humbert's character. Richard Rorty's notion of the sin of lacking curiosity is one such window. Critics discuss a single sentence-long scene probably because Nabokov himself, in his afterword to *Lolita*, refers to it as a key moment in the novel, adding that it took him a month of work: "In Kasbeam a very old barber gave me a very mediocre haircut: he babbled of a baseball-playing son of his, and, at every explodent, spat into my neck, and every now and then wiped his glasses on my sheet-wrap, or interrupted his tremulous scissor work to produce faded newspaper clippings, and so inattentive was I that it came as a shock to realize as he pointed to an easeled photograph among the ancient gray lotions, that the mustached young ball player had been dead for the last thirty years."[74] Humbert's inattentiveness betrays him: his lack of attention to or consideration for other people's despair, for Charlotte's dead son, and, of course, for Lolita.

Important to remember that the narrator is addressing an audience. It was Humbert's intention to use "these tragic notes" in a court of law, before the jury who is to judge him. Every now and then he speaks to the jury directly, but not reactively, and his tone is consistently satirical. As there is no jury, the reader gradually assumes that role, and is ultimately tasked with reaching a verdict. In the beginning of the novel, Humbert calls upon the "ladies and gentlemen of the jury" and regrets that the "angels" have not tolerated his pure love and have snatched Annabel from him. But at the end of the first half of the novel he cries out, "Human beings, attend!" and refers to the "gentlemen of the jury" as "winged."[75] This reinforces the theme of heaven and hell, and the way in which they are apportioned. Thus the reader who is acquainted with Humbert's standpoint finds him or herself in the judgment seat, whether willingly or not. A judge must be impartial but eventually must also take a side, and no matter which side that is, the judge is drawn into the novel in the guise of another character, entangled in the destiny of the protagonist. This calls a familiar theme to mind: the relationship between the writer and his readers. As we have seen in other novels by Nabokov, the tone here is serious and satirical at once. He deceives yet convinces his readers and, at the same time, pokes fun at them.

Humbert, at the Enchanted Hunters hotel, begs the reader to imagine him: "I shall not exist if you do not imagine me,"[76] he says. Elsewhere, he quotes "greater authors" than he who have said: "Let readers imagine," but goes on to say "On second thought, I may as well give those imaginations a kick in the pants."[77] Appel counts no fewer than twenty-nine times in the novel that Humbert addresses the reader directly, excluding when he addresses the jury, humankind in general, or even his car. Humbert's practice of directly speaking to the reader counters Henry James's more self-conscious idea of a protagonist being a "central intelligence" or "sentient center."[78] Or indeed a fiction that is carried forward without the writer's apparent intervention because the character is so strong. This is done by the technique of showing, not telling, with the idea that direct address blights the realistic atmosphere of a narration and emphasizes, inevitably, the fact that the story is but a device, an illusion. *Lolita* foregrounds Nabokov's ploy of maximizing contrasts in narrative devices. As many critics have observed, the novel parodies older traditions of fiction, transmogrifies deliberate anachronisms. In other words, James's "sentient center" theory, meant to maintain an authorial distance, is inverted in *Lolita,* entangling the reader inside Nabokov's intricacies of perspective and position. *Lolita* is like a chessboard between writer and reader; the reader cannot remain impartial, and the rules of the game arise from within the game itself and are therefore unrelated to readers' expectations.

The relationship the narrator establishes with the reader reaches a point where Humbert can shout "Reader! *Bruder!*"[79] This alludes to Baudelaire's poem "To the Reader" from his collection *The Flowers of Evil,* where he addresses his "hypocritical" reader as "mon semblable, — mon frère."[80] In the relationship between narrator and reader, there are always

at once manifest and latent elements. In almost all the novels produced by
Nabokov after his migration to America, especially in *Lolita,* both seeming
and real relationships are revealed. In *Lolita,* the narrator not only sub-
sumes the reader in the novel and calls on that reader to pass judgment,
but eventually he persuades the "good reader" to face his or her own hidden self. It is easy to feel sorrow over Lolita's lost childhood and to condemn Humbert's sins, but how is it possible at the same time to finish the
novel and not be emotionally involved with Humbert, in some way complicit? And how not to become ensnared by the "earnestness" of Dr. Ray,
the manuscript's editor? In fact, even the reader cannot help being earnest. The earnest reader inevitably accepts, at least in some instances, feeling
"sympathy" for Humbert. "Reader! *Bruder!*" Is a reader's peace of mind
not the strongest indication ultimately of guilt? The moralistic reader may
place him or herself in a position of judgment, be considered innocent, but
who among us is truly innocent?

6: Time, Place, Atmosphere

In *Lolita,* the narrative proceeds in metaphoric form, a characteristic that
can be observed in Nabokov's other novels, too. In *Lolita,* however, the
metaphoric structure is not merely a formal device. Rather, it rises from
the depth of the novel's central ambivalence. Structure aside, metaphor
also denotes the bond between two parties in a relationship. In *Lolita,* the
two sides appear to be not only unrelated but contradictory; still, each is
a reflection of the other. Heaven is seen in hell, and beauty is observed in
ugliness. Compassion and cruelty are expressed in opposition. The plot of
the novel appears to be sequential, but the narration is confessional (and
the confession at the outset is itself unconventional in revealing the ending,
which would be made known only at the end of a conventional sequential plot) or, in other words, personal: the subjective and the objective elements intermingle. Humbert conveys the character of Lolita with the help
of the present, the present time with the help of the past, and the material
world with the aid of what is immaterial. On the other hand, what Humbert
evokes transcends his narrative style. Not only has no effort been made to

remove, or even to lift, the narrator's veil (as happens in novels that claim to be entirely subjective), but, on the contrary, emphasis is placed on the auras that encircle the other characters as Humbert depicts them.

Dr. Ray's foreword further complicates this metaphoric duality. Humbert's present time is, in fact, the past. The reader is reading the book after all its principal characters have died. We read the narrator's words, addressed to the jury and the reader when the narrator is no more. By the time Humbert appeals to the reader's sympathy, it is too late; he no longer requires it. Isn't this a measure of Humbert's success? Humbert's foremost desire is to gain access to the past and turn the impossible into the possible. He does not accept that the past exists only in memory. He wants to reinvent time yet he yearns for timelessness. He wants the Annabel of the past in the Lolita of the present. But the impossible cannot be transformed into the possible, the past cannot be retrieved. Even Humbert is no longer the Humbert of the past. Yet the metaphoric mirrors that face each other will glint and sparkle for an eternity. In art, they are always alive. The dead Annabel lives in Lolita, who lives on, and the dead Lolita is, at the end of it all, an Annabel. Humbert synthesizes, in an eternal present, his lost past and his volatile present, his heaven and his hell. In this way, he immortalizes both his past and his present.

According to Dr. Ray, Lolita lived in a remote settlement in the Northwest called Gray Star (again, the place Nabokov called the "capital town of the book"), named as if shrouded in haze. Within the first few pages of his book, Humbert recalls his first tryst with Annabel. Both thirteen years old, they meet in a mimosa grove in the darkness of night. Annabel is sitting farther up than Humbert, and above them, "a cluster of stars palely glowed." Humbert sees Annabel's face in the sky, now recalling "the haze of stars, the tingle, the flame, the honey-dew, and the ache remained with me, and that little girl with her seaside limbs and ardent tongue haunted me ever since."[81] Toward the end of the novel, when Lolita and Humbert meet for the last time, she tells him that she and her husband will fly to Jupiter (or, at least, Humbert records the name of the city as Jupiter).[82] In a note, Appel adds that in fact they are going to Juneau, but that it might as well be Jupiter, as both are always veiled by haze.[83] This is how the novel's "haze" expands, as though the key locations in the narrative, when connected to Lolita in some way, are shrouded in nimbuses of mist. Or as if Lolita, like Annabel, were a distant star that looks to Humbert at once like the nearest one and the farthest. Naturally, beside these mythical locations, numerous "real" locations are also presented, and in a realistic style. One example is the description (and the *poshlust*) of Charlotte's house, which, in total contrast to the overall atmosphere of *Lolita,* is entirely realistic and representative of Charlotte herself.

Neither accidental nor meaningless, these misty places provide background for the fairy-tale theme of the novel.[84] Lolita's birthplace is a town with the well-considered name of Pisky, conjuring the word *pixie,* a djinn or fairy.[85] Humbert loses Lolita finally in a town with another fictitious name, Elphinstone, where, at the hospital, Lolita successfully deceives Humbert and runs away, accompanied by Quilty.[86] The name Elphinstone calls *elf* and *elfin* to mind, and there is, naturally, a precedent for this image: in the beginning of the book, Humbert calls Annabel "the initial fateful elf in my life."[87] Humbert and Lolita spend their first night on the road in a hotel called Enchanted Hunters.[88] Quilty who, as we gradually learn, is pursuing Humbert and Lolita, writes a play of the same name, *Enchanted Hunters.*[89] Humbert, who considers himself an enchanted hunter, refers to the hotel and play's name in various ways.[90] On the first night, Humbert notices a purplish spot on Lolita's neck "where a fairytale vampire had feasted."[91] Other fairy-tale references are even more direct. Humbert's birthday gift to Lolita is *The Little Mermaid* by Hans Christian Andersen,[92] and Quilty's Pavor Manor is located on Grimm Road.[93]

Appel raises two related points in his notes: First, "the themes of deception, enchantment, and metamorphosis are akin to the fairy tale." Second, "the recurrence of places and motifs and the presence of three principal characters recall the formalistic design and symmetry of those archetypal tales."[94] The plot of *Lolita* reverses the fairy-tale process, however. Humbert offers Lolita a happy ending ("we will live happily ever after"), but she rejects the offer. Appel then pursues the fable or fairy-tale motif in Nabokov's other novels, especially those set in imaginary lands: the utopia of *Bend Sinister,* the Zembla of *Pale Fire,* and, most important, the completely imaginary world of *Ada.* Beyond these lands lies *Alice's Adventures in Wonderland.* To Appel's first point, we should add that the fairy-tale world of *Lolita* is in fact the egoistic world of Humbert's mind, a world that revolves around Annabel. This reminds us of Kinbote's Zembla, a kingdom that never belonged to him. Neither character is capable of reconciling with reality, so they fabricate their own personal fairy tales. This is what makes them so dangerous; they try to impose their fairy tales on others, to dismantle the barrier between reality and fantasy. This is why the fairy tale *Lolita* appears to move in opposition to the plot of a traditional fairy tale, and why the fairy tales of the mad protagonists of Nabokov's novels (like Humbert or Kinbote) are at once so seductive and destructive. There is only a short distance between the madness of one of these characters and the genius of an author, with the latter capable of navigating the barrier that exists between reality and the imagination. The artist's goal is to attain unquestioned domination: over reality and imagination, over the past and the future.

In *Lolita,* time and space operate similarly, creating two distinct zones (now/then; a "real America"/an imagined utopia), even when they are not contradictory, which they often are. On the one hand, the writer re-creates part of America in realistic detail and with great accuracy. On the other, he shrouds everything in mist to create a magical climate. An overview of the novel reveals how a location or space serves a particular theme. Similarly, one can see how fluid the design of the novel is, how each element keeps its own shape and preserves its independence but like a wave facilitates the progress of other components that go on to repeat themselves in the overall structure of the novel. This lends a sense of reality to the most mythical of plotlines and gives credibility even to what seems incredible. It is credible because *Lolita* possesses an internal intelligence, a fluent logic, which becomes most evident in the way the characters are delineated (notwithstanding the importance of time, space, and atmosphere).

7: Characterization

An accomplished writer's ability to familiarize his reader with the inner life or mental qualities of his characters is more or less taken for granted as part of his craft. In an interview with Penelope Gilliatt of *Vogue,* Nabokov explains that he meticulously researches and identifies "such local ingredients as would allow me to inject a modicum of average 'reality' (one of the few words which [according to Nabokov] mean nothing without quotes) into the brew of individual fancy."[95] However, *Lolita* draws upon more than the author's prefabricated "reality" for this confection of a character's past and psychological makeup. Lolita's past is not solely historical or individual, she has the added ancestry of a literary past, too. We can imagine Lolita when she is twelve years old, but presenting a character's prehistory to the reader is not literature's sole objective. Portraying Lolita in the past does not mean simply depicting her at a younger age. The plot discloses that Lolita has a particular past or perceived past or forebear as Humbert's first love incarnate: Annabel. In providing her with literary antecedents, Nabokov structures her character with the support of others, from Annabel Lee to Alice in Wonderland.

To build Lolita's character, Nabokov draws on a variety of images, which seem to be in motion, as in a film. But each image also has the quality of a still, becoming fixed as it passes through the filter of Humbert's mind: Humbert, as we know, prefers to keep Lolita captive on an island untouched by time. Images of Lolita are all in color, overflowing with a playful use of light. The dominant color is gold; she appears to be always radiating sunshine. When Humbert meets Lolita for the first time, he has come to the town to rent a room at the McCoo residence, drawn to that particular house when he learns of the proprietor's twelve-year-old daughter, an "enigmatic nymphet." The house burns down as he travels by train to Ramsdale, and Charlotte Haze offers to take him in, but Humbert is not interested in her room. All the same, as he is, according to himself, a polite European, he accepts her invitation to visit Lawn Street. He dislikes Charlotte and the house, and the *poshlust* of both of them squares his resolve to get away as soon as he can. Humbert's unanticipated encounter with Lolita is imminent, but the author makes us wait; Humbert's hopes have been foiled, but fate is at play to change his fortunes. Charlotte shows him room after room, first hers, then Lo's — he thinks she is referring to the maid — and the house is not tidy or even clean; he sees a white sock lying on the floor, and the only thing in the fruit bowl is a glistening plum pit. Humbert surreptitiously fishes the train's timetable from his pocket. Charlotte, noticing that Humbert is unimpressed with the interior, takes him out to see the garden, which she calls, trying to be chic, "the piazza." There is a sudden rush of greenery, "and then, without the least warning, a blue sea-wave swelled under my heart and, from a mat in a pool of sun, half-naked, kneeling, turning about on her knees, there was my Riviera love peering at me over dark glasses." Humbert describes Lolita as if the same child as Annabel: "the same frail, honey-hued shoulders, the same silky supple bare back, the same chestnut head of hair." Charlotte introduces her "Lo" and adds, "These are my lilies." Humbert, enchanted, finds the flowers "beautiful, beautiful, beautiful!"[96]

In this encounter, Lolita's image is suffused with light and color, which is especially acute in the eyes of someone who has spent a long time in darkness. The depiction seems to belong to the "real" world, but in fact the sunny spectacle of the garden, the verdant green of the plants, and the blue of the sea are fragments of Humbert's dreamlike memories. Lolita's golden glimmer in the sunshine blends with the blue water of the pool to evoke Humbert's memory of Annabel. This is why from the outset both Lolita and Annabel are one image. The scene depicts neither Lolita's personality nor her past. Instead, it reconstructs Annabel's personality and Humbert's past. The details that follow — "frail, honey-hued shoulders, the same silky supple bare back, the same chestnut head of hair" — describe not only Lolita but the recollected Annabel. In his "adult disguise," Humbert manages to "suck in every detail of her bright beauty, and these I checked against the features of my dead bride." Immediately the concept of a fairy tale unfolding is evinced; Humbert in his rapture says he feels like a "fairy-tale nurse of some little princess (lost, kidnaped, discovered in gypsy rags through which her nakedness smiled at the king and his hounds), I recognized the tiny dark-brown mole on her side. With awe and delight (the king crying for joy, the trumpets blaring, the nurse drunk) . . ."[97] Humbert is no longer a child, but in his joyful delusion the princess has remained unchanged; he sees himself, in disguise, as though the "real" Humbert is still only thirteen years old. Thus Lolita is constructed here, as are associative images with Humbert at their center. The images of Lolita, re-created on the

easel of memory, are our conduit to the core of Humbert's self-portrait. The
painter paints the painting and the painting paints the painter.

In Humbert's "exhibit number two" is an image in which Lolita
moves and his vision of Annabel retreats. It opens with Humbert at the
bathroom window, and Lolita is seen in the context of Humbert's gaze until
she leaves the frame. Lolita is taking washing from the line; Humbert steps
out, and Lolita comes to sit beside him on the porch. She first picks up
pebbles between her feet, then "a curled bit of milk-bottle glass resembling a snarling lip—and chuck[s] them at a can. *Ping.*" Humbert bets
she cannot hit it twice. She can: "*Ping.*" When Lolita gets up to take the
washing inside, Charlotte arrives and snaps a photo of Humbert looking
at her. Here we see Lolita through Humbert's eyes and Humbert through
Charlotte's.[98] The plot advances as these freeze-frames and descriptions
grow; before long, Humbert and Charlotte are married. Let us return to the
scene's detailed description: "that silky shimmer above her temple grading
into bright brown hair. And the little bone twitching at the side of her dust-
powdered ankle." The reader often observes the act of painting with words
in Nabokov's novels, especially in *Lolita* and *Ada*. Detailed "sketches" or
"paintings" make even his most abstract novels become tangible. Nabokov
referred to himself, first and foremost, as a painter, telling Appel that he
was born a landscape painter. In an interview with the BBC in 1962 he described spending most of the day drawing and painting, and revealed his
condition of synesthesia, through which he saw specific letters as colors,
as his mother did. "It's called color hearing," Nabokov explained in the
interview.[99]

In the second half of the novel, after Charlotte's death and his fall
from grace, Humbert, no longer cutting the figure of leading man for Lolita,
can no more assert or prove his hold over her without threats and machina-
tions. Humbert visits Lolita's school to discuss her poor performance, and
afterward finds her in "Mushroom," which is the nickname for a "smelly"
classroom with a sepia print by Sir Joshua Reynolds above the blackboard.
A character study, the print depicts a little girl, barefoot and wearing a yellow dress, her hands clasped to her chest, sitting under a tree gazing away at
something outside the frame. Humbert does not describe the painting but

reveals its name: *Age of Innocence.* Humbert describes in detail another girl sitting a few rows ahead of Lolita: "a very naked, porcelain-white neck and wonderful platinum hair." She is deeply absorbed in reading, "absolutely lost to the world and interminably winding a soft curl around one finger." Humbert sits down beside Lolita just behind that neck and that hair, and has "Dolly put her inky, chalky, red-knuckled hand under the desk."[100] She consents to Humbert's sexual request only after securing sixty-five cents and permission to participate in the school play, *The Enchanted Hunters,* which is the work of the novel's antagonist, Clare Quilty. Here, Lolita's image is part of a reflected series that includes the silent girl in the painting and the girl who is sitting and reading, oblivious to what is taking place a few rows behind. Each image mirrors the others. And these reflections elucidate elements concealed in each — What is Reynolds's girl looking at? What is the platinum blond reading? What is Lolita doing? — to the extent that Humbert appears to taint all three. This scene, only a few lines long and without further detail, naturally depicts Lolita's innocence, even when she is, apparently, no longer innocent: the only description of her is of her hands, exactly at the moment when she moves her arm under the desk. In this way, a full portrait of Lolita is constructed here in an extremely delicate way.[101]

V describes Sebastian Knight's novel *The Prismatic Bezel* thus: "I'm going to show you not the painting of a landscape, but the painting of different ways of painting a certain landscape, and I trust their harmonious fusion will disclose the landscape as I intend you to see it."[102] Lolita's personality, too, is not a fixed image, but a collection of images: an innocent American girl, a magical fairy, an adolescent temptress, and a lonely, sad young woman. All these different Lolitas can be found within the one character; at every moment, the reader is confronted with a fixed image and, at the same time, its infinite reproductions through the *mise en abyme* structure to Humbert's narrative. This is how Lolita makes her way into the reader's mind and heart: she is not "real" in the sense of someone you encounter in everyday life, but she becomes real to the reader because being real entails being a recognizable composite of different features, an amalgam of contrasts and contradictions. Nabokov's nymphet enters the con-

ceptual domains of culture, encyclopedias, and dictionaries, but the pre-
requisite for her becoming fully real is her possession of an entirely unique
character. Early in the novel, Humbert refers to the "twofold nature of this
nymphet," a mixture of "tender dreamy childishness and a kind of eerie
vulgarity, stemming from the snub-nosed cuteness of ads and magazine
pictures, from the blurry pinkness of adolescent maidservants in the Old
Country (smelling of crushed daisies and sweat); and from very young har-
lots disguised as children in provincial brothels; and then again, all this
gets mixed up with the exquisite stainless tenderness seeping through the
musk and the mud, through the dirt and the death, oh God, oh God."[103]
By the end of the novel, what Humbert finds extraordinary is that his object has metamorphosed into a real unique individual, and what he tells us
is that "*this* Lolita, *my* Lolita" now defines the narrator's old desire, to the
extent that she acquires a status above everything else, everything that has
come before.[104]

How can characters that represent "methods of composition" seem
tangible, credible, and, above all, alive? Nabokov's answer is that one must
"caress the details, the divine details." To begin, every character is shaped
around a nucleus or core, made up of a mixture comprising a transient
state or mood and the particular intensity of a temporary shade or color.
These feelings and tones nourish the reader's notion of the nucleus. To
this mixture are added a set of metamorphoses undergone by the character in question, changes that exhibit various (or contrasting) aspects of
personality, all of this presented not in a vacuum but in very specific locations created with great care and meticulousness. The settings in *Lolita* are
more than mere backdrops, and time does not only sequence events. Nabokov begins to describe Charlotte even before she appears in view, through
the presentation of her home. Humbert derides the door chime, "a white-
eyed wooden thingamabob of commercial Mexican origin, and that banal
darling of the arty middle class, van Gogh's 'Arlésienne.'" This is careless
poshlust. Charlotte's voice topples melodiously from upstairs, emphasizing
the word "Monsieur" to Humbert, dropping cigarette ash from on high as
she speaks. "Presently, the lady herself—sandals, maroon slacks, yellow
silk blouse, squarish face, in that order—came down the steps, her index

finger still tapping upon her cigarette."[105] Here, Humbert's scornful tone
is of a piece with the description he provides. When he describes Charlotte directly, as a "weak solution of Marlene Dietrich," he does so "right
away, to get it over with." Yet the core of Charlotte's personality has already
been conveyed through Humbert's reaction to the surroundings. Charlotte
shows Humbert around her home, and the fixtures and fittings that contex-
tualize Charlotte's personality inform the larger dual portrait in progress in
which the subsequent relationships between landlady and tenant will take
shape. Meanwhile, the reader is given a cursory sketch of the as yet unseen
Lolita. The narrator is Humbert, of course, but the depiction is twofold: the
narrator is inadvertently divulging knowledge about himself.

The tone of the language that Humbert uses is central to our understanding of character. When he first meets Lolita, his tenor is not only amor-
ous but poetic. Through Humbert's passion, Nabokov finds a hidden poem
in the quotidian. As Humbert's obsession with nymphet love is replaced by
love for "*this* Lolita," the specific details about her grow increasingly important. Every item of clothing, her every trait, becomes a poem in its own
right. With this transition, Humbert the narrator becomes inseparable from
Humbert the lover (despite the complexities of his character), usurped into
the poem of Lolita's slightest movement. Yet when the narrator considers
Charlotte, his tone is petty, subjective, and disparaging. Humbert's description of Quilty is rife with toxic fervor and righteous indignation, pep-
pered with affected shock and incredulity. (The novel's story line advances
because of all that Humbert ignores about Quilty, and what he gradually
comes to know.) Humbert evolves through the variations in tone between
Humbert the narrator and Humbert the character. As readers, we interact
with Humbert's vacillating tone, these variations reflecting not other characters so much as Humbert's own capricious personality. His tone, too,
lays the foundations for the introduction of new characters. For example,
in the beginning of *Lolita*, Humbert details the books he finds in the prison
library. Obviously, Agatha Christie's novel *A Murder Is Announced* may signify in this context, as may a book by Percy Elphinstone titled *A Vagabond
in Italy,* a prelude to the (imaginary) city of Elphinstone. Humbert's complex task intensifies; he comes across *Who's Who in the Limelight,* with a

list of producers and playwrights, and shots of static scenes. He quotes an entire page of the book, including a woman with Lolita's given name "Quine, Dolores," who comes immediately after "Quilty, Clare, American dramatist," and a list of his plays. Humbert also finds a list of Lolita's classmates at Ramsdale School and delights to note that she is halfway down the list, between Mary Rose Hamilton and Rosaline Honeck. He memorizes the names like a poem. "So strange and sweet was it to discover this 'Haze, Dolores' (she!) in its special bower of names, with its bodyguard of roses — a fairy princess between her two maids of honor."[106] Beyond the narrator's ardor, however, this simple list of names contains several clues and associations. Lolita has tried to draw a map of the United States on the other side of the page with the list. It is an unfinished outline, but in the second part of the novel it comes to be completed over the course of their road trip.

On the question of character portrayal in *Lolita,* Humbert's nemesis, Quilty, certainly requires a more detailed description. Quilty is mysterious, so much so that Humbert for a long time remains oblivious of his existence. For the attentive reader, however, Quilty's presence can be felt more or less everywhere, in the shadows lurking in the novel's crevices. On the surface, his character appears simple: Quilty is a playwright whose work is largely meant for young audiences. He becomes acquainted with Lolita at her school and, like Humbert, pursues her. He discreetly follows Humbert and Lolita on their road trips and tricks Humbert in the city of Elphinstone, where he escapes with Lolita. Years later we learn more about Quilty from Lolita, who had been initially fascinated by him but soon found his behavior repulsive and grew tired of his constant entourage expecting "crazy things, filthy things."[107] The point is that we have no contact with Quilty except at the end of the novel, yet his presence pervades the book from start to finish. He trails Humbert like a private detective, everywhere, hiding behind a tree, sitting in the lobby of a hotel, behind the wheel of his car. The device of a narrator introducing a character indirectly reaches its fullest example in Quilty even if he is introduced inadvertently through the narrator, without the narrator's knowing quite what he is divulging. Quilty's personality is formed through multiple allusions; Appel gives a list of forty-four.[108] What sort of character is a seemingly anonymous shadow hidden from the narrator while maintaining an invisible presence in most of the scenes? How is such a character constructed?

A character who emerges through allusions and is shaped by associative meanings is arguably less "real" than substantiated characters that have been portrayed realistically to accompany him or her. *Lolita*, of course, is a study in contrasting images, textures, and even interpretations. For example, the way the novel reveres Poe coincides with a parody of Poe, just as it interprets tragedy through comedy, and tetchy realism blended with allegory and burlesque. *Lolita* makes the most of Quilty's shadow, moving to the edge of caricature when describing Quilty's personality. Yet he is not one-dimensional; clearly Humbert's Quilty is not Lolita's Quilty, and to other characters acquainted with Quilty the playwright, Lolita's Quilty would probably seem fanciful and indeed entirely unrecognizable. Quilty, present or in shadow, brings humor to even the most serious of scenes, especially the last. Quilty contributes different motifs to the novel precisely because his character, unlike others, is not portrayed using the devices of realism. Most important, there is the juxtaposition of two contrasting personalities: Humbert's and Quilty's, which posits the doppelgänger motif, itself nothing new in Nabokov's work specifically (we may recall Cincinnatus and his doppelgänger). This device has a long tradition in fiction, and if Nabokov is indifferent to Dostoevsky, he remains fond of Stevenson's *Dr. Jekyll and Mr. Hyde* (1886), which he taught, and Poe is an even better point of reference, given Humbert's invocation of Annabel. Poe is also the inventor of the detective story, a genre we encounter in *Lolita*, alongside its parody, and "William Wilson" (1839), one of Poe's most masterful stories, is another important doppelgänger tale that anticipates *Lolita*. If Jekyll's twin is the horrific Hyde, Wilson's twin is his own conscience, and Wilson's murder of him a kind of suicide. Quilty clearly plays the role of Humbert's nemesis and doppelgänger, though in this case, the borderline between good and evil is obliterated: who is guilty and who is innocent? Despite Humbert's insistence on considering Quilty the only evil one, the traditional doppelgänger poles (good versus bad) are collapsed. Again, a premise encounters its contradiction or parody as *Lolita* convolutes questions of moral values and innocence.[109]

Eventually, Quilty steps into the foreground. The murder scene in *Lolita* was written early on and out of sequence, Nabokov later explained, because Quilty's death "had to be clear in my mind in order to control his earlier appearances."[110] When Humbert sets off to find Quilty, the narrative gains pace and the novel undergoes a transformation, growing less and less realistic, and even following certain gothic conventions; a thunderstorm builds and follows Humbert, though the sun comes out when he arrives at Pavor Manor, "burning like a man, and the birds screamed in the drenched and steaming trees."[111] He walks to the front door, which, "how nice, . . . swung open as in a medieval fairy tale." The atmosphere of the house possesses Humbert immediately, and he describes himself as "lucidly insane, crazily calm, an enchanted and very tight hunter."[112] After a tour in search of Quilty, he finally sees him walking out of a bathroom. Quilty is suffering a hangover from his excesses the previous night, and Humbert is clearly drunk. Gun in hand, Humbert sits down facing Quilty in order to make him aware of his "crime" before killing him, but the entire scene then unfolds like a farce. Quilty thinks that Humbert has been sent by the telephone company to collect for unpaid long-distance calls. When Humbert names Lolita, Quilty replies, "Sure, she may have made those calls, sure. Any place. Paradise, Wash., Hell Canyon. Who cares?" Yet the farce cannot undermine what Humbert and Quilty have in common. They start to fight and "rolled all over the floor, in each other's arms, like two huge helpless children. He was naked and goatish under his robe, and I felt suffocated as he rolled over me. I rolled over him. We rolled over me. They rolled over him. We rolled over us."[113]

The spectacle reaches a peak when Humbert hands Quilty the text of his "sentence," which he has written out in verse form, and asks him to read aloud. (It is revealed to be an amusing parody of T. S. Eliot's *Ash Wednesday*.) Humbert finally shoots Quilty several times, and Quilty, "trudging from room to room, bleeding majestically," steers the scene toward grotesque farce right up to the moment of his death, when "a big pink bubble with juvenile connotations formed on his lips, grew to the size of a toy balloon, and vanished."[114] Meanwhile, a number of people have shown up and are helping themselves to drinks. Humbert announces that he has killed their host, but no one takes him seriously. The murder has not brought the relief he expected; instead, "a burden even weightier than the one I had hoped to get rid of was with me, upon me, over me." As he leaves Pavor Manor and the newly arrived guests, he remarks, "This . . . was the end of the ingenious play staged for me by Quilty."[115] Quilty thus foils Humbert's carefully crafted plans for Lolita, and fulfills a serious objective in the novel by extending the fairy-tale motif that calls into question Humbert's idea of "reality" and makes a farce of Humbert's tragedy, facilitating our understanding of Humbert and even enabling sympathy and empathy for him. The novel, however, does not leave Humbert in peace after Quilty's death. Generally, the doppelgänger device offers an escape route for the protagonist; here, on the contrary, the device constructs a barrier that prevents him from escaping. Quilty's travesty of a death prevents Humbert from simply washing away his guilt and hiding behind his doppelgänger's murder. The crime does not end in or lead to punishment—or redemption—and the reader remains entangled by questions of Humbert's "guilt."

In the novel's final chapter, Humbert departs Quilty's Pavor Manor and gets into his car. He has disregarded "all laws of humanity" and determines to disregard "the rules of traffic" too, driving over to the wrong side of the road, "that queer mirror side." Once there he checks the feeling of it, "and the feeling was good." He is now without his doppelgänger and has fully entered the world of the mirror. He is arrested almost immediately, though not without avoiding a roadblock, and "with a graceful movement I turned off the road, and after two or three big bounces, rode up a grassy slope, among surprised cows, and there I came to a gentle rocking stop." Journey's end. The whole series of events linking up two dead women— Charlotte and Lolita—creates a "thoughtful Hegelian synthesis," a new liberty for Humbert. As he waits for the police, he recalls "a last mirage of wonder and hopelessness." Its description is the novel's most beautiful: "One day, soon after her disappearance, an attack of abominable nausea forced me to pull up on the ghost of an old mountain road . . ." He describes the scene meticulously: "And then, thinking the sweet air might do me good, [I] walked a little way toward a low stone parapet on the precipice side of the highway." And then he hears the sound:

As I approached the friendly abyss, I grew aware of a melodious unity of sounds rising like vapor from a small mining town that lay at my feet, in a fold of the valley. One could make out the geometry of the streets between blocks of red and gray roofs, and green puffs of trees, and a serpentine stream, and the rich, ore-like glitter of the city dump, and beyond the town, roads crisscrossing the crazy quilt of dark and pale fields, and behind it all, great timbered mountains. But even brighter than those quietly rejoicing colors—for there are colors and shades that seem to enjoy themselves in good company—both brighter and dreamier to the ear than they were to the eye, was that vapory vibration of accumulated sounds that never ceased for a moment, as it rose to the lip of granite where I stood wiping my foul mouth. And soon I realized that all these sounds were of one nature, that no other sounds but these came from the streets of the transparent town, with the women at home and the men away. Reader! What I heard was but the melody of children at play, nothing but that, and so limpid was the air that within this vapor of blended voices, majestic and minute, remote and magically near, frank and divinely enigmatic—one could hear now and then, as if released, an almost articulate spurt of vivid laughter, or the crack of a bat, or the clatter of a toy wagon, but it was all really too far for the eye to distinguish any movement in the lightly etched streets. I stood listening to that musical vibration from my lofty slope, to those flashes of separate cries with a kind of demure murmur for background, and then I knew that the hopelessly poignant thing was not Lolita's absence from my side, but the absence of her voice from that concord.[116]

In his afterword to *Lolita*, Nabokov refers to this scene as being a "secret point," and one of the "nerves" of the novel.[117] What remain are Humbert's closing words, in which he makes a point of noting that he has reread his story and realizes that there are "bits of marrow sticking to it," and "beautiful bright-green flies."[118]

8: Language

Humbert says he can only play with words, which is his creator's and indeed any author's predilection. But in *Lolita,* the language usage and prose style can be considered the novel's most important element, representing not only the aesthetic purposes of word choices but also their sentient, conscious use.[119] To recap, *Lolita* is Nabokov's love affair with the English language; Anthony Burgess observes that Lolita's personality lies not in her flesh and bones but in the two "allophones" in her name, and, in a letter to Vera, Nabokov calls the English language, by comparison with Russian, "an illusion, ersatz." So in *Lolita,* language becomes a veritable protagonist. It is remarkable that for Nabokov language, like character, is not real, ersatz, when written in English and not Russian. Yet the style of English in *Lolita* is an extraordinary performance that shows the Russian influence, a latent language illuminating the visible pages of the novel from within.

For Burgess, the beauty of Lolita's character depends on language, but so, too, does her "reality." *Lolita* is so true to life, so real, so tangible, precisely because of an intangible detail: language. What Nabokov observes in *Lectures in Russian Literature* of Gogol and his work becomes particularly relevant when considering *Lolita:* "If you are interested in 'ideas' and 'facts' and 'messages,' keep away from Gogol. The awful trouble of learning Russian in order to read him will not be repaid in your kind of hard cash. Keep away, keep away. He has nothing to tell you. Keep off the tracks. High tension. Closed for the duration. Avoid, refrain, don't." But he welcomes the "right sort" of reader, advising that "you will first learn the alphabet, the labials, the linguals, the dentals, the letters that buzz, the drone and the bumblebee, and the Tse-tse Fly. One of the vowels will make you say 'Ugh!' You will feel mentally stiff and bruised after your first declension of personal pronouns. I see however no other way of getting to Gogol (or to any other Russian writer for that matter). His work, as all great literary achievements, is a phenomenon of language and not one of ideas."[120]

Language is the tool of literature. From Nabokov's perspective, while words carry clear meanings, literature permits a different approach. Everyday language has the task of imparting information, communicating. For this reason, it always refers the listener to an application or a phenomenon that is outside of language. The more we focus, and eliminate immaterial details, the better we impart precise information. Literary or poetic language, however, does not have the exclusive intention of imparting information in a functional way nor does it feel dependent on certain familiar words or expressions. Poetic language embraces the full spectrum of rich verbal associations, to alter the nature of familiar words and distort common usages. For Nabokov, literature searches for freedom. Victor Erlich in *Russian Formalism* (1965) cites Edmund Husserl's conviction that meaning resides within words while their application lies outside, and the language of literature, for Nabokov, is therefore in its own world, distinct from reality and the quotidian application of words. This clarifies Nabokov's prose style, his use of language, and even the structure of his novels.[121] Nabokov's language sees most of the words move to the interior of themselves, recursive and self-reflecting, instead of aiming at external phenomena. Appel refers to Nabokov's work as "involuted" — it "turns in upon itself, is self-referential."[122] Every word carries a number of different consignments: mood, etymology, associative meanings, sound, and others. In Nabokov's usage, meaning is equal in importance to these additional consignments. Consequently, each word has a number of levels and ways of exerting its influence, not only mentally but sensually. Language in literature acquires the bulk and heft of these multiple consignments for Nabokov.

This perhaps explains Nabokov's objection to what is generally referred to as "realist theory." From this perspective, the type of "realist" literature that aims only at external truth is literature that deceives the reader. Literature of this "realist" type maintains, in his view, that there is only one truth, the truth as presented by the writer. This is objectionable, as words carry multiple loads and pointers or double indicators. Words refer to something outside of themselves (application) and, at the same time, attract the reader's attention to the existence of this apparently contradictory correspondence (between, for example, the word "butterfly" and an actual colorful winged insect in reality). Neither the word nor its application is an absolute. The type of literature that claims to imitate reality accepts, in fact, only one reality and only one way of expressing this unique reality. In this scenario, ordinary language and literary language (and finally even reality itself) are deprived of all associations of meanings. The movement of language that is used to relate a "realist" story can clearly be seen in this simple instruction: from inside to outside and back inside again.[123]

Literature narrates an experience and seeks to create something tangible. Jane Austen's method primarily used conversation instead of character description or setting to reveal information through tone. Nabokov, as we have seen, paints, and in *Lolita,* the tension lies in the contrast between fixed and moving images. Nonetheless, Nabokov's only paintbrush is made of words, and their strings of meaning and associative networks. For example, Lolita's names: Dolores, Dolly, Lola, Lo. The novel begins with a list of these names (and the sentiments and the mental states that each name summons inside Humbert's mind). From among these names, Humbert opts for a melodious and suggestive name, Lolita, a name that Humbert brings, in a way, into his possession — just as Lolita herself is the little fairy that Humbert captures (and does not capture). Nabokov, in an exchange with Alvin Toffler in 1964, returned to his thoughts on Joyce and the similarities of atmosphere in his own and Joyce's novels: "We think not in words but in shadows of words. James Joyce's mistake in those otherwise marvelous mental soliloquies of his consists in that he gives too much verbal body to thoughts."[124] For Nabokov, then, a writer ought not to confine words to their own boundaries but to allow them to bring their shadows into play as well. Nabokov's "paintings" are lit not only by external light but by internal light too. Just as natural daylight moves with the sun and shadows accordingly vary their position and length, so too the shadows of words are transformed by variations in internal light and internal color. This is the nature of the movement of language in *Lolita.*

Every word, then, is a hoard of attitudes, affections, and experiences and a cache that conveys meaning. Literary language is a language of metaphors; Nabokov's literary language is poetic. But this does not mean that Nabokov imitates poetry in the prose of his novels — rather, he truly *discovers* poetry through the language of his fiction. Nabokov's language is not content merely to narrate the story and move the plot forward but has other, deeper motivations. Nabokov's relationship with Russian and English is not unlike Humbert's relationship with his Annabel and Lolita. Just as Humbert loses his childhood love, Nabokov was compelled to abandon his cherished Russian. Nothing can replace that first love. However, the despair over a lost love gives way to hope for a love that appears attainable. Love is requited through the narrative process, and at the end of the novel, Humbert immortalizes Lolita. *Lolita* is Humbert's handiwork, but the peculiar brand of English used in *Lolita* bears Nabokov's personal seal. The memory of the Russian language flows through the novel like an internal poem, like the blue memory of Annabel before the golden presence of Lolita.

In *Lolita* not only is the language metaphoric, but the novel itself is too. Typically, an author will vary the tenor and mood as different characters and different states or conditions are introduced. In *Lolita,* it is not the tones that change but the combinations of tone and character or state, their uses unexpected. Nabokov's particular use of language creates a new kind of tonal fluency that encompasses different styles and leads to a sense of defamiliarization. Apparently incoherent words are given prominence by association, charging them with new and unexpected power. Bathos and pathos are interchanged, one disrupting the natural flow of the other, giving rise to entirely new moods or tones. The same unsettling approach is applied to characters and events: Charlotte's personality is rendered realistically, while Quilty is introduced absurdly. Humbert travels from despair in his last encounter with Lolita to pure farce and slapstick in his murder of Quilty. Other games are being played out too: Humbert alludes to Poe and parodies Eliot. Language is employed to synthesize itself, and also the language that opposes or contradicts it, or that remains in the shadowy reaches of another language. Nabokov's magic, his enchantment, begins with his use of language, to pool all these diverse and divergent elements together.[125] *Lolita* exemplifies the qualities or the characteristics to which Nabokov refers in *Speak, Memory* as inherent to a creative mind: "from the charting of dangerous seas to the writing of one of those incredible novels where the author, in a fit of lucid madness, has set himself certain unique rules that he observes, certain nightmare obstacles that he surmounts, with the zest of a deity building a live world from the most unlikely ingredients — rocks, and carbon, and blind throbbings."[126]

SEVEN

Heaven and Hell

Ada or Ardor

1

The sun has just risen and the autumn morning is clear and bright. I am sitting at an old metal desk in an empty, curtainless room looking out on Mount Damavand. The notes and drafts of this chapter are scattered over the desk, alongside a neat, clean copy of *Ada* that is not mine. My own copy is a mess; I have covered it in notes, dog-eared so many pages, and high-lighted sentences throughout with crooked or curvy lines. I am diligently rewriting this chapter, hopefully for the last time, and I must behave myself with this copy of the novel, which is a loan. Mr. R. (*Transparent Things*) is on my mind as I rewrite, and I hope for his cooperation. This is yet another "final" draft on yet another morning in the mountains, here under the roof of the sky, so close I could almost touch it. The firmament appears at once like a closed circle and an infinite expanse. The sun is inching up through a gap between two peaks; its vanguard and herald is a bright pyramid that paints the mountain slopes with faint shades of color. This is not the only patch of sky that is gaining color. Vibrant rays of light gradually animate not only the mountaintops but also the wandering clouds; eventually, the entire expanse of the sky is illumined. Even in the extreme west, where the cold, white moon dangles above pale, lavender mountains.

Reality, or its reflection, possesses a similar allure in Nabokov's novels. Nabokov reflects his own previous work and that of other writers in his novels in a manner similar to the scattering of sunbeams across the sky, without exactly repeating or multiplying. Light spreads throughout with its own range of hues, yet also acquires the unique shape of each crevice or rock it touches. In *Ada,* arguably one of the most ambitious of Nabokov's novels (along with *Lolita* and *Pale Fire*), we find all Nabokov's principal themes, with their variegated shades of color and reflections: the passage of time, exile, memory, *poshlust,* cruelty, pain, languages (Russian, English, and French), art, and love, and also the multifaceted prism of "reality." *Ada* is deeply indebted to *Speak, Memory,* as if both books were cut from the same fabric, with the same texture, even though one is an autobiography and the other a novel. They complement each other. In *Speak, Memory,* we see how reality, in its multiple guises, gives rise to the numerous voids in Nabokov's life. *Ada* is his attempt to fill those voids, a fairy tale that creates its own, independent reality.[1]

The plot of *Ada* (1969) can be summarized in a few lines, though not easily.[2] It is a familiar story of everlasting love between a girl and a boy who at first think they are cousins but later discover that they are siblings. They come from an aristocratic family. They first fall in love when Van (short for Ivan) is fourteen years old and Ada (short for Adelaida) almost twelve. Their love story lasts until they are both in their late nineties and in a sense extends even beyond their deaths. The novel opens on Ada's family estate and summer residence, Ardis Manor, which casts a long shadow over all subsequent times and settings in the book. Ada and Van are products of a passionate love affair—between Marina and Demon—and cannot seem to live with or without each other. Demon, a form of Demian or Dementius, is a word with its own significance in English. Demon marries Marina's less pretty twin, her "far more dotty" sister Aqua. Marina then exchanges the stillborn child to whom Aqua gives birth for her own newborn son, Van. Later, when already pregnant with Ada, Marina marries Demon's equally "opulent, but much duller" cousin. The outcome of this marriage is a red-haired girl called Lucette (short for Lucinda). Throughout her short life, Lucette is madly in love with Van, a love that is unrequited; Ada and Van are always looking to steal away together. Eventually, Lucette despairingly renounces her love for Van and commits suicide, as had her Aunt Aqua before her. Nevertheless, after two magical summers in Ardis Manor, Ada and Van are compelled to separate, reunited only briefly and agonizingly. The

years come and go, until finally they meet again after a seventeen-year hiatus, when Van is fifty-two and Ada is fifty. (Demon, Marina, and Ada's husband are by now all dead.) They subsequently spend the rest of their lives
together. Van becomes a renowned psychologist, professor of philosophy,
and author of several books. His last work is a book of memoirs touching
on his lifelong love affair with Ada. He writes it over the last few years of
his life, with Ada's help.

If *Ada* seems magical, it is because the childhood of the novel's protagonists, especially their time at Ardis Manor, is infused with Nabokov's
own memories of childhood summers spent at Vyra. In *Ada,* both time and
space are metaphoric. In a letter from Cambridge to his mother in 1920, the
young Nabokov writes about having awakened in the middle of the night to
ask "someone—I don't know whom—the night, the stars, God: will I really
never return, is it really all finished, wiped out, destroyed . . . ?" He goes
on to plead, "Mother, we must return, mustn't we, it cannot be that this has
all died, turned to dust—such an idea could drive one mad!" Then he confesses his desire to describe and remember "every little bush, every stalk
in our divine park at Vyra—but no one can understand this. . . . How little
we valued our paradise . . . —we should have loved it more pointedly, more
consciously."[3] Initially, I had intended to analyze Nabokov's oeuvre in this
book with the primary notion of turning "fate" on its head, confronting the
meaning of "reality," challenging the idea of "exile," and picking apart the
received sense of "time." There is, after all, a present that is not filled with
the past (and, of course, the future). I have not confined myself to these
questions. All the same, these knots are all untangled in *Ada.* As Alter puts
it, it is in *Ada* that Nabokov eventually regains his paradise lost.[4]

In *Ada,* we reside in a different time and a different space. The novel
begins toward the end of the nineteenth century; Van is born in 1870 and
Ada in 1872. Slowly but surely, however, it becomes clear that the time is
actually an amalgam of the nineteenth century and an imaginary future; although time moves on as expected in the nineteenth century, we repeatedly
encounter highly advanced twentieth-century inventions and innovations.[5]
In fact, the novel takes place on a different planet, one that confronts or opposes Terra, called Antiterra (or Demonia). The inhabitants of Antiterra

are more or less familiar with Terra, though they treat it lightly, and some even confuse it with Antiterra. The geographies are similar, as are their histories; there are other superficial resemblances. On closer look, however, we observe fundamental differences. For example, the fact that on Terra, Russia and America are two separate countries astounds the Antiterrestrians: in Antiterra, Russia is the outmoded name of the northern province of America, Estoty. Amerussians speak English as easily as they speak Russian or French. There is a gap of up to a hundred years one way or the other between the two planets, although, according to the narrator, not all the "no-longers" of one world correspond to the "not-yets" of the other.[6]

In the beginning of *Ada*, the narrator notes that "even the deepest thinkers, the purest philosophers" of Antiterra are divided on the subject of whether there "existed a distortive glass of our distorted glebe."[7] "Distortion" is one of Nabokov's key words, and essential for describing his style during the last period of his writing. There remain Nabokov's ever-present "thesis" and "antithesis," yet they appear different now; one is the misquoted or distorted version of the other; one imitates the other. We thus encounter parody once more, one of the fundamentals of Nabokov's art, something that throws us into a world of affection and compassion. This is how Terra casts a shadow over Antiterra. If Antiterrestrials doubt whether Terra actually exists, this doubt lengthens Terra's shadow and lends it more heft than any feeling of certitude. On a more tangible level, Antiterra traces the outline of Nabokov's ideal world. For example, if Amerussia is located on one side of Antiterra, on the opposite side is located the region of Tartary that stretches from the Baltic and Black Seas to the Pacific Ocean, an "independent inferno," "touristically unavailable."[8] Nabokov's three cultures—Russian, English, and French—come together in Amerussia, a space largely devoid of politics. No wonder then that the main characters speak these three languages with ease and their words constantly reference a colossal number of literary and artistic allusions from these three cultures. Only in a place like this could paradise lost be regained, and only by way of artistic tradition.

Only those prepared to step into the abyss, those deluded, sick minds, actually believe in the existence of Terra. Aqua, Marina's sister and Demon's wife, is one such believer. Aqua was not quite twenty when the "exaltation of her nature had begun to reveal a morbid trend."[9] Doubts about whether Van is really her child make life even more difficult for her, and she commits suicide. She leaves a note signed "My sister's sister who *teper' iz ada* ('now is out of hell')."[10] According to Hyde, the word "Ada" brings various (contradictory) notions to mind: in Russian, "ad" means hell or Hades, "da" means "yes," and the combination "a da!" is a Russian expression of joy. In Latin "aqua" means water and "marina" means marine. Aqua can never overcome the "despair of desire"; in a way, Aqua's suicide foreshadows Lucette's.[11] Lucette jumps overboard into the Atlantic when she realizes that Van will never reciprocate her love. Aqua and Lucette, the most positive characters in the novel, fall victim to the cruelty of those around them. Ada and Van make Lucette suffer just as Marina and Demon make Aqua suffer, though their methods are different. Van, narrating, explains that "no sooner did all the fond, all the frail, come into close contact with him (as later Lucette did, to give another example) than they were bound to know anguish and calamity, unless strengthened by a strain of his father's demon blood."[12]

Most of Van's working life is passionately devoted to terrology, a branch of psychiatry involving mental patients who see Terra recurrently in their dreams.[13] He reports on the "transcendental delirium" of his patients.[14] The narrator detects in himself the same passion for the insane as "some have for arachnids or orchids."[15] It is important to keep this profession in mind when analyzing Van's philosophical novel entitled *Letters from Terra,* which tells the story of a scholar from Antiterra who begins a more or less loving relationship with Theresa, a roving reporter on Terra. "Poor Van! In his struggle to keep the writer of the letters from Terra strictly separate from the image of Ada, he gilt and carmined Theresa until she became a paragon of banality."[16] Van is similarly obliged, with respect to the character of the scholar's betrayed wife, Antilia, to extract "all traces of Ada, thus reducing yet another character to a dummy with bleached hair."[17] The novel's narrator is Van, and Van has a creator, Nabokov. So does that mean Nabokov creates Van to be an unsuccessful novelist? If we compare Van to Sebastian, who transcribes his deepest emotions, we see that Van's Nabokovian distance from his characters is not synonymous with noninvolvement.

Theresa is able to transport herself to Antiterra. But she is so tiny that her scholar admirer can see her only through a powerful microscope. Their affair ends in tragedy when another one-dimensional female character throws away the test tube, with Theresa in it, by mistake. At first, Theresa offers a pleasant image of Terra, praise and praise alone, but eventually she confesses that she has not been entirely truthful, and has exaggerated the bliss as an instrument of "cosmic propaganda."[18] Van, too, compiled reports based on the visions of his patients, which meant relaying many things in garbled and botched form, and this is how they appear in the book. Nevertheless, Nabokov's "good reader" will identify "Athaulf the Future" as Adolf Hitler. Nabokov amuses himself here by satirizing European communism and wartime Nazism. Fifty years later, Van's novel is adapted for film, which proves controversial because it depicts Terra's political history during the first half of the twentieth century as a farce.[19] When Appel writes about *Ada,* he praises this reconstituted history, considering parts of it a "brilliant stroke, unhappily enough, since history is indeed a mad dream, a bad movie, and World War II a mythical happening or pop extravaganza, as anyone in touch with the under-thirties generation knows, since 'Casablanca' exists for them, but not Auschwitz."[20]

Van publishes *Letters from Terra* under the pseudonym Voltemand, taken from a courtier bearing news to Claudius in Shakespeare's *Hamlet,* a role mirrored in Theresa, who brings messages from Terra; Lucette, who delivers Ada's letter to Van to restore their relationship; and finally in Aqua, who appears to carry messages from another world.[21] This alludes to an obsession that envelops Nabokov's works: the existence of other spaces and other times that exert pressure on this world and this present time. Beyond the novel's present, which is inevitably referred to as "reality," another world is also felt, one that is no less real, a world that guides our thoughts and our actions and is sometimes called "fate." "Fate" provides an explanation for scattered events and life's unexpected (and seemingly unrelated) occurrences. "Fate" is given voice through Theresa and her messages and, beyond Theresa, through Voltemand. Yet *Ada* is not allegorical: the messages are not symbolical. *Ada* is committed purely to literature. There is, however, a dimension beyond the known parameters of "reality," and it is a sense of this dimension that is conveyed in *Ada,* even at the simplest levels of the novel.

2

Ada is the first Nabokov novel I ever read. It was the gift of a friend who considered himself one of Nabokov's staunchest admirers and who, like the author, spoke a number of European languages. We were students together, and had both registered for a seminar on Samuel Beckett. Our professor had an intoxicating (and, of course, helpless) fascination for Beckett, as if he were in love, and we imagined, despite being so young, that we were Beckett lovers too. The professor was a tall man, recently graduated from Yale, who cut a perfect figure with his glossy blond hair. He walked the halls of our faculty with a confident stride, stooping slightly as some tall people do. It seemed as though anyone in his path should just step aside. He appeared to beam and radiate something that wasn't quite happiness. We knew nothing about the professor, except that Beckett was his sole passion. Sometimes the cheek and antagonism of our questions seemed to irritate him. Now I realize that it was our ignorance that annoyed him. Whenever he would raise examples of oriental philosophy in Beckett's works, I, as the self-appointed sole representative of the East among his students, felt it was my duty to disagree with him. A seminar that would begin with great enthusiasm would turn sour for no reason. Consequently, we all heaved a sigh of relief when the semester came to an end. It was just before the next semester that we learned that the professor had shut himself in his garage, turned his car on, and killed himself. The details are fuzzy now, but thinking of and writing about *Ada* now causes me to recall the tall, stooping, Beckett-loving professor, who had at least one student who did not understand him, and it knocks me off balance.

Reading *Ada* obliged me to confront an unexpected feeling. As if some distant past had spread itself out before me, a past at once unfamiliar and yet very familiar (or as if I had lost the memory of a familiar feeling that was now unknown to me), I was suddenly addressed by a series of bright images that looked like paintings, evoking memories I thought had been lost. Yet nothing in *Ada* corresponded to my past. Instead, the quality that *Ada* evoked was, in essence, memory itself, something beyond the images of a particular past, like the immediate effect of a melody you have never heard before, or the sudden, penetrating scent of a flower you have never smelled before. No novel had ever influenced me so deeply. To me, the novel did not merely portray quotidian realities—it articulated the reader's subjective realities. It reminded me of my own make-believe fairy tales: a princess who can be awakened only by a prince, a hope that forever sprinkles not from a real rain cloud but from the mists of the imagination. Recalling Nabokov's declaration that "great novels are above all great fairy tales,"[22] I asked myself whether this need to tell and hear stories originates precisely from this familiar-unfamiliar feeling, the feeling that somewhere there is a paradise lost. At the same time, a story—any story—draws us unwittingly down a particular path, perhaps without our wish or consent; a story may not show us the way, but it can still offer hope.

The fairy-tale-like nature of *Ada* prompts another, sometimes vexing inkling. The novel closely resembles "Sleeping Beauty" and, at the same time, ridicules the impact of this impression on the reader. Just when the reader becomes absorbed in its colorful world of spaces and lights, a faint, mischievous voice from behind the shadows of the trees laughs, spritelike, at one's simpleminded credulity. Over the years as I have reread *Ada* and become familiar with Nabokov's other works, I have caught myself reacting repeatedly to that irritation. On one level the experience of being immersed in Nabokov's worlds filled me with wonder and the impression of beauty, but I gradually discovered that on another level that beauty is like the alluring mermaid song meant to pull the reader into the abyss, into the dark reality lurking behind the story. Nabokov's novels are like life's truths, overflowing with real mirages and miragelike realities. To Nabokov, the security and happiness of his childhood are as real as the helplessness and pain of his years in exile. This is evident in *Speak, Memory,* a book I read many years after *Ada*. As I moved from his novels to his autobiography, I understood that I was exploring the hell that cast its shadow over his paradise lost. But his paradise was regained in/via art, and hope thus rubbed shoulders with despair. This is what turns Nabokov's novels into such peculiar blends of comedy and tragedy, sweetness and bitterness, elation and shadow. This accessible and inaccessible paradise provides the origin of Nabokov's latent and sometimes overt satire, like photographs inside letters of condolence, recalling life amid death.

Ada believes that Van will go to heaven: "I know there's a Van in Nirvana." But she also says: "I'll be with him in the depths *moego ada,* of my Hades."[23] Aqua's suicide note, meanwhile, states that she is now out of hell.[24] *Ada* is a story not only of paradise regained but also of the hell inherent to this worldly paradise. The dichotomy of heaven and hell means that while one cannot exist without the other, they are not harmonious or tolerant of each other, they constantly sabotage the other's actions. This sabotage or interruption extends beyond the thematic to disorder the novel's entire structure. This is how it casts its spell, engaging unwitting readers in a peculiar game that no one can actually win. Nabokov's "good reader" is already familiar with his method of interruption in other novels. But *Ada* is where the device plays its most fundamental part because here it encompasses Nabokov's interpretation of the concept of time. In *Ada,* arguably, time is the novel's underlying protagonist. Appel believes that part 4, which deals directly with the concept of time, was written before the other sections of *Ada,* much as in *Lolita,* Quilty's murder scene was written first.[25]

Speak, Memory opens, as we know, with the image of an infinite, timeless abyss, its first sentence pausing to contemplate existence, shackled in the everlasting darkness of time's prison. A few sentences farther on, Nabokov revolts against this state of affairs; he feels "the urge to take my rebellion outside and picket nature."[26] *Ada* is part of Nabokov's rebellion, as can be seen in part 4, *The Texture of Time.*[27] As Fyodor's book on Chernyshevsky forms a separate chapter in *The Gift* and Shade's poem is incorporated into *Pale Fire,* so on a plot level does Van's treatise function in *Ada.* His novella in the form of a treatise is reproduced almost entirely in *Ada.* The treatise incorporates one of Van's speeches, and his journey to meet Ada after seventeen years apart, when he takes the wrong road, then again veers east in error; and it features Ada's voice, at the other end of the telephone line, which "resurrects" the past and links it to the present.[28] Their planned encounter is unsuccessful: Ada leaves the hotel and Van spends the night working on his treatise. At daybreak, he decides to go after Ada, but she has in fact already returned to the hotel in the middle of the night. Not only has Van finished his first draft, but the knots of the novel's plot have been untied. The treatise and the novel effectively end here, as the next chapter (the last) is, in essence, an epilogue in which Ada and Van live happily ever after.

The lost paradise of Ada and Van's childhood is called Ardis Park. Ardis means "arrow" in Greek, and it is as if the arrow of time, like that of love, aims directly at the heart, and that experiencing it fully is what causes death. *The Texture of Time* objects, simply, to the one-way nature of time, and Van's treatise, as part of *Ada* and as something at the service of the novel, has a purely literary use, less important for the philosophical issues it raises than for what it means for the creative process. For Van, the progress of time is "something that looks useful to me one moment, but dwindles the next to the level of an illusion obscurely related to the mysteries of growth and gravitation." Time's irreversibility, he says, is "a parochial affair."[29] Van says he intends to investigate the essence of time, not its passing, which is to say its essence does not merely comprise its lapse; "I wish to caress Time," he says.[30] Moreover, he tries to reject time's relativity; he tries to separate time from space, arguing that although time can be measured, it cannot be understood.[31] Van propounds an isolated, distinct aural notion of time: "If my eye tells me something about Space, my ear tells me something about Time. But while Space can be contemplated, naively, perhaps, yet directly, I can listen to Time only between stresses." Time is not the recurrent beats of a rhythm "but the gap between two such beats, the gray gap between black beats: the Tender Interval."[32]

Van does not believe that time is a triptych of Past, Present, and Future. There is only a diptych, in his view, because the future is a "'not-yet' that may never come," a loss of consciousness, or death, which exists beyond Van's (and our) sensate capacity.[33] Van will not die in this scenario; Nabokov himself believed self-consciousness to be the distinguishing human factor that separates us from animals, the fact of "being aware of being aware of being."[34] Present time, then, is volatile, Van reasons, and in order to apprehend it, "I must move my mind in the direction opposite to that in which I am moving, as one does when one is driving past a long row of poplars and wishes to isolate and stop one of them, thus making the green blur reveal, and offer, yes offer, its every leaf." It is only through conscious reconstruction, the "Deliberate Present," that one can attain the present time, or a sense of "nowness."[35] There is also the past, the second panel in his diptych. Van illustrates his idea of the past by telling the story of Zembre, "a quaint old town on the Minder River, near Sorcière." New buildings have been constructed around the old town, and it has transformed into a modern-looking city. People interested in historical preservation carefully reconstruct a replica of old Zembre on the opposite side of the river, so the modern city lies on one bank, the old city on the other, and a bridge connects the two. Van believes that by making a model of the old town, "all we do is to spatialize it." The city's past can be seen in the modern city, using the imagination, through the prism of memory. "The Past, then," Van asserts, "is a constant accumulation of images."[36] We reconstruct the past, consciously, at every moment because "time is but memory in the making."[37] So for Van and Nabokov, time is not a straight line that cuts through the past, present, and the future. Van says that his is "Motionless Time." "The Time I am concerned with is only the Time stopped by me and closely attended to by my tense-willed mind."[38]

Heaven and hell correspond to "Flowing Time" and "Motionless Time," respectively. If Flowing Time evokes the everyday nature of life, Motionless Time is the chronometer of memory and art. In *Ada*, hell signifies exile, an exile imposed by the passage of time, exile not only from Ardis but also from youth and love.[39] Van accepts the fact that the past will not return, and interprets it as a repository of thought and feeling. The time that belongs to Van and Ada is a private log, or an accumulated individual time, extending beyond death, acquired and kept alive through memory, then given voice through metaphor: in most of Nabokov's novels memory speaks through the magical language of art. Van tells us toward the end of *Ada* that the process of dying comes in three stages. In the first stage, one forever relinquishes memories, a commonplace problem, "but what courage man must have had to go through that commonplace again and again and not give up the rigmarole of accumulating again and again the riches of consciousness that will be snatched away!" The second stage is "hideous physical pain," and finally there is the "featureless, pseudo-future, blank and black, an everlasting nonlastingness, the crowning paradox of our boxed brain's eschatologies!"[40] Van refers to the Sisyphean struggle of

memory as "courage" — a futile endeavor that is an indication of the perseverance of memory and tantamount to memory imposing its will on the
despotism of time. Van also argues that to forfeit memory means to lose any
prospect of immortality. This is why Humbert longed to send Lolita forever
to the "intangible island of entranced time."[41]

Humbert, the narrator and lover, tries to assert his ownership over
Lolita by the way he describes her, by turning her into a still photograph. If
this manner of description is generally referred to as "painting with words,"
it is conceptually more complex than that, as we see in *Ada,* where characters are similarly painted. It entails "fixing" a scene and holding it motionless, freeing it from the despotic clutches of Flowing Time to capture it. Van
pursues such an objective, and we encounter direct or indirect allusions
to paintings throughout *Ada.*[42] Boyd recalls that before embarking on the
novel, Nabokov, on a trip to Italy with Vera, spent a few weeks looking at
paintings in various museums and art galleries.[43] We come across some of
these artworks in *Ada,* and color and colorful descriptions play an essential
narrative role. Ada and Lucette are associated with certain colors: Ada's
black hair and ivory pallor in contrast with Lucette's red hair and sandy
skin. In a scene where Ada, Van, and Lucette are playing, the reader comes
across objective moments where life suddenly stands still, as if in paintings
or photographs. The novel keeps moving forward by plaiting and unplaiting
the black and red strands of the two girls' hair.[44]

This descriptive device increases in conceptual complexity in one
particular scene, where the adolescent Van sees Ada washing her face and
arms. He had not meant to see her, and she is unaware of his presence.
Van observes her. "A fat snake of porcelain curled around the basin, and
as both the reptile and he stopped to watch Eve and the soft woggle of her
bud-breasts in profile, a big mulberry-colored cake of soap slithered out
of her hand, and her black-socked foot hooked the door shut with a bang
which was more the echo of the soap's crashing against the marble board
than a sign of pudic displeasure."[45] Van's voyeurism ends here, as does the
scene. The precision of the description renders the brief scene real, tangible, appealing. Yet it overflows simultaneously with associative meanings:
a porcelain snake curls round the washbasin, and, according to the narrator,

both Van and the snake remain motionless to watch Eve.[46] Soon, then, this Adam and Eve will be expelled from the Garden of Eden, though they are not so innocent. They both seduce and are seduced. Here, one of Nabokov's "divine details" is the color of the soap, as Motionless Time, with its accumulated associations of meanings, imposes itself on Flowing Time before Van's eyes.

Nabokov blends heterogeneous elements in *Ada* as a device, identifiable in a scene at Ardis that deals with the passage of time, and therefore memory. Ada and Van spend only two summers together at Ardis, with a four-year gap between them. A brief description of Van at the start of the second summer alludes to the porcelain snake: he returns on a cloudy June afternoon, "unexpected, unbidden, unneeded; with a diamond necklace coiled loose in his pocket." When Van sees Ada, he notices that she has an independent life "without him, not for him." Without any additional explanation, the narrator gives a brief description of Ada's dress: "Against the white cape Ada's new long figure was profiled in black—the black of her smart silk dress with no sleeves, no ornaments, no memories."[47] A few sentences later he observes that "the low cut of her black dress allowed the establishment of a sharp contrast between the familiar mat whiteness of her skin and the brutal black horsetail of her new hair-do."[48] The unexpected effect of this device is accomplished when two unrelated phenomena are juxtaposed; in this instance, proximity underscores distance.

Nabokov continues to put forward Van's concept of time, familiarizing the reader with Van's thought processes, and how the three stages of time constantly disrupt each other. We experience the passage of time, how cruel a process it is, both in lengthy descriptions and in brief, apparently inconsequential sentences too.[49] Van becomes a ghost on his return to Ardis, observing life as it unfolds without him, unwatched, autonomous. The Ardis of *Ada* is not a parallel for the Vyra of *Speak, Memory*, because Nabokov is not working symmetrically but rather amassing heterogeneous ingredients. Russia remains a dreamland to which one cannot return except by way of the imagination. When Vadim in *Look at the Harlequins!* returns to the Soviet Union, for example, the result is disastrous. Nabokov's fiction does not depict the "real" Russia but instead describes a dreamscape, conjured up by narrative art. In *The Gift,* Nabokov describes the city of Berlin realistically, as he does North America in *Lolita,* alongside (in both cases) a magical or imaginary Russia. In *Ada,* our locations are two different worlds, Terra and Antiterra. The entire novel takes place in a dyadic fairy-tale world, revealed in an orderly manner.

Near the end of Van's treatise, after he and Ada are reunited, Van tells her that he intends to compose a kind of novella in the form of a treatise on the texture of time, "an investigation of its veily substance, with illustrative metaphors gradually increasing, very gradually building up a logical love story, going from past to present, blossoming as a concrete story, and just as gradually reversing analogies and disintegrating again into bland abstraction."[50] Nabokov has undertaken exactly what Van is proposing, presenting the transformation of an abstract idea into a novel's concrete story and vice versa, converting a scene in *Ada* into an abstract idea. In fact, Van's novella about time is a miniature conceit on the same principles as Nabokov's long novel about Ada and Van, whose predominant metaphor takes shape with the help of their relationship with Ardis, or time's arrow. Within the framework of metaphor, all these apparently unrelated themes come together. Before writing *Ada,* when he was still putting notes together and expected the novel to be titled *The Texture of Time,* Nabokov spoke to reporters and echoed something similar to what Van says; as he later told Brian Boyd: "The difficulty about it is that I have to devise an essay, a scholarly-looking essay on time and then gradually turn it into the story I have in mind. The metaphors start to live. The metaphors gradually turn into the story because it's very difficult to speak about time without using similes or metaphors. And my purpose is to have these metaphors breed to form a story of their own, gradually, and then again to fall apart, and to have it all end in this rather dry though serious and well-meant essay on time. It proves so difficult to compose that I don't know what do about it."[51]

Metaphors are a central device in Nabokov's novels. His use of metaphor is not a casual choice from a grab bag of literary techniques or an arbitrary framework for an assortment of ideas, but a wide-ranging conceptual vision, a way of approaching and interpreting literary experience and, more important, understanding the experience of life and death, a way of confronting life's abysses, of seeking to comprehend life in exile, which cannot be considered anything other than an abyss. It is not contrast alone that matters in metaphor, or dualities like place and void, color and shadow, past and present, but where these opposites can overlay and superimpose, unite in a single image. Van reaches this conclusion while writing his treatise, finding "real time's being connected with the interval between events, not with their 'passage,' not with their blending, not with their shading the gap wherein the pure and impenetrable texture of time transpires."[52] The metaphoric texture of Nabokov's novels, especially *Ada*, depends on the gulf between events, and not the events themselves, as the author perceives or narrates this gulf.

The Nabokovian metaphor is the result of a process that renders the present reality unacceptable. Why? What more convincing answer is there than the cruel events of the twentieth century and the bitterness of exile? It is a difficult solution, and an inevitable harbor: for Nabokov's characters, there has to be another place and another time beyond the ordinary here and now. It is a place often evoked when a character passes away, an aura that emanates to enrobe Nabokov's protagonists even when they are absorbed in the reality of their everyday lives. Hence, the connection between "good" spirits like Fyodor's father (*The Gift*) or Mira (*Pnin*) or Lucette (*Ada*) and the main characters is not severed through death. (One of these good spirits is Mr. R. in *Transparent Things*, who serves as Nabokov's substitute at one level of the novel.) For the lepidopterist author, death is not an end but a metamorphosis. Nabokov is trying not to run away from reality, to escape the inevitable, but to reconfigure our idea of time, of the present, as a complex accumulation of both the past and the future; by rejecting a simple sense of time as a straight line, we refuse to accept that the past is lost, and that the future is unpreventable. Using metaphor instead of the mathematics of chronology to consider reality perhaps allows for a more layered perception of it, a multidirectional reality, encompassing all the contradictory elements of life: Flowing Time, Motionless Time, memory and art, heaven and hell.

Multidirectional reality applies equally to the inset narrative of Van's treatise and the greater world of the novel itself. Nabokov's descriptive style weaves this metaphoric vision into the texture of every scene in *Ada*. Every moment involves another moment and every scene another scene, so much so that thinking uniquely in terms of heroes or villains, protagonists or antagonists, is meaningless because Terra cannot be thought of without Antiterra, nor hell without heaven. Van's *The Texture of Time* is a structural trick; it has no existence beyond the framework of *Ada*.[53] Time, one of Nabokov's key themes (probably more than for any other of the great novelists of his era), refutes the realism of the nineteenth-century novel that moved forward on the basis of linear time, a narration seemingly incongruous in the twentieth century. The tradition of the nineteenth-century English-language novel developed greater complexity and ambiguity with Henry James's narrative art. The twentieth-century novel engaged the notion of time in a central way: Proust added the texture of individual memory, Joyce the texture of collective memory. Nabokov's idea of the texture of time was not the same as Proust's "lost" time but something that can be felt, handled even, in everyday life. Few writers have infused time with the level of wonder and enchantment that Nabokov did in his work. As Van explains, "Time is a fluid medium for the culture of metaphors."[54]

3

During the autumn days I have spent rewriting this last chapter on *Ada*, I have also been thinking of when, two decades ago, I read *Ada* for the first time and gradually discovered Nabokov. At the time, I could never have imagined that I would come to write about *Ada*. Nevertheless, something must have been percolating even then. With *Ada*, my present time has always encompassed future expectations, and it remains the case. I have returned to *Ada* after every fundamental change in my life; this novel always causes me to combine and reconsider unrelated times and different relationships. *Ada* finds an acceptable association of them. That spring when I was twenty, and I had just discovered *Ada*, has the green and red background of an unforgettable natural world, or so it is in my memory: the red soil and the wide brooks that turn the ground into a gigantic chessboard, reminiscent of the world of *Alice's Adventures in Wonderland*. In *Ada*, the narrator, comparing the present to the past, says that "that complete collapse of the past, the dispersal of its itinerant court and music-makers, the logical impossibility to relate the dubious reality of the present to the unquestionable one of remembrance" aggrieves him.[55]

So long as the past is interpreted through memory, the language of art, it will always belong to us. Time moves through our thoughts and our words, yet the present is never entirely ours: we do not control it; we are not immune to its unexpected twists and turns. When I first read *Ada,* I was still anticipating the future impatiently, but when the future arrives, it never really looks the way one expects. Van, who excludes the future from his consideration of time, is correct in this respect. Many years later, I found a paperback copy of *Ada* in a bookshop unexpectedly, with the same pink orchid on the cover. As an act of gratitude toward the past, I gave it to a friend, envisaging her future acquaintance with the book. I found copies for other, younger friends, too. This process continued until *Ada* gradually settled and became something to which I owe my sense of my past and maybe even my own present self-awareness. Similarly, I owe to it many of my friendships and acquaintances. The nearer I get to my elusive present time — to memories that are, in fact, in the process of becoming memories though they are not quite there yet — the harder it is to see the connection in writing between past and present, and between reality and imagination.

Ada also elaborates the complexity of living in the elusive present. A scene early in the novel (through which the narrator swiftly passes but that has an essential role in the structure of *Ada*) anticipates the book's principal theme, Ada's and Van's love for each other. It describes Van's first feeling of love, even before he sees Ada. He is thirteen years old. A French widow (who speaks English with a Russian accent) owns a shop near his school, where she sells antique furniture and *objets d'art*. At various points in the shop there are crystal vases of artificial flowers. In a magical sentence, Van considers it "puzzling that such imitations always pander so exclusively to the eye instead of also copying the damp fat feel of live petal and leaf." Then, one day, he touches one of the roses and is "cheated of the sterile texture his fingertips had expected when cool life kissed them with pouting lips."[56] The widow explains that her daughter always places a few real flowers among the fake ones *"pour attraper le client,"* to capture customers. A moment later, the daughter appears, a schoolgirl with brown shoulder-length ringlets. They never speak, but Van falls "madly" in love with her for "at least one term." Van thus experiences love, normal and mysterious, for the first time. At the same time, the narrator recounts Van's first experience of sex: without love or sentiment, and costing "a Russian green dollar."[57] Here we are dealing with two extremes of the same experience, thesis and antithesis. It is through his love for Ada that Van attains synthesis, and achieves maturity, in every sense of the word.

Again, a familiar Nabokovian trick: the shop of the artificial and natural flowers moves the plot forward and, at the same time, recalls a central device in *Ada,* that art's reality often appears in unexpected and, of course, pleasing ways. Very simply, art and reality reveal themselves as deceitful or charming. As we have seen, Nabokov often compares the allure, mimicry, and mischief of art with the same qualities in nature. In nature, many insects and animals (butterflies and moths included) mimic plants, like chameleons who change color to blend in with the environment, or insects that look like tree bark. Art, like nature, reflects its surroundings, to ward off the banal threats both of life and death. The widow's daughter hides real flowers among artificial ones to attract real customers. Nabokov's approach is figurative, wherein one flower repeats and explains the other. This heralds another device, the skill or artistry of asymmetry, no mere juxtaposition of opposites such as dream and reality. The farther we move from symmetry, the closer we get to metaphor. No longer is subject or context the means by which an image or state of mind revives another. In the flower scene, the reader encounters juxtaposition, but even the image of the flowers in a vase (a combination of reality and art) involves half-hidden allusions to more complex structures and figures that lead to metaphors.

On Ada's twelfth birthday, during Van's first summer at Ardis, the return from the group picnic requires Ada to sit on Van's knee, as there is not enough room in the carriage. This is the first time they touch. The narrator describes the pleasant agony of the situation.[58] Four years later, the second summer at Ardis again features a picnic, on Ada's sixteenth birthday, and again there is not enough room in the carriage. This time, twelve-year-old

Lucette sits on Van's knee, while Ada, sitting beside Van, leafs through a book.[59] The childish love of the first picnic has gone through a number of stages before (and during) the second, making it flourish and grow. At the same time, Van has been away from Ada for some years and has come to know infidelity and jealousy. He cannot help but remember the summer four years earlier, cannot help but regret the loss of the twelve-year-old Ada, even though he has now gained the sixteen-year-old Ada, and is trying to locate the past Ada in the present Lucette. The scene highlights the different colors of Ada and Lucette, and the visible and hidden variances between the sisters. Lucette's hair carries the scent of that past summer, and Van not only finds the past Ada in Lucette but also loses the present Lucette in the past he imagines. Inadvertently, Lucette brings a message from the past Ada, and transmits a message to her. In this second carriage scene we see how metaphor is founded on heterogeneity: Van experiences not only the Ada of the past or the Ada of the present but both of them. The narrator points out that we see and hear everything from Van's point of view, as if we were under his skin, while "his Ada sits within Lucette, and both sit within Van." The sentence is written by the elderly Van many years later. In a footnote to which, the elderly Ada adds "and all three in me."[60]

In the first part of *Ada*, four characters are at dinner. They are Ada and Van (young lovers concealing their love), together with the secret lovers of a generation earlier, Marina and Demon. Sixteen years have elapsed since Marina and Demon's last encounter. The narrator explains that Demon is trying to find in the present Marina the image of the woman whom he had loved more keenly than any other. He is not successful.[61] The narrator gives a description of the present Marina in detail and a little cruelly. She is no longer young, and her efforts to look youthful and desirable are futile. But the effects of aging are not the issue; the point is that whatever passion Marina and Demon once shared no longer exists. Time has conquered their love, a love that is now only a cause for bewilderment and resentment because it brings to mind all that was and is no more. Demon revisits his moments of desire and fervor, but a dead love cannot be revived even through memories: "How strange that when one met after a long separation a chum or fat aunt whom one had been fond of as a child the unimpaired human warmth of the friendship was rediscovered at once, but with an old mistress this never happened—the human part of one's affection seemed to be swept away with the dust of the inhuman passion, in a wholesale operation of demolishment."[62] Demon looks at Marina now and sees a stranger. In contrast to a love that ends, Ada and Van's love is enduring, a love that, like art and as art, opposes time. Love and art, art and love, both go to battle against reality in their desire to resist time and decay, both create their own inner worlds, their imaginary worlds, despite bitter everyday reality.

Toward the end of *Ada* is another dinner scene. With numerous events and adventures behind them, Ada and Van eventually reencounter each other seventeen years since they parted, meeting again at the same hotel as before. Van is fifty-two and Ada fifty. Now, at last, Ada can remain by Van's side; they are both free of other commitments, though Van is busy writing *The Texture of Time*. Like Marina and Demon, the erstwhile lovers have changed with time. The narrator gives a detailed description of Ada now, with the same degree of cruelty. Ada has gained weight and wears unusual clothes and too much makeup; she has cropped her hair and bobbed it pageboy fashion, and dyed it a brilliant bronze (reminiscent of Lucette, dead for many years). Both she and Van have gold-capped teeth. Ada's skin is still pale, but the veins in her hands are fibrous and pronounced, while Van's skin is covered with liver spots. Their conversation stalls and is wasted on trivialities. When Van talks about his investigation on the nature of time, Ada peeks at her wristwatch. In the past, whenever they met after a long period of separation, the initial inevitable strangeness was subsumed by the shared ache of sexual desire. Now desire does not come to the rescue; "they were on their own."[63] Eventually, Ada makes her excuses: she cannot stay for the night. Her suitcases have been sent to Geneva and she has to retrieve them. She promises that they will see each other again, and leaves the hotel. Van goes back to his room and his unfinished work, asking himself, "Does the ravage and outrage of age deplored by poets tell the naturalist of Time anything about Time's essence?" He answers: "Very little."[64]

Has time, then, ravaged Van and Ada's love? In an interview, Nabokov explained that although he had begun work on the section entitled "The Texture of Time" ten years earlier, in Ithaca, New York, not until

February 1966 did "the entire novel leap into the kind of existence that can and must be put into words. Its springboard was Ada's telephone call."[65] This conversation occurs exactly before the dinner scene, when Ada, who has just arrived at the hotel, calls Van. The narrator, Van, reminds us that she has "never—never, at least, in adult life—spoken to him by phone; hence the phone had preserved the very essence, the bright vibration, of her vocal cords." He hears the timbre of their shared past, "as if the past had put through that call, a miraculous connection." Ada's voice resurrects the past and grafts it to the present time, transforming it into Van's deepest experience of tangible time, "the glittering 'now' that was the only reality of Time's texture."[66] Ada's voice is that very butterfly that Nabokov lost when he was seven years old, the swallowtail that resurfaced forty years later posed atop an "immigrant dandelion" near Boulder, Colorado. Although Van and Ada separate after an unsuccessful dinner, the reader knows that the separation is going to be temporary.

Van spends the night with his treatise, and, before long, he reaches the conclusion: "Physiologically the sense of Time is a sense of continuous becoming." And then he adds, "Philosophically, on the other hand, Time is but memory in the making." Finally, he says: "'To be' means to know one 'has been.'"[67] At daybreak, he wakes abruptly, goes out onto the balcony, and realizes that if he does not go after Ada immediately, he will lose her forever. Ada, meanwhile, had traveled a certain distance that night, but then turned around and come back. She is on her balcony, one floor below, looking out at the same view. Ada looks up, and in one of Nabokov's magical sentences, "He saw her bronze bob, her white neck and arms, the pale flowers on her flimsy peignoir, her bare legs, her high-heeled silver slippers. . . . All her flowers turned up to him, beaming, and she made the royal-grant gesture of lifting and offering him the mountains, the mist and the lake with three swans."[68] Van runs down to her, and from then on they are never apart. In the lovers' perpetual present time, there always appears to be an air or a movement that carries a message from their other earlier selves. It is with the weapon of these other selves that the lovers put up a fight against time. As the chapter draws to a close, Van remarks, "All that matters just now is that I have given new life to Time by cutting off Siamese

Space and the false future."[69] The present time is the only time for lovers, overflowing with both the realities and the potentialities of the past. Finally, Ada says, "We can know the time, we can know a time. We can never know Time." She adds that our senses "are simply not meant to perceive it. It is like—."[70] The chapter ends with this incomplete sentence, as if anything that follows might explain what it's like, complete her analogy. The novel is near its end.

4

I started writing to avoid the loneliness that accompanies self-consciousness and introspection. I think one cannot truly love literature without feeling the need to share a book with a friend, an acquaintance, or even with a stranger. I gave copies of *Ada* to my friends and decided to teach Nabokov to a small class of doctoral students. First we read *Alice's Adventures in Wonderland* and, studying it together, formed a circle of empathy connecting students, teacher, and book; the "kids" brought sweets and flowers to class, even when we had heated debates. After *Alice,* I plucked up the courage to venture into *Invitation to a Beheading.* The "kids" soon discovered that Nabokov's novels, though like total strangers at first, are in fact familiar and that, at times, they can even become confidants. *Invitation to a Beheading* was not, is not, an easy novel. For the "kids," however, it was more lucid and more tangible than any so-called "realistic" novel.

The class moved on to the adventures of my adored Pnin. It was a powerful experience, like a stroll down a familiar street interrupted by a sudden, strange sound from behind, prompting you to look back, where you see a fast-flowing river has formed out of nowhere, a spontaneous waterfall at its end. The "kids" complained amusingly that we should have allocated more time to *Pnin.* So for the next study group, I did so—and I still do, every autumn when I return to the university. I come back to the wide street that ends in mountains, the mountains whose changes of color I have used so many times in class to wake up the ones who have fallen asleep. I come back to the lawn and to the decrepit pond used as a background for all group photographs. And I come back to the stairwell that goes up five floors. Even as I plan Sunday's lesson, these repeat journeys are all being transformed, slowly and calmly, into memories, at once elusive and warm. This is like the paradise in *Ada* that also constitutes the hell in *Ada*, the hell in *Ada* that recalls the paradise in *Ada*. Likewise, the book that you are holding now has not been written solely as an exercise in tenderness, like sharing a cool coffee-and-chocolate ice cream cone with a best friend. It has to be a reckoning with oneself, too.

About halfway through the novel, Ada is suddenly confronted by a former kitchen boy at Ardis Hall who blackmails her with photographs he has taken of Van making love to Ada. Van says that he will either "horsewhip his eyes out or redeem our childhood by making a book of it: *Ardis, a family chronicle*."[71] The book he writes is, of course, *Ada* (subtitled "A Family Chronicle"). Naturally, revenge is greater than a petty settling of personal scores or scoffing at that "Viennese quack," as he called Freud, or even rejecting totalitarianisms.[72] Nabokov exacts revenge against human pain or suffering, against *poshlust*, cultural poverty, and cruelty. In other words, he has his revenge not against a particular era or time, but against time itself. Not meaning to make a comparison, I admit that I began writing with a similarly ambitious revenge in mind. But every book almost immediately demands its independence, and eventually attains it, and in each draft, I have had to come face to face with aspects of myself I had failed to see. Instead, I saw their reflection in other people, the flaws of the bad teacher and the bad critic with a superficial vision, or my personal willingness to compromise, my taste for the banal. I might add laziness to the list. I wish to (and I must) redeem my better self from all these things (if I can, if we can). It is against centers of pain and suffering that we must have our revenge, as Pnin does.

Pain is the principal theme in *Pnin*. Pnin has to grapple with the bitterness of exile, with love and art as his only ammunition. Pain is the central theme in *Ada*, too, but it is configured differently: in *Ada*, love and art are also sources of pain. In Nabokov's later novels, hero and villain are brought together in the same person: think of Humbert or Kinbote. At its most basic, *Ada* is a love story, with the passage of time its central theme. However, as detailed, the themes of time and love are not separate. If in *Ada* the lovers prevail over their antagonist, which is time, where should we locate the epicenter of pain? In most of Nabokov's novels, pain manifests itself in two forms, conceptual and actual, and this is clearly the case in *Ada*. On an ontological level, time and the texture of the passage of time bring to mind the pain of separation from the self that we once were, and with respect to linear time, every case of separation remains an open, bleeding wound. In the last few pages of *Ada*, however, the two elderly lovers are in physical pain. Van and Ada are using morphine to manage otherwise unbearable pain. They discuss Lucette and realize that Van did not contemplate pain in *The Texture of Time*. The omission was a pity, Van says, because "an element of pure time enters into pain, into the thick, steady, solid duration of I-can't-bear-it-pain."[73] Later we encounter sentences where the word "pain" takes the place of "time" without explanation: "In the latest *Who's Who* the list of his main papers included by some bizarre mistake the title of a work he had never written, though planned to write many pains: *Unconsciousness and the Unconscious*. There was no pain to do it now—and it was high pain for *Ada* to be completed."[74]

Alongside the time-and-pain theme in *Ada*, there is the theme of creative pain. What is the relationship between pain and art and love? The pain of separation is alleviated by art. The wound of love might be healed by art. Most women in Nabokov's novels are muses, even his contrary women, whose insincere love, abandonment, or infidelity leads to artistic creation. The "positive" women, meanwhile, accompany the author (narrator?) and think like him, so much so that they become microcosmic of the novels they inhabit: Zina in *The Gift*, Clare in *The Real Life of Sebastian Knight*, or "You" in *Look at the Harlequins!* (as well, of course, as "You" in the memoir *Speak, Memory*). It is as if the memory of first love, first separation, and first unfaithfulness must be repeated over and over again, as if to alleviate pain through repetition. The narrators in love with Lolita and Ada ignore the reality of these women in preference to their ideal appearance in imagination, however unrepresentative. As a result, the women become frozen images, like trapped butterflies. But the relationship is reciprocal: they are both prisoners and jailers. This is how Hyde describes Ada: "As the embodiment of desire she is the progenitor of pain (longing, loss) as well as the creative drive, her infidelities (real and imagined) move Van to despair; in this, her relationship to Proust's Albertine is evident."[75] When Lucette tries to seduce Van aboard an ocean liner, they watch a film together and Ada appears to him on screen in a minor role as a little gypsy girl named Dolores. The scene is so entrancing that it ensnares Van, once again, in the memory of his lost childhood.[76]

Humbert, Kinbote, and Van are among Nabokov's most creative characters, beneficiaries of the brilliant prose of Nabokov's last period of writing. As sensitive characters, they express, in the best possible way and with the most beautiful imagery, the love, the happiness, and the sorrow they feel. But what about the happiness and the sorrow of other people? And to what extent is an artist's genius useful? Increasingly, Nabokov is engaged with negative characters, deaf and blind to others' needs and emotions. These characters began in the shadows of other protagonists, but gradually moved from background to foreground until transformed into protagonists themselves. Even as these monster-heroes of Nabokov's later fiction inspire ambivalence, accepted norms and standards are called into question too: Is love both the source of salvation and the epicenter of pain? Can art hurt? Does tragedy bring death or simply enforce the passage of time? Or does tragedy usher in love and art? If we prevail over life and death by way of eternal love and art, where is pain sited?

Van is a trained psychologist, working with people who cultivate Terrestrian dreams of another world. Van is also a philosopher, involved with the question of time. And of course he is the writer at work on *The Texture of Time*. Moreover, like Humbert and Kinbote, Van is surrounded by art and is aesthetically minded. As a child, he learns how to walk on his hands, and during the period of his first separation from Ada, he tours his performance, becoming famous under the pseudonym Mascodagama (a conflation, it seems, of "mask" and the Portuguese explorer Vasco da Gama). The show, though remarkable, is simple: a masked monster like a colossus enters the stage and struts up and down until the stride changes to the "restless walk of a caged madman, then he whirled, and to a clash of cymbals in the orchestra and a cry of terror (perhaps faked) in the gallery, Mascodagama turned over in the air and stood on his head." Upside down, he jumped "pogo-stick fashion—and suddenly came apart."[77] The monster eventually removes his mask to reveal Van, who is in fact standing upright in a magical reversal. The narrator likens this to a "standing of a metaphor on its head not for the sake of the trick's difficulty, but in order to perceive an ascending waterfall or a sunrise in reverse: a triumph, in a sense, over the ardis of time." Mascodagama overcoming gravity "was akin to that of artistic revelation."[78] If Humbert and Kinbote live in a way on the margins of the world of art, with Van we arrive at the essence of art. For Van (and, of course, for Ada), art is a way of life in its own right; through art and love they are able to confront life. When Ada discusses acting, she says: "In 'real life' we are creatures of chance in an absolute void—unless we be artists ourselves, naturally."[79]

The theme of the freeze-frame aesthetic that takes shape with Humbert and Kinbote develops further with Ada and Van: though the spiral of pain in *Ada* begins with time, it does not move forward with time or in time. As mentioned, Richard Rorty brings Nabokov the theorist face to face with Nabokov the novelist to question whether it is possible to combine the joy of creating a work of art with curiosity about other people's lives and feelings. Is the ecstasy of love and art inevitably cruel or not? The solution Rorty himself articulates is that the experience of art and curiosity builds emotions of empathy and sympathy. But is that sufficient? Is art too complex and contradictory to settle for Rorty's solution? Despite being an oxymoron, the "pitiless poet"—an artist indifferent to the plight or suffering of others—may be more accurate. Is the source of compassion (the artist's work) itself the result of selfishness and self-centeredness in its creator? In the novel's closing pages, when Ada and Van talk about publishing *Ada,* we come across these three sentences: "I'm afraid we're going to wound a lot of people (openwork American lilt)! Oh come, art cannot hurt. It can, and how!"[80] Humbert, in love with Lolita, is unkind to her. Kinbote has a creative and artful mind, but is devoid of everyday kindness. Yet Nabokov generates compassion for both in the heart of the "good reader." How does the "good reader" react toward Ada and Van? Ada and Van are not likable; aristocratic and rich, they are beautiful and successful, endowed with more or less superhuman gifts and knowledge, and perfectly self-centered and cruel. Yet strangely, despite all this, we are engaged by and with them.[81]

In *Ada,* Nabokov moves farther away than ever from everyday life, as if Kinbote's Zembla were holding sway over Shade's real world. Only the imaginary world of Antiterra is considered real, unlike *Lolita* or *Pale Fire,* constructed upon the premise of two complementary worlds. In *Ada,* the pale shadow of Terra narrows to such an extent that it becomes almost unbelievable to the novel's protagonists. With *Ada,* we enter a world that spirals into itself and has no exit, a world that is devoid of pointers to human qualities like the compassion that Shade cherishes, a world occupied by narcissistic characters, which gradually comes to suggest a world with a narcissistic creator. Boyd reported that Nabokov himself noted— while explaining the weaknesses of Pasternak's celebrated translations of Shakespeare—"the metaphors. Unattached comparisons. Suppose I were to say, 'as passionately adored and insulted as a barometer in a mountain hotel.' . . . It would be a beautiful metaphor. But who is it about? The image is top-heavy. There is nothing to attach it to."[82] This quotation reminds the reader of two things: Nabokov's self-awareness and the (apparent) problem with *Ada.* Few critics doubt the beauty of the linguistic combinations (in three languages) and imagery in *Ada.* But could Nabokov be propelling his narrative toward the impasse of *Finnegans Wake* without the slightest connection to human sentiments and the real world? Do the doors of art remain closed here to the reader, even Nabokov's ideal reader?

Nabokov knows how to avoid a narrative cul-de-sac for a straight highway, and what opens and saves *Ada* is his power as a storyteller.[83] Nabokov is, among other things, an heir to the nineteenth-century tradition of the Russian novel, and a writer of few peers, a creator of beauty, and a narrator of both beauty and sadness. It is the created, and not the creator, that remains trapped. The magic of *Ada* is unconnected to human emotion; it is in the charged atmosphere. Ada and Van's allure (unlike that of Humbert or Kinbote) arises not from their pain but from the extraordinary quality of their characters and their story, in the magic of art and through the magic of love. Humbert's love for Lolita is destructive and his artistry cruel, yet the novel is narrated with compassion. Their love, and Humbert's confessional art, allow Lolita to attain a certain redemption and immortality. But with *Ada,* Nabokov explores largely uncharted and prohibited terrain: the absolute values of pure love and pure art repel all interference and resist external factors, turning endlessly in a vicious circle around their own untarnished essence. In an archetypal love story of narration depicting an ideal, such as *Romeo and Juliet,* the cruel, blind, and deaf centers of pain in the outside world continue to interact with the narrative core, the love story: art does not stand in isolation. What artist is there who can create a complete work (the totality of art like the totality of death) without art itself becoming the sole obsession of all the hours of all the days of their life?

Nabokov, to reveal what he considers a fundamental literary inviolability, uses the character of Ada to taunt the reader with questions of pure love and pure art, which often defy or flout prevailing social or cultural notions and norms. Ada and Van are passionately, madly in love, which makes them blind and deaf to others. Their love literally obliterates reality—it is so exclusive that it negates the outside world. Here, there is no struggle against reality or tension between art and reality: "In his lovemaking with Ada he discovered the pang, the *ogon'*, the agony of supreme 'reality.' Reality, better say, lost the quotes it wore like claws—in a world where independent and original minds must cling to things or pull things apart in order to ward off madness or death (which is the master of madness). For one spasm or two, he was safe. The new naked reality needed no tentacle or anchor."[84] The warmth and allure of this new reality depend entirely on Ada's identity as seen and understood by Van. This is reminiscent of Vadim in *Look at the Harlequins!,* who considers "You" to be the essence of reality, the natural outcome when love and genius are self-containing, exclusive, and no longer need the outer world. However, Nabokov does not allow Ada and Van to withdraw to their private world so easily (though as characters they are not so removed from himself; he understands them very well). Lucette is the third central character in *Ada.* The reader cannot forget Lucette's tragic involvement in Ada and Van's world, which aspires to total exclusivity; Lucette repeats a Nabokovian role already familiar to us from Marina and Demon's love affair, the role of Aqua, the unrequited lover. The narrator ensures that we do not lose sight of either sacrifice.

Why does love demand sacrifice? Ada addresses Lucette as "pet," a term of endearment that also denotes a domestic animal. Ada and Van behave like two smug, clever children with their "pet," which, despite being likable, is nevertheless intrusive. Lucette's natural curiosity prompts her to spy on the young lovers from behind doors, through keyholes, and outside, using branches and leaves as camouflage. Ada and Van forever seek to evade her, locking her in the bathroom, tying her to a tree, and tormenting her variously. They exclude her whenever they are together, play upon her devotion, ensnare her fatally: when Lucette despairs over her unrequited passion for Van, she commits suicide. The novel's tension resides in how Ada, Van, and the (complicit) reader are allowed no respite from answerability for Lucette's fate. Toward the end of the novel, while they endure acute physical pain bearable only with morphine, Ada admits to Van that they never loved her enough. Van might have married Lucette, and Ada could have "stayed with you both in Ardis Hall, and instead of that happiness, handed out gratis, instead of all that, we *teased* her to death!"[85] Ada and Van are not alone in feeling remorse over Lucette's suicide. In interviews, Nabokov remarked several times that Lucette was his favorite character in *Ada*.[86] Lucette appears to be a character unable to escape a role as tragic victim: those who are stronger than she may appreciate her beauty but are compelled to torment her.

What *Ada* so nakedly presents is the contradiction within the writer — in fact any genuine writer who does not wear the deceitful mask of committed literature or does not hide behind the convenient fable of exalted art.

Lucette's character function is more intricate than it might initially appear, and the more one reads the more one realizes that she is no mere footnote to Ada and Van's liaison.[87] She becomes a standard of conduct for the other characters, by which their behavior, locked in their own private world, is measured. This is the case, for example, when Lucette and Van watch the film aboard the ocean liner before Lucette jumps overboard. Why does she not pursue Van when he leaves? Because at that moment an elderly couple sit down beside her in the theater, "melting in smiles of benevolence and self-effacement." Lucette offers them "her last, last, last free gift of staunch courtesy that was stronger than failure and death."[88] Earlier, on Van's first visit to Ardis, when Ada and Van are attempting to outmaneuver Lucette, Van plays a particularly cruel trick. He hands a book to the eight-year-old girl and, mustering his most charming self, says, " 'You and

I' (whispering) 'are going to prove to your nasty, arrogant sister that stupid little Lucette can do anything. If' (lightly brushing her bobbed hair with his lips), 'if, my sweet, you can recite it and confound Ada by not making one single slip — you must be careful about the "here-there" and the "this-that," and every other detail — if you can do it then I shall give you this valuable book for keeps.'"[89] Seventeen years later, Lucette, still fully remembering the poem, recalls the incident in the letter she posts Van before boarding the fateful ocean liner to seduce him. The letter, of course, arrives after her death. The poem concerns a guide who explains the history of the place to a visitor:

> Here, said the guide, was the field
> There, he said, was the wood.
> This is where Peter kneeled,
> That's where the Princess stood.
> No, the visitor said,
> *You* are the ghost, old guide.
> Oats and oaks may be dead,
> But she is by my side.[90]

In designating her its reader, Van affirms Lucette's perpetual status as outsider-onlooker.

5

I last read *Ada* to locate my references, and it was a peculiar experience to read bits and pieces in no particular order, from the middle, beginning, and end. I was reminded of how beautiful the sentences were. Are. Still are. I was busy re-creating *Ada,* my *Ada,* stealing *Ada* from its author just to prove the veracity of my own reading, stealing of course with the deepest respect and love. I also wanted to step into Nabokov's world to offer a different angle, another point of view. The last time I skimmed through the novel, it seemed as though the *Ada* that I had read and reread was in transformation. Now that I was fashioning my own version of the novel for this chapter, how distant that first spring seemed when I read *Ada* without any pressure or tension. The book was in mint condition, no dog-eared pages. No scribbles and underscores. How silly to think the book could remain that way forever, how naïve the inscription on the first page: "My *Ada.*" During that youthful spring, associative meanings and concepts were unassuming: borrow the writer's imagination, and live life with the help of stories. Do we understand a book any better when casually rereading it? Nabokov took the view that the good reader was, of necessity, a rereader.

In rereading *Ada,* I wanted to detect, even narrate, the different *Ada*s over time — the *Ada* of my adolescence, the *Ada* of now, the *Ada* I revisited for the citations in this book. I should add other people's *Ada*s to the list, too. *Ada* differs with the passage of time, and the way we read it reflects those differences; as we change, so does the novel. The first chapter of this book was ready by the time I started to write this last chapter on *Ada.* All the scattered, interrupted thoughts had at last been given some sort of order. Words and sentences in black ink followed in monotonous lines over white sheets of paper. Deep into *Ada,* I thought about Nabokov's comments on the novel's plethora of associative meanings. Should we believe, as Nabokov docs, in some sort of hidden pattern hiding behind life's trials and tribulations? Another spring, years after my first spring with *Ada,* another luminous, sunshiny afternoon: I walked down a hill along a tree-lined street and thought to myself that I would begin my book, "The first time I read Nabokov . . ." The sentence, incomplete, has stayed with me over the years, despite the book's many different iterations in my mind and on the page. So too has the note I thought I would use before the introduction, where I qualify the writer as being an enchanter, a charmer, a magician, a note I have never finished; the words did not settle properly. In this fall of rewriting, I have moved from thinking of the first time to the last time, and I am still without the proper note. Here I am, at the end of the book, though there are still several folders of notes.

The themes of "time," "love," and "pain" in *Ada* are also explored in the novel's references, its allusions, and Nabokov's intertextual conversations. This starts with the very first sentence. "All happy families are more or less dissimilar; all unhappy ones are more or less alike."[91] This openly distorts the first sentence of *Anna Karenina*, which in Rosemary Edmond's translation reads, "All happy families are alike but an unhappy family is unhappy after its own fashion."[92] The narrator's puns and parodies continue: "Anna Arkadievna Karenina" is wrongly transliterated as "Anna Arkadievich Karenina" to ridicule the work of shoddy translators who garble and sabotage great works of literature when they fall prey to "pretentious and ignorant versionists," as Vivian Darkbloom observes in *Footnotes to Ada*.[93] The narrator goes on to warn us, though, that *Anna Karenina* has little if any relation to this novel, which he refers to as a "family chronicle" whose first part is probably closer in his view to another Tolstoy work, *Childhood and Fatherland*, published by Pontius Press![94] We are thus introduced to one of the novel's central concerns from the first paragraph. It opens with reference to the tradition of nineteenth-century realism, but the narrator speaks in paradoxes, and, more important, the truth does not arrive through the narrator, but through tangential references. In other words, a serious reader cannot be content merely with reading and rereading *Ada*, but would have to know its references and sources as well.

Nabokov references certain features and characters from his earlier novels in *Ada*. We find that a "lolita" is a style of skirt, and also a town in Texas whose name had been changed—"I believe," writes Vivian Darkbloom in the notes, "after the appearance of the notorious novel."[95] Sirin appears in the guise of Ben Sirine, an "obscene ancient Arab, expounder of anagrammatic dreams";[96] Ada and Van translate a passage of John Shade's now "famous poem" into Russian.[97] We also come across marginal allusions. Borges is reconfigured as "Osberg," a "Spanish writer of pretentious fairy tales and mystic-allegoric anecdotes."[98] Among many writerly references, Russian writers, especially Tolstoy, have a special status in this novel.[99] Nabokov also parodies Maupassant's "The Necklace."[100] Flaubert becomes Floeberg and his style is mimicked,[101] as is that of Henry James, termed Dr. Henry.[102] *Mansfield Park* is mentioned repeatedly, and at one point Ada even refers to herself as the heroine Fanny Price.[103] Although the protagonists of *Mansfield Park* are cousins, the differences with *Ada* are so numerous that the allusion should be taken more as a joke. Aside from the mimicry and insouciance in these authorly games, the core themes of love, time, and loss in *Ada* are present in the repeated allusions to two of Chateaubriand's works, particularly, *Atala* and *René*. We are told that Ada calls Van "*cher, trop cher René,*" referencing the love of Amélie for her brother René in Chateaubriand's novella.[104] Van also composes a poem in English that includes verses from a poem by Chateaubriand ("Souvenir du pays de France"), which Vivian Darkbloom tells us is one of the leitmotivs of the novel: "*Oh! Qui me rendra mon Héléne. Et ma montagne et le grand chêne*" (Oh! Who will give me back my Helen, / And my mountain, and the big oak?).[105]

The constant literary references and intertextual conversations are Nabokovian trademarks, and the several self-conscious devices in *Ada* detailed below follow in the tradition that Alter considers to have begun with *Don Quixote* and continued through *Tristram Shandy, Tom Jones,* and *Jacques the Fatalist,* and, in the twentieth century, Queneau and Nabokov. But *Ada* is particular in that it is not meant to deceive the reader: it never pretends to be a real story but instead emphasizes its own artificiality. *Ada* declares itself to be a novel, whose fundamental concerns are literature and words. The characters will exist only until the novel comes to an end. Consequently, an awareness of decline and death are central to the novel, however much the novel seeks to defy time.

Sebastian Knight "used parody as a kind of springboard for leaping into the highest emotion," and in *Ada,* too, parody enables contrast, stylistic juxtaposition. *Ada* is not merely a love story in the style of traditional novels. It is a novel that consciously accommodates all the usual tropes of love stories of the eighteenth and nineteenth centuries: love is forbidden, obstacles and difficulties are customary, the background and the foreground are dreamlike, there are diversions and parenthetic statements, rivals and successors, and, for lovers, separations as well as reunions. There are narrative devices including epistolary relationships and duels. As Hyde explains, the love in *Ada* is incestuous, recalling the Romantic relationship between poet and muse, the muse descended from the goddess of memory, enabling the poet's recollections.[106] "Old storytelling devices," Van says, "may be parodied only by very great and inhuman artists, but only close relatives can be forgiven for paraphrasing illustrious poems."[107] A parodic challenge to writers of previous generations requires an author of at least the same degree of ability as his subject. Van considers, moreover, the originality of literary style to constitute the only real honesty in a writer. What form does all this take in *Ada?* At the beginning of the novel, when Van visits Ardis for the first time, the narrator provides a description of Ardis, where, "at the next turning, the romantic mansion appeared on the gentle eminence of old novels."[108] Appel has collected a number of examples that show *Ada*'s parody of traditional novels throughout, arguing that *Ada* is, fundamentally, a "self-contained survey course, a completion of the syllabus (Literature 311–312, 'The Novel: Austen to Nabokov')."[109] Other critics, however, find the novel's scope even greater, observing that Nabokov shows no restraint in parodying the popular novel.[110]

Despite the puns and wisecracks, the underlying concern is serious: the age of the great realist novel has come to an end, unfortunately, yet it is inevitable that imitation should end in parody. *Ada* partly conceals a glorification of the great realist novels; it parodies, satirizes, and burlesques them, demonstrating, too, appreciation and gratitude, debt. It puts realism to the test. *Ada* is a story of paradise lost, and, as such, a return to the styles of writers of a bygone age is not possible. As Alter puts it, a free, unbridled artist creates not only heavenly birds but monsters too. It is not possible to escape from Nabokov's metaphoric vision.[111] We naturally return to the epi-center of pain: to the irreversible passage of time.

In *Ada,* the narrator — Van — is apparently writing a chronicle. The plot of the novel, then, is deceptively linear, proceeding chronologically. But every narrative moment is overlaid with commentary; linear time is constantly interrupted by Ada and Van's reflections on their memories in old age. The past exerts its weight on the present, and the present constantly reassesses the past, testing it and reconstructing it. Van and Ada's interruptions and disruptions denote the past's interference in the present. Effectively, Ada and Van impose their desired time on the "real" time of the novel, not only re-creating reality in memory, but re-creating time too. The novel's time does not register on calendar or clock because it is timeless, reliant on creativity, not chronology. The representation of time is in dialogue with the dyads of reality and art, and heaven and hell, the direct, visible movement of the arrow of time versus the hand of time with regard to the imperceptible advance and accumulation of memories. The main theme of *Ada* cannot be separated from the structure of *Ada*.

All the familiar themes of Nabokov's earlier novels find in *Ada* consolidation and a fluency that is not surprising, but is astonishing. If the structure of *Ada* is founded upon the parodies of novels from other eras, the sheer number of references to them, not only the masterpieces of a genius like Tolstoy, whom Nabokov deeply admires, but also the banal examples of mediocre writers, is self-explanatory. In addition to the great realist novel and the great romantic novel, we also find melodrama: Nabokov playing with bathos and commonplace tropes to illustrate the difference between what is literature and what is not. In the episode of the photographs taken by the kitchen boy, the images convey a different version of Van and Ada's love story: Ada and Van find out that the boy who took the photographs is not their only witness: "Their first summer in the orchards and orchidariums of Ardis had become a sacred secret and creed, throughout the countryside. Romantically inclined handmaids, whose reading consisted of *Gwen de Vere* and *Klara Mertvago,* adored Van, adored Ada, adored Ardis's ardors in arbors. Their swains, plucking ballads on their seven-stringed Russian lyres under the racemosa in bloom or in old rose gardens (while the windows went out one by one in the castle), added freshly composed lines — naïve, lackey-daisical, but heartfelt — to cyclic folk songs."[112] By contrast, the governess at Ardis is a woman of literary taste, and she reads one of her stories to Ada and Van, modeled on Maupassant's "La Parure."[113] The implied originality of the story does not fool Ada and Van even when young, although the story and its author become famous. Later, the aged Van asks, "Had a grotesque governess really written a novel entitled *Les Enfants Maudits*? To be filmed by frivolous dummies, now discussing its adaptation? To be made even triter than the original Book of the Fortnight, and its gurgling blurbs?"[114]

Poshlust is the point of all these different versions; which is why we cannot judge a story based only on its subject matter, for the subject matter when separated from its form is nothing but *poshlust*. Nabokov reiterates this time and again in his novels, articles, lessons, and interviews. The writer's point of view, whether open or concealed, depends on the final form the novel takes. Without an elevated and distinct perspective, Nabokov, or any other great writer, would be dependent on common clichés. True art is attained only through what Van refers to as "third sight," which he defines as "individual, magically detailed imagination."[115] Yet all these different genres or versions of stories act as barriers to block the narrator. *Ada* confronts not only the traditional barriers of old love stories but also the barriers of melodramatic love stories. It is not only the passage of time that steals reality away from the lovers: as a literary writer, Van has no other choice but to reclaim the reality of Ada's childhood, and his own, not only from time but also from hackneyed art. By writing *Ada,* Van and Ada are able to re-create reality and have their revenge on both time and *poshlust.* When Ada and Van are being blackmailed, Van regrets the photographs because they "vulgarized our own mind-pictures." His response is to take revenge, to "redeem our childhood by making a book of it: *Ardis,* a family chronicle."[116] Love and art meet and complement each other because Van safeguards the past and his teenage love from the despotic clutches of time, and protects them against ignorance and cruelty.

6

Ada's ending presents an interesting problem. *Mansfield Park* ends with the two cousins, Fanny and Edward, marrying, presumably to live happily ever after. *Anna Karenina* ends in tragedy and death. In *Ada,* the lovers end up living together happily for many years, but their happy ending is not the happy ending of the book. Behind every happy ending lurks an unhappy one because life, all life, ends in death; the end of any life story is death. The lovers in *Ada* face the unreliable reality of life. But what can they do with the reality of death? At the end of the novel, the elderly Ada and the elderly Van discuss the future. Which one of them will die first? Their defiant reaction to the inevitability of death is not so unexpected. Ada and Van merge, to become Vaniada. "Ada. Van. Ada. Vaniada. Nobody. Each hoped to go first, so as to concede, by implication, a longer life to the other, and each wished to go last, in order to spare the other the anguish, or worries, of widowhood."[117] Who will die first? The answer is: neither. Before long, the question no longer applies. The narrator of the following lines, who could be either Van or Ada, says that "the hero and heroine should get so close to each other by the time the horror begins, so organically close, that they overlap, intergrade, interache, and even if Vaniada's end is described in the epilogue, we, writers and readers, should be unable to make out (myopic, myopic) who exactly survives, Dava or Vada, Anda or Vanda."[118] As the past and the present intermingle, Ada and Van declare they will not die but merge with art as well as with each other, and "if [they] ever intended to die they would die, as it were, *into* the finished book."[119] In other words, our lovers fade into the book itself, *Ada*.

On the penultimate page of the book and with a magical turn of phrase, the narrator fades into the editor, himself to disappear soon. The next paragraphs are a description of the book, together with a summary of the plot, the subject, a summary of the characters and description of the writer's style, the paratexts of a book typical of a back cover or catalogue text. Our "time-racked, flat-lying couple" die into the finished book, entering the "Eden or Hades, into the prose of the book or the poetry of its blurb."[120] These paragraphs introduce and publicize the book and seek to persuade the reader, who has now reached the end, to read *Ada*. For Nabokov, salvation is possible only for lovers and only through art. This is also the conclusion we reached in *Lolita*. By writing *Lolita*, Humbert immortalizes *his* Lolita and himself. In a sense, Kinbote, too, fades into the index at the end of *Pale Fire*. The only indication of his death is that the entry on Zembla, the last entry in the index and the last letter of the alphabet, is left incomplete. His Zembla is tailor-made. In *Look at the Harlequins!* Vadim, unlike Kinbote, is able to fall in love and can reach the end of the book in a happy state, having eventually regained reality. He kisses reality's hand and falls into the dream of death.

Among the characters in the earlier novels, Fyodor can probably be considered the happiest. At the end of *The Gift*, when Fyodor has, at last, found love (and the ability to write), he begins to work on the novel. In the last few lines he imitates *Eugène Onegin* in bidding farewell to his book. The protagonists of *Invitation to a Beheading* and *Bend Sinister*, however, require the writer to rush to their rescue at the end of each book. Nabokov forces the hero of *Invitation to a Beheading*, albeit indirectly, to stand on his own two feet. When the farce eventually collapses, Cincinnatus can leave the flimsy world of totalitarianism behind and join the writer. Krug, the hero of *Bend Sinister,* faces a more horrible fate, and the author has no choice but to enter the book to save him. The novel ends with a moth alighting on the windowsill. Does this point toward metamorphosis? This ending resembles the case of "V," the narrator of *The Real Life of Sebastian Knight,* who merges with Sebastian as the novel closes. In fact, both fade into the writer. It is only the lovable Pnin who withstands cruelty single-handedly. He escapes the malevolent enchanters of the narrative to create another world in another place. In a way, Pnin is a harbinger of the heroes of Nabokov's later works in which a happy ending becomes feasible, happy in the sense of outmaneuvering worlds that are imposed on us. At the end of *Speak, Memory,* the forty-one-year-old Nabokov, accompanied by Vera and Dmitry, escapes the pain and suffering of Europe to create, despite all the difficulties that follow and at the cost of losing his mother tongue, an ideal world in a foreign language.

What kind of ending can I write for this book? I can return to a poem Nabokov composed in 1933, in which he writes: "My Muse does not blame me: in the study of life's quivers, all is beauty."[121] Perhaps this is the best ending for this book, whose main goal is to invite readers to read, reread Nabokov's work. I've borrowed the title, themes, and even form from Nabokov, but responsibility for the book ultimately belongs to the writer of these lines, in the same way a school notebook bears the name and address of a student. The address is particularly important in this case: Iran, Asia, Earth (in other words, the Terra that is dreamt of in Antiterra). I hope now for a final gesture of kindness from Mr. "R," the broken-hearted hero of *Transparent Things.* I feel I can now empathize with his disquieting temptation and pain. Everything begins with curiosity. And curiosity prompts Mr. R to extend a helping hand. Is this a happy ending? I hope Mr. R will accompany the "beginner" who is writing these lines (and all who come to read them) not only as far as the last, and the most difficult, sentence of this last chapter but even beyond the confines of the book.

Notes

Translated by Dorna Khazeni

1. Life

1. Nabokov, *Speak, Memory*, 275.
2. Boyd, *The American Years*, 564.
3. Seidel, "Stereoscope," 238. Original citation: "We are free citizens of our dreams."
4. Nabokov, *Strong Opinions*, 254. In answer to a question about his Proustian sense of places, Nabokov responds to an interview with Simona Morini for *Vogue:* "My sense of places is Nabokovian rather than Proustian."
5. Nabokov, *Speak, Memory*, 19.
6. Ibid., 21-22.
7. As a result of the changes made to the Russian calendar, establishing dates of birth is difficult. For birthday, see Nabokov, *Speak, Memory*, 13; and Boyd, *The Russian Years*, 37-38, footnotes. For brothers' and sisters' dates of birth, see Boyd, *The Russian Years*, 43-44, 61, 96.
8. Boyd, *The Russian Years*, 38-40, for Konstantin Stanislavsky, Moscow Art Theater.
9. Nabokov, *Speak, Memory*, 174.
10. Boyd, *The Russian Years*, 19-33.
11. Ibid., 56-57, for Kishinyov pogrom.
12. Ibid., 76, for Vladimir Dmitrievich in prison and Vyborg Manifesto.
13. Nabokov, *The Gift*, 420-421.
14. Quoted in Boyd, *The American Years*, 42.
15. Nabokov, *Glory*, 4-5; Nabokov, *Speak, Memory*, 86.
16. Nabokov, *Speak, Memory*, 34-35.
17. Ibid., 36.
18. Ibid., 33-50, for Nabokov's mother, Elena Ivanovna Rukavishmikov; 40, for her whisper.
19. Boyd, *The Russian Years*, 46.
20. Nabokov, *Nabokov's Dozen*.

21. Nabokov, *Speak, Memory,* 149–152.

22. Boyd, *The Russian Years,* 110–135, for Valentina Evgenievna Shulgin, "Lyussya."

23. Nabokov, *Speak, Memory,* 229–251.

24. Ibid., 215–227. Boyd believes the experiences of approximately five years are condensed into this chapter; see *The Russian Years,* 108.

25. Nabokov, *Speak, Memory,* 229–241.

26. Ibid., 250–251.

27. Boyd, *The Russian Years,* 79.

28. Nabokov, *Lectures on Russian Literature,* 110; Boyd, *The Russian Years,* 150.

29. Nabokov, *Strong Opinions,* 64. See his answer to the first question of his August 18 *Life Magazine* interview with Jane Howard, 1964.

30. Boyd, *The Russian Years,* 90–91.

31. Nabokov, *Lectures on Russian Literature,* 142, footnote.

32. Boyd, *The Russian Years,* 93–95.

33. Nabokov, *The Gift,* viii.

34. Nabokov, *Speak, Memory,* 92–94.

35. Boyd, *The Russian Years,* 86–109; Nabokov, *Speak, Memory,* 185–186.

36. Nabokov and Wilson, *Dear Bunny, Dear Volodya,* 102–103; Boyd, *The Russian Years,* 100.

37. Boyd, *The Russian Years,* 118.

38. Ibid., 121. According to Field, *V N,* 37–38, "over a million, in cash." Boyd writes, "the equivalent of several million dollars," and in a footnote adds, "The bookkeeper told him in 1917 that he was worth £2 million."

39. Nabokov, *Speak, Memory,* 238–239.

40. Boyd, *The Russian Years,* 142–144.

41. Ibid., 133.

42. Nabokov, *The Nabokov-Wilson Letters,* ed. 33, to Wilson; see Boyd, *The Russian Years,* 148, footnote, for further explanation.

43. Boyd, *The Russian Years,* 130–131.

44. Ibid., 134.

45. Ibid., 134–139.

46. Ibid., 136–160; 143, for night patrol; 137, for first chess problem.

47. Nabokov, *Speak, Memory,* 251.

48. Ibid., 253, for the jewels; see Boyd, *The Russian Years,* 165, for the string of pearls.

49. Boyd, *The Russian Years,* 168.

50. Nabokov, *Speak, Memory,* 261.

51. Ibid., 73.

52. Ibid., 261–262.

53. Boyd, *The American Years*, 143; Nabokov, *Speak, Memory*, 263–264.

54. Nabokov, *Speak, Memory*, 179; Boyd, *The Russian Years*, 168–169.

55. Boyd, *The Russian Years*, 180–181.

56. Ibid., 190.

57. Nabokov, *Speak, Memory*, 188–193; Boyd, *The Russian Years*, 194.

58. Boyd, *The Russian Years*, 195.

59. Ibid., 196.

60. Nabokov, *Speak, Memory*, 283; Boyd, *The Russian Years*, 197.

61. Field, *VN*, 34.

62. Boyd, *The Russian Years*, 206–208, 212.

63. Ibid., 213–214.

64. Ibid., 239; Boyd, *The American Years*, 629–630. In Boyd's opinion, the "you" in *Speak, Memory* and the "you" in *Look at the Harlequins!* are the same.

65. For Nabokov's reaction, see (as an example) his reply to Matthew Hodgart in Nabokov, *Selected Letters*, 450–451, or a complaint about John Updike's critique, in a 1969 interview, in Nabokov, *Strong Opinions*, 191.

66. Nabokov, *Speak, Memory*, 295–298.

67. Nabokov, *Strong Opinions*, 168; see the 1969 interview with Martha Duffy and R. Z. Sheppard.

68. Boyd, *The Russian Years*, 395.

69. Nabokov, *Strong Opinions*, 115, 116, the 1967 interview with Alfred Appel.

70. Boyd, *The Russian Years*, 504; Nabokov, *Strong Opinions*, 96–97.

71. Boyd, *The Russian Years*, 425.

72. For example, see Rampton, *A Critical Study of the Novels*, 133–134, for language; or Hyde, *Vladimir Nabokov*, 217–218, for the novel that negates itself; or see Alter, "*Ada* or the Perils of Paradise," 176, for language in *Ada*.

73. Boyd, *The Russian Years*, 496.

74. Field, *Nabokov*, 86.

75. Ibid., 88; Nabokov, *Speak, Memory*, 257–258.

76. Boyd, *The American Years*, 483, for Kirill's passing; see Boyd, *The Russian Years*, 354, for Kirill; see Boyd, *The American Years*, 126, 89, for Olga.

77. Boyd, *The Russian Years*, 511, 514, 521.

78. Nabokov, *Speak, Memory*, 309.

79. Boyd, *The Russian Years*, 522–523.

80. Nabokov, *Speak, Memory*, 287.

81. Boyd, *The Russian Years*, 343.

82. Nabokov, *Speak, Memory*, 287–288.

83. Nabokov, *Lectures on Russian Literature*, 304.

84. Nabokov, *Poems and Problems*, 15, for the introduction.

85. Boyd, *The Russian Years*, 74.

86. Ibid., 83.

87. Nabokov, *Strong Opinions*, 18.

88. Chudacoff, "Schmetterlinge sind wie Menschen."

89. Nabokov, *Speak, Memory*, 120.

90. Boyd, *The Russian Years*, 68.

91. Nabokov, *Speak, Memory*, 192.

92. Boyd, *The Russian Years*, 71, 78.

93. Boyd, *The American Years*, 28–29.

94. Ibid., 37–38, 45, 53, for the museum and the poem "On Discovering a Butter-fly."

95. Ibid., 43–44.

96. Nabokov and Wilson, *Dear Bunny, Dear Volodya*, 72, June 16, 1942.

97. Nabokov, *Lectures on Literature*, 1.

98. Ibid., 3.

99. Nabokov and Wilson, *Dear Bunny, Dear Volodya*, 105, March 10, 1943.

100. Wetzsteon, "Nabokov as Teacher," 242.

101. Nabokov, *Lectures on Literature*, 1–6.

102. Wetzsteon, "Nabokov as Teacher," 245.

103. Nabokov, *Lectures on Literature*, 385, appendix.

104. Boyd, *The American Years*, 173–175, 184; Nabokov, *Strong Opinions*, 77, the September 1965 interview with Robert Hughes.

105. Boyd, *The American Years*, 181, 311, 138–139.

106. Vladimir Nabokov, "Sartre's First Try," 3, 19; Nabokov, *Strong Opinions*, 226.

107. Boyd, *The American Years*, 138.

108. Nabokov, *Strong Opinions*, 79–80.

109. Ibid., 223–226.

110. The article titled "Inspiration" was written for *Saturday Review* on November 20, 1972, and adapted as the ninth chapter of Nabokov, *Strong Opinions*, 403–404. Ibid., 104, footnote, to the 1966 interview in Montreaux with Alfred Appel, for Pynchon. See Boyd, *The American Years*, 316.

111. Boyd, 39, for the poem "Softest of Tongues."

112. Nabokov, *The Annotated Lolita*, 316–317.

113. Walker, "The Person from Porlock," 261, for "the critics it scared," e.g., Diana Trilling.

114. Nabokov, *Selected Poems*, 134.

115. Boyd, *The American Years*, 269–273, 272, for "pain."

116. Ibid., 149.

117. Ibid., 226. Nabokov, *The Annotated Lolita*, 312, Nabokov's epilogue; Nabokov, *Strong Opinions*, 140, for the 1966 *Paris Review* interview.

118. Nabokov, *Selected Letters*, 173–265.
119. Diderot, *Jacques le Fataliste*, 201.
120. Boyd, *The American Years*, 265, for Sylvia Beach.
121. Appel, in Nabokov, *The Annotated Lolita*, xxxiv; or Moynahan, "*Lolita* and Related Memories," 52.
122. Boyd, *The American Years*, 295–296.
123. Ibid., 301; Nabokov, *Selected Letters*, 200–201.
124. Boyd, *The American Years*, 359–360.
125. Nabokov, *Ada or Ardor*, 625.
126. Boyd, *The American Years*, 364–365, 370, 387.
127. Ibid., 420.
128. Nabokov, *Strong Opinions*, 32, 33, for the 1964 interview with Alvin Toffler for *Playboy;* 130, 131, for the 1966 *Paris Review* interview and remaining American; 195, for the 1969 BBC interview.
129. Ibid., 144, for the 1968 interview with Martin Esselin.
130. Nabokov, *Selected Letters*, 259.
131. Nabokov, *Strong Opinions*, 124, for the *Paris Review* interview.
132. Boyd, *The American Years*, 318.
133. Ibid., 319.
134. Nabokov, *Invitation to a Beheading*, 8, introduction.
135. Boyd, *The American Years*, 321, 328.
136. Ibid., 492–499, for literary quarrels; and Nabokov and Wilson, *Dear Bunny, Dear Volodya*, 1–25, Karlinsky's introduction for additional background.
137. Nabokov, *Selected Letters*, 180–181.
138. Nabokov and Wilson, *Dear Bunny, Dear Volodya*, 320.
139. Boyd, *The American Years*, 321, 348–349.
140. Ibid., 648–649.
141. Nabokov, *Strong Opinions*, 250. Unpublished 1972 interview.
142. Nabokov, *Selected Letters*, 562.
143. Boyd, *The American Years*, 661.
144. Ibid., 663, for the unpublished, unfinished continuation of *The Gift*.
145. Nabokov, *Strong Opinions*, 229, for the April 1971 interview with Alden Whitman for the *New York Times*.
146. Boyd, *The American Years*, 662.

2. Reality

1. Nabokov, *Speak, Memory*, 26–27.
2. Ibid., 27.

3. Nabokov, *The Real Life of Sebastian Knight*, 155.

4. Nabokov, *The Annotated Lolita*, 312.

5. Rampton, *A Critical Study of the Novels*, 100.

6. Nabokov, *Speak, Memory*, 280.

7. Ibid., 280.

8. Ibid., 282.

9. Nabokov, *Lectures on Russian Literature*, 18.

10. Nabokov, *The Gift*, viii.

11. Ibid., ix.

12. The book's female protagonist's name, Zina, can be considered an abbreviation of Mnemosyne, the Greek goddess of memory.

13. Nabokov, *The Gift*, ix.

14. Ibid., 43.

15. Ibid., 104.

16. Ibid., 424.

17. Hyde, *Vladimir Nabokov*, 26–30, for humor in *The Gift*; Hyde cites Bergson's study on the comic sensibility.

18. Nabokov, *The Gift*, 195.

19. Ibid., 495–496.

20. Nabokov, *The Annotated Lolita*, 39.

21. Nabokov, *The Gift*, 496.

22. Ibid., 496.

23. Ibid., 189.

24. The views of Nabokov's critics on the subject of Chernyshevski have generally been in line with Nabokov's own. For contrary views, see Rampton, *A Critical Study of the Novels*, 65–84.

25. Nabokov, *The Gift*, vii.

26. Ibid., 210.

27. Ibid., 103.

28. Nabokov, *Look at the Harlequins!* 7.

29. Ibid., 71. In Barton Johnson's analysis, "dementia" (along with incest) is the novel's main theme: a madman by the name of Vadim dreams up and fakes a life and (an imaginary) body of work for himself based on Nabokov's work and life; see Johnson, "*Look at the Harlequins!*" 223–234.

30. Nabokov, *Look at the Harlequins!* 212.

31. Ibid., 81.

32. Ibid., 71.

33. Ibid., 7.

34. Ibid., prior to the first page, "Part One."

35. Ibid., 192.

36. Ibid., 75–78.

37. Ibid., 80.

38. Ibid., 210–211.

39. Rampton, *A Critical Study of the Novels*, 178–180.

40. Boyd, *The American Years*, 640–642; Boyd believes that Vadim, with the help of the "You," arrives at a spirituality that is beyond life and death.

41. Nabokov, *Lectures on Russian Literature*, 42.

42. Ibid., 43.

43. Nabokov, *The Real Life of Sebastian Knight*, 82.

44. Nabokov, *Lectures on Russian Literature*, 57.

45. Nabokov, *The Real Life of Sebastian Knight*, 54–55.

46. Ibid., 98.

47. Ibid., 120.

48. Ibid., 120.

49. Ibid., 121.

50. Boyd, *The Russian Years*, 501, footnote.

51. Nabokov, *The Real Life of Sebastian Knight*, 152.

52. Ibid., 43–44.

53. Ibid., 56.

54. Ibid., 79.

55. Ibid.

56. Ibid., 15.

57. Ibid., 79.

58. Ibid., 82.

59. Ibid., 83.

60. Ibid., 104.

61. Ibid., 91.

62. Ibid., 153–160.

63. Bader, "*Sebastian Knight*," 23–25, for Bader's analysis of Sebastian's last novel.

64. Boyd, *The Russian Years*, 499–500. The expression Boyd employs is a philosophical riddle: Nabokov, the creator of Sebastian, and Sebastian, the creator of V—who strives through Sebastian's novels to himself access Sebastian, and Nabokov.

65. Nabokov, *The Real Life of Sebastian Knight*, 100.

66. Ibid., 90.

67. Bader, "*Sebastian Knight*," 20. In Bader's opinion, the Siller/Silberman character also appears in other forms throughout the novel.

68. Nabokov, *The Real Life of Sebastian Knight*, 97.
69. Ibid., 98.
70. Ibid., 128.
71. Ibid., 163.
72. Ibid., 167.
73. Nabokov, *The Annotated Lolita*, xli. See "popular literature" in Appel's introduction.
74. Nabokov, *The Real Life of Sebastian Knight*, 165.
75. Ibid., 161.
76. Ibid., 180–181.
77. Nabokov, *Lectures on Russian Literature*, 11.
78. Carroll, *The Annotated Alice*, 11.
79. Nabokov, *Speak, Memory*, 19.
80. Hyde, *Vladimir Nabokov*, 84–85.
81. Ibid., 86–89, for the resemblance between Sebastian and the white horse.
82. Nabokov, *The Real Life of Sebastian Knight*, 3.
83. Ibid., 28.
84. Ibid., 73.
85. Nabokov, *Lectures on Russian Literature*, 54–56.
86. Carroll, *The Annotated Alice*, 188–189.
87. Hyde, *Vladimir Nabokov*, 93–94, on the similarity of the endings of *The Real Life of Sebastian Knight* and *Through the Looking Glass* (chapter 8, 233–249).

3. The Oppressor and the Oppressed

1. Nabokov, *The Real Life of Sebastian Knight*, 33.
2. Nabokov, *Nikolai Gogol*, 63–74, for Nabokov's earliest and most complete explanation of *poshlust* or *poshlost*.
3. Nabokov, *Strong Opinions*, 93, for the 1967 interview; see Boyd, *The Russian Years*, 408–409, for further explanation.
4. Nabokov, *Invitation to a Beheading*, vii.
5. Boyd, *The Russian Years*, 416.
6. Nabokov, *The Gift*, 274.
7. Nabokov, *Invitation to a Beheading*, 61. Boyd, *The Russian Years*, 410, mentions the original Russian spelling, *gnoseologicheskaya gnusnost,* whose opening *gn's,* have an unpleasant ring in the Russian language. For further explanation, see Hughes, "Notes on the Translation of Invitation to a Beheading."
8. Nabokov, *Invitation to a Beheading*, 1.
9. Ibid., 4.

10. Ibid., 25.

11. Ibid., 12.

12. Ibid., 32.

13. Carroll, *The Annotated Alice*, 124.

14. Nabokov, *Lectures on Russian Literature*, 313.

15. Ibid., 309.

16. Ibid., 309–311.

17. Ibid., 16.

18. Ibid., 7.

19. Nabokov, *Lectures on Literature*, 376.

20. Nabokov repudiates any influence from Kafka, asserting that he had not yet read his work; see Nabokov, *Invitation to a Beheading*, Introduction, vii. See Boyd, *The Russian Years*, 415–416, for an additional explanation (and confirmation of Nabokov's statement). See Rampton, *A Critical Study of the Novels*, 60, 61, for an explanation of the differences, including Nabokov's "optimism" versus Kafka's "pessimism."

21. Nabokov, *Invitation to a Beheading*, 104.

22. Ibid., 49.

23. Ibid., 13.

24. Ibid., 135.

25. Ibid., 95.

26. Hyde, *Vladimir Nabokov*, 138–141, for further explanation and examples of real versus imitative art from *Invitation to a Beheading* and *Bend Sinister*.

27. Peterson, "Nabokov's Invitation," 97, for Iris Murdoch's sentence.

28. Ibid., 98, for Nabokov quotation on Pushkin.

29. Nabokov, *Invitation to a Beheading*, 35.

30. Boyd, *The American Years*, 91, for Mildred Horton.

31. Boyd, *The Russian Years*, 116.

32. Ibid., 116.

33. Nabokov, *Invitation to a Beheading*, 27.

34. Ibid., 17, 177, for some examples.

35. Ibid., 75.

36. Ibid., 77.

37. Ibid., 75.

38. Ibid., 3.

39. Ibid., 21.

40. Ibid., 52.

41. Ibid., 16.

42. Ibid., 163–165.

43. Ibid., 176.

44. Ibid., 179, 180.

45. Ibid., ix.

46. Ibid., 71.

47. Nabokov, *Bend Sinister,* xii. Putting aside the literal meanings of "bend," "twist," "twisted," and "sinister," it is a term used in heraldry. Nabokov explains in the introduction: "The term 'bend sinister' means a heraldic bar or band drawn from the left side (and popularly, but incorrectly, supposed to denote bastardy). This choice of title was an attempt to suggest an outline broken by refraction, a distortion in the mirror of being, a wrong turn taken by life, a sinistral and sinister world."

48. Ibid., 8.

49. Ibid., 6, introduction.

50. Nabokov, *Lectures on Russian Literature,* 60.

51. Nabokov, *Bend Sinister,* 127.

52. Ibid., 181.

53. Ibid., 200.

54. Ibid., 201.

55. Ibid., 6.

56. Ibid., 7.

57. Most critics do not consider the author of *Bend Sinister,* Nabokov, as distinct from its narrator. See Walker, "The Person from Porlock," for the opposite point of view.

58. Nabokov, *Bend Sinister,* 11.

59. Boyd, *The American Years,* 94–95, for "narrative disruptions."

60. Nabokov, *Bend Sinister,* 7.

61. Nabokov, *Invitation to a Beheading,* epigraph and 6.

62. Boyd, *The American Years,* 104.

63. Nabokov, *Bend Sinister,* 8.

64. Nabokov and Wilson, *Dear Bunny, Dear Volodya,* 210.

65. Ibid., 215, for Nabokov's letter.

66. Nabokov, *Invitation to a Beheading,* 7. Nabokov does not consider George Orwell's novel to be more than "publicistic fiction." For a defense of Orwell's sincerity as an example of Nabokov's artfulness, see Rampton, *A Critical Study of the Novels,* 52–53.

67. Rampton, *A Critical Study of the Novels,* 62. Rampton does not take Nabokov's optimism seriously, for the simple reason that in the year 1984, the Bolshevik government was still standing.

68. Erlich, *Russian Formalism,* 171–191, 212–229.

69. Shklovsky, "Art as Technique."
70. Ibid., 11–13, specifically for "habit" and "perception."
71. Alter, "Invitation to a Beheading," 56, for further explanations of totalitarianism's need for *poshlust*.
72. Rampton, *A Critical Study of the Novels,* 63.
73. Nabokov, *Invitation to a Beheading,* 104.

4. Cruelty

1. Nabokov, *Invitation to a Beheading,* 105.
2. Hyde, *Vladimir Nabokov,* 139.
3. Nabokov, *Lectures on Literature,* 251.
4. Alter presents a detailed comparison of *Don Quixote* and Nabokov's novels (especially *Pale Fire*) in *Partial Magic,* 1–29, for *Don Quixote;* 180–218, for *Pale Fire.*
5. Nabokov, *Lectures on Don Quixote,* xiv.
6. Boyd, *The American Years,* 272.
7. Nabokov, *Lectures on Don Quixote,* 27–28.
8. Ibid., 8.
9. Ibid., 52.
10. Ibid., 56.
11. Ibid., 112.
12. Maddox, "*Pnin,*" 149–150. Maddox sees hidden references in *Pnin* to two plays by Arthur Schnitzler (the author of the *Libelei,* which is being staged by friends of Pnin's); in both plays (*The Green Cockatoo* and *Literature*), the "reality" of life, when compared to the "reality" of art, appears unreal.
13. Boyd, *The American Years,* 237, footnote.
14. Nabokov, *Pnin,* 7.
15. Nabokov, *Selected Letters,* 190–192. When *Pnin* was ready to be published, Nabokov sent the publisher such a precise description of Pnin—including the shape of his nose, the length of his chin, and more—that the book's graphic designer was able to produce a cover image conforming to his wishes.
16. Nabokov, *Pnin,* 12.
17. Ibid., 17.
18. Ibid., 19.
19. Ibid., 27.
20. Ibid., 169.
21. Nabokov, *Lectures on Don Quixote,* 17.
22. Nabokov, *Pnin,* 31.

23. Hyde, *Vladimir Nabokov,* 161.

24. Ibid.

25. Nabokov, *Pnin,* 26.

26. Nabokov, *Lectures on Russian Literature,* 56.

27. Ibid., 56.

28. Nabokov, *Pnin,* 3.

29. Ibid., 6.

30. Ibid., 30.

31. Ibid., 27.

32. Ibid., 24.

33. Ibid., 35; Nabokov mischievously parodies a few of Liza's fake Akhmatova poems, which Boyd, citing Lydia Chukovsky, claims hurt Akhmatova's feelings; see Boyd, *The American Years,* 276, footnote.

34. Nabokov, *Pnin,* 35.

35. Ibid., 36.

36. Ibid., 37.

37. Ibid., 47.

38. Ibid., 47.

39. Ibid., 50.

40. Rorty, *Contingency, Irony, and Solidarity,* xvi.

41. Nabokov, *Lolita,* 315.

42. Rorty, *Contingency, Irony, and Solidarity,* 158.

43. Nabokov, *Pnin,* 41.

44. Ibid., 74.

45. Ibid., 12.

46. Ibid., 148.

47. Ibid., 161.

48. Ibid., 154.

49. Ibid., 162.

50. Ibid., 168–169.

51. Ibid., 125.

52. Ibid., 126, 127.

53. Ibid., 148.

54. Ibid., 97.

55. Ibid., 98.

56. Ibid., 101.

57. Ibid., 112.

58. Grams, "The Biographer as Meddler," 194, footnote. Grams believes that based on the narrator's description, the genus of butterfly is identifiable, one

that, because it was discovered and classified by Nabokov, has been named after him. See Boyd, *The American Years*, 107, for a description of the butterfly.

59. Nabokov, *Pnin*, 111.

60. Ibid., 115.

61. Ibid., 116, 117.

62. Ibid., 116, 117.

63. Ibid., 19.

64. Ibid., 41.

65. Ibid., 118.

66. Ibid., 85.

67. Ibid., 93.

68. Ibid., 71–72.

69. The "beach on the Bohemian Sea" may be a reference to Shakespeare's *A Winter's Tale* (act III, scene 3). As those critics who never tire of pointing out Shakespeare's "mistakes" have noted, there is no sea in Bohemia. The next reference, "At Tempest Point," not only alludes to Shakespeare's *The Tempest* but also prompts the question: Is Nabokov's narrator/Pnin not a response and a reaction to Shakespeare's Prospero/Caliban?

70. Nabokov, *Strong Opinions*, 113. Nabokov himself explains the "telepathy" of these dream passages in the 1967 interview with Alfred Appel.

71. Nabokov, *Pnin*, 94. Boyd considers the Anna/Vronski dreams in *Anna Karenina*, and the Stephen/Bloom dreams in *Ulysses* to be the sources of these "twinned dreams"; see Boyd, *The American Years*, 274, footnote.

72. Nabokov, *Pnin*, 74.

73. Ibid., 75–76.

74. Ibid., 80–82.

75. Ibid., 82.

76. Nabokov, *Speak, Memory*, 275.

77. Nabokov, *The Real Life of Sebastian Knight*, 104.

78. Nabokov, *Pnin*, 82, 83.

79. Nabokov, *Nikolai Gogol*, 41.

80. Nabokov, *The Real Life of Sebastian Knight*, 167.

81. Rowe, "Pnin's Uncanny Looking Glass." Rowe implies that the squirrels are perhaps "fairy-tale-like reincarnations of Mira Belochkin." His source is the article by Charles D. Nicol, "Pnin's History." I did not have access in Iran to what is, apparently, the best explanation of the squirrels in Bader, *Crystal Land*.

82. Nabokov, *Pnin*, 47.

83. See Chapter 4, Section 2, of this book for "childhood room"; Section 3 for "meeting Liza"; Chapter 1, Section 2, for "Martin."

84. Nabokov, *Pnin*, 64.

85. Ibid., 155.

86. Boyd, *The American Years*, 282.

87. Nabokov, *Pnin*, 75.

88. Ibid., 138.

89. Ibid., 152.

90. Ibid., 4.

91. Hyde, *Vladimir Nabokov*, 149–151.

92. Shklovsky, "Sterne's *Tristram Shandy*."

93. Hyde, *Vladimir Nabokov*, 153–154.

94. Ibid., 160.

95. Nabokov, *Pale Fire*, 162.

96. Nabokov, *Pnin*, 23.

97. Hyde, *Vladimir Nabokov*, 152.

98. Ibid., 163–165.

99. Nabokov, *Lectures on Literature*, 251.

5. Genius and Madness

1. Nabokov, *Pnin*, 71.

2. Ibid., 94.

3. Ibid., 72, for *Solus rex*. See Nabokov, *Pale Fire*, 92, for *Solus rex;* 100, for the motorboat.

4. Nabokov, *Strong Opinions*, 113, for the 1967 interview in which Nabokov himself notes that the king in *Pale Fire* finds his way to *Pnin* before he wrote *Pale Fire*.

5. Nabokov, *Pale Fire*, 232.

6. Boyd, *The Russian Years*, 516–520.

7. Nabokov, *The Enchanter*, ix, Authors Note One, and xi, Author's Note Two.

8. Nabokov, *Strong Opinions*, 122.

9. Nabokov, *Collected Stories*, 585, for the story "Ultima Thule."

10. Ibid., *Collected Stories*, 781.

11. Ibid., 782.

12. Nabokov, *Pale Fire*, 238.

13. Mr. Harold Skimpole is a main character in the novel *Bleak House* by Charles Dickens.

14. Rorty, *Contingency, Irony, and Solidarity*, 161.

15. Whatever the structure of *Pale Fire,* it is not unexpected. Remember that in *The Gift* Nabokov is not content with creating Fyodor but also presents the book Fyodor is writing (as well as the opinions of his critics). This combination of the writer and the writing is present again later in *Ada.*

16. Nova Zembla (Novya Zemlya in Russian, meaning "new land") refers to a group of islands in the frozen waters of the Arctic Ocean, north of Russia, where a river is named after Vladimir Nabokov's paternal great-grandfather, who, on an expedition, apparently discovered and named it Nabokov River. In *Speak, Memory,* 52, Nabokov calls this paternal great-grandfather an "explorer." However, Boyd, *The Russian Years,* 17, reminds us that the information to which Nabokov had access was not accurate; in fact, a friend of his paternal great-grandfather discovered the river and named it Nabokov out of that friendship. Further, the paternal great-grandfather was not an explorer.

17. Boyd, *The American Years,* 443.

18. Nabokov, *Pale Fire,* 5.

19. Boyd, *The American Years,* 602–622.

20. Johnson, *Johnson on Shakespeare,* 2: 706–746, for Dr. Johnson's headnote to *Timon of Athens.*

21. Nabokov, *Pale Fire,* 59, for Shade's reference to the title.

22. Ibid., 68.

23. Ibid., 23.

24. *Pale Fire,* in a variety of ways, brings to mind Pope's *The Dunciad* (1728) — with its notes by an imaginary critic, and an amusing index. For additional explanations about the eighteenth-century background to *Pale Fire,* see Hyde, *Vladimir Nabokov,* 178–184.

25. Nabokov, *Pale Fire,* 11.

26. Ibid., 31.

27. Ibid., 33.

28. Ibid., 59.

29. Ibid., 23.

30. Ibid., 234.

31. Ibid., 59.

32. Ibid., 220.

33. Ibid., 222.

34. Ibid., 139, 227. The butterfly that sits on Shade's sleeve is Nabokov's favorite, Red Admirable.

35. Ibid., 233–235.

36. Ibid., 14.

37. Some critics consider Shade and Kinbote to be a single character. For ex-

ample, Boyd tries to prove that Shade, in reality, is the creator of Kinbote; see Boyd, *The American Years,* 443–456.

38. Ibid., 709, notes.

39. Not only is Kinbote the mirror image of Botkin, but considering the indications in the index, both names conjure the same association of images. Boyd (using Webster's dictionary, which was also Nabokov's point of reference) provides definitions: for example, a *bote* is a form of compensation or damage paid to the *kin* of a murder victim; a Botkin (as bodkin) can refer to a person who is stuck between two others. Ibid., *The American Years,* 444.

40. Nabokov, *Pale Fire,* 246.

41. Nabokov, *Strong Opinions,* 18.

42. Rampton, *A Critical Study of the Novels,* 149–164, for the opposite view. Rampton believes the tricks and devices leave no room for "human reality" and storytelling.

43. Berberova, "The Mechanics of *Pale Fire.*"

44. Hyde, *Vladimir Nabokov,* 171.

45. "Augustan," as in the reign of Augustus (the first Roman emperor) and ascendance of Roman literature, applied to the golden age of Queen Anne (the early eighteenth century) and the glory of English literature.

46. Alter, *Partial Magic,* 202.

47. Beyond revealing the novel's structure and allusions, the majority of critics believe that *Pale Fire* is about the difficulty of communication; the reader's relationship to the work or the critic's to the author. As an example, see Kernan, "The Audience Disappears in Nabokov's *Pale Fire*"; and others, like Pilon, "A Chronology of *Pale Fire,*" who writes a chronology of the novel from the early nineteenth century through October 19, 1959; or Sprowles, "Preliminary Annotation to Charles Kinbote's Commentary on *Pale Fire,*" who writes footnotes to Kinbote's footnotes.

48. Alter, *Partial Magic,* 187–189.

49. Nabokov, *Pale Fire,* 27.

50. Ibid., 63.

51. Ibid.

52. Ibid., 128.

53. Ibid., 23.

54. Ibid., 63, 64.

55. Ibid.

56. Ibid., 180.

57. Ibid., 64.

58. Ibid., 23.

59. Ibid., 29, 30.
60. Hyde, *Vladimir Nabokov,* 174. And Hyde considers that Victor's crystal bowl in *Pnin* is a foreshadowing of Zembla and Aunt Maude's paperweight (30).
61. Nabokov, *Pale Fire,* 30.
62. Ibid.
63. Ibid., 36.
64. Ibid., 48.
65. Ibid., 44.
66. Ibid., 47.
67. Ibid., 53.
68. Ibid., 53–54.
69. Ibid., 55.
70. Ibid., 58. See Nabokov, *Strong Opinions,* 28, for an interview in which Nabokov acknowledges that he agrees with Shade on the ideas written here.
71. Nabokov, *Pale Fire,* 58.
72. Ibid., 214.
73. Rorty, *Contingency, Irony, and Solidarity,* 161.
74. Nabokov, *Pale Fire,* 138.
75. Ibid., 69.
76. Ibid., 208. While "zemlya," earth in Russian, is an actual word, the English *Semblerland* seems made up, a construct of *semble,* possibly related to the French *sembler* (to seem, seeming to), plus "land." And as a reminder, the word *semble* is also used in relation to butterflies, short for "assemble."
77. Ibid., 30.
78. Ibid., 191.
79. Ibid., 224.
80. Ibid., 22.
81. Nabokov, *The Real Life of Sebastian Knight,* 64.
82. Nabokov, *Pale Fire,* 209.
83. Ibid., 138.
84. Ibid., 36.
85. Ibid., 165.
86. Ibid., 165.
87. Ibid., 209.
88. Nabokov, *The Gift,* 475.
89. Nabokov, *Pale Fire,* 233.
90. Ibid., 170.
91. Ibid., 171.
92. Ibid., 170–171.

93. Ibid., 210.

94. Ibid., 186.

95. Ibid., 245.

96. Ibid., 93.

97. Ibid., 158; for the giraffe, 198.

98. Ibid., 122.

99. Ibid., 124.

100. Ibid.

101. Ibid.

102. Rampton, *A Critical Study of the Novels,* 149. Alfred Appel, quoting Nabokov, says the novel's simple message lies in the name of the other town in Zembla: Yeslove.

103. Boyd, *The American Years,* 456.

104. Nabokov, *Pale Fire,* 237–246. An excuse to linger (as Kinbote might) on *Pale Fire*'s index. We know Nabokov himself drew up the index for *Speak, Memory,* because he wanted to highlight certain themes; see Nabokov, *Speak, Memory,* 15–16, foreword. But it is useful to delve into the index of names in *Pale Fire.* The index Kinbote provides at the end is another one of the numerous mirrors the novel contains, one that reflects a ridiculous image of Kinbote. For example, in two whole pages he refers to himself, but Sybil is disposed of with a single *passim* ("all over, everywhere," in Latin). Or he fails to include people he does not like. Or he provides references to names absent from the actual book. Or with repeated *q.v.*'s (refer to), he imitates the sound made by a crow. The best illustration of the absurdity of the index may be the entry for "crown jewels," and the place where they may be buried—considered one of Charles's secrets, so to speak. The entry directs the reader to "hiding place," which in turn sends the reader to *potaynik* (hiding place in Zemblan?), and the entry for "Potaynik" sends the reader to "Taynik." The entry for Taynik explains the Russian word for "hiding place," and sends the reader to . . . "crown jewels." The joke is not limited to the book's pages. When Nabokov's old student and critic Alfred Appel, at the end of his 1967 interview, asked, "Where, please are the crown jewels hidden?" Nabokov answered, "In the ruins, sir, of some old barracks near Kobaltana (q.v.) but do not tell it to the Russians." The name is of a town in Zembla, which though it does not appear in the text, does appear in the index—maybe with a view to this future interview? See Nabokov, *Strong Opinions,* 123.

105. Nabokov, *Pale Fire,* 199.

106. Ibid., 216.

107. Ibid., 215.

108. Ibid., 235.

109. Ibid.

110. Ibid., 235–236.

111. Rorty, *Contingency, Irony, and Solidarity,* 157. This section is a continued commentary on chapter 7: "The barber of Kasbeam: Nabokov on cruelty," 147–168.

112. Ibid., 158.

113. Ibid., 160.

114. Nabokov, *Pale Fire,* 178.

115. Ibid., 180.

116. Many critics believe that Shade's poem is a "limited" work. For an opposing view that considers Shade's collection among the best poems in the English language, see Boyd, *The American Years,* 439–443.

117. Nabokov, *Pale Fire,* 232.

118. Ibid., 73.

119. Ibid., 126.

120. Ibid., 163.

121. Ibid., 166.

122. Ibid., 167. Alter comments on this sentence in *Partial Magic,* 213–214.

123. Nabokov, *Pale Fire,* 203.

124. Ibid., 188.

125. Ibid.

6. Love

1. Nabokov, *The Annotated Lolita,* 320, Appel's notes. Alfred Appel was Nabokov's student at Cornell in 1953–1954, and he edited *Lolita* in 1970 with an introduction and elaborate notes. As a result, critics writing about *Lolita,* including the author of the present volume, consider themselves in Appel's debt for the information he provided.

2. Ibid., 316, Nabokov's epilogue. When excerpts of *Lolita* were first published in a magazine in the United States, Nabokov decided to write a note "On a Book Entitled *Lolita,*" which later appeared as the final pages of all editions of the novel. This is the text of the "epilogue" I refer to.

3. Nabokov, *Strong Opinions,* 37.

4. Nabokov, *The Annotated Lolita,* 328, Appel's notes, for Burgess poem. See Burgess, "To Vladimir Nabokov on his 70th Birthday," for the complete poem.

5. Nabokov, *The Annotated Lolita,* 316, epilogue.

6. Ibid., 32.

7. Ibid., 328, Appel's notes.

8. Ibid., 364.

9. Ibid., xxiii, Appel's introduction.

10. Ibid., 9.

11. Ibid.

12. For references to Edgar Allan Poe, see ibid., 329–332, Appel's notes.

13. Poe, *The Complete Tales and Poems.* For "Annabel Lee," 957–958; for "Ligeia," 654–666; for "William Wilson," 626–641.

14. This quotation is from one of Poe's essays, "The Philosophy of Composition" (1864), but can be referenced in Nabokov, *The Annotated Lolita,* 331, Appel's note.

15. Ibid., 3–6.

16. Ibid., 17.

17. Ibid., 338–340, Appel's notes for wood nymph and etymology of the word "nymphet."

18. Ibid., 339, Appel's notes.

19. Ibid., 39.

20. Ibid., 308.

21. Ibid., 309.

22. The topos of love immortalizing the loved one enjoys a long history in English literature. Critics—for example, Sharpe, *Vladimir Nabokov,* 76–77—often refer to John Keats and "Ode on a Grecian Urn" (1820), and of course to Shakespeare, for example, Sonnet 18: "So long as men can breathe or eyes can see, / So long lives this, and this gives life to thee." Or to Robert Browning's poem "My Last Duchess" (1842), wherein a jealous husband substitutes the beautiful portrait of his wife for his actual wife, whom he has murdered. (Browning's "Porphyria's Lover," in which the protagonist murders his wife not out of jealousy but to make her immortal, may be a better example.) Or the story of Pygmalion, whose sculptor with the help of Aphrodite brings the statue he has built to life. Immortalizing *Lolita* takes the place of killing her.

23. Nabokov, *The Annotated Lolita,* 332–334, Appel's notes.

24. Ibid., 296.

25. Boyd, *The American Years,* 237–238.

26. Nabokov, *The Annotated Lolita,* 364, Nabokov's note in Appel's endnotes.

27. Ibid., 135, for Humbert's explanation.

28. Hyde, *Vladimir Nabokov,* 115–122. Hyde constructs his interesting thesis of *Lolita* on the basis of the dual nature of Humbert's character (similar to the protagonists of *The Eye* and *Despair*), and proceeds to the stage of schizophrenia, naturally referencing the opinions of R. D. Laing (in *The Divided Self*).

29. Nabokov, *The Annotated Lolita,* 311, epilogue. Nabokov had written the first draft of *Lolita* as a novella in Paris in the fall of 1939, in Russian, calling it *The Enchanter.* At the time of writing *Lolita,* he was convinced he had destroyed *The Enchanter,* but in 1959 he found the only existing draft of the story. Even though in the epilogue to *Lolita* he states that he was not satisfied with the work, upon rereading the story, he changed his mind, and *The Enchanter,* in a translation by Dmitri, was published in 1986 after Nabokov's death. According to Nabokov, the story was prompted by a newspaper story he had read about an ape who, following the efforts of a scientist, at last and for the first time, produces a drawing: of the bars of his cage.

30. Rampton, *A Critical Study of the Novels,* 79–80. Rampton compares the general atmosphere and, of course, the confessional tone of *Lolita* to Jean-Jacques Rousseau's *Confessions* (1765–1770), especially because on one occasion, Humbert calls himself Jean-Jacques Humbert (Nabokov, *The Annotated Lolita,* 122). Explaining the character of Humbert, Rampton cites a well-known story from the *Confessions:* Rousseau steals a ribbon from the lady of the house and accuses an innocent maid of the crime; consequently, the maid is severely punished; Rousseau not only judges and condemns himself but states that this was all prompted by the intense affection he bore the maid.

31. Hyde, *Vladimir Nabokov,* 119–120. Nabokov was unimpressed by the poetry of Eliot (and by Ezra Pound's). In Nabokov, *Strong Opinions,* 60, he takes every opportunity in that 1964 *Playboy* interview to poke fun at them, especially Eliot. In Nabokov, *Ada,* 575, for example, Eliot's *The Waste Land* becomes *The Waistline.* All the same, Hyde presents a different view; he tries to demonstrate the commonalities between the work of Eliot and Nabokov based on their Bergsonian backgrounds, and strives to highlight themes common to Eliot that also appear in Nabokov's work.

32. Nabokov, *The Annotated Lolita,* lxi–lxvii; Appel's introduction for additional explanations. Nabokov's parodies are a favorite topic with critics.

33. Ibid., 309.

34. Ibid., 277. As opposed to critics like Appel, who generally speak of the unimportance of the subject in *Lolita,* Rampton emphasizes the "humanist" character of the novel. One of the scenes he examines in support of this view is this last meeting between Humbert and Lolita, as well as an account from a lesser known interview with the *National Observer,* in 1964, in which Nabokov states that *Lolita* is a moral novel and that in his last stage, Humbert becomes moral because he realizes he loves Lolita as a woman should be loved. "But it is too late, he has destroyed her childhood. There is certainly this kind of morality in it." See Rampton, *A Critical Study of the Novels,* 113–115; and for the interview, 202.

35. Nabokov, *Bend Sinister*, 133. Appel explains (citing Nabokov) that the "poem" is not truly poetry; rather, it is composed of random "iambic incidents" that Nabokov lifted from Melville's *Moby-Dick*. See Nabokov, *The Annotated Lolita*, xlvi, Appel's introduction.

36. Nabokov, *The Annotated Lolita*, 264.

37. Ibid., 264.

38. Ibid., 17.

39. Ibid., 21.

40. Ibid., 15.

41. Ibid., 314–315, epilogue.

42. Nabokov, *The Real Life of Sebastian Knight*, 167.

43. Nabokov, *The Annotated Lolita*, 194.

44. Ibid., 176.

45. Ibid., 283–284.

46. Ibid., 286.

47. Ibid., 284.

48. Nabokov, *The Real Life of Sebastian Knight*, 79.

49. Nabokov, *The Annotated Lolita*, 316, epilogue.

50. There are, nonetheless, critics who consider Humbert to be a "weak" character, a dupe of the bewitching Lolita, especially given the end of the first night that Humbert and Lolita spend together, when it becomes clear Humbert is not the first man to have entered her life. For further explanation, and a rejection of these views, see Boyd, *The American Years*, 230. Boyd specifically notes that outside the context of the book, Nabokov is categorical; he considers Humbert "a vain and cruel wretch who manages to appear 'touching.'" See Nabokov, *Strong Opinions*, 126, for the 1966 interview with Harold Gold and George Plimpton.

51. Nabokov, *The Annotated Lolita*, 62.

52. Ibid., 308.

53. Ibid., 283–284.

54. Ibid., 32.

55. Ibid., 308–309.

56. Nabokov, *Pnin*, 85.

57. Nabokov, *The Annotated Lolita*, 316, epilogue.

58. Quoted in Boyd, *The American Years*, 52.

59. Ibid., 47. The Nabokov statement does not appear in his published biography.

60. Nabokov, *The Gift*, 362.

61. Nabokov, *The Annotated Lolita*, 283.

62. Ibid., 257.

63. Nabokov, *Speak, Memory*, 290-291.

64. Nabokov, *The Annotated Lolita*, 4.

65. Ibid., 309.

66. Ibid., 135.

67. Nabokov, *Nikolai Gogol*, 141.

68. Ibid., 140.

69. Nabokov, *The Annotated Lolita*, 32.

70. Ibid., 3.

71. Ibid., 4.

72. Ibid., 323, Appel's footnotes, for additional explanation on Vivian Dark-bloom.

73. Ibid., 3-6.

74. Ibid., 213.

75. Ibid., 124-125.

76. Ibid., 129.

77. Ibid., 65.

78. For James's theorizing about point of view, see his introduction to *Portrait of a Lady* (1880).

79. Nabokov, *The Annotated Lolita*, 262.

80. Ibid., lvii-lviii, Appel's introduction. "Reader! *Bruder!*": the famous verse of Baudelaire's is the last line of his poem "Au Lecteur" (to the reader) and serves as an introduction to his book *Les Fleurs du Mal* (1857).

81. Nabokov, *The Annotated Lolita*, 15.

82. Ibid., 280.

83. Ibid., 443, Appel's notes.

84. Ibid., 346, Appel's notes, for a list of names.

85. Ibid., 46.

86. Ibid., 246.

87. Ibid., 18.

88. Ibid., 117.

89. Ibid., 200.

90. Ibid., 109.

91. Ibid., 139.

92. Ibid., 174.

93. Ibid., 291.

94. Ibid., 346-347, Appel's notes.

95. Ibid., xl, Appel's introduction, in which he cites this interview from *Vogue* (December 1966), 280.

96. Nabokov, *The Annotated Lolita*, 35-40.

97. Ibid., 39.

98. Ibid., 41.

99. Nabokov, *Strong Opinions*, 26–27.

100. Nabokov, *The Annotated Lolita*, 198.

101. See Rampton, *A Literary Life*, 106–117, for more information on mirroring in this scene.

102. Nabokov, *The Real Life of Sebastian Knight*, 82.

103. Nabokov, *The Annotated Lolita*, 44.

104. Ibid., 45.

105. Ibid., 36–37.

106. Ibid., 31–33.

107. Ibid., 277.

108. Ibid., 349–350, Appel's footnotes for "Quilty."

109. Ibid., lx–lxiv, Appel's introduction for additional explanations about the doppelgänger motif.

110. Ibid., 349, Appel's notes.

111. Ibid., 293.

112. Ibid., 294.

113. Ibid., 298–299.

114. Ibid., 303–304.

115. Ibid., 304–305.

116. Ibid., 306–308.

117. Ibid., 316.

118. Ibid., 308.

119. For a different view, see Boyd, *The American Years*, 252–254. Since Boyd sees the Humbert/Quilty encounter as the exact equivalent of Humbert/Lolita's first night, he is not moved by the final scene and continues to condemn Humbert. I would add that numerous critics have attempted to extract more meaning out of the Humbert/Lolita relationship; Nabokov himself refers in his epilogue (see Nabokov, *The Annotated Lolita*, 314) to an "otherwise intelligent reader who flipped through the first part [and] described *Lolita* as 'Old Europe debauching young America,'" while another flipper saw in it "Young America debauching old Europe." This is possibly a reference to Mary McCarthy's note to Wilson (Nabokov and Wilson, *Dear Bunny, Dear Volodya*, 320–321). Nabokov's jab aside, in *Lolita* we are obviously faced with the confrontation of Europe and America, and this is a return to the central theme of James's novels, especially his first major novel, *Roderick Hudson* (1875).

120. Nabokov, *Lectures on Russian Literature*, 60–61.

121. Erlich, *Russian Formalism*, 185.

122. Nabokov, *The Annotated Lolita*, xxiii, Appel's introduction.

123. Roland Barthes, "The Reality Effect" (1968).

124. Nabokov, *Strong Opinions*, 43.

125. As an example, it is enough to compare the scene of Humbert and Lolita's first night in *Lolita* to a similar scene in *The Enchanter*. With the help of the same associations (and of course comic motifs) the relatively straightforward scene in *The Enchanter* acquires enormous depth in *Lolita;* see Nabokov, *The Annotated Lolita*, 128–134, and Nabokov, *The Enchanter*, 53–59.

126. Nabokov, *Speak, Memory*, 290–291.

7. Heaven and Hell

1. Hyde, *Vladimir Nabokov*, 192–201, for the relationship between *Speak, Memory* and *Ada*.

2. Appel, "*Ada* Described," 162. Appel reminds us that several of the first critics to write about *Ada* provide incorrect summaries.

3. Boyd, *The Russian Years*, 177, for the letter.

4. Alter, "*Ada* or the Perils of Paradise," 175.

5. Appel, "*Ada* Described," 166–167, for further explanation regarding *Ada* and other works by Nabokov, including many characteristics of the science fiction genre in *Ada*.

6. Nabokov, *Ada*, 23.

7. Ibid., 23.

8. Ibid., 25.

9. Ibid., 25.

10. Ibid., 36. Proffer points out that the composition of *teper' iz ada* recalls the Russian pronunciation of Scheherezade (shexerizada) the storyteller; see Proffer, "*Ada* as Wonderland," 256. Proffer indexes more or less all the Russian expressions and references in *Ada*, and provides explanations for them, 249–279.

11. Hyde, *Vladimir Nabokov*, 199–200.

12. Nabokov, *Ada*, 25.

13. Ibid., 23.

14. Ibid., 387.

15. Ibid., 384.

16. Ibid., 385.

17. Ibid., 386.

18. Ibid., 388.

19. Ibid., 657.

20. Appel, *"Ada* Described," 165–166.

21. Nabokov, *Ada,* 389. Appel points out that Volte (in German) means "sleight of hand"; see *"Ada* Described," 165, footnote.

22. Appel, "Ada Described," 160; according to Appel, Nabokov always began his first lecture at Cornell with this statement.

23. Nabokov, *Ada,* 662.

24. Ibid., 36.

25. Appel "Ada Described," 164, footnote.

26. Nabokov, *Speak, Memory,* 19–20.

27. Nabokov, *Ada,* 609.

28. Ibid., 633.

29. Ibid., 613.

30. Ibid., 610.

31. Rampton, *A Critical Study of the Novels,* 141–142, for a different theory, in defense of Einstein. And Rampton, *A Literary Life,* 118–119, for a defense of Freud, in relation to *Ada's* narrator.

32. Nabokov, *Ada,* 612–613. See Zeller, "The Spiral of Time in *Ada,*" for a focus on these pauses.

33. Nabokov, *Ada,* 638–639.

34. Nabokov, *Strong Opinions,* 185.

35. Nabokov, *Ada,* 626.

36. Ibid., 620–621. See Seidel, "Stereoscope," 240, for more on this scene and time.

37. Nabokov, *Ada,* 638.

38. Ibid., 614.

39. Seidel, "Stereoscope," 239, for further explanations on the subject of exile.

40. Nabokov, *Ada,* 664.

41. Nabokov, *The Annotated Lolita,* 17.

42. Appel, *"Ada* Described," 161.

43. Boyd, *The American Years,* 512–513.

44. Nabokov, *Ada,* 231–234. See Alter, *"Ada* or the Perils of Paradise," 177, for additional analysis of this scene.

45. Nabokov, *Ada,* 70. See Alter, *"Ada* or the Perils of Paradise," 185–186, for additional explanations of the "snake" in this scene.

46. Appel, *"Ada* Described," 182, reminds us that Ada's "AD" is also present in "Adam."

47. Nabokov, *Ada,* 212.

48. Ibid., 213.

49. Ibid., 427–428.

50. Ibid., 642.

51. Boyd, *The American Years,* 487.

52. Nabokov, *Ada,* 383.

53. Nabokov, *Strong Opinions,* 376–378. The note is Nabokov's relatively strong reaction to an article by Jeffrey Leonard, "In Place of Lost Time: *Ada,*" in *Triquarterly,* 136–146, about *The Texture of Time.* Nabokov points out that Van's theorizing about time is necessarily a "structural trick" that has no meaning outside this particular part of the novel, explains that Van's *Texture of Time* bears no relation to Proust's *Lost Time,* and adds that he considers himself in no way indebted to Borges (for instance, to his "Refutation of Time"), citing his actual sources: Berkeley and Bergson.

54. Nabokov, *Ada,* 611.

55. Ibid., 284–285.

56. Ibid., 38.

57. Ibid., 39.

58. Ibid., 98.

59. Ibid., 317.

60. Ibid., 319.

61. Ibid., 267–301, for the dinner scene.

62. Ibid., 286.

63. Ibid., 635.

64. Ibid., 637.

65. Nabokov, *Strong Opinions,* 161.

66. Nabokov, *Ada,* 633–634.

67. Ibid., 638.

68. Ibid., 641.

69. Ibid., 642.

70. Ibid., 642.

71. Ibid., 462.

72. One of the interesting aspects of the novel that I would like to emphasize is that the utterly imaginary *Ada* suddenly turns "real": there is no longer talk of Russian empires, even the meaning of Amerussia is no longer obscure. Tartary is in a sense credible, and, here at present, as I am writing these lines, if Freud's status as a quack is not yet altogether acknowledged, based on the publication of new works examining his contributions, the question is again relevant.

73. Nabokov, *Ada,* 666.

74. Ibid., 667.

75. Hyde, *Vladimir Nabokov,* 199.

76. Nabokov, *Ada,* 558.

77. Ibid., 208. Standing upside down calls to mind Alice, who while falling down the hole at the start of the story wonders whether she's going to fall through the earth and come out the other side where people are upside down.

78. Ibid., 209.

79. Ibid., 485.

80. Ibid., 457.

81. Rampton, *A Critical Study of the Novels*, 122–147, for an opposite view. Rampton objects to the notion that the characters in *Ada* are not real (or even human).

82. Boyd, *The American Years*, 513.

83. In Rampton, *A Literary Life*, 116–119, his second book about Nabokov, the author explains that both the supporters and the detractors of *Ada* bring up principles that *Ada* in fact combats and attempts to overturn. Rampton himself, to describe *Ada*, turns to Frye's examples for help and consequently calls the novel a kind of Menippean satire, referencing the satires of Menippus, the Greek cynic from the third century B.C., none of whose works remain. See Frye, *Anatomy of Criticism*, 230.

84. Nabokov, *Ada*, 248.

85. Ibid., 666.

86. Nabokov appeared with Bernard Pivot on the French television show *Apostrophes* (1975) to talk about *Ada*, which was published in France that year. Nabokov at seventy-six, looking pale, his forehead high, his eyes lusterless even, read off his replies (albeit secretly) but was nonetheless an extraordinary "presence," in front of the camera—and appeared, still, to be under the sway of the Lucette character. See Vladimir Nabokov, Interview with Bernard Pivot, *Apostrophes*, accessed July 4, 2018, https://vimeo.com/23608897.

87. Boyd, *The American Years*, 550–555, for Boyd's analysis of Ada's coldheartedness toward Lucette at the center of the story.

88. Nabokov, *Ada*, 560.

89. Ibid., 165.

90. Ibid., 166.

91. Ibid., 5.

92. Tolstoy, *Anna Karenin*, 13.

93. Nabokov, *Ada*, 671, footnotes.

94. Ibid., 5.

95. Ibid., 673, 88, 21.

96. Ibid., 391.

97. Ibid., 665.

98. Ibid., 675.

99. Ibid., 71, 674, in Darkbloom's footnotes. *Ada*'s narrator, like Nabokov, insists on teaching in his lectures that the term *monologue intérieur,* or "stream of consciousness," was an invention of Tolstoy.

100. Ibid., 675.

101. Ibid., 677.

102. Ibid., 554.

103. Ibid., 683.

104. Ibid., 677. See Appel, *"Ada* Described," 176–181, for more on the importance of Chateaubriand in *Ada.*

105. Nabokov, *Ada,* 678.

106. Hyde, *Vladimir Nabokov,* 199.

107. Nabokov, *Ada,* 279.

108. Ibid., 42.

109. Appel, *"Ada* Described," 170–175.

110. Rampton, *A Critical Study of the Novels,* 205–206, footnote 41. Rampton, as opposed to most critics, believes that Nabokov in *Ada* is exclusively dealing with popular novels. But the more examples one gathers, the more one feels inclined to come down on the side of Alter, who sees the scope of the novels as being much broader; see Alter, *"Ada* or the Perils of Paradise," 179–180.

111. Alter, *"Ada* or the Perils of Paradise," 188.

112. Nabokov, *Ada,* 465.

113. Ibid., 675. Vivian Darkbloom, in the notes, connects the story to Maupassant's. The necklace borrowed by the story's heroine, which she loses, is in fact a fake, but the protagonist returns something like half a million francs to the owner of the necklace and spends a lifetime in destitution as a result of the debt she incurs to do this.

114. Ibid., 225.

115. Ibid., 286. "Third sight" rests upon and extends the familiar construction "second sight," meaning clairvoyance.

116. Ibid., 462.

117. Ibid., 663.

118. Ibid.

119. Ibid., 667.

120. Ibid.

121. Karlinsky, "Nabokov and Chekhov," 13. From an untranslated Russian poem whose English title is "Biology" in Karlinsky's translation.

Bibliography

By Vladimir Nabokov

Ada or Ardor: A Family Chronicle. London: Penguin, 2012.

The Annotated Lolita. Edited by Alfred Appel. New York: Vintage, 1991.

Bend Sinister. London: Penguin, 2012.

Collected Poems. Translated by Thomas Karshan and Dmitri Nabokov. London: Penguin, 2012.

Collected Stories. London: Penguin, 2001.

Despair. Translated by Dmitri Nabokov. London: Penguin, 2012.

The Enchanter. Translated by Dmitri Nabokov. London: Penguin, 2009.

The Eye. Translated by Dmitri Nabokov and the author. London: Penguin, 2010.

The Gift. Translated by Michael Scammell and Dmitri Nabokov. London: Penguin, 2012.

Glory. Translated by Dmitri Nabokov and the author. London: Penguin, 1974.

Invitation to a Beheading. Translated by Dmitri Nabokov and the author. London: Penguin, 2001.

King, Queen, Knave. Translated by Dmitri Nabokov and the author. London: Penguin, 2010.

Laughter in the Dark. Translated by the author. London: Penguin, 2010.

Lectures on Don Quixote. Edited by Fredson Bowers. New York: Harcourt Brace Jovanovich, 1983.

Lectures on Literature. Edited by Fredson Bowers. New York: Harcourt Brace Jovanovich, 1980.

Lectures on Russian Literature. Edited by Fredson Bowers. New York: Harcourt, 1981.

Lolita: A Screenplay in *Plays*. London: Penguin, 2012.

Look at the Harlequins! London: Penguin, 2011.

The Luzhin Defense. Translated by Michael Scammell and the author. London: Penguin, 1994.

Mary. Translated by Michael Glenny and the author. London: Penguin, 2012.

Nabokov's Dozen. New York: Doubleday, 1958.

Nikolai Gogol. New York: New Directions, 1961.

The Original of Laura. Edited by Dmitri Nabokov. London: Penguin, 2009.

Pale Fire. London: Penguin, 1973.

Pnin. London: Penguin, 2010.

Poems and Problems. New York: McGraw-Hill, 1981.

The Real Life of Sebastian Knight. London: Penguin, 2001.

A Russian Beauty and Other Stories. Translated by Dmitri Nabokov, Simon Karlinsky, and the author. New York: McGraw-Hill, 1973.

"Sartre's First Try," *New York Times Book Review,* April 24, 1949, 3.

Selected Letters, 1940–1977. Edited by Dmitri Nabokov and Matthew J. Bruccoli. New York: Harcourt Brace Jovanovich, 1989.

Selected Poems. Translated by Thomas Karshan. New York: Knopf, 2012.

Speak, Memory. New York: Vintage, 1989.

Strong Opinions. London: Penguin, 2012.

The Tragedy of Mister Morn. Translated by Anastasia Tolstoy and Thomas Karshan. London: Penguin, 2012.

Transparent Things. London: Penguin, 2012.

(with Edmund Wilson) *Dear Bunny, Dear Volodya: The Nabokov-Wilson Letters, 1940–1971.* Edited by Simon Karlinsky. Berkeley: University of California Press, 2001.

(with Edmund Wilson) *The Nabokov-Wilson Letters: Correspondence between Vladimir Nabokov and Edmund Wilson, 1940–1971.* Edited by Simon Karlinsky. London: Weidenfeld and Nicolson, 1979.

About Vladimir Nabokov and Other Works

Alter, Robert. *"Ada* or the Perils of Paradise." In *Modern Critical Views: Vladimir Nabokov,* edited by Harold Bloom, 175–190. New York: Chelsea House, 1987.

———. "Invitation to a Beheading: Nabokov and the Art of Politics." *Triquarterly: For Vladimir Nabokov on His Seventieth Birthday.* Number 17 (Winter 1970): 41–59.

———. *Partial Magic: The Novel as a Self-Conscious Genre.* Berkeley: University of California Press, 1975.

Appel, Alfred. *"Ada* Described." *Triquarterly: For Vladimir Nabokov on His Seventieth Birthday.* Number 17 (Winter 1970): 160–186.

Bader, Julia. *Crystal Land: Artifice in Nabokov's English Novels.* Berkeley: University of California Press, 1972.

———. *"Sebastian Knight:* The Oneness of Perception." In *Modern Critical Views: Vladimir Nabokov,* edited by Harold Bloom, 15–26. New York: Chelsea House, 1987.

Berberova, Nina. "The Mechanics of *Pale Fire." Triquarterly: For Vladimir Nabokov on His Seventieth Birthday.* Number 17 (Winter 1970): 154–155.

Boyd, Brian. *Vladimir Nabokov: The American Years.* London: Vintage, 1993.

————. *Vladimir Nabokov: The Russian Years.* London: Vintage, 1993.

Burgess, Anthony. "To Vladimir Nabokov on His 70th Birthday." *Triquarterly: For Vladimir Nabokov on His Seventieth Birthday.* Number 17 (Winter 1970): 336–337.

Carroll, Lewis. *The Annotated Alice.* Edited by Martin Gardner. New York: W. W. Norton, 2000.

Chudacoff, Helga. "Schmetterlinge sind wie Menschen," *Die Welt,* September 26, 1974, iii.

Diderot, Denis. *Jacques le Fataliste.* Translated by Michael Henry. London: Penguin, 1986.

Erlich, Victor. *Russian Formalism: History-Doctrine.* Second edition. The Hague: Mouton, 1965.

Field, Andrew. *Nabokov: His Life in Part.* New York: Penguin, 1978.

————. *V N: The Life and Art of Vladimir Nabokov.* London: Futura, 1987.

Frye, Northrop. *Anatomy of Criticism: Four Essays.* Princeton: Princeton University Press, 1971.

Grams, Paul. "The Biographer as Meddler." In *A Book of Things about Vladimir Nabokov,* edited by Carl R. Proffer, 193–202. Ann Arbor: Ardis, 1974.

Hughes, Robert P. "Notes on the Translation of Invitation to a Beheading." *Triquarterly: For Vladimir Nabokov on His Seventieth Birthday.* Number 17 (Winter 1970): 284–292.

Hyde, G. M. *Vladimir Nabokov: America's Russian Novelist.* London: Marion Boyars, 1977.

Johnson, Barton. "*Look at the Harlequins!* Dementia's Incestuous Children." In *Modern Critical Views: Vladimir Nabokov,* edited by Harold Bloom, 330–340. New York: Chelsea House, 1987.

Johnson, Samuel. *Johnson on Shakespeare.* Edited by Arthur Sherbo. Two volumes. New Haven: Yale University Press, 1968.

Karlinsky, Simon. "Nabokov and Chekhov: The Lesser Russian Tradition." In *Triquarterly: For Vladimir Nabokov on His Seventieth Birthday.* Number 17 (Winter 1970): 7–16.

Kernan, Alvin B. "The Audience Disappears in Nabokov's *Pale Fire.*" In *Modern Critical Views: Vladimir Nabokov,* edited by Harold Bloom, 101–125. New York: Chelsea House, 1987.

Maddox, Lucy. "*Pnin.*" In *Modern Critical Views: Vladimir Nabokov,* edited by Harold Bloom, 143–156. New York: Chelsea House, 1987.

Moynahan, Julian. "*Lolita* and Related Memories." *Triquarterly: For Vladimir Nabokov on His Seventieth Birthday.* Number 17 (Winter 1970): 247–252.

Nicol, Charles D. "Pnin's History." In *Novel: A Forum for Fiction.* Number 4 (Spring 1971): 197-208.

Peterson, Dale E. "Nabokov's Invitation: Literature as Execution." In *Modern Critical Views: Vladimir Nabokov,* edited by Harold Bloom, 83-99. New York: Chelsea House, 1987.

Pilon, Kevin. "A Chronology of *Pale Fire.*" In *A Book of Things about Vladimir Nabokov,* edited by Carl R. Proffer, 218-225. Ann Arbor: Ardis, 1974.

Poe, Edgar Allan. *The Complete Tales and Poems.* New York: Modern Library, 1938.

Proffer, Carl. "*Ada* as Wonderland: A Glossary of Allusions to Russian Literature." In *A Book of Things about Vladimir Nabokov,* edited by Carl R. Proffer, 249-279. Ann Arbor: Ardis, 1974.

Rampton, David. *Vladimir Nabokov: A Critical Study of the Novels.* Cambridge: Cambridge University Press, 1984.

———. *Vladimir Nabokov: A Literary Life.* New York: Palgrave Macmillan, 2012.

Rorty, Richard. *Contingency, Irony, and Solidarity.* Cambridge: Cambridge University Press, 1993.

Rowe, William W. "Pnin's Uncanny Looking Glass." In *A Book of Things about Vladimir Nabokov,* edited by Carl R. Proffer, 182-192. Ann Arbor: Ardis, 1974.

Seidel, Michael. "Stereoscope: Nabokov's *Ada* and *Pale Fire.*" In *Modern Critical Views: Vladimir Nabokov,* edited by Harold Bloom, 235-258. New York: Chelsea House, 1987.

Sharpe, Tony. *Vladimir Nabokov.* London: E. Arnold, 1991.

Shklovsky, Viktor. "Art as Technique" (1917). In *Russian Formalist Criticism: Four Essays,* trans. Lee T. Lemon and Marion J. Reis, 3-24. Lincoln: University of Nebraska Press, 1965.

———. "Sterne's *Tristram Shandy:* Stylistic Commentary" (1921). In Lemon and Reis, *Russian Formalist Criticism,* 25-57.

Sprowles, Alden. "Preliminary Annotation to Charles Kinbote's Commentary on *Pale Fire.*" In *A Book of Things about Vladimir Nabokov,* edited by Carl R. Proffer, 226-247. Ann Arbor: Ardis, 1974.

Tolstoy, Leo. *Anna Karenin.* Translated by Rosemary Edmonds. London: Penguin, 2009.

Walker, David. "The Person from Porlock: *Bend Sinister* and the Problem of Art." In *Modern Critical Views: Vladimir Nabokov,* edited by Harold Bloom, 259-282. New York: Chelsea House, 1987.

Wetzsteon, Ross. "Nabokov as Teacher." *Triquarterly: For Vladimir Nabokov on His Seventieth Birthday.* Number 17 (Winter 1970): 240-246.

Zeller, Nancy Anne. "The Spiral of Time in *Ada.*" In *A Book of Things about Vladimir Nabokov,* edited by Carl R. Proffer, 280-290. Ann Arbor: Ardis, 1974.

Acknowledgments

In reviewing the translation for publication in English, I realized that it needed considerable revision. I would like to thank the following people for making the process of revision so much easier and smoother. Sarah Chalfant, my agent at The Wylie Agency, as always offered her unwavering support, wise advice, and patient encouragement. I am also grateful to Charles Buchan of The Wylie Agency for his continuous support and brilliant suggestions. Charles, Jessica Friedman, and Sarah Watling went through the whole manuscript, each of them offering insightful comments and helpful edits. It was a joy collaborating with Valerie Miles. I appreciate her support and friendship. I would like to thank my publishers at Yale for their support and patience, especially my editor Dan Heaton for his judgment, clarity, and precision. And Erica Hanson for her excellent fact checking.

This book would not have existed in its present form without my students in Iran. Their passion for literature and particular appreciation of Vladimir Nabokov were the main sources of encouragement and inspiration in its writing.

And my family, Bijan, Negar, and Dara Naderi, I thank for their love, patience, and sense of humor.

Credits

Index